FIVE HUNDRED POINTES

OF

GOOD HUSBANDRIE, 1580

Including

A HUNDREDTH GOOD POINTES OF HUSBANDRIE,
1557

by

THOMAS TUSSER

Edited (with introduction, notes and glossary) by
W. Payne, ESQ., and Sidney J. Herrtage, ESQ., B.A.

CONTENTS.

BIOGRAPHICAL SKETCH OF THE AUTHOR.

THOMAS TUSSER, the Author of the "Five Hundred Points of Good Husbandry," was born at Rivenhall,[1] near Kelvedon and Witham, in the County of Essex, about the year 1525. The exact date of his birth is uncertain, Warton[2] placing it in 1523, and Dr. Mavor in 1515, in which he is supported by the inscription on the mural tablet erected to the memory of Tusser in the church of Manningtree, where he is stated to have been sixty-five years of age at the time of his death, which took place in 1580.

Tusser, however, appears to have been elected to King's College, Cambridge, in 1543, and as he would have become ineligible at nineteen, his birth cannot have taken place earlier than 1523, and, most probably, did not take place before 1524 or 1525.

It appears from the pedigree recorded by his nephew, John Tusser, the son of his eldest brother Clement, at the Herald's Visitation of Essex in 1570, which is the only record we have

[1] The name of Tusser does not appear in the parochial registers at Rivenhall, which only extend back to 1634. According to Dr. Mavor, the name and race have long been extinct.

[2] History of English Poetry, 1840, vol. iii. p. 248.

of the family, that "William Tusser, the father, had five sons, Clement, Andrew, John, THOMAS, and William, and four daughters; the marriages of the daughters are set down, but no wives assigned to the sons, except to Clement, who married Ursula Petts, and had issue John (who entered the pedigree), Edward, and Jane, all three unmarried in 1570. The mother of THOMAS was [Isabella], a daughter of Thomas Smith, of Rivenhall, in Essex, Esq., whose elder brother, Hugh, was ancestor of Smith, Lord Carrington (not the present lord), sister of Sir Clement Smith, who married a sister of the Protector Somerset, and first cousin of Sir John Smith, one of the Barons of the Exchequer in the reign of Edward the Sixth. This match with Smith I take to have been the chief foundation of gentility in the Tussers, for I can find no traces of them or their arms before this connexion."[1]

At a very early age, and notwithstanding his mother's tears and entreaties, he was placed by his father as a singing-boy in the Collegiate Chapel of the Castle of Wallingford, in Berkshire, which, according to Warton,[2] consisted of a dean, six prebendaries, six clerks, and four choristers, and was dissolved in 1549. He has himself recorded[3] in his homely and quaint style the hardships which he had to endure at this school, the bare robes, the college fare, the stale bread, and the penny ale. The excellence of his voice appears to have attracted the notice of some of those persons to whom at that time "placards" or commissions were

[1] Letter from J. Townsend, Esq., Windsor Herald, to Dr. Mavor, quoted in his edition of Tusser, p. 7.

[2] History of English Poetry, 1840, vol. iii. p. 248.

[3] See chapter 113, stanza 5.

issued, authorizing them to impress singing-boys for the King's Chapel.[1] Afterwards, by the good offices of some friend, he was admitted into the choir of St. Paul's Cathedral, where he acquired a considerable proficiency in music under the tuition of John Redford, the organist and almoner, of whom he speaks in terms of the highest praise. From St. Paul's he was sent to Eton, probably in 1540 or 1541, "to learn the Latin phrase," and was for some time a pupil of Nicholas Udall,[2] the author of "Roister Doister," who appears to have been a second Orbilius, and by whom he was unmercifully thrashed, receiving on one occasion, "for fault but small, or none at all," no fewer than fifty-three stripes.

From Eton he passed on to Cambridge, and, as already stated, was elected to King's College in 1543,[3] but afterwards removed to Trinity Hall, of which he appears to have retained pleasant memories. Being obliged by a long illness to discontinue his studies, he left the University, and joined the Court as a retainer of William, Lord Paget,[4] by whom he was probably employed as

[1] Dr. Rimbault, in his Cheque Book of the Chapel Royal, quotes the following from *Liber Niger Domini Regis* (temp. Edward VI.): "The children of the Chappelle were 8 in number, with a Master of Songe to teach them. And when any of the children comene to be xviij yeares of age, and their voices change, ne cannot be preferred in this Chappelle, the nombere being full, then, yf they will assente, the kyng assynethe them to a College of Oxford or Cambridge of his fundatione, there to be at fynding and studye both suffycyently, tylle the king may otherwise advanse them."—Query, was Tusser assigned in this way to King's College, Cambridge?

[2] Nicholas Udall took his degree of M.A. at Oxford in 1534.

[3] Hatcher, MSS. Catalog. Præpos. Soc. Schol. Coll. Regal. Cant.

[4] Of this nobleman, the ancestor of the Earl of Uxbridge, a very full account is given in Dugdale, from which it appears that he was born at Wednesbury in Staffordshire, his father being one of the Serjeants-at-Mace of the city of London. Under Henry VIII. he was Ambassador to France, and Master of the Post. In 1549 he obtained a grant of the fee of the house without Temple Bar, first called

a musician, and of whom he speaks in terms of praise and affection. In this manner the next ten years were passed, and during this time his parents died. At the end of this period, either from disgust at the vices of the Court, or finding, to use his own words, "the Court began to frown," he retired into the country, married,[1] and settled down as a farmer at Cattiwade,[2] a hamlet in the parish of Brantham, in Suffolk, and on the borders of Essex, where he composed his "Hundredth Good Pointes of Husbandrie," the first edition of which appeared in 1557.

In consequence of his wife's ill-health, he removed to Ipswich, "a town of price, like Paradise." Here his wife died, and he married Amy, daughter of Edmond Moon, and settled down at West Dereham in Norfolk. On leaving this town, on account of the litigious character of his neighbours, he became, probably

Paget House, then Leicester House, and lastly Essex House. Two years afterwards he was Ambassador to the Emperor Charles V., and in the same year was called by writ to Parliament by the title of Lord Paget of Beaudesert, *Com. Salop.*, and soon after sent to treat for peace with France. On the fall of the Duke of Somerset, he was charged with designing the murder of several noblemen at Paget House, and in consequence was sent to the Tower, deprived of his honours and offices, and fined £6000, one-third of which was remitted. On the death of Edward VI. he joined the Earl of Arundel, the chief champion of Queen Mary, and gained her favour by his activity. Soon after her marriage with Philip, he was sent Ambassador to the Emperor at Brussels, to consult Cardinal Pole respecting the restoration of Popery. In this reign he was made Lord Privy Seal. Lord Paget died very aged, in 1563, and was buried at Drayton in Middlesex. He left issue by Anne, daughter of — Prestin, Esq., *Com. Lanc.*, three sons and five daughters. His eldest son Henry succeeded him in the title; but dying in 1568, the peerage descended to his next brother, Thomas, whom Tusser claims also for a patron. Thomas being zealously affected to Popery, and implicated in the plots in favour of Mary Queen of Scots, fled and was attainted 1587, and died three years after at Brussels, leaving one son, Thomas, who succeeded him.

[1] Of the name and family of his first wife we are entirely ignorant.

[2] In later editions printed Ratwade, and transferred to Sussex, a mistake into which Warton has fallen.

through the influence of his patron, Sir Robert Southwell,[1] a lay-clerk or singing-man in the Cathedral at Norwich, the Dean of which, John Salisbury, appears to have befriended him in every way.

From Norwich a painful illness caused him to remove to Fairsted, about four miles from Witham, in Essex, the tithes of which parish he farmed; becoming involved in "tithing strife," he left that village, and once more returned to London, where we find him living in St. Giles's, Cripplegate, in 1572.[2] The plague, however, breaking out,[3] he returned to Cambridge, where he at last found "a resting plot" in his favourite College, Trinity Hall, in the choir of which he appears to have been employed, as he was matriculated as a servant of the College, probably on May 5th, 1573.[4]

His death, as appears from a paper read before the London and Middlesex Archæological Society, took place in London, on the 3rd May, 1580, in the fifty-fifth or fifty-sixth year of his age. His will,[5] which is dated 25th April of that year, was proved by his son on the 8th August following.

He was buried in the Church of St. Mildred, in the Poultry,

[1] Tusser is generally supposed to have addressed Sir *Richard* Southwell as "Thou worthy wight, thou famous knight," but it is clear that Sir *Robert* Southwell is intended, for in 1573 Tusser alludes to Southwell's death as having occurred some years before, but Sir Richard Southwell did not die till 1579, while Sir Robert died twenty years previously.—Cooper, Ath. Cant.

[2] His second son, Edmond, was baptized at St. Giles's, Cripplegate, 13th March, 1572-3.

[3] The plague to which Tusser evidently alludes (in stanza 31 of Autobiogaphy), according to Maitland, raged in London in 1573 and 1574.

[4] Cooper, Ath. Cantab. vol. i. p. 422.

[5] See p. xxix.

where was formerly, according to Stow,[1] a monument to his memory, inscribed as follows:

"Here Thomas Tusser, clad in earth doth lie,
That sometime made the Poyntes of Husbandrie;
By him then learne thou maist, here learne we must,
When all is done we sleepe and turne to dust,
And yet through Christ to heaven we hope to go,
Who reades his bookes, shall find his faith was so."

This inscription is perfectly in character with the man, and was probably written by Tusser himself.

A mural tablet to his memory has been erected in Manningtree Church in Essex, with the following inscription: "Sacred to the memory of Thomas Tusser, Gent., born at Rivenhall, in Essex, and occupier of Braham Hall[2] near this town, in the reign of King Edward the Sixth, where he wrote his celebrated poetical treatise, entitled, *Five Hundred Points of Good Husbandry, etc.* His writings show that he possessed a truly Christian spirit, and his excellent maxims and observations on rural affairs evince that he was far in advance of the age in which he lived. He died in London in 1580, at the age of 65, and was interred in the parish church of St. Mildred in the Poultry, where the following epitaph, said to have been written by himself, recorded his memory;" then follows a copy of the epitaph already given.

[1] Survey of London, ed. 1618, p. 474. The church of St. Mildred was destroyed in the Great Fire.

[2] Braham Hall was in 1460 the residence of Sir John Braham, and is about a mile and a half from Manningtree, and in the parish of Brantham, where Tusser first introduced the culture of barley;

"In *Brantham* where rye but no barley did grow,
Good barley I had, as a many did know.
Five seam of an acre, I truly was paid,
For thirty load muck of each acre so laid."—Chapt. 19, st. 9.

The field where barley first grew at Brantham is still pointed out by tradition.

The statement in this inscription that he wrote the "Five Hundred Points" at Braham Hall is incorrect; what he did write there was the "One Hundred Points of Good Husbandrie," afterwards enlarged to "Five Hundred Points."

It has been a very generally received opinion that Tusser died in great poverty. Fuller, in his "Worthies of Essex," p. 334, says, "Whether he bought or sold, he lost, and when a renter impoverished himself, and never enriched his landlord; he spread his bread with all sorts of butter; yet none could stick thereon." Warton also says:[1] "Without a tincture of careless imprudence, or vicious extravagance, this desultory character seems to have thrived in no vocation."

Again, in Peacham's "Minerva," a book of emblems printed in 1612, there is a device of a whetstone and a scythe, with these lines:—

"They tell me, Tusser, when thou wert alive,
And hadst for profit turned every stone,
Where'er thou camest, thou could'st never thrive,
Though hereto best thou could'st counsel every one,
As it may in thy Husbandry appear;
Wherein afresh thou liv'st among us here.
So like thy self, a number more are wont,
To sharpen others with advice of wit,
When they themselves are like the whetstone blunt."[2]

These statements, however, appear to be scarcely borne out by Tusser's will. By it we find that, at the time of his death,

[1] Hist. of Eng. Poetry, vol. iii. p. 249.

[2] Thus altered in "Recreations for ingenious Head Pieces; or a pleasant Grove for their Wits to walk in, etc.," 8vo. 1644:—

"Tusser, they tell me, when thou wert alive
Thou, teaching thrift, thyself could'st never thrive:
So, like the whetstone, many men are wont,
To sharpen others, when themselves are blunt.

his brother William owed him £330, a large sum in those days, and, further, that he was the owner of two small copyhold and leasehold farms. Had he been so unfortunate in all his undertakings, and been, as Fuller terms him, "a stone which gathers no moss," Tusser would hardly have been able to lend his brother such a sum of money. If, however, it be true that he lived and died poor, we may, in all probability, attribute it to his love of hospitality, a prominent feature in his character, as well as to a roving and unsteady disposition.

Dr. Mavor states in the introduction to his edition of 1810, p. 11, that "it may be inferred from his [Tusser's] own words, that his happiness was not permanently promoted by this match [his second marriage]. He seems to complain of the charges incident 'to a wife in youth,' and had she transmitted her thoughts to posterity, we should probably have heard some insinuations against an old husband." I fail, however, to see sufficient grounds for this assertion: on the contrary, Tusser's words on the only occasion on which he speaks of his second wife seem to bear an opposite construction:—

> "I chanced soon to find a Moon
> of cheerful hue;
> Which well a fine me thought did shine
> And never change—(a thing most strange)
> Yet kept in sight her course aright,
> And compass true."—Chapt. 113, stanza 19.

It is true that in several passages he speaks of the increased expenses and responsibilities incident to a married life, but only, as it appears to me, with the view of deterring others from entering into that state without carefully considering beforehand the cost and probable consequences of such a step.

By his first wife Tusser had no children, but by the second, who survived him, he had three sons, Thomas, John and Edmond, and one daughter Mary.

His will, which is exceedingly characteristic, is given in full at the end of this introduction, p. xxix, from a copy in the British Museum,[1] privately printed in 1846 by Mr. Charles Clark, of Great Totham, Essex, from a transcript furnished to him by Mr. E. Ventris, of Cambridge, by whom the original was discovered in the Registry at Ely.[2] At the end of the will were printed Tusser's metrical Autobiography, and a few notices from nearly contemporary authors. Mr. Clark also printed in 1834 a few copies of the original edition of 1557 of the "Hundredth good Poyntes of Husbandrie."

Tusser was, as may be seen from his writings, a man of high religious principles, good-natured and cheerful, of a kindly and generous disposition, and hospitable to a fault. Although he constantly inculcates economy, he was entirely free from the meanness and pitiful spirit, which, according to Stillingfleet, made farmers of his time starve their cattle, their land and everything belonging to them; choosing rather to lose a pound than spend a shilling. "Mirth and good cheer," seems to have been his motto, and although he may have been imprudent in allowing his love of hospitality to be carried to such an excess as to keep him from independence, yet we cannot help loving the man, and admiring the justness of his sentiments on every subject connected with life and morals. Strict as he appears to have been in all matters connected with religion, he

[1] Shelf-mark, 10817, g.

[2] Notes and Queries, 1st Ser. vol. xii. p. 193.

was far from being what he terms "fantastically scrupulous," or, as we should now say, of a puritanical disposition. He prefers a merry fellow to a grave designing villain:—

"Play thou the good fellow! seeke none to misdeeme;
Disdaine not the honest, though merie they seeme;
For oftentimes seene, no more verie a knave,
Than he that doth counterfeit most to be grave."[1]

How strongly, too, does he support the keeping up of the old "feasting-daies," "Olde customes that good be let no man dispise," the festivities of Christmas,[2] the Harvest Home, etc. His maxims on the treatment of servants and dependents are conceived in a truly Christian spirit, as when he says:—

"Once ended thy harvest, let none be beguil'd,
Please such as did help thee—man, woman, and child;
Thus doing with alway such help as they can,
Thou winnest the praise of the labouring man."

"Good servants hope justly some friendship to feel,
And look to have favour, what time they do well."

And again, such as these—

"Be lowly, not sullen, if aught go amiss,
What wresting may lose thee, that win with a kiss."

"Remember the poor that for God's sake do call,
For God both rewardeth and blesseth withall.
Take this in good part, whatsoever thou be,
And wish me no worse than I wish unto thee."

The versification of Tusser does not call for any lengthened remarks. The greater portion of his work is written in the same anapæstic metre, which, though rough, is well adapted

[1] Chapter 30, stanza, 3.

[2] "What season then better of all the whole yeere
Thy needie poor neighbour to comfort and cheere?"

for retention in the memory. There are, however, two exceptions worthy of special notice: firstly, the "Preface to the Buier" (see p. 14) and the "Comparison between Champion Countrie and Severall" (see p. 140), which are the first examples of a metre afterwards adopted by Prior and Shenstone, and generally believed to have originated with the latter: secondly, the "Author's linked verses" (see p. 204), a species of what Dr. Guest calls Inverse Rhime in the following passage from his "History of English Rhythms":[1] "Inverse Rhime is that which exists between the last accented syllable of the first section, and the first accented syllable of the second. It appears to have flourished most in the fifteenth and sixteenth centuries. I do not remember any instance of it in Anglo-Saxon, but it is probably of native growth.[2] A kindred dialect, the Icelandic, had, at an early period, a species of rhime closely resembling the present—the second verse always beginning with the last accented syllable of the first. It is singular that the French had in the sixteenth century a rhime like the Icelandic, called by them *la rime entrelassée.* The present rhime differed from it, as it was contained in one verse . . . Thus:—

> 'These steps| both *reach*|| and *teach*| thou shalt|
> To come| by *thrift*|| to *shift*| withal|.'—Tusser.
>
> 'The pi|pers *loud*|| and *loud*|er blew|,
> The dan|cers *quick*|| and *quick*|er flew|.'—Burns."

The following are Tusser's principal peculiarities:—

1. The use of a plural noun with a verb singular. This very frequently occurs. "*Some,*" too, is almost invariably treated thus.

[1] Vol. i. pp. 136, 7.

[2] A very curious example is printed from Harl. MS. 913 in "Early English Poems," ed. Furnivall, pp. 21, 2.

2. His omissions and elliptical phrases, such as [while] *plough-cattle* [are] *a-baiting* (85/2); *thy market* [having been] *despatched,* 57/45; *a small* [income] 65/11; in the mottoes of the months, [work] *forgotten* [in the] *month past*; and in such expressions as "*fault known*" 47/22, "*that done*" 55/2, "*who living*" 26/1, etc.

3. Peculiarities of rime. Tusser appears to have attributed far more importance to the *outward appearance* of his riming words, than to the *reality* of the rimes. So long as they *appeared* to rime, it seems to have mattered little that in *pronunciation* they were widely different. We thus find them constantly (*a*) changing the spelling of words in order to make them *look like* others; and again (*b*) using as rimes words which, though similarly spelt, are totally unlike in pronunciation. The following examples will suffice. In alterations of orthography we find *weight* (for wait) to rime with *eight; raies* (for raise); *mutch* to rime with *hutch; thease* to rime with *ease; ise* (for ice) to rime with *device; flo* (for flow) to rime with *fro; feere* (for fire or fier) to rime with *Janiveere*; *tought* (for taught) to rime with *thought; cace* (for case) to rime with *place; waight* (for wait) to rime with *straight; bilde,* to rime with *childe; thoes* (for those) to rime with *sloes,* etc.

On the other hand, we find such rimes as the following: *plough, rough; shew, few; have, save; have, crave; feat, great; overthwart, part; shal, fal;* and a very curious instance in Chapter 69, stanza 1, where *thrive* is made to rime with *atchive.*

If the number of editions through which an author's works pass be a proof of merit, as it certainly is of popularity, few writers of his time can enter into competition with Tusser. During the forty years from the appearance of the first edition of the "One Hundreth Poyntes" in 1557 to the end of the sixteenth century, no fewer than *thirteen* editions of his work are known to have been published. Yet all are scarce, and few of those surviving are perfect; a proof that what was intended for practical use had been sedulously applied to that purpose. "Some books," says Mr. Haslewood, in the "British Bibliographer," No. iii., "become heir-looms from value; and Tusser's work, for useful information in every department of agriculture, together with its quaint and amusing observations, perhaps passed the copies from father to son, till they crumbled away in the bare shifting of the pages, and the mouldering relic only lost its value by the casual mutilation of time." Subjoined is a list of all the various recorded editions, extracted from Mavor's introduction and other sources.

1557. A Hundreth Good Pointes of Husbandrie. Reprinted here (see p. 219) from the unique copy in the British Museum.

1561. Thomas Hacher had licence for a "dyalogue of wyuynge and thryuynge of Tusshers, with ij lessons for olde and yonge." Ritson, though improperly, considers this as a different work from the piece which appears under the same title in later editions.[1]

1562. It appears probable that this edition, though its existence is disputed by some, contained the original germ of the Book of Huswifery, as we find, on the authority of Warton, that in the preceding year Richard Totell had licence to print "a booke entituled one hundreth good

[1] This was probably a broadside edition of the Dialogue found in the Book of Husbandry.

poyntes of housbondry lately maryed unto a hundreth poyntes of huswiffry, newly corrected and amplyfyed." [1]

1564. The existence of an edition of this date rests on the authority of Otridge's Catalogue, 1794. It is probably a misprint for 1562.

1570. A hundreth good pointes of husbandry, lately maried unto a hundreth good poynts of huswifery: newly corrected and amplified, with dyuers proper lessons for householders, as by the table at the latter ende more plainly may appeare. Set foorth by Thomas Tusser, gentleman, servant to the right honorable lorde Paget of Beudesert. In ædibus Richardii Tottyli, cum privilegio, Anno 1570.

1573. Five hundreth pointes of good husbandry united to as many of good huswifery, first devised and more lately augmented, with divers approved lessons, concerning hopps and gardening and other needful matters, together with an abstract before every moneth, containing the whole effect of the sayd moneth, with a table and a preface in the beginning, both necessary to be reade, for the better understanding of the booke. Set forth by Thomas Tusser, gentleman, servant to the honorable lorde Paget of Beudesert. Imprinted at London in Flete Strete within Temple Barre, at the signe of the hand and starre, by Richard Tottell. Anno 1573. Cum privilegio. [2]

1577. A reprint of the above, by the same person [but with some alterations, W.P.].

1580. The edition here reprinted, 4to.

1585. Five hundred pointes, etc. Newly set foorth by Thomas Tusser, gentleman. At London, printed in the now dwelling house of Henrie Denham, in Aldersgate Street, at the signe of the Starre. [3]

[1] No copy of this date is known to be extant, though it is mentioned both in Weston's and King's Catalogues.

[2] This is the first edition of "Five Hundred Points."

[3] Differing very little from the preceding. It is probable that Tusser might have left, before his death, some corrections on the ed. of 1580, which were introduced into this. After this edition, errors seem to have multiplied in every successive issue.

1586. By Denham, as before. 4to., pp. 164.

1590. By the assignees of Serres.[1]

1593. By Yardley. 4to. (in the Bodleian Library, M.)

1597. By Peter Short. 4to.

1599. Again by Peter Short.[2] Also by Waldegrave in Scotland. 4to.

1604. Printed for the Companie of Stationers. Five hundreth points of good husbandrie: as well for the Champion or open countrie, as also for the Woodland or Severall, mixed in every Month with Huswiferie, over and besides the booke of Huswiferie. Corrected, better ordered and newly augmented to a fourth part more, with divers other lessons, as a diet for the farmer, of the properties of winds, plants, hops, herbs, bees, and approved remedies for sheepe and cattell, with manie other matters both profitable and not unpleasant for the Reader. Also two tables, one of husbandrie, and the other of Huswiferie, at the end of the booke; for the better and easier finding of any matter contained in the same. Newlie set foorth by Thomas Tusser, gentleman, etc. (Public Library, Cambridge, M.).

1610. Printed for the Company of Stationers. 4to.[3]

1614. id. id. 4to.

1620. id. id. The orthography in the title in some respects more obsolete than in earlier impressions: thus we have *moneth* for *month*, and *hearbs* for *herbs*. 4to. In British Museum.

1638. For the Company of Stationers. 4to.[4]

1672. Printed for T. R. and M. D. for the Company of Stationers. 146 pp., exclusive of the tables, closely printed.[5]

1692. Bibliotheca Farmeriana, No. 7349. Haslewood.

[1] In White's Catalogue, 1788; Mr. Ashby saw a copy in possession of Dr. Lort.

[2] Extremely incorrect. Reprinted in "Somers' Tracts" by Sir W. Scott, vol. iii. p. 403.

[3] An edition little known, but certainly existing.

[4] Payne's Catalogue, 1773; Deck's, 1792, little known.

[5] In this edition some errors are corrected, and the orthography is considerably modernized.

All the foregoing editions are in small 4to. black-letter [with roman and italic headlines and occasional verses, W.P.].

1710. Tusser Redivivus. The Calendar of the twelve months with notes, published in as many numbers, by Daniel Hilman, a Surveyor of Epsom in Surry. 8vo. Lond. pp. 150.

1744. The same with a new title-page only. Printed for M. Cooper, in Paternoster Row; and sold by J. Duncan, in Berkley Square, near Grosvenor Gate. The title runs thus: Five Hundred points of Husbandry: directing what grass, corn, etc., is proper to be sown; what trees to be planted; how land is to be improved; with whatever is fit to be done for the benefit of the FARMER, in every month of the YEAR. By Thomas Tusser, Esq. To which are added notes and observations, explaining many obsolete TERMS used therein, and what is agreeable to the present practice in several counties of this kingdom. A work very necessary and useful for gentlemen, as well as occupiers of land, whether wood-ground or tillage and pasture.

1810. A very correct reprint of the First Edition of 1557 was issued by R. Triphook and William Sancho.

1812. Five Hundred Points of good Husbandry, as well for the champion or open country, as for the woodland or several; together with a Book of Huswifery. Being a Calendar of rural and domestic Economy, for every month in the year; and exhibiting a Picture of the Agriculture, Customs, and Manners of England, in the Sixteenth Century. By Thomas Tusser, Gentleman. A New Edition, with notes, Georgical, Illustrative and Explanatory, a Glossary, and other Improvements. By William Mavor, LL.D.,[1] Honorary Member of the Board of Agriculture, etc.

"Multa renascentur, quæ jam cecidêre, cadentque,
Quæ nunc sunt in honore."—*Hor.*

London, printed for Lackington, Allen & Co., Temple of the Muses, Finsbury-Square, 8vo. 1812. Dedicated to the President and Members of the Board of Agriculture. pp. 36, xl., and 338.

[1] Rector of Woodstock.

1834. Mr. Charles Clark of Great Totham, Essex, printed at his private press a few copies of the original edition of 1557.

1848. A Selection was published at Oxford with the following title: Five Hundred Points of Good Husbandry, by Thomas Tusser. Now newly corrected and edited and heartily commended to all true lovers of country life and honest thrift. By H. M. W. Oxford, 1848, 16mo.

The work is also included in Southey's Select Works of the British Poets, 143–199.

Extracts from the Registers of the Stationers' Company.

1557. John Daye had licence to print "the Hundreth poyntes of good '*Husserie.*'" Regist. Station. A. fo. 23*a*.

1559–60. June 20. T. Marshe had licence "to print the boke of Husbandry." Ibid. fo. 486. This last title occurs in these registers much lower.

1561. Richard Tottell was to print "A boke intituled one hundreth good poyntes of husboundry lately maryed unto a hundreth good poyntes of Huswiffry newly corrected and amplyfyed." Ibid. fo. 74*a*.

1565. A licence to Alde to print "An hundreth poyntes of evell huswyfraye," probably a satire or parody on Tusser. Ibid. fo. 131.

ERRATUM.

Page 265, line 8, for *Fonte-bonne* read *Toute-bonne.*

FIVE HUNDRED POINTES
OF
GOOD HUSBANDRIE,
1580

Including

A HUNDREDTH GOOD POINTES OF HUSBANDRIE,
1557

Fiue hundred pointes of *good Huſbandrie, as well for* the Champion, or open coun-*trie, as alſo for the woodland, or Seue-*rall, mixed in euerie Month with Hus-*wiferie, ouer and beſides the booke of Huſwife-*rie, corrected, better ordered, and newly augmented to a fourth part more, with diuers other lessons, as a diet for the fermer, of the properties of winds, planets, hops, herbes, bees, and approoued remedies for sheepe & cattle, with many other matters both profitable, and not vnpleasant for the Reader. Also a table of husbandrie at the beginning of this booke : and another of huswiferie at the end : for the better and easier finding of any matter conteined in the same.

Newly ſet foorth by Thomas Tuſſer Gentleman, ſeruant to the Honorable Lorde Paget of Beaudeſert.

Imprinted at London, by Henrie *Denham, dwelling in Pater-*noster Row, at the signe *of the Starre.*

1580.

A lesson how to confer euery abstract *with his month, & how to finde* out huswiferie verses by the *Pilcrowe, and Champion* from Woodland.

IN euerie month, er[1] in aught be begun,
Reade ouer that month, what auailes to be dun.
So neither this trauell[2] shall seeme to be lost:
Nor thou to repent of this trifeling cost.

The figure of abstract and month doo agree,
Which one to another relations bee.
These verses so short, without figure that stand,[3]
Be points of themselues, to be taken in hand.

¶ [4]In husbandrie matters, where Pilcrowe ye finde,
That verse appertaineth to huswiferie kinde.
So haue ye mo lessons, (if there ye looke well),
Than huswiferie booke doth vtter or tell.

Of Champion husbandrie now doo I write,
Which heretofore neuer this booke did recite.
With lessons approoued, by practise and skill:
To profit the ignorant, buie it that will.

The Champion differs from Seuerall much,
For want of partition, closier and such.
One name to them both doo I giue now & than,
For Champion countrie, and Champion man.

[1] yer. 1585. [2] trauail. 1577.
[3] The lessons that after those figures so stand. 1577.
[4] The edition of 1577 contains only the first two verses.

A Table of the pointes of husbandrie *mentioned in this booke.*

*** Roman words in [ ] are wanting in 1577 edition; *italics* in [ ] are additions in the edition of 1577, in which *y* is substituted for *ie*, and accented é is unused.

The Table of Huswiferie you shall finde at the ende of the booke.

FINIS.

*** Tusser's references to pages are omitted.

1.

❡ The Author's Epistle to the late Lord *William Paget, wherein he doth discourse* of his owne bringing vp, and of the good- *nes of the said Lord his master vnto him,* and the occasion of this his booke, *thus set forth of his owne* long practise.

Chap. 1.

T *Time trieth the troth, in euerie thing,*
H *Herewith let men content their minde,*[1]
O *Of works, which best may profit bring,*
M *Most rash to iudge, most often blinde.*
A *As therefore troth in time shall craue,*
S *So let this booke iust fauor haue.*

T *Take you my Lord and Master than,*
U *Vnlesse mischance mischanceth me,*
S *Such homelie gift, of me your man,*
S *Since more in Court I may not be,*
E *And let your praise, wonne heretofore,*
R *Remaine abrode for euermore.*

M *My seruing you, (thus vnderstand,)*
A *And God his helpe, and yours withall,*
D *Did cause good lucke to take mine hand,*
E *Erecting one most like to fall.*

M *My seruing you, I know it was,*
E *Enforced this to come to pas.*

[1] How euery man doth please his mind. 1577.

4 *Since being once at Cambridge taught,*
Of Court ten yeeres I made assaie,
No Musicke then was left vnsaught,
Such care I had to serue that waie.
When ioie gan slake, then made I change,
Expulsed[1] *mirth, for Musicke strange.*

5 *My Musicke since hath bene the plough,*
Entangled with some care among,
The gaine not great, the paine ynough,
Hath made me sing another song.
Which song, if well I may auow,
I craue it iudged be by yow.

Your seruant Thomas Tusser.

[1] Expelled. 1585.

2.

To the Right Honorable and my speciall *good Lord and Master, the Lord* Thomas Paget of Beaudesert, *sone and heire to his late*[1] father deceased.

Chap. 2.

MY Lord, your father looued me,
and you my Lord haue prooued me,
and both your loues haue mooued me,
to write as here is donne:
Since God hath hence your father,
such flowers as I gather,
I dedicate now rather,
to you my Lord his sonne.

2 Your father was my founder,
till death became his wounder,
no subiect euer sounder,
whome Prince aduancement gaue:
As God did here defend him,
and honour here did send him,
so will I here commend him,
as long as life I haue.

3 His neighbours then did blisse him,
his seruants now doe misse him,
the poore would gladlie kisse him,
aliue againe to be:
But God hath wrought his pleasure.
and blest him, out of measure,
with heauen and earthlie treasure,
so good a God is he.

[1] In the edition of 1575 the word Thomas, and the words following Beaudesert, do not occur. and the whole Epistle precedes that to Lord William Paget.

Ceres the Goddesse of husbandrie.

4 His counsell had I vsed,
and *Ceres* art refused,
I neede not thus haue mused,
nor droope as now I do:
But I must plaie the farmer,
and yet no whit the warmer,
although I had his armer,
and other comfort to.

Æsops fable

5 The Foxe doth make me minde him,
whose glorie so did blinde him,
till taile cut off behinde him,
no fare could him content:
Euen so must I be proouing,
such glorie I had in loouing,
of things to plough behoouing,
that makes me now repent.

Salust.

6 Loiterers I kept so meanie,
both Philip, Hob, and Cheanie,
that, that waie nothing geanie,
was thought to make me thriue:
Like *Iugurth*, Prince of *Numid*,
my gold awaie consumid,
with losses so perfumid,
was neuer none aliue.

7 Great fines so neere did pare me,
great rent so much did skare me,
great charge so long did dare me,
that made me at length crie creake:
Much more [1] of all such fleeces,
as oft I lost by peeces,
among such wilie geeces
I list no longer speake.

[1] mort. 1620.

8 Though countrie health long staid me,
yet lesse[1] expiring fraid me,
and (*ictus sapit*) praid me
to seeke more steadie staie:
New lessons then I noted,
and some of them I coted,[2]
least some should think I doted,
by bringing naught awaie.

9 Though *Pallas* hath denide me,
hir learned pen to guide me,
for that she dailie spide me,
with countrie how I stood:
Yet *Ceres* so did bold me,
with hir good lessons told me,
that rudenes cannot hold me,
from dooing countrie good.

Pallas, Goddesse of wisdome and cunning.

10 By practise and ill speeding,
these lessons had their breeding,
and not by hearesaie, or reeding,
as some abrode haue blowne:
Who will not thus beleeue me,
so much the more they greeue me,
because they grudge to geeue me,
that is of right mine owne.

11 At first for want of teaching,
at first for trifles breaching,
at first for ouer reaching,[3]
and lacke of taking hid,[4]
was cause that toile so tost me,
that practise so much cost me,
that rashnes so much lost me,
or hindred as it did.

[1] lease. 1585 and 1620.
[2] quoted. 1585 and 1620.
[3] reacing. 1599.
[4] hede. 1577.

12 Yet will I not despaier
thorough Gods good gift so faier
through friendship, gold, and praier,
in countrie againe to dwell :
Where rent so shall not paine me,
but paines shall helpe to gaine me,
and gaines shall helpe maintaine me,
New lessons mo to tell.

13 For citie seemes a wringer,
the penie for to finger,
from such as there doe linger,
or for their pleasure lie :
Though countrie be more painfull,
and not so greedie gainfull,
yet is it not so vainfull,
in following fansies eie.

14 I haue no labour wanted
to prune this tree thus planted,
whose fruite to none is scanted,
in house or yet in feeld :
Which fruite, the more ye taste of,
the more to eate, ye haste of,
the lesse this fruite ye waste of,[1]
such fruite this tree doth yeeld.

15 My[2] tree or booke thus framed,
with title alreadie named,
I trust goes forth vnblamed,
in your good Lordships name :
As my good Lord I take you,
and neuer will forsake you,
so now I craue to make you
defender of the same.

Your seruant Thomas Tusser.

[1] Which fruite to say (who hast of)
though nere so much they taste of
yet can they make no waste of. 1577.
[2] this. 1573. 1577.

3.

¶ *To the Reader.*

Chap. 3.

I Have been praid
to shew mine aid,
in taking paine,
not for the gaine,
but for good will,
to shew such skill
as shew I could:
That husbandrie
with huswiferie
as cock and hen,
to countrie men,
all strangenes gone,
might ioine in one,
as louers should.

2 I trust both this
performed is,
and how that here
it shall appere,
with iudgement right,
to thy delight,
is brought to passe:
That such as wiue,
and faine would thriue,
be plainly taught
how good from naught
may trim be tride,
and liuely spide,
as in a glasse.

3 What should I win,
by writing in
my losses past,
that ran as fast
as running streame,
from reame to reame
that flowes so swift?
For that I could
not get for gould,
to teach me how,
as this doth yow,
through daily gaine,
the waie so plaine
to come by thrift.

4 What is a grote
or twaine to note,
once in the life
for man or wife,
to saue a pound,
in house or ground,
ech other weeke?
What more for health,
what more for wealth,
what needeth lesse,
run Iack, helpe Besse,
to staie amis,
not hauing this,
far off to seeke?

5 I do not craue
mo thankes to haue,
than giuen to me
alreadie be,
but this is all
to such as shall
  peruse this booke:
That for my sake,
they gently take,
where ere they finde
against their minde,
when he or she
shall minded be
  therein to looke.

6 And grant me now,
thou reader thow,
of termes to vse,
such choise to chuse,
as may delight
the countrie wight,
  and knowledge bring:
For such doe praise
the countrie phraise,
the countrie acts,
the countrie facts,
the countrie toies,
before the ioies
  of anie thing.

7 Nor looke thou here
that euerie shere
of euerie verse
I thus reherse
may profit take
or vantage make
  by lessons such:
For here we see
things seuerall bee,
and there no dike,
but champion like,
and sandie soile,
and claiey toile,
  doe suffer[1] much.

8 This[2] being waid,
be not afraid
to buie to proue,
to reade with loue,
to followe some,
and so to come
  by practise true:
My paine is past,
thou warning hast,
th' experience mine,
the vantage thine,
may giue thee choice
to crie or reioice:
  and thus adue.

Finis T. Tusser.

[1] differ. 1573; suffer. 1577.

[2] Thus. 1577.

4.

¶ An Introduction to the Booke *of Husbandrie.*[1]

Chap. 4.

GOod husbandmen must moile & toile,
to laie to liue by laboured feeld:
Their wiues at home must keepe such coile,
as their like actes may profit yeeld.
For well they knowe,
as shaft from bowe,
or chalke from snowe,
A good round rent their Lords they giue,
and must keepe touch in all their paie:
With credit crackt else for to liue,
or trust to legs and run awaie.

2 Though fence well kept is one good point,
and tilth well done, in season due;
Yet needing salue in time to annoint,
is all in all and needfull true:
As for the rest,
thus thinke I best,
as friend doth gest,
With hand in hand to leade thee foorth
to *Ceres* campe, there to behold *Ceres,* Goddesse of husbandry.
A thousand things as richlie woorth,
as any pearle is woorthie gold.

[1] This Introduction is not in the editions of 1573 or 1577.

5.

¶ A Preface to the buier of *this booke.*

Chap. 5.

WHat lookest thou herein to haue ?
Fine verses thy fansie to please ?
Of many my betters that craue,
Looke nothing but rudenes in thease.

2 What other thing lookest thou then ?
Graue sentences many to finde ?
Such, Poets haue twentie and ten,
Yea thousands contenting the minde.

3 What looke ye, I praie you shew what ?
Termes painted with Rhetorike fine ?
Good husbandrie seeketh not that,
Nor ist any meaning of mine.

4 What lookest thou, speake at the last ?
Good lessons for thee and thy wife ?
Then keepe them in memorie fast,
To helpe as a comfort to life.

5 What looke ye for more in my booke ?
Points needfull and meete to be knowne ?
Then dailie be suer to looke,
To saue to be suer thine owne.

*** Mason remarks that this metre was peculiar to Shenstone.

6.

The commodities of Husbandrie.

Chap. 6.

Let house haue to fill her,
Let land haue to till her.

NO dwellers, what profiteth house for to stand ?
What goodnes, vnoccupied, bringeth the land ?

2.

No labor no bread,
No host we be dead.

No husbandry vsed, how soone shall we sterue ?
House keeping neglected, what comfort to serue ?

3.

Ill father no gift,
No knowledge no thrift.

The father an vnthrift, what hope to the sonne ?
The ruler vnskilfull, how quickly vndonne ?

7.

Chap. 7.

As true as thy faith
This riddle thus saith.

I Seeme but a drudge, yet I passe any King — The praise of husbandrie.
To such as can vse me, great wealth I do bring.
Since Adam first liued, I neuer did die,
When Noe was shipman, there also was I.
The earth to susteine me, the sea for my fish :
Be readie to pleasure me, as I would wish.[1]
What hath any life, but I helpe to preserue,
What wight without me, but is ready to sterue.

[1] The earth is my storehouse, the sea my fishpond,
What good is in either, by me it is found. 1577.

In woodland, in Champion, Citie, or towne
If long I be absent, what falleth not downe?
If long I be present, what goodnes can want?
Though things at my comming were neuer so scant.
So many as looue me, and vse me aright,
With treasure and pleasure, I richly acquite.
Great kings I doe succour, else wrong it would go,
The King of al kings hath appointed it so.

8.

¶ The description of Husbandrie.

Chap. 8.

OF husband, doth husbandrie challenge that name,
  of husbandrie, husband doth likewise the same:
Where huswife and huswiferie, ioineth with thease,
  there wealth in abundance is gotten with ease.

2 The name of a husband, what is it to saie?
  of wife and the houshold the band and the staie:
Some husbandlie thriueth that neuer had wife,
  yet scarce a good husband in goodnes of life.

3 The husband is he that to labour doth fall,
  the labour of him I doe husbandrie call:
If thrift by that labour be any way caught,
  then is it good husbandrie, else it is naught.

4 So houshold and housholdrie I doe define,
  for folke and the goodes that in house be of thine:
House keeping to them, as a refuge is set,
  which like as it is, so report it doth get.

5 Be house or the furniture neuer so rude,
  of husband and husbandrie, (thus I conclude:)
That huswife and huswiferie, if it be good,
  must pleasure togither as cosins in blood.

9.

¶ The Ladder to thrift.

Chap. 9.

TO take thy calling thankfully,
and shun[1] the path to beggery.

2 To grudge in youth no drudgery,
to come by knowledge perfectly.

3 To count no trauell slauerie,
that brings in penie sauerlie.

4 To folow profit earnestlie
but meddle not with pilferie.

5 To get by honest practisie,
and kéepe thy gettings couertlie.

6 To lash not out too lashinglie,
for feare of pinching penurie.

7 To get good plot to occupie,
and store and vse it husbandlie.

8 To shew to landlord curtesie,
and kéepe thy couenants orderlie.

9 To hold that thine is lawfullie,
for stoutnes or for flatterie.

10 To wed good wife for companie,
and liue in wedlock honestlie.

11 To furnish house with housholdry,
and make prouision skilfully.

12 To ioine to wife good familie,
and none to kéepe for brauerie.

13 To suffer none liue idlelie,
for feare of idle knauerie.

14 To courage wife in huswiferie,
and vse well dooers gentilie.

15 To kéepe no more but néedfullie,
and count excesse vnsauerie.

16 To raise betimes the lubberlie,
both snorting Hob and Margerie.[2]

17 To walke thy pastures vsuallie,
to spie ill neighbours subtiltie.

18 To hate reuengement hastilie,
for loosing loue and amitie.

19 To loue thy neighbor neighborly,
and shew him no discurtesy.

20 To answere stranger ciuilie,
but shew him not thy secresie.

21 To vse no friend deceitfully,
to offer no man villeny.

22 To learne how foe to pacifie,
but trust him not too trustilie.

23 To kéepe thy touch substanciallie,
and in thy word vse constancie.

24 To make thy bandes aduisedly,
& com not bound through suerty.

25 To meddle not with vsurie,
nor lend thy monie foolishlie.

26 To hate to liue in infamie,
through craft, and liuing shiftingly.[3]

27 To shun all kinde of treachery,
for treason endeth horribly.

28 To learne to eschew ill cōpany,
and such as liue dishonestly.

29 To banish house of blasphemie,
least crosses crosse vnluckelie.

30 To stop mischance, through policy,
for chancing too vnhappily.

31 To beare thy crosses paciently,
for worldly things are slippery.

32 To laie to kéepe from miserie,
age comming on so créepinglie.

33 To praie to God continuallie,
for aide against thine enimie.

34 To spend thy Sabboth holilie,
and helpe the needie pouertie.[4]

35 To liue in conscience quietly,
and kéepe thy selfe from malady.

36 To ease thy sicknes spéedilie,
er helpe be past recouerie.

37 To séeke to God for remedie,
for witches prooue vnluckilie.

[38] These be the steps vnfainedlie:
to climbe to thrift by husbandrie.

[39] *These steps both reach, and teach thee shall:*
To come by thrift, to shift withall.

*** Stanzas 25, 27, 28, 32, 37 are not in the edition of 1577. After 31 the edition of 1577 has:—

29 To train thy child vp vertuously
that vertue vice may qualifie.

30 To bridle wild otes fantasie,
to spend thee naught vnthriftely.

[1] shonne. 1577.
[2] To rise betimes up readely. 1577.
[3] naughtily. 1573, 1557.
[4] poore in misery. 1577.

10.

¶ *Good husbandlie lessons worthie to be* followed of such as will thriue.

Chap. 10.

GOD sendeth and giueth both mouth and the meat,
and blesseth vs al with his benefits great:
Then serue we that God that so richly doth giue,
shew loue to our neighbors, and lay for to liue.

2[1] As bud by appearing betokneth the spring,
and leafe by her falling the contrarie thing:
So youth bids vs labour, to get as we can,
for age is a burden to laboring man.

3[1] A competent liuing, and honestly had,
makes such as are godlie both thankfull and glad:
Life neuer contented, with honest estate,
lamented is oft, and repented too late.

4[1] Count neuer wel gotten that naughtly is got,
nor well to account of which honest is not:
Looke long not to prosper, that wayest not this,
least prospering faileth, and all go amisse.

Laie wisely to marrie.

5 True wedlock is best, for auoiding of sinne,
the bed vndefiled much honour doth winne:
Though loue be in choosing farre better than gold,
let loue come with somewhat, the better to hold.

Concord bringeth foyson.

6 Where cooples agree not is ranker and strife,
where such be together is seldome good life:
Where cooples in wedlock doe louelie agree,
there foyson remaineth, if wisedome there bee.

[1] Stanzas 2, 3, and 4 are wanting in 1573 and 1577.

7 Who looketh to marrie must laie to keepe house,
for loue may not alway be plaieing with douse:
If children encrease, and no staie of thine owne,
what afterwards followes is soone to be knowne.

Wife and children craue a dwelling.

8 Once charged with children, or likelie to bee,
giue ouer to sudgerne, that thinkest to thee:
Least grutching of hostis, and crauing of nurse,
be costlie and noisome to thee and thy purse.

Thee for thriue.

Hostisses grudge: nurses craue.

9 Good husbands that loueth good houses to keepe
are oftentimes careful when other doe sleepe:
To spend as they may, or to stop at the furst,
for running in danger, or feare of the wurst.

Live within thy Tedder.

10 Go count with thy cofers,[1] when haruest is in,
which waie for thy profite, to saue or to win:
Of tone of them both, if a sauer wee smel,
house keeping is godlie where euer we dwel.

By haruest is ment al thy stock.

11 Sonne, think not thy monie purse bottom to burn,
but keepe it for profite, to serue thine owne turn:
A foole and his monie be soone at debate,
which after with sorrow repents him too late.

Be thine own purs bearer.

12 Good bargaine a dooing, make priuie but few,
in selling, refraine not abrode it to shew:
In making make haste, and awaie to thy pouch,
in selling no haste, if ye dare it auouch.

13 Good Landlord who findeth, is blessed of God,
A cumbersome Landlord is husbandmans rod:
He noieth, destroieth, and al to this drift,
to strip his poore tenant of ferme and of thrift.

Euill landlord.

[1] coefers. 1577.

Rent corne.

14[1] Rent corn who so paieth, (as worldlings wold haue,
so much for an aker) must liue as a slaue:
Rent corne to be paid, for a reasnable rent,
at reasnable prises is not to lament.

Foure beggers.

15 Once placed for profit, looke neuer for ease,
except ye beware of such michers as thease:
Unthriftines, Slouthfulnes, Careles and Rash,
that thrusteth thee headlong to run in the lash.

Thrifts officers.

16 Make monie thy drudge, for to follow thy warke,
Make wisedome controler, good order thy clarke:
Prouision Cater, and skil to be cooke,
make steward of all, pen, inke, and thy booke.

Thrifts phisicke.

17 Make hunger thy sauce, as a medcine for helth,
make thirst to be butler, as physick for welth:
Make eie to be vsher, good vsage to haue,
make bolt to be porter, to keepe out a knaue.

Thrifts bailie.

18 Make husbandrie bailie, abrode to prouide,
make huswiferie dailie at home for to guide:
Make cofer fast locked, thy treasure to keepe,
make house to be sure, the safer to sleepe.

Husbandly armors.

19 Make bandog thy scoutwatch, to barke at a theefe,
make courage for life to be capitaine cheefe:
Make trapdore thy bulwarke, make bell to begin,[2]
make gunstone and arrow shew who is within.

Théeues to thrift.

20 The credite of maister, to brothell his man,
and also of mistresse, to minnekin Nan,
Be causers of opening a number of gaps,
That letteth in mischiefe and many mishaps.

[1] St. 14 is not in ed. of 1577.

[2] be ginne. 1577.

Friends to thrift.

21 Good husband he trudgeth, to bring in the gaines,
good huswife she drudgeth, refusing no paines:
Though husband at home be to count[1] ye wote what,
yet huswife within is as needfull as that.

Enimie to thrift.

22 What helpeth in store to haue neuer so much,
halfe lost by ill vsage, ill huswiues, and such:
So, twentie lode bushes, cut downe at a clap,
such heede may be taken, shall stop but a gap.

Sixe noiances to thrift.

23 A retcheles[2] seruant, a mistres that scowles,
a rauening mastife, and hogs that eate fowles:
A giddie braine maister, and stroyal his knaue,
brings ruling to ruine, and thrift to hir graue.

Inough is a praise.

24 With some vpon Sundaies, their tables doe reeke,
and halfe the weeke after, their dinners to seeke:
Not often exceeding, but alwaie inough,
is husbandlie fare, and the guise of the plough.

25 Ech daie to be feasted, what husbandrie wurse,
ech daie for to feast, is as ill for the purse:
Yet measurely feasting with neighbors among,
shal make thee beloued, and liue the more long.

Thrifts aduises.

26 Things husbandly handsom let workman contriue,
but build not for glorie, that thinkest to thriue:
Who fondlie in dooing consumeth his stock,
in the end for his follie doth get but a mock.

Spoilers to thrift.

27 Spend none but your owne, howsoeuer ye spend,
for bribing[3] and shifting, haue seldom good end:
In substance although ye haue neuer so much,
delight not in parasites, harlots, and such.[4]

[1] compt. 1577. [2] reachelesse. 1577. [3] bringing. 1577.
[4] In lieu of last two lines, the edition of 1577 reads:

Tithe duely and truely with harty good will,
that god and his blessing may dwell with thee still.

28 Be suretie seldome, (but neuer for much)
for feare of purse penniles hanging by such :
Or Skarborow warning, as ill I beleeue,
when (sir I arest yee) gets hold of thy sleeue.

29 Use (*legem pone*) to paie at thy daie,
but vse not (*Oremus*) for often delaie :
Yet (*Præsta quæsumus*) out of a grate,
Of al other collects, the lender doth hate.

30[1] Be pinched by lending, for kiffe nor for kin,
nor also by spending, by such as come in ;
Nor put to thy hand betwixt bark and the tree,
least through thy owne follie so pinched thou bee.

31[1] As lending to neighbour, in time of his neede,
winnes love of thy neighbour, and credit doth breede,
So neuer to craue, but to liue of thine owne,
brings comforts a thousand, to many vnknowne.

32 Who liuing but lends ? and be lent to they must ;
else buieng and selling might lie in the dust ;
But shameles and craftie, that desperate are,
make many ful honest the woorser to fare.

33 At some time to borow, account it no shame,
if iustlie thou keepest thy touch for the same :
Who quick be to borow, and slow be to paie,
their credit is naught, go they neuer so gaie.

34[2] By shifting and borrowing, who so as liues,
not well to be thought on, occasion giues :
Then lay to liue warily, and wisely to spend,
for prodigall liuers haue seldom good end.

[1] Stanzas 30 and 31 are wanting in 1573 and 1577.
[2] Stanza 34 is not in 1577.

35[1] Some spareth too late, and a number with him,
the foole at the bottom, the wise at the brim :
Who careth nor spareth, till spent he hath all,
Of bobbing, not robbing, be fearefull he shall.

36[1] Where welthines floweth, no friendship can lack,
whom pouertie pincheth, hath friendship as slack :
Then happie is he by example that can
take heede by the fall of a mischieued man.

37 Who breaketh his credit, or cracketh it twise,
trust such with a suretie, if ye be wise :
Or if he be angrie, for asking thy due,
once euen, to him afterward, lend not anue.

38 Account it wel sold that is iustlie well paid,
and count it wel bought that is neuer denaid :
But yet here is tone, here is tother doth best,
for buier and seller, for quiet and rest.

39 Leaue Princes affaires undeskanted on,
and tend to such dooings as stands thee vpon :
Feare God, and offend not the Prince nor his lawes,
and keepe thyselfe out of the Magistrates clawes.[2]

40 As interest or vsurie plaieth the dreuil,
so hilback and filbellie biteth as euil :
Put dicing among them, and docking the dell :
and by and by after, of beggerie smell.[3]

41 Once weekelie remember thy charges to cast, Thrifts Auditor.
once monthlie see how thy expences may last :
If quarter declareth too much to be spent,
for feare of ill yeere take aduise of thy rent.

[1] Stanzas 35 and 36 are not in 1577.
[2] In lieu of last two lines, the edition of 1577 reads—
In substance, although ye have never so much,
delight not in parasites, harlots, and such.
[3] and smell of a begger where ever ye dwell. 1577.

42 Who orderlie entreth his paiment in booke,
may orderlie find them againe (if he looke.)
And he that intendeth but once for to paie:
shall find this in dooing the quietest waie.

43 In dealing vprightlie this counsel I teach,
first recken, then write, er[1] to purse yee doe reach,
Then paie and dispatch him, as soone as ye can:
for lingring is hinderance to many a man.

44 Haue waights, I aduise thee, for siluer & gold,
for some be in knauerie now a daies bold:
And for to be sure good monie to pay:
receiue that is currant, as neere as ye may.

45 Delight not for pleasure two houses to keepe,
least charge without measure vpon thee doe creepe.
And Jankin and Jenikin coosen thee so
to make thee repent it, er yeere about go.

46 The stone that is rouling can gather[2] no mosse,
who often remoooueth is sure of losse.
The rich it compelleth to paie for his pride;
the poore it vndooeth on euerie side.

47 The eie of the maister enricheth the hutch,
the eie of the mistresse auaileth as mutch.
Which eie, if it gouerne, with reason and skil,
hath seruant and seruice, at pleasure and wil.

48 Who seeketh reuengement of euerie wrong,
in quiet nor safetie continueth long.
So he that of wilfulnes trieth the law,
shall striue for a coxcome, and thriue as a daw.

[1] or. 1577.

[2] gether. 1577.

49 To hunters and haukers, take heede what ye saie,
milde answere with curtesie driues them awaie:
So, where a mans better wil open a gap,
resist not with rudenes, for feare of mishap.

50 A man in this world for a churle that is knowne,
shall hardlie in quiet keepe that is his owne:
Where lowlie and such as of curtesie smels,
finds fauor and friendship where euer he dwels.

51 Keepe truelie thy Saboth, the better to speed,
Keepe seruant from gadding, but when it is need.
Keepe fishdaie and fasting daie, as they doe fal:
what custome thou keepest, let others keepe al.

52[1] Though some in their tithing be slack or too bold,
be thou vnto Godward not that waie too cold:
Euill conscience grudgeth, and yet we doe see
ill tithers ill thriuers most commonlie bee.

53 Paie weekelie thy workman, his houshold to feed,
paie quarterlie seruants, to buie as they need:
Giue garment to such as deserue and no mo,
least thou and thy wife without garment doe go.

54 Beware raskabilia, slothfull to wurke,
purloiners and filchers, that loueth to lurke.
Away with such lubbers, so loth to take paine,
that rouies in expences, but neuer no gaine.

55 Good wife, and good children, are worthie to eate,
good seruant, good laborer, earneth their meate:
Good friend, and good neighbor, that fellowlie gest,
with hartilie welcome, should haue of the best.

[1] St. 52 is not in 1577; sts. 56, 58, 59 not in 1573 (M.); 56, 58, 59, 60, 61, 62 not in 1577.

56 Depart not with al that thou hast to thy childe,
much lesse vnto other, for being beguilde:
Least, if thou wouldst gladlie possesse it agen,
looke for to come by it thou wottest not when.

57 The greatest preferment that childe we can giue,
is learning and nurture, to traine him to liue:
Which who so it wanteth, though left as a squier,
consumeth to nothing, as block in the fier.

58 When God hath so blest thee, as able to liue,
and thou hast to rest thee, and able to giue,
Lament thy offences, serue God for amends,
make soule to be readie when God for it sends.

59 Send fruites of thy faith to heauen aforehand,
for mercie here dooing, God blesseth thy land:
He maketh thy store with his blessing to swim,
and after, thy soule to be blessed with him.

60 Some lay to get riches by sea and by land,
and ventreth his life in his enimies hand:
And setteth his soule vpon sixe or on seauen,
not fearing nor caring for hell nor for heauen.

61 Some pincheth, and spareth, and pineth his life,
to cofer vp bags for to leaue to his wife:
And she (when he dieth) sets open the chest,
for such as can sooth hir and all away wrest.

62 Good husband, preuenting the frailnes of some,
takes part of Gods benefits, as they doo come,
And leaueth to wife and his children the rest,
each one his owne part, as he thinketh it best.

63 These lessons approoued, if wiselie ye note,
may saue and auantage ye many a grote.
Which if ye can follow, occasion found,
then euerie lesson may saue ye a pound.

11.

¶ An habitation inforced better late than neuer,

vpon these words Sit downe Robin and rest thee.

Chap. 11.

MY friend, if cause doth wrest thee,
Ere follie hath much opprest thee:
Farre from acquaintance kest thee,
Where countrie may digest thee,
Let wood and water request thee,
In good corne soile to nest thee,
Where pasture and meade may brest thee,
And healthsom aire inuest thee.
Though enuie shall detest thee,
Let that no whit molest thee,
Thanke God, that so hath blest thee,
And sit downe Robin & rest thee.

*** The title in the edition of 1577 reads:
An habitation enforced aduisedly to be followed better late than never, &c.

12.

[Not in 1577.]

¶ The fermers dailie diet.

Chap. 12.

1 A Plot set downe, for fermers quiet,
as time requires, to frame his diet:
With sometime fish, and sometime fast,
that houshold store may longer last.

Lent.

2 Let Lent well kept offend not thee,
for March and Aprill breeders bee:
Spend herring first, saue saltfish last,
for saltfish is good, when Lent is past.

Easter.

3 When Easter comes, who knowes not than,
that Veale and Bakon is the man:
And Martilmas beefe[1] doth beare good tack,
when countrie folke doe dainties lack.

Midsommer.

4 When Mackrell ceaseth from the seas,
John Baptist brings grassebeefe and pease.

Mihelmas.

Fresh herring plentie, Mihell brings,
with fatted Crones,[2] and such old things.

Hallomas.

5 All Saints doe laie for porke and souse,
for sprats and spurlings for their house.

Christmas.

At Christmas play and make good cheere,
for Christmas comes but once a yeere.

A caueat.

6 Though some then doe, as doe they would,
let thriftie doe, as doe they should.

Fasting.

For causes good, so many waies,
keepe Embrings wel, and fasting daies:

Fish daies

7 What lawe commands, we ought to obay,
for Friday, Saturne, and Wednesday.

A thing needful.

The land doth will, the sea doth wish,
spare sometime flesh, and feede of fish.

The last remedie.

Where fish is scant, and fruit of trees,
Supplie that want with butter and cheese.

q, Tusser.

[1] "Dry'd in the Chimney as Bacon, and is so called because it was usual to kill the Beef for this Provision about the Feast of St. Martin, Nov. 11th."—T.R.

[2] "A Crone is a Ewe, whose teeth are so worne down that she can no longer keep her sheep-walk."—T. R.

13.

[Not in 1577.]

A description of the properties of windes *all the times of the yeere.*

Chap. 13.

1 North winds send haile, South winds bring raine, In winter.
East winds we bewail, West winds blow amaine:
North east is too cold, South east not too warme,
North west is too bold, South west doth no harme.

2 The north is a noyer to grasse of all suites, At the spring.
The east a destroyer to herbe and all fruites:
The south with his showers refresheth the corne, Sommer.
The west to all flowers may not be forborne.

3 The West, as a father, all goodnes doth bring, Autumne.
The East, a forbearer, no manner of thing:
The South, as vnkind, draweth sicknesse too neere,
The North, as a friend, maketh all againe cleere.

4 With temperate winde we be blessed of God, God is the gouerner of winde and weather.
With tempest we finde we are beat with his rod:
All power we knowe to remaine in his hand,
How euer winde blowe, by sea or by land.

5 Though windes doe rage, as windes were wood,
And cause spring tydes to raise great flood,
And loftie ships leaue anker in mud,
Bereafing many of life and of blud;
Yet true it is, as cow chawes cud,
And trees at spring doe yeeld forth bud,
Except winde stands as neuer it stood,
It is an ill winde turnes none to good.

14.

[Not in 1577.]

¶ Of the Planets.

Chap. 14.

1 AS huswiues are teached, in stead of a clock,
how winter nights passeth, by crowing of cock;
So here by the Planets, as far as I dare,
some lessons I leaue for the husbandmans share.

Of the rising and going down of the sun.

2 If day star appeareth, day comfort is ny,
If sunne be at south, it is noone by and by:
If sunne be at westward, it setteth anon,
If sunne be at setting, the day is soone gon.

Of the Moone changing.

3 Moone changed, keepes closet three daies as a Queene,
er she in hir prime will of any be seene:
If great she appereth, it showreth out,
If small she appereth, it signifieth drout.
At change or at full, come it late or else soone,
maine sea is at highest, at midnight and noone:
But yet in the creekes it is later high flood,
through farnesse of running, by reason as good.

Of flowing and ebbing to such as be verie sick.

4 Tyde flowing is feared, for many a thing,
great danger to such as be sick it doth bring:
Sea eb by long ebbing some respit doth giue,
and sendeth good comfort to such as shal liue.

15.

¶ Septembers Abstract.

Chap. 15.

1[1] Now enter John,
old fermer is gon.

2[1] What champion vseth,
that woodland refuseth.

3 Good ferme now take,
kéepe still, or forsake.

4 What helpes to reuiue
the thriuing to thriue.

5 Plough, fence, & store
aught else before.

6 By tits and such
few gaineth much.

7 Horse strong and light
soone charges quite.[2]
Light head and purse,
what lightnes wurse.

8 Who goeth[3] a borrowing,
goeth a sorrowing.
Few lends (but fooles)
their working tooles.[4]

9 Gréene rie haue some,
er Mihelmas come.

10 Grant soile hir lust,
sowe rie in the dust.

11 Cleane rie that sowes,
the better crop mowes.

12 Mix rie aright,
with wheat that is whight.

13 Sée corne sowen in,
too thick nor too thin.
For want of séede,
land yéeldeth wéede.

14 With sling or bowe,
kéepe corne from Crowe.

15 Trench hedge and forrow,
that water may thorow.
Déepe dike saues much,
from drouers and such.

16 Amend marsh wall,
Crab holes and all.

[1] Stanzas 1 and 2 not in 1577.
[2] quight. 1577. [3] goes. 1577.
[4] After st. 8, in 1577, follow sts. 36, 37, of August's Abstract. Many stanzas of Sept. Abst, 1577, occur as Aug. Works after harvest in 1580.

17 Geld bulles and rams,
sewe ponds, amend dams.
Sell webster thy wull,
fruite gather, grapes pull.
For fear of drabs,
go gather thy crabs.

18 Plucke fruite to last,
when Mihell[1] is past.

19 Forget it not,
fruit brused will rot.
Light ladder and long
doth trée least wrong.
Go gather with skill,
and gather that will.

20 Driue hiue, good conie,
for waxe and for honie.
No driuing of hiue,
till yéeres past[2] fiue.

21 Good dwelling giue bée,
or hence goes[3] shée.

22 Put bore in stie,
for Hallontide nie.

23 With bore (good Cisse)
let naught be amisse.

24 Karle hempe, left gréene,
now pluck vp cléene.
Drowne hemp as ye néed,
once had out his séed.
I pray thee (good Kit)
drowne hempe in pit.

25 Of al the rest,
white hempe is best.
Let skilfull be gotten
least hempe prooue rotten.

26 Set strawberies, wife,
I loue them for life.

27 Plant Respe and rose,
and such as those.

28 Goe gather vp mast,
er[4] time be past.
Mast fats vp swine,
Mast kils vp kine.

29 Let hogs be roong,
both old and yoong.

30 No mast vpon oke,
no longer[5] vnyoke.
If hog doe crie,
giue eare and eie.

31 Hogs haunting corne
may not be borne.

32 Good neighbour thow
good custome alow,
No scaring with dog,
whilst mast is for hog.

[1] Migchel. 1577. [2] nere. 1577. [3] goeth. 1577.
[4] or. 1577. [5] lenger. 1577.

33 Get home with the brake,
to brue with and bake,
To couer the shed
drie ouer the hed,
To lie vnder cow,[1]
to rot vnder mow,[1]
To serue to burne,
for many a turne.

34 To sawpit drawe
boord log, to sawe.
Let timber be haile,
least profit doe quaile.
Such boord and pale
is readie sale.

35 Sawne slab let lie,
for stable and stie,
sawe dust spred thick,
makes alley trick.

36 Kéepe safe thy fence,
scare breakhedge thence.
A drab and a knaue
will prowle to haue.

37 Marke winde and moone,
at midnight and noone.
Some rigs thy plow,
some milks thy cow.

38 Red cur or black,
few prowlers lack.

39 Some steale, some pilch,
some all away filch,
Mark losses with gréefe,
through prowling théefe.

Thus endeth Septembers abstract, agréeing with Septembers husbandrie.[2]

¶ Other short remem-*brances.*[2]

[40] Now friend, as ye wish,
goe seuer thy fish:
When friend shall come,
to be sure of some.

[41] Thy ponds renew,
put éeles in stew,
To léeue[3] till Lent,
and then to be spent.

[42] Set priuie or prim,
set boxe like him.
Set Giloflowers[4] all,
that growes on the wall.

[43] Set herbes some more,
for winter store.
Sowe séedes for pot,
for flowers sowe not.

Here ends Septembers short remembrances.[2]

[1] To lie under mow,
to rot under kow. 1577.
[2] These and similar notes under other months do not occur in 1577.
[3] liue. 1577.
[4] Gelliflowers. 1577.

16.

¶ Septembers husbandrie.

Chap. 15.

September blowe soft,
Till fruite be in loft.

Forgotten, month past,
Doe now at the last.[1]

1[2] AT Mihelmas lightly new fermer comes in,
new husbandrie forceth him new to begin:
Old fermer, still taking the time to him giuen,
makes August to last vntill Mihelmas euen.

2[2] New fermer may enter (as champions say)
on all that is fallow, at Lent ladie day:
In woodland, old fermer to that will not yeeld,
for loosing of pasture, and feede of his feeld.

Ferme take or giue over.

3 Prouide against Mihelmas,[3] bargaine to make,
for ferme to giue ouer, to keepe or to take:
In dooing of either, let wit beare a stroke,
for buieng or selling of pig in a poke.

Twelue good properties.

4 Good ferme and well stored, good housing and drie,
good corne and good dairie, good market and nie:
Good shepheard, good tilman, good Jack and good Gil,
makes husband and huswife their cofers[4] to fil.

Haue euer a good fence.

5 Let pasture be stored, and fenced about,
and tillage set forward, as needeth without:
Before ye doe open your purse to begin,
with anything dooing for fancie within.

[1] In 1577 these and similar couplets at the beginning of each month's *Husbandrie*, precede the month's *Abstract* instead.
[2] Sts. 1 and 2 not in 1577.
[3] Mighelmas. 1577.
[4] coefers. 1577.

6 No storing of pasture with baggedglie tit,
with ragged,[1] with aged, and euil athit:[2]
Let carren and barren be shifted awaie,
for best is the best, whatsoeuer ye paie.

Best cattle most profit.

7 Horse, Oxen, plough, tumbrel, cart, waggon, & waine,
the lighter and stronger, the greater thy gaine.
The soile and the seede, with the sheafe and the purse,
the lighter in substance, for profite the wurse.

Strong and light.

8 To borow to daie and to-morrow to mis,
for lender and borower, noiance it is:
Then haue of thine owne, without lending vnspilt,
what followeth needfull, here learne if thou wilt.[3]

Hate borowing.

*** The stanzas of No. 16 are continued after the following *Digression*.

17.

A digression to husbandlie furniture.

1 Barne locked, gofe ladder, short pitchforke and long,
flaile, strawforke and rake, with a fan that is strong:
Wing, cartnaue and bushel, peck, strike readie hand,
get casting sholue, broome, and a sack with a band.

Barne furniture.

2 A stable wel planked, with key and a lock,
walles stronglie wel lyned,[4] to beare off a knock:
A rack and a manger, good litter and haie,
swéete chaffe and some prouender euerie daie.

Stable furniture.

3 A pitchfork, a doongfork, seeue, skep and a bin,
a broome and a paile to put water therein:
A handbarow, wheelebarow, sholue and a spade,
a currie combe, mainecombe, and whip for a Jade.

[1] rakged. 1577. [2] at hyt. 1577.
[3] Or borow with sorow as long as thou wilt. 1577.
[4] liened. 1577.

4 A buttrice[1] and pincers, a hammer and naile,
an aperne and siszers for head and for taile:
Hole bridle and saddle, whit lether and nall,
with collers and harneis, for thiller and all.

5 A panel and wantey, packsaddle and ped,
A line to fetch litter, and halters for hed.
With crotchis and pinnes, to hang trinkets theron,
and stable fast chained, that nothing be gon.

Cart furniture.

6 Strong exeltred cart, that is clouted[2] and shod,[3]
cart ladder and wimble, with percer and pod:
Wheele ladder for haruest, light pitchfork and tough,
shaue, whiplash[4] wel knotted, and cartrope ynough.

A Coeme is halfe a quarter.

7 Ten sacks, whereof euerie one holdeth a coome,
a pulling hooke handsome, for bushes and broome:
Light tumbrel and doong crone, for easing sir wag,
sholue, pickax, and mattock, with bottle and bag.

Husbandry tooles.

8 A grinstone, a whetstone, a hatchet and bil,
with hamer and english naile, sorted with skil:
A frower of iron, for cleauing of lath,
with roule for a sawpit, good husbandrie hath.

9 A short saw and long saw, to cut a too logs,
an ax and a nads, to make troffe for thy hogs:
A Douercourt beetle, and wedges with steele,
strong leuer to raise vp the block fro the wheele.

Plough furniture.

10 Two ploughs and a plough chein, ij culters, iij shares,
with ground cloutes & side clouts for soile that so tares:
With ox bowes and oxyokes, and other things mo,
for oxteeme and horseteeme, in plough for to go.

[1] To pare horse's hoofs with.—"Tusser Redivivus."

[2] "Clouting is arming the Axle-Tree with Iron plates."—T.R.

[3] "Arming the Fellowes with Iron Strakes, or a Tire as some call it."—T.R. Strakes are segments of a tire.

[4] "Of a tough piece of Whitleather."—T.R.

11 A plough beetle, ploughstaff, to further the plough,
great clod to a sunder that breaketh so rough;
A sled for a plough, and another for blocks,
for chimney in winter, to burne vp their docks.

12 Sedge collers[1] for ploughhorse, for lightnes of neck,
good seede and good sower, and also seede peck:
Strong oxen and horses, wel shod and wel clad,
wel meated and vsed, for making thee sad.

13 A barlie rake toothed, with yron and steele,
like paier of harrowes, and roler doth weele:
A sling for a moether, a bowe for a boy.
a whip for a carter, is hoigh de la roy.

14 A brush sithe and grasse sithe, with rifle to stand, Haruest tooles.
a cradle for barlie, with rubstone and sand:
Sharpe sikle and weeding hooke, haie fork and rake,
a meake for the pease, and to swinge vp the brake.

15[2] Short rakes for to gather vp barlie to binde,
and greater to rake vp such leauings behinde:
A rake for to hale vp the fitchis that lie,
a pike for to pike them vp handsom to drie.

16[3] A skuttle or skreine, to rid soile fro the corne,
and sharing sheares readie for sheepe to be shorne:
A fork and a hooke, to be tampring in claie,[4]
a lath hammer, trowel, a hod, or a traie.

[1] "Lightest and coolest, but indeed not so comly as those of Wadmuś." —T.R.

[2] St. 15 not in 1577, but as follows:—

Rakes also for barley, long toothed in hed,
and greater like toothed for barley so shed.

and first couplet of st. 16.

[3] St. 16 not thus in 1577; see note 2, and next note.

[4] In 1577 the second couplet of st. 16 makes a stanza with the following:

Strong fetters and shakles, with horslock and pad;
Strong soles, and such other thinges, meete to be had.

17 Strong yoke for a hog, with a twicher and rings,
with tar in a tarpot, for dangerous things:[1]
A sheepe marke, a tar kettle, little or mitch,
two pottles of tar to a pottle of pitch.

18 Long ladder to hang al along by the wal,
to reach for a neede to the top of thy hal:
Beame, scales, with the weights, that be sealed and true,
sharp moulspare with barbs, that the mowles do so rue.

19[2] Sharpe cutting spade, for the deuiding of mow,
with skuppat and skauel, that marsh men alow:
A sickle to cut with, a didall and crome
for draining of ditches, that noies thee at home.

20[3] A clauestock and rabetstock, carpenters craue,
and seasoned timber, for pinwood to haue:
A Jack for to saw vpon fewell for fier,
for sparing of firewood, and sticks fro the mier.

21 Soles, fetters, and shackles, with horselock and pad,
a cow house for winter, so meete to be had:
A stie for a bore, and a hogscote for hog,
a roost for thy hennes, and a couch for thy dog.

Here endeth husbandlie furniture.

[1] Hog yokes, and a twicher, and ringes for a hog,
with tar in a pot, for the byeting of dog. 1577.

[2] St. 19 not in 1577.

[3] St. 20 not in 1577.

*** In the edition of 1577 stanzas 31–46 of Augusts Husbandrie (*post*) are found here.

[**16** *contd.*]

9 Thresh seed and to fanning, September doth crie,
get plough to the field, and be sowing of rie:
To harrow the rydgis, er euer ye strike,
is one peece[1] of husbandrie Suffolk doth like. Sowing of rie.

10 Sowe timely thy whitewheat, sowe rie in the dust,
let seede haue his longing, let soile haue hir lust:
Let rie be partaker of Mihelmas spring,
to beare out the hardnes that winter doth bring.

11[2] Some mixeth to miller the rie with the wheat, Myslen.
Temmes lofe on his table to haue for to eate:
But sowe it not mixed, to growe so on land,
least rie tarie wheat, till it shed as it stand.

12 If soile doe desire to haue rie with the wheat,
by growing togither, for safetie more great,
Let white wheat be ton, be it deere, be it cheape,
the sooner to ripe, for the sickle to reape.

13 Though beanes be in sowing but scattered in, Sowing.
yet wheat, rie, and peason, I loue not too thin:
Sowe barlie and dredge, with a plentifull hand,
least weede, steed of seede, ouer groweth thy land.

14[3] No sooner a sowing, but out by and by,
with mother[4] or boy that Alarum can cry:
And let them be armed with sling or with bowe, Keeping of crowes.
to skare away piggen, the rooke and the crowe.

15 Seed sowen, draw a forrough, the water to draine, Water furrough.
and dike vp such ends as in harmes[5] doe remaine:
For driuing of cattell or rouing that waie,
which being preuented, ye hinder their praie.

[1] This point of good husbandry, etc. 1577. [2] St. 11 not in 1577.
[3] Sts. 14 and 15 not in 1577, but nine stanzas which do not occur here.
[4] Cf. *ante*, ch. 17, st. 13. [5] Cf. *post*, ch. 19, st. 6.

Amend marsh walles.

16 Saint Mihel[1] doth bid thee amend the marsh wal,
the brecke and the crab hole, the foreland and al:
One noble in season bestowed theron,
may saue thee a hundred er winter be gon.

Gelding of rams.

17 Now geld with the gelder the ram and the bul,
sew ponds, amend dammes, and sel webster thy wul:
Out fruit go and gather, but not in the deaw,
with crab and the wal nut, for feare of a shreaw.

Gathering of fruit.

18 The Moone in the wane, gather fruit for to last,
but winter fruit gather when Mihel[1] is past:
Though michers that loue not to buy nor to craue,
makes some gather sooner, else few for to haue.

Too early gathering is not best.

19 Fruit gathred too timely wil taste of the wood,
wil shrink[2] and be bitter, and seldome prooue good:
So fruit that is shaken, or beat off a tree,
with brusing in falling, soone faultie wil bee.

Driuing of hiues.

20 Now burne vp the bees that ye mind for to driue,
at Midsomer driue them and saue them aliue:
Place hiue in good ayer, set southly and warme,
and take in due season wax, honie, and swarme.

Preseruing of bées.

21 Set hiue on a plank, (not too low by the ground)
where herbe with the flowers may compas it round:
And boordes to defend it from north and north east,
from showers and rubbish, from vermin and beast.

Stie up the bore.

22 At Mihelmas safely go stie vp thy Bore,
least straying abrode, ye doo see him no more:
The sooner the better for Halontide nie,
and better he brawneth if hard he doo lie.

[1] Mighel. 1577.

[2] "If Fruit stand too long it will be mealy, which is worse than shrively, for now most Gentlemen chuse the shriveled Apple."—T.R.

23 Shift bore (for il aire) as best ye do thinke,
and twise a day giue him fresh vittle and drinke:
And diligent Cislye, my dayrie good wench,
make cleanly his cabben, for measling and stench.

24 Now pluck vp thy hempe, and go beat out the seed,
and afterward water it as ye see need:
But not in the riuer where cattle should drinke,
for poisoning them and the people with stinke.

Gathering of winter hempe.

25 Hempe huswifely vsed lookes cleerely and bright,
and selleth it selfe by the colour so whight:
Some vseth to water it, some do it not,[1]
be skilful in dooing, for feare it do rot.

Whitest hempe best sold.

26 Wife, into thy garden, and set me a plot,
with strawbery rootes, of the best to be got:
Such growing abroade, among thornes in the wood,
wel chosen and picked prooue excellent good.

Setting of strawberies & roses, &c.

27 The Barbery, Respis, and Goosebery too,
looke now to be planted as other things doo:
The Goosebery, Respis, and Roses, al three,
with Strawberies vnder them trimly agree.

Gooseberies & Respis.

28 To gather some mast, it shal stand thee vpon,
with seruant and children, er mast be al gon:
Some left among bushes shal pleasure thy swine,
for feare of a mischiefe keepe acorns fro kine.

Gathering of mast.

29 For rooting of pasture ring hog ye had neede,
which being wel ringled the better do feede:
Though yong with their elders wil lightly keepe best,
yet spare not to ringle both great and the rest.

Rooting of hogs.

[1] "Ther is a Water-retting and a Dew-retting, which last is done on a good Rawing, or aftermath of a Meadow Water."—T.R.

Yoking of swine.

30 Yoke seldom thy swine while the shacktime[1] doth last,
for diuers misfortunes that happen too fast:
Or if ye do fancie whole eare of the hog,
giue eie to il neighbour and eare to his dog.

Hunting of hogs.

31 Keepe hog I aduise thee from medow and corne,
for out aloude crying that ere he was borne:
Such lawles, so haunting, both often and long,
if dog set him chaunting he doth thee no wrong.

32 Where loue among neighbors do beare any stroke,
whiles shacktime indureth men vse not to yoke:

Ringling of hogs.

Yet surely ringling is needeful and good,
til frost do enuite them to brakes in the wood.

Carriage of brakes.

33[2] Get home with thy brakes, er an sommer be gon,
for teddered cattle to sit there vpon:
To couer thy houel, to brewe and to bake,
to lie in the bottome, where houel ye make.

Sawe out thy timber.

34 Now sawe out thy timber, for boord and for pale,
to haue it vnshaken, and ready to sale:
Bestowe it and stick it,[3] and lay it aright,
to find it in March, to be ready in plight.

Slabs of timber.

35 Saue slab[4] of thy timber for stable and stie,
for horse and for hog the more clenly to lie:
Saue sawe dust, and brick dust, and ashes so fine,
for alley to walke in, with neighbour of thine.

Hedge breakers.

36 Keepe safely and warely thine vttermost fence,
with ope gap and breake hedge do seldome dispence:
Such runabout prowlers, by night and by day,
see punished iustly for prowling away.

[1] "After Harvest."—T.R.
[2] This is placed before st. 9 in 1577.
[3] "Laying the Boards handsomely one upon another with sticks between."—T.R.
[4] The outermost piece.

37 At noone if it bloweth, at night if it shine,
out trudgeth Hew make shift, with hooke & with line: Learne to know Hewe prowler.
Whiles Gillet, his blouse, is a milking thy cow,
Sir Hew is a rigging thy gate or the plow.

38 Such walke with a black or a red little cur, Black or red dogs.
that open wil quickly, if anything stur;
Then squatteth the master, or trudgeth away,
and after dog runneth as fast as he may.

39 Some prowleth for fewel, and some away rig
fat goose, and the capon, duck, hen, and the pig:
Some prowleth for acornes, to fat vp their swine,
for corne and for apples, and al that is thine.

Thus endeth Septembers husbandrie.[1]

*** Many stanzas do not occur or are not in the same order in 1577.

18.

¶ Octobers abstract.

Chap. 16.

1 LAY drie vp and round,
for barlie thy ground.
Flaies lustily thwack,
least plough séede lack.

2 Too late doth kill,
too soone is as ill.

3 Maides little and great,
pick cleane séede wheat.
Good ground doth craue
choice séede to haue.

4[2] Séede first go fetch,
for edish or etch,
Soile perfectly knowe,
er edish ye sowe.

5 White wheat, if ye please,
sowe now vpon pease.

[1] Cf. note 2, p. 33.
[2] 1577 inserts— Plie sowing a pace,
in euery place.

Sowe first the best,
and then the rest.

6[1] Who soweth in raine,
hath wéed to his paine.
But worse shall he spéed,
that soweth ill séed.

7 Now, better than later,
draw furrow for water.
Kéepe crowes, good sonne,
sée fencing[2] be donne.

8[3] Each soile no vaine
for euerie graine.
Though soile be but bad,
some corne may be had.

9 Naught proue, naught craue,
naught venter, naught haue.

10 One crop and away,
some countrie may say.

11 All grauell and sand,
is not the best land.
A rottenly mould
is land woorth gould.

12 Why wheat is smitten
good lesson is written.

13 The iudgement of some
how thistles doe come.

14 A iudgement right,
of land in plight.
Land, all forlorne,
not good for corne.

15 Land barren doth beare
small strawe, short eare.

16 Here maist thou réede
for soile what séede.

17 Tis tride ery hower,
best graine most flower.

18 Grosse corne much bran
the baker doth ban.

19[4] What croppers bée
here learne to sée.

20[4] Few after crop much,
but noddies and such.

21 Som woodland may crake,
thrée crops he may take.

22 First barlie, then pease,
then wheat, if ye please.

[1] St. 6 is not in 1577.
[2] furrowing. 1577.
[3] Sts. 8–30 do not occur here in 1577; but sts. 32–37 follow.
[4] Sts. 19 and 20 are in Septembers Abstract in 1577.

23 Two crops and away,
must champion say.

24[1] Where barlie did growe,
laie[2] wheat to sowe.
Yet better I thinke,
sowe pease after drinke.
And then, if ye please,
sowe wheat after pease.

25 What champion knowes
that custome showes.

26 First barlie er rie,
then pease by and by.
Then fallow for wheat,
is husbandrie great.

27 A remedie sent,
where pease lack vent.
Fat peasefed swine
for drouer is fine.

28 Each diuers soile
hath diuers toile.

29 Some countries vse
that some refuse.

30 For wheat ill land,
where water doth stand.
Sowe pease or dredge
belowe in that redge.

31 Sowe acornes to prooue
that timber doe looue.

32 Sowe hastings now,
if land[3] it alow.

33 Learne soone to get
a good quickset.

34 For feare of the wurst
make fat away furst.

35 Fat that no more
ye kéepe for store.

36 Hide carren in graue,
lesse noiance to haue.

37 Hog measeled kill,
for flemming that will.

38[4] With peasebolt and brake
some brew and bake.

39 Old corne[5] worth gold,
so kept as it shold.

40 Much profit is rept,
by sloes well kept.

41 Kéepe sloes vpon bow,
for flixe of thy cow.

[1] In Septembers Abstract in 1577.
[2] strike. 1577.
[3] ground. 1577.
[4] In 1577, sts. 38 to the end are much transposed.
[5] graine. 1577.

42 Of vergis be sure,
poore cattel to cure.

Thus endeth Octobers abstract, agréeing with Octobers husbandrie.[1]

¶ Other short remem-
brances.[1]

[43] Cisse, haue an eie
to bore in the stie.
By malt ill kept,
small profit is rept.

[44] Friend, ringle thy hog,
for feare of a dog.
Rie straw up stack,
least Thacker doe lack.

[45] Wheat straw drie saue,
for cattell to haue.
Wheat chaffe lay vp drie,
in safetie to lie.

[46] Make handsome a bin,
for chaffe to lie in.

[47] (Séede thresht) thou shalt
thresh barlie to malt.
Cut bushes to hedge,
fence medow and redge.

[48] Stamp crabs that may,
for rotting away.
Make vergis and perie,
sowe kirnell and berie.

[49] Now gather vp fruite,
of euerie suite.
Marsh wall too slight,
strength now, or god night.

[50][2] Mend wals of mud,
for now it is good.
Where soile is of sand,
quick set out of hand.

[51] To plots not full
ad bremble and hull.
For set no bar
whilst month hath an R.
Like note thou shalt
for making of malt.
Brew now to last
till winter be past.

Here ends Octobers short remembrances.[1]

[1] Cf. note 2, p. 33.
[2] First couplet of st. 50 not in 1577

19.

¶ Octobers husbandrie.

Chap. 17.

October good blast,
To blowe the hog mast.

Forgotten month past,
Doe now at the last.

1 NOW lay vp thy barley land, drie as ye can, Laie vp barlie land.
when euer ye sowe it so looke for it than:
Get daily aforehand, be neuer behinde;
least winter preuenting do alter thy minde.

2 Who laieth vp fallow too soone or too wet,
with noiances many doth barley beset.
For weede and the water so soketh and sucks,
that goodnes from either it vtterly plucks.

3 Greene rie in September when timely thou hast,
October for wheat sowing calleth as fast. Wheat sowing.
If weather will suffer, this counsell I giue,
Leaue sowing of wheat before Hallomas eue.

4 Where wheat vpon edish ye mind to bestowe, Sowe edish betimes.
let that be the first of the wheat ye do sowe:
He seemeth to hart it and comfort to bring,
that giueth it comfort of Mihelmas spring.

5 White wheat vpon peaseetch doth grow as he wold, Best wheat first sowen.
but fallow is best, if we did as we shold:[1]
Yet where, how, and when, ye entend to begin,
let euer the finest be first sowen in.[2]

6[3] Who soweth in raine, he shall reape it with teares,
who soweth in harmes,[4] he is euer in feares,
Who soweth ill seede or defraudeth his land,
hath eie sore abroode, with a coresie at hand.

[1] White wheat upon pease etch is willing to grow:
though best upon fallow as many do knowe. 1577.

[2] After st. 5, 1577 has st. 31 *post*.

[3] St. 6 not in 1577.

[4] "In harms or harms way, whether of Roads, ill Neighbours, Torrents of Water, Conies, or other Vermin."—T.R. Cf. *ante*, ch. 16, st. 15.

7[1] Seede husbandly sowen, water furrow[2] thy ground,
that raine when it commeth may run away round,
Then stir about Nicoll, with arrow and bowe,
take penie for killing of euerie crowe.

[Not in 1577.]

A digression to the usage of diuers countries, concerning Tillage.

8 Each soile hath no liking of euerie graine,
nor barlie and wheat is for euerie vaine:
Yet knowe I no countrie so barren of soile
but some kind of corne may be gotten with toile.

9 In Brantham, where rie but no barlie did growe,
good barlie I had, as a meany did knowe:
Five seame of an aker I truely was paid,
for thirtie lode muck of each aker so laid.

10 In Suffolke againe, where as wheat neuer grew,
good husbandrie vsed good wheat land I knew:
This Prouerbe experience long ago gaue,
that nothing who practiseth nothing shall haue.

11 As grauell and sand is for rie and not wheat,
(or yeeldeth hir burden to tone the more great,)
So peason and barlie delight not in sand,
but rather in claie or in rottener land.

12 Wheat somtime is steelie or burnt as it growes,
for pride[3] or for pouertie practise so knowes.
Too lustie of courage for wheat doth not well,
nor after sir peeler he loueth to dwell.

[1] In Septembers Husbandry, 1577.
[2] "Furrows drawn cross the Ridges in the lowest part of the Ground."—T.R.
[3] "or too much Dung."—T.R.

13 Much wetnes, hog rooting, and land out of hart,
makes thistles a number foorthwith to vpstart.
If thistles so growing prooue lustie and long,
it signifieth land to be hartie and strong.

14 As land full of tilth and in hartie good plight,
yeelds blade to a length and encreaseth in might,
So crop vpon crop, vpon whose courage we doubt,
yeelds blade for a brag, but it holdeth not out.

15 The straw and the eare to haue bignes and length,
betokeneth land to be good and in strength.
If eare be but short, and the strawe be but small,
it signifieth barenes and barren withall.

16 White wheat or else red, red riuet or whight,
far passeth all other, for land that is light.
White pollard or red, that so richly is set,
for land that is heauie is best ye can get.

17 Maine wheat that is mixed with white and with red
is next to the best in the market mans hed:
So Turkey or Purkey wheat many doe loue,
because it is flourie, as others aboue.

18 Graie wheat is the grosest, yet good for the clay,
though woorst for the market, as fermer may say.
Much like vnto rie be his properties found,
coorse flower, much bran, and a peeler of ground.

19 Otes, rie, or else barlie, and wheat that is gray,
brings land out of comfort, and soone to decay:
One after another, no comfort betweene,
is crop vpon crop, as will quickly be seene.

Crop vpon crop.

20 Still crop vpon crop many fermers do take,
and reape little profit for greedines sake.
Though breadcorne & drinkcorn such croppers do stand:
count peason or brank, as a comfort to land.

21 Good land that is seuerall, crops may haue three,
in champion countrie it may not so bee:
Ton taketh his season, as commoners may,
the tother with reason may otherwise say.

22 Some vseth at first a good fallow to make,
to sowe thereon barlie, the better to take.
Next that to sowe pease, and of that to sowe wheat,
then fallow againe, or lie lay for thy neat.

23 First rie, and then barlie, the champion saies,
or wheat before barlie be champion waies:
But drinke before bread corne with Middlesex men,
then lay on more compas, and fallow agen.

24 Where barlie ye sowe, after rie or else wheat,
if land be vnlustie,[1] the crop is not great,
So lose ye your cost, to your coresie and smart,
and land (ouerburdened) is cleane out of hart.

25 Exceptions take of the champion land,
from lieng alonge from that at thy hand.
(Just by) ye may comfort with compas at will,
far off ye must comfort with fauor and skill.

26 Where rie or else wheat either barlie ye sowe,
let codware be next, therevpon for to growe:
Thus hauing two crops, whereof codware is ton,
thou hast the lesse neede, to lay cost therevpon.

[1] "There is a sort of Barley, called Sprat Barley, or Battledore Barley, that will grow very well on lusty land."—T. R.

27 Some far fro the market delight not in pease,
for that ery chapman they seeme not to please.
If vent of the market place serue thee not well,
set hogs vp a fatting, to drouer to sell.

28 Two crops of a fallow enricheth the plough,
though tone be of pease, it is land good ynough:
One crop and a fallow some soile will abide,
where if ye go furder lay profit aside.

29 Where peason ye had and a fallow thereon,
sowe wheat ye may well without doong therevpon:
New broken vpland, or with water opprest,
or ouer much doonged, for wheat is not best.

30 Where water all winter annoieth too much,
bestowe not thy wheat vpon land that is such:
But rather sowe otes, or else bullimong there,
gray peason, or runciuals, fitches, or tere.

31 Sowe acornes ye owners, that timber doe looue, Sowing of acorns.
sowe hawe and rie with them the better to prooue;
If cattel or cunnie may enter to crop,
yong oke is in daunger of loosing his top.

32 Who pescods delighteth to haue with the furst, Sowing of Hastings or fullams.
if now he do sowe them, I thinke it not wurst.
The greener thy peason and warmer the roome,
more lusty the layer, more plenty they come.

33 Go plow vp or delue vp, aduised with skill,
the bredth of a ridge, and in length as you will.
Where speedy quickset for a fence ye wil drawe,
to sowe in the seede of the bremble and hawe.

A disease in fat hogs.

34 Through plenty of acornes, the porkling to fat,
not taken in season, may perish by that,
If ratling or swelling get once to the throte,
thou loosest thy porkling, a crowne to a grote.

Not to fat for rearing.

35 What euer thing fat is, againe if it fall,
thou ventrest the thing and the fatnes withall,
The fatter the better, to sell or to kil,
but not to continue, make proofe if ye wil.

Burieng of dead cattell.

36 What euer thing dieth, go burie or burne,
for tainting of ground, or a woorser il turne.
Such pestilent smell of a carrenly thing,
to cattle and people great peril may bring.

Measeled hogs.

37 Thy measeled bacon, hog, sow, or thy bore,
shut vp for to heale, for infecting thy store:
Or kill it for bacon, or sowce it to sell,
for Flemming, that loues it so deintily well.

Strawwisps and peas-bolts.

38 With strawisp and peasebolt, with ferne and the brake,
for sparing of fewel, some brewe and do bake,
And heateth their copper, for seething of graines:
good seruant rewarded, refuseth no paines.

Olde wheat better than new.

39 Good breadcorne and drinkcorne, full xx weekes kept,
is better then new, that at harvest is rept:
But foisty the breadcorne and bowd eaten malt,
for health or for profit, find noysome thou shalt.

40[1] By thend of October, go gather vp sloes,
haue thou in a readines plentie of thoes,
And keepe them in bedstraw, or still on the bow,
to staie both the flixe of thyselfe and thy cow.

[1] Stanza 40 is not in 1577.

41 Seeith water and plump therein plenty of sloes,
mix chalke[1] that is dried in powder with thoes.
Which so, if ye giue, with the water and chalke,
thou makest the laxe fro thy cow away walke.

A medicen for the cow flixe.

42[2] Be sure of vergis (a gallond at least)
so good for the kitchen, so needfull for beast,
It helpeth thy cattel, so feeble and faint,
if timely such cattle with it thou acquaint.

Thus endeth Octobers husbandrie.

20.

¶ Nouembers abstract.

Chap. 18.

1 LET hog once fat,
loose nothing of that.
When mast is gon,
hog falleth anon,
Still fat vp some,
till Shroftide come.
Now porke and souse,
beares tack in house.

2 Put barlie to malting,
lay flitches a salting.
Through follie too beastlie
much bacon is reastie.[3]

3 Some winnow, some fan,
some cast that can.[4]
In casting prouide,
for séede lay aside.

4 Thresh barlie thou shalt,
for chapman to malt.
Else thresh no more
but for thy store.

5[5] Till March thresh wheat,
but as ye doo eat,
Least baker forsake it
if foystines take it.

[1] chawlk. 1577. [2] Stanza 42 is not in 1577. [3] resty. 1577
[4] 1577 reads—

Let husbandly man
make clene as he can.

[5] Not in 1577.

6 No chaffe in bin,
makes horse looke thin.

7[1] Sowe hastings now,
that hastings alow.

8 They buie it full déere,
in winter that réere.

9 Few fowles, lesse swine,
rere now, friend mine.

10 What losse, what sturs,
through rauening curs.

11 Make Martilmas béefe,
déere meate is a théefe.

12 Set garlike and pease,
saint Edmond to please.

13 When raine takes place,
to threshing apace.

14 Mad braine, too rough,
marres all at plough.
With flaile and whips,
fat hen short skips.

15 Some threshing by taske,
will steale and not aske:
Such thresher at night
walkes seldom home light.
Some corne away lag
in bottle and bag.
Some steales, for a iest,
egges out of the nest.

16 Lay stouer vp drie
in order to lie.
Poore bullock[2] doth craue
fresh straw to haue.

17 Make wéekly vp flower,
though threshers do lower:
Lay graine in loft
and turne it oft.

18 For muck, regard,
make cleane foule yard.
Lay straw to rot,
in watrie plot.

19 Hedlond vp plow,
for compas ynow.

20 For herbes good store,
trench garden more.

21 At midnight trie
foule priuies to fie.

22 Rid chimney of soot,
from top to the foot.

23 In stable, put now
thy horses for plow.

24 Good horsekeeper will
laie muck vpon hill.

25[3] Cut molehils that stand
so thick vpon land.

Thus endeth Nouembers abstract, agréeing with Nouembers husbandrie.

[1] Stanzas 7–10 are not in 1577.

[2] kow.

[3] St. 25 is not in 1577.

¶ Other short remem-
brances.

26 Get pole, boy mine,
beate hawes to swine.
Driue hog to the wood,
brake rootes be good.

27 For mischiefe that falles,
looke well to marsh walles.
Drie laier get neate,
and plentie of meate.

28 Curst cattel that nurteth,
poore wennel soon hurteth.
Good neighbour mine,
ring well thy swine.

29 Such winter may serue,
hog ringled[1] will sterue.
In frost kéepe dog
from hunting of hog.

Here ends Nouembers short remembrances.

21.

¶ Nouembers husbandrie.

Chap. 19.

Nouember take flaile,
Let ship no more saile.

Forgotten month past,
Doe now at the last.

1 AT Hallontide, slaughter time entereth in,
and then doth the husbandmans feasting begin:
From thence vnto shroftide kill now and then some,
their offal for houshold the better wil come.

Slaughter time.

2 Thy dredge and thy barley go thresh out to malt,
let malster be cunning, else lose it thou shalt:
Thencrease of a seame is a bushel for store,
bad else is the barley, or huswife much more.

Dredge is otes and barlie.

[1] ringd. 1577.

Winnowing, fanning, and casting.

3 Some vseth to winnow,[1] some vseth to fan,
some vseth to cast it as cleane as they can:
For seede goe and cast it, for malting not so,
but get out the cockle,[2] and then let it go.

Threshing of barlie.

4 Thresh barlie as yet but as neede shal require,
fresh threshed for stoouer thy cattel desire:
And therefore that threshing forbeare as ye may,
till Candelmas comming, for sparing of hay.

5 Such wheat as ye keepe for the baker to buie,
vnthreshed till March in the sheafe let it lie,
Least foistnes take it if sooner yee thresh it,
although by oft turning ye seeme to refresh it.

Chaffe of corn.

6 Saue chaffe of the barlie, of wheate, and of rie,
from feathers and foistines, where it doth lie,
Which mixed with corne, being sifted of dust,
go giue to thy cattel, when serue them ye must.

7[3] Greene peason or hastings at Hallontide sowe,
in hartie good soile he requireth to growe:
Graie peason or runciuals cheerely to stand,
at Candlemas sowe, with a plentifull hand.

8 Leaue latewardly rering, keepe now no more swine,
but such as thou maist, with the offal of thine:
Except ye haue wherewith to fat them away,
the fewer thou keepest, keepe better yee may.

9 To rere vp much pultrie, and want the barne doore,
is naught for the pulter and woorse for the poore.
So, now to keepe hogs and to sterue them for meate,
is as to keepe dogs for to bawle in the streate.

[1] winnew. 1557.
[2] "If the Cockle be left in, it will work, and some say make the Drink the stronger."—T. R.
[3] Stanzas 7–10 are not in 1577.

10 As cat a good mouser is needfull in house,
   because for hir commons she killeth the mouse,
So rauening curres, as a meany doo keepe,
   makes master want meat, and his dog to kill sheepe.

11 (For Easter) at Martilmas hang vp a beefe, — Martilmas beefe.
   for stalfed and pease fed plaie pickpurse the theefe:
With that and the like, er an grasse biefe come in,
   thy folke shal looke cheerelie when others looke thin.

12 Set garlike and beanes, at S. Edmond[1] the king, — ¶ Set garlike and beanes.
   the moone in the wane, thereon hangeth a thing:
Thencrease of a pottle (well prooued of some)
   shal pleasure thy houshold er peskod time come.

13 When raine is a let to thy dooings abrode, — Threshing.
   set threshers a threshing to laie on good lode:
Thresh cleane ye must bid them, though lesser they yarn,
   and looking to thriue, haue an eie to thy barne.

14 Take heede to thy man in his furie and heate, — Cattle beaters.
   with ploughstaff and whipstock, for maiming thy neate:
To thresher for hurting of cow with his flaile,
   or making thy hen to plaie tapple vp taile.

15 Some pilfering thresher will walke with a staffe, — Corne stealers.
   will carrie home corne as it is in the chaffe,
And some in his bottle of leather so great
   will carry home daily both barlie and wheat.

16 If houseroome will serue thee, lay stouer vp drie, — Kéepe dry thy straw.
   and euerie sort by it selfe for to lie.
Or stack it for litter, if roome be too poore,
   and thatch out the residue noieng thy doore.[2]

[1] 20th November.

[2] "The rest may lie in the open Yard, for the Cattle to tread into Dung, which is the practice now a days, so that our Farmers are not so afraid of noying their Doors it seems as formerly, and that not without good reason." —T. R.

Euerie wéeke rid thy barne flower.

17 Cause weekly thy thresher to make vp his flower,
though slothfull and pilferer thereat doo lower:
Take tub for a season, take sack for a shift,
yet garner for graine is the better for thrift.

18 All maner of strawe that is scattered in yard,
good husbandlie husbands haue daily regard,
In pit full of water the same to bestowe,
where lieng to rot, thereof profit may growe.

Digging of hedlonds.

19 Now plough vp thy hedlond,[1] or delue it with spade,
where otherwise profit but little is made:
And cast it vp high, vpon hillocks to stand,
that winter may rot it, to compas thy land.

Trenching of garden.

20 If garden requier it, now trench it ye may,
one trench not a yard from another go lay:
Which being well filled with muck by and by,
go couer with mould for a season to ly.

Clensing of priuies.

21 Foule priuies are now to be clensed and fide,
let night be appointed such baggage to hide:
Which buried in garden, in trenches alowe,
shall make very many things better to growe.

Sootie chimneyes.

22 The chimney all sootie would now be made cleene,
for feare of mischances, too oftentimes seene:
Old chimney and sootie, if fier once take,
by burning and breaking, soone mischeefe may make.

Put horse into stable.

23 When ploughing is ended, and pasture not great,
then stable thy horses, and tend them with meat:
Let season be drie when ye take them to house,
for danger of nittes, or for feare of a louse.

[1] T.R. thinks that here is meant "such Ground in Common Field-land, which the whole Shot (or parcel of Land belonging to many Men against which it lies) turn upon."

24 Lay compas vp handsomly, round on a hill,
to walke in thy yard at thy pleasure and will,
More compas it maketh and handsom the plot,
if horsekeeper daily forgetteth it not. Sauing of doong.

25[1] Make hillocks of molehils, in field thorough out,
and so to remaine, till the yeere go about.
Make also the like whereas plots be too hie,
all winter a rotting for compas to lie.

Thus endeth Nouembers husbandrie.

22.

¶ Decembers abstract.

Chap. 20.

1 NO season to hedge,
get béetle and wedge.
Cleaue logs now all,
for kitchen and hall.

2 Dull working tooles
soone courage cooles.

3 Leaue off tittle tattle,
and looke to thy cattle.
Serue yoong poore elues
alone by themselues.

4 Warme barth for neate,
woorth halfe their meate.
The elder that nurteth
the yonger soone hurteth.

5 Howse cow that is old,
while winter doth hold.

6 Out once in a day,
to drinke and to play.

7 Get trustie to serue,
least cattle doo sterue.
And such as in déede
may helpe at a néede.

8 Obserue this law,
in seruing out straw.

9 In walking about,
good forke spie out.

[1] St. 25 is not in 1577.

10 At full and at change,
spring tides are strange.
If doubt ye fray,
driue cattle away.

11 Dank ling forgot
will quickly rot.

12 Here learne and trie
to turne it and drie.

13 Now stocks remooue,
that Orchards looue.

14 Set stock to growe
too thick nor too lowe.
Set now, as they com,
both cherie[1] and plom.

15 Shéepe, hog, and ill beast,
bids stock to ill feast.[2]

16 At Christmas is good
to let thy horse blood.

17 Mark here what rable
of euils in stable.

18 Mixe well (old gaffe)
horse corne with chaffe.
Let Jack nor Gill
fetch corne at will.

19[3] Some countries gift
to make hard shift.
Some cattle well fare
with fitches and tare.
Fitches and tares
be Norfolke wares.

20 Tares threshed with skill
bestowe as yée will.

21 Hide strawberies, wife,
to saue their life.

22 Knot, border, and all,
now couer ye shall.

23 Helpe bées, sweet conie,
with licour and honie.

24 Get campers a ball,
to campe therewithall.

Thus endeth Decembers abstract, agréeing with Decembers husbandrie.

¶ Other short remem-
brances.

[25] Let Christmas spie
yard cleane to lie.
No labour, no sweate,
go labour for heate.
Féede dooues, but kill not,
if stroy them ye will not.
Fat hog or (er ye kill it)
or else ye doo spill it.

[1] chearrey. 1577.
[2] St. 15. Wind north, north east
bids stock to il feast. 1577.
[3] Sts. 19 and 20 are not in 1573 (M.); sts. 19, 20, and 24 are not in 1577.

[26] Put oxe in stall,
er oxe doo fall.
Who séetheth hir graines,
hath profit for paines.
Rid garden of mallow,
plant willow and sallow.

[27] Let bore life render,
sée brawne sod tender,
For wife, fruit bie,
for Christmas pie.

Ill bread and ill drinke,
makes many ill thinke.
Both meate and cost
ill dressed halfe lost.

[28] Who hath wherewithall,
may chéere when he shall:
But charged man,
must chéere as he can.

Here ends Decembers
short remembrances.

23.

¶ Decembers husbandrie.

Chap. 21.

O dirtie December
For Christmas remember.

Forgotten month past,
Doe now at the last.

1 WHEN frost will not suffer to dike and to hedge,
then get thee a heat with thy beetle and wedge:
Once Hallomas come, and a fire in the hall,
such sliuers doo well for to lie by the wall. Béetle and wedges.

2 Get grindstone and whetstone, for toole that is dull,
or often be letted and freat bellie full.
A wheele barrow also be readie to haue
at hand of thy seruant, thy compas to saue. Grinding stone and whetston.

3 Giue cattle their fodder in plot drie and warme,
and count them for miring or other like harme.
Yoong colts with thy wennels together go serue,
least lurched by others they happen to sterue.[1] Seruing of cattle.

1 "The old will be apt to hunge or gore the younger."—T.R.

Woodland countrie.

4 The rack is commended for sauing of doong,
so set as the old cannot mischiefe the yoong:
In tempest (the wind being northly or east)
warme barth vnder hedge is a sucker[1] to beast.

Housing of cattel.

5 The housing of cattel while winter doth hold,
is good for all such as are feeble and old:
Champion.
It saueth much compas, and many a sleepe,
and spareth the pasture for walke of thy sheepe.[2]

Champion.

6 For charges so little much quiet is won,
if strongly and handsomly al thing be don:
But vse to vntackle them once in a day,
to rub and to lick them, to drink and to play.

Ordering of cattel.

7 Get trustie to tend them, not lubberlie squire,
that all the day long hath his nose at the fire.
Nor trust vnto children poore cattel to feede,
but such as be able to helpe at a neede.

8 Serue riestraw out first, then wheatstraw and pease,
then otestraw and barlie, then hay if ye please:
But serue them with hay while the straw stouer last,
then loue they no straw, they had rather to fast.

Forkes and yokes.

9 Yokes, forks, and such other, let bailie spie out,
and gather the same as he walketh about.
And after at leasure let this be his hier,
to beath them and trim them at home by the fier.

10 As well at the full of the moone as the change,
sea rages in winter be sodainly strange.
Going of cattel in marshes.
Then looke to thy marshes, if doubt be to fray,
for feare of (*ne forte*) haue cattel away.

[1] succor. 1620.
[2] and trimly refresheth the walk of the sheepe. 1577.

11 Both saltfish and lingfish (if any ye haue)
through shifting and drieng from rotting go saue: Looke to thy ling and saltfish.
Least winter with moistnes doo make it relent,
and put it in hazard before[1] it be spent.

12 Broome fagot is best to drie haberden on, How to vse ling and haberden.
lay boord vpon ladder if fagots be gon.
For breaking (in turning) haue verie good eie,
and blame not the wind, so the weather be drie.

13 Good fruit and good plentie doth well in the loft,
then make thee an orchard and cherish it oft:
For plant or for stock laie aforehand to cast, Remoouing of trées.
but set or remooue it er Christmas be past.

14 Set one fro other full fortie foote wide, An orchard point.
to stand as he stood is a part of his pride.
More faier, more woorthie, of cost to remooue,
more steadie ye set it, more likely to prooue.

15 To teach and vnteach in a schoole is vnmeete,
to doe and vndoe to the purse is vnsweete.
Then orchard or hopyard, so trimmed with cost, Orchard and hopyard.
should not through follie be spoiled and lost.

16 Er Christmas be passed let horse be let blood, Letting horse blood.
for many a purpose it doth them much good.
The daie of S. Stephen old fathers did vse:
if that doe mislike thee some other daie chuse.

17 Looke wel to thy horses in stable thou must, Bréeding of the bots.
that haie be not foistie, nor chaffe ful of dust:
Nor stone in their prouender, feather, nor clots,
nor fed with greene peason, for breeding of bots.

[1] er ere. 1577.

Hog and hennes meate.

18 Some horsekeeper lasheth out prouender so,
some Gillian spendal so often doth go.
For hogs meat and hens meat, for that and for this,
that corne loft is empted er chapman hath his.

19[1] Some countries are pinched of medow for hay,
yet ease it with fitchis as well as they may.
Which inned and threshed and husbandlie dight,
keepes laboring cattle in verie good plight.

20[1] In threshing out fitchis one point I will shew,
first thresh out for seede of the fitchis a few:
Thresh few fro thy plowhorse, thresh cleane for the cow,
this order in Norfolke good husbands alow.

¶ Strawberies.

21 If frost doe continue, take this for a lawe,
the strawberies looke to be couered with strawe.
Laid ouerly trim vpon crotchis and bows,
and after vncouered as weather allows.

¶ Gilleflowers.

22 The gilleflower also, the skilful doe knowe,
doe looke to be couered, in frost and in snowe.
The knot, and the border, and rosemarie gaie,
do craue the like succour for dieng awaie.

¶ How to preserue bees.

23 Go looke to thy bees, if the hiue be too light,
set water and honie, with rosemarie dight.
Which set in a dish ful of sticks in the hiue,
from danger of famine[2] yee saue them aliue.

24[3] In medow or pasture (to growe the more fine)
let campers be camping[4] in any of thine:
Which if ye doe suffer when lowe is the spring,
you gaine to your selfe a commodious thing.

Thus endeth Decembers husbandrie.

[1] Sts. 19 and 20 are not in 1577.
[2] from famen and daunger. 1577.
[3] St. 24 is not in 1577.
[4] "Football playing, at which they are very dextrous in Norfolk."—T.R.

24.

¶ A digression to hospitalitie.

Chap. 22.[1]

LEAUE husbandrie sleeping a while ye must doo,
to learne of housekeeping a lesson or twoo.
What euer is sent thee by trauell and paine,
a time there is lent thee to rendrit againe.
Although ye defend it, vnspent for to bee,
another shall spend it, no thanke vnto thee.
How euer we clime, to accomplish the mind,
we haue but a time thereof profit to find.

25.

¶ A description of time, and the yeare.

Chap. 23.

1 OF God to thy dooings a time there is sent,
which endeth with time that in dooing is spent.
For time is it selfe but a time for a time,
forgotten ful soone, as the tune of a chime.

2 In Spring time we reare, we doo sowe, and we plant, Spring.
in Sommer get vittels, least after we want. Sommer.
In Haruest we carie in corne and the fruit, Haruest.
in Winter to spend as we neede of ech suit. Winter.

[1] Chap. 22 is wanting in 1573 (M). In 1577 it is printed in twice the number of lines.

3 The yeere I compare, as I find for a truth,
the Spring vnto childhood, the Sommer to youth,
The Haruest to manhood, the Winter to age:
all quickly forgot as a play on a stage.

Childhood. Youth. Manhood. Age.

4 Time past is forgotten, er men be aware,
time present is thought on with woonderfull care,
Time comming is feared, and therefore we saue,
yet oft er it come, we be gone to the graue.

26.

¶ *A description of life and riches.*

Chap. 24.

1 WHO liuing but daily discerne it he may,
how life as a shadow doth vanish away;
And nothing to count on so suer to trust
as suer of death and to turne into dust.

2 The lands and the riches that here we possesse
be none of our owne, if a God we professe,
But lent vs of him, as his talent of gold,
which being demanded, who can it withhold?

3 God maketh no writing that iustly doth say
how long we shall haue it, a yeere or a day;
But leaue it we must (how soeuer we leeue)
when Atrop shall pluck vs from hence by the sleeue.

Atrop, or death.

4 To death we must stoupe, be we high, be we lowe,
but how and how sodenly, few be that knowe:
What carie we then, but a sheete to the graue,
to couer this carkas, of all that we haue?

27.

¶ *A description of housekeeping.*

Chap. 25.

1 WHAT then of this talent, while here we remaine,
to studie to yeeld it to God with a gaine?
And that shall we doo, if we doo it not hid,
but vse and bestow it, as Christ doth vs bid.

2 What good to get riches by breaking of sleepe,
but (hauing the same) a good house for to keepe?
Not onely to bring a good fame to thy doore,
but also the praier to win of the poore.

3 Of all other dooings house keeping is cheefe,
for daily it helpeth the poore with releefe;
The neighbour, the stranger, and all that haue neede,
which causeth thy dooings the better to speede.

4 Though harken[1] to this we should euer among,
yet cheefly at Christmas, of all the yeare long.
Good cause of that vse may appeare by the name,
though niggerly niggards doo kick at the same.

28.

¶ *A description of the feast of the birth* of Christ, commonly called Christmas.[2]

Chap. 26.

1 OF Christ cometh Christmas, the name with the feast,
a time full of ioie to the greatest and least:
At Christmas was Christ (our Sauiour) borne,
the world through sinne altogether forlorne.

[1] hardnes. 1577. [2] A description of Christmas. 1577.

2 At Christmas the daies doo[1] begin to take length,
of Christ doth religion cheefly[2] take strength.
As Christmas is onely a figure or trope,
so onely in Christ is the strength of our hope.

3 At Christmas we banket, the rich with the poore,
who then (but the miser) but openeth [h]is doore?
At Christmas of Christ many Carols we sing,
and giue many gifts in the ioy of that King.

4 At Christmas in Christ we reioice and be glad,
as onely of whom our comfort is had;
At Christmas we ioy altogether with mirth,
for his sake that ioyed vs all with his birth.

29.

¶ *A description of apt time to spend.*

Chap. 27.

1 LET such (so fantasticall) liking not this,
nor any thing honest that ancient is,
Giue place to the time that so meete we doo see
appointed of God as it seemeth to bee.

2 At Christmas good husbands haue corne on the ground,
in barne, and in soller, woorth many a pound,
With plentie of other things,[3] cattle and sheepe,
all sent them (no doubt on) good houses to keepe.

3 At Christmas the hardnes of Winter doth rage,
a griper of all things and specially age:
Then lightly poore people, the yoong with the old,
be sorest oppressed with hunger and cold.

[1] the day doth. 1577.
[2] Of Christ our faith doth begin, etc. 1577.
[3] Things plentie in house. 1577.

4 At Christmas by labour is little to get,
  that wanting, the poorest in danger are set.
What season then better, of all the whole yeere,
  thy needie poore neighbour to comfort and cheere?

30.

¶ *Against fantasticall scruplenes.*

Chap. 28.

1 AT this time[1] and that time[1] some make a great matter,
  som help not but hinder the poore with their clatter.
Take custome from feasting, what commeth then last,
  where one hath a dinner, a hundred shall fast.

2 To dog in the manger some liken I could,
  that hay will eate none, nor let other that would;
Some scarce in a yeere giue a dinner or twoo,
  nor well can abide any other to doo.

3 Play thou the good fellow, seeke none to misdeeme,
  disdaine not the honest, though merie they seeme:
For oftentimes seene, no more verie a knaue
  than he that doth counterfait most to be graue.

31.

¶ *Christmas husbandlie fare.*

Chap. 29.

1 GOOD husband and huswife now cheefly be glad,
  things handsom to haue, as they ought to be had;
They both doo prouide against Christmas doo come,
  to welcome good neighbour, good cheere to haue some.

[1] thing. 1577.

Christmas cuntrie fare.

2 Good bread and good drinke, a good fier in the hall,
brawne, pudding and souse, and good mustard withall.

3 Beefe, mutton, and porke, shred pies of the best,
pig, veale, goose and capon, and turkey well drest;
Cheese, apples and nuts, ioly Carols to heare,
as then in the countrie is counted good cheare.

4 What cost to good husband is any of this?
good houshold prouision onely it is.
Of other the like, I doo leaue out a menie,
that costeth the husbandman neuer a penie.

32.

¶ *A Christmas Caroll of the birth of Christ* vpon the tune of King Salomon.

Chap. 30.

1 WAS not Christ our Sauiour
sent to vs fro God aboue?
not for our good behauiour,
but onely of his mercie and loue.
If this be true, as true it is,
truely in deede,
great thanks to God to yeeld for this,
then had we neede.

2 This did our God for very troth,
to traine to him the soule of man,
and iustly to performe his oth
to Sara and to Abram than,
That through his seed all nations should
most blessed bee:
As in due time performe he would,
as now wee see.[1]

[1] all flesh should see. 1577.

3 Which woonderously is brought to pas,
and in our sight alredie donne,
by sending as his promise was
(to comfort vs) his onely sonne,
Euen Christ (I meane) that virgins child,
in Bethlem[1] borne,
that Lambe of God, that Prophet mild,
with crowned thorne.

4 Such was his loue to saue vs all,
from dangers of the curse of God,
that we stood in by Adams fall,
and by our owne deserued rod,
That through his blood and holie name
who so beleeues,[2]
and flie from sinne and abhors the same,
free mercie he geeues.

5 For these glad newes this feast doth bring:
to God the Sonne and holy Ghost
let man giue thanks, reioice, and sing,
from world to world, from cost to cost:
for all good gifts so many waies
that God doth send,
let vs in Christ giue God the praies,
till life shall end.

T. Tusser.

[6] At Christmas be merie and thankfull withall,
And feast thy poore neighbors, the great with the small,
Yea, all the yeere long, to the poore let vs giue,
Gods blessing to folow vs while wee doo liue.

[1] Bethelem. 1577.
[2] to such as beleues. 1577.

33.

¶ Januaries abstract.

Chap. 31.

1 BID Christmas adew,
thy stock now renew.

2 Who killeth a neat,
hath cheaper his meat.
Fat home fed souse,
is good in a house.

3 Who dainties loue,
a begger shall proue.
Who alway selles,
in hunger dwelles.

4 Who nothing saue,
shall nothing haue.

5 Lay durt vpon heapes,
some profit it reapes.
When weather is hard,
get muck out of yard.
A fallow bestowe,
where pease shall growe.
Good peason and white,
a fallow will quite.

6 Go gather quickset,
the yongest go get.
Dig garden, stroy mallow,
set willow and sallow.
Gréene willow for stake
in bank will take.[1]

7 Let Doe go to buck,
with Conie[2] good luck.
Spare labour nor monie,
store borough with conie.
Get warrener bound
to vermin thy ground.
Féed Doues, but kill not,
if loose them ye will not.
Doue house repaire,
make Douehole faire.
For hop ground cold,
Doue doong woorth gold.

8 Good gardiner mine,
make garden fine.
Set garden pease,
and beanes if ye please.
Set Respis and Rose,
yoong rootes of those.

9 The timelie buier
hath cheaper his fier.

[1] Green set as a stake
in banke they wil take. 1577.

[2] conney. 1577.

10 Some burns without wit,
some fierles sit.

11 Now season is good
to lop or fell wood.
Prune trées some allows
for cattle to brows.

12 Giue shéepe to their fées
the mistle of trées.

13 Let lop be shorne
that hindreth corne.
Saue edder and stake,
strong hedge to make.

14 For sap as ye knowe,
let one bough growe.
Next yéere ye may
that bough cut away.

15 A lesson good
to encrease more wood.

16[1] Saue crotchis of wud,
saue spars and stud.
Saue hop for his dole,
the strong long pole.

17 How euer ye scotch,
saue pole and crotch.

18 From Christmas to May,
weake cattle decay.

19 With vergis acquaint
poore bullock so faint;
This medcin approoued
is for to be looued.

20 Let plaister lie
thrée daies to trie:
too long if ye stay,
taile rots away.

21 Eawes readie to yeane
craues ground rid cleane.
Kéepe shéepe out of briers,
Kéepe beast out of miers.[1]

22 Kéepe bushes from bill,
till hedge ye will:
Best had for thy turne,
their rootes go and burne.[1]

23 No bushes of mine,
if fence be thine.

24 In stubbed plot,
fill hole with clot.[2]

25 Rid grasse of bones,
of sticks and stones.

26 Warme barth giue lams,
good food to their dams,
Look daily well to them,
least dogs vndoo them.

[1] St. 16 and the second couplets in sts. 21 and 22 are not here in 1577.
[2] Here follows in 1577, Take for thy turne,
their roots go burne.

27 Yoong lamb well sold,
fat lamb woorth goold.

28 Kéepe twinnes for bréed,
as eawes haue néed.[1]

29 One calfe if it please ye,
now reared shall ease ye.
Calues likely reare,
at rising of yeare.
Calfe large and leane
is best to weane.

30 Calfe lickt take away,
and howse it[2] ye may.
This point I allow
for seruant and cow.

31 Calues yonger than other
learne one of another.

32 No danger at all
to geld as they fall.
Yet Michel cries
please butchers eies.

33 Sow ready to fare,
craues huswiues[3] care.

34 Leaue sow but fiue,
the better to thriue.

35 Weane such for store
as sucks before.
Weane onely but thrée
large bréeders to bée.

36 Lamb, bulchin, and pig,
geld vnder the big.

37 Learne wit, sir dolt,
in gelding of colt.

38 Geld yoong thy filly,
else perish will ginny.
Let gelding alone,
so large of bone.
By breathely tits
few profit hits.

39 Bréede euer the best,
and doo of the rest,
Of long and large,
take huswife a charge.

40 Good cow & good ground[4]
yéelds yéerely a pound.
Good faring sow
holds profit with cow.

41 Who kéepes but[5] twaine,
the more may gaine.

42[6] Tith iustly, good garson,
else driue will the parson.

43 Thy garden twifallow,
stroy hemlock and mallow.

44 Like practise they prooue,
that hops doe looue.

45 Now make and wand in
trim bower to stand in.

[1] feede. 1577.
[2] if. 1577.
[3] huswifes. 1577.
[4] Good milch kow and sound. 1577.
[5] both. 1577.
[6] St. 42 is not in 1577.

Leaue wadling about,
till arbor be out.

46 Who now sowes otes,
gets gold and grotes.
Who sowes in May
gets little that way.

47 Go breake vp land,
get mattock in hand,
Stub roote so tough,
for breaking of plough.

48 What greater crime
then losse of time?

49[1] Lay land or[2] lease
breake vp if ye please.
But fallow not yet,
that hast any wit.

50[1] Where drink ye sowe,
good tilth bestowe.

51 Small profit is found,
by péeling of ground.

52 Land past the best
cast vp to[3] rest.

Thus endeth Januaries abstract, agréeing with Januaries husbandrie.

¶ Other short remembrances.

53 Get pulling hooke (sirs),
for broome and firs.
Pluck broome, broome still,
cut broome, broome kill.

54 Broome pluckt by and by,
breake vp for rie.
Friend ringle thy hog,
or looke for a dog.

55 In casting prouide,
for séede lay aside.
Get doong, friend mine,
for stock and vine.

56 If earth be not soft,
go dig it aloft.
For quamier get bootes,
stub alders and rootes.

57 Hop poles waxe scant,
for poles mo plant.
Set chestnut and walnut,
set filbeard and smalnut.

58 Peach, plumtrée, & cherie,
yoong bay and his berie.
Or set their stone,
vnset leaue out none.

59 Sowe kirnels to beare,
of apple and peare.
All trées that beare goom
set now as they coom.

60 Now set or remooue
such stocks as ye looue.[4]

Here ends Januaries short remembrances.

[1] Sts. 49 and 50 are not in 1577.
[2] for. M.
[3] the. 1577.
[4] And set or remoue
what fruite ye loue. 1577.

34.

Of trees or fruites to be set or remooued.

1 Apple trées of all sorts.
2 Apricocks.
3 Barberies.
4 Boollesse, black & white.
5 Cheries, red and black.
6 Chestnuts.
7 Cornet plums.
8 Damsens,[1] white & black.
9 Filbeards, red and white.
10 Goose beries.
11 Grapes, white and red.
12 Gréene or grasse plums.
13 Hurtillberies.
14 Medlars or marles.
15 Mulberie.
16 Peaches, white and red.
17 Peares of all sorts.
18 Perareplums,[2] black & yelow.
19 Quince trées.
20 Respis.
21 Reisons.
22 Small nuts.
23 Strawberies, red and white.
24 Seruice trées.
25 Walnuts.
26 Wardens, white and red.
27 Wheat plums.

[28] Now set ye may
the box and bay,
Haithorne and prim,
for clothes trim.

35.

¶ Januaries husbandrie.

Chap. 32.

A kindly good Janiuéere,
Fréeseth pot by the féere.

Forgotten month past,
Doe now at the last.

Husbandly lessons.

1 WHEN Christmas is ended, bid feasting adue,
goe play the good husband, thy stock to renue.
Be mindfull of rearing, in hope of a gaine,
dame profit shall giue thee reward for thy paine.

[1] Damisens. 1577.

[2] *sic* also in 1577.

2 Who both by his calfe and his lamb will be knowne,
may well kill a neate and a sheepe of his owne.
And he that can reare vp a pig in his house,
hath cheaper his bacon and sweeter his souse.

3 Who eateth his veale, pig and lamb being froth,
shall twise in a weeke go to bed without broth.[1]
Vnskilfull that passe not, but sell away sell,
shall neuer haue plentie where euer they dwell.

4 Be greedie in spending, and careles to saue,
and shortly be needie and readie to craue.
Be wilfull to kill and vnskilfull to store,
and looke for no foison,[2] I tell thee before.

5 Lay dirt vpon heapes, faire yard to be seene,
if frost will abide it, to feeld with it cleene.
In winter a fallow some loue to bestowe,
where pease for the pot[3] they intend for to sowe.

6 In making or mending as needeth thy ditch, Quick set now.
get set to quick set it, learne cunningly whitch.[4]
In hedging (where clay is) get stake as ye knowe,
of popler and willow, for fewell to growe.

7 Leaue killing of conie,[5] let Doe go to buck,
and vermine thy burrow, for feare of ill luck.
Feed Doue (no more killing), old Doue house repaire, Kéepe cleane thy douehous.
saue doue dong for hopyard, when house ye make faire.

[1] "Broath is still us'd in some Farm Houses for Supper Meat, and Roast Meat look'd upon as very ill Husbandry."—T.R.

[2] looke not for foyzen. 1577. "*Foyzon* is Winter Food."—T.R.

[3] Pease boyling or not boyling is one of the Farmers occult Qualities; but fresh, and next to it, well dunged Grounds are observed to produce the best Boylers, perhaps because they retain most moisture."—T.R.

[4] "By Experience Garden Quicksets are found to be the best, ... because they are all of an age."—T.R.

[5] "The common time of ending their Slaught (or Slaughter as the Warreners term it) is *Candlemas*."—T.R.

¶ Runciual peason.

8 Dig garden, stroy mallow, now may ye at ease,
and set (as a daintie) thy runciuall pease.[1]
Go cut and set roses, choose aptly thy plot,
the rootes of the yoongest are best to be got.

Timelie prouision for fewell.

9 In time go and bargaine, least woorser doo fall,
for fewell, for making, for carriage and all.
To buie at the stub is the best for the buier,
more timelie prouision, the cheaper is fier.

Ill husbandrie.

10 Some burneth a lode at a time in his hall,
some neuer leaue burning til burnt they haue all.
Some making of hauock, without any wit,
make many poore soules without fire to sit.

Pruning of trées.

11 If frost doo continue, this lesson doth well,
for comfort of cattel the fewell to fell:
From euerie tree the superfluous bows
now prune for thy neat therevpon to go brows.[2]

12 In pruning and trimming all maner of trees,
reserue to ech cattel their properly fees.

Mistle and Iuie.

If snowe doo continue, sheepe hardly that fare
craue Mistle and Iuie for them for to spare.

Lopping of pollengers.

13 Now lop for thy fewell old pollenger growen,
that hinder the corne or the grasse to be mowen.
In lopping and felling, saue edder and stake,
thine hedges as needeth to mend or to make.

14 In lopping,[3] old Jocham, for feare of mishap,
one bough stay vnlopped, to cherish the sap:
The second yeere after then boldly ye may,
for driping his fellowes, that bough cut away.

[1] "The most forward Pea is the Rogue, they are pick'd from the Hasting and Hotspur."—T.R.

[2] "Since the use of Turneps Cattel need not be hard put to it in snowy weather as formerly."—T.R.

[3] "This is more proper in Underwood than Pollards, at least more in use at present; few Pollards perish for want of it, but Runt-wood will."—T.R.

15 Lop popler and sallow, elme, maple, and prie,
well saued from cattle, till Sommer to lie.
So far as in lopping, their tops ye doo fling,
so far without planting yoong copie will spring.

The propertie of soft wood.

16[1] Such fewell as standing a late ye haue bought,
now fell it, and make it, and doo as ye ought.
Giue charge to the hewers (that many things mars),
to hew out for crotches, for poles, and for spars.

17 If hopyard or orchard ye mind for to haue,
for hoppoles and crotches in lopping go saue.
Which husbandlie spared may serue at a push,
and stop by so hauing two gaps with a bush.

Hoppoles and crotches.

18 From Christmas, till May be well entered in,
some cattle waxe faint, and looke poorely and thin.
And cheefly when prime grasse[2] at first doth appeere,
then most is the danger of all the whole yeere.

19 Take vergis and heate it, a pint for a cow,
bay salt a hand full,[3] to rub tong ye wot how.
That done, with the salt, let hir drinke off the rest:
this manie times raiseth the feeble vp best.

A medicen for faint cattell.

20 Poore bullock with browsing and naughtily fed,
scarce feedeth, hir teeth be so loose in hir hed:
Then slise ye the taile where ye feele it so soft,
with soote and with garlike bound to it aloft.[4]

To fasten loose téeth in a bullock.

[1] St. 16 is not in 1577.

[2] "Prime Grass appears commonly in woody moist Grounds, on Hedge Banks, and is so called from its earliness; when Cattle have tasted this they begin to loath their dry food. It is often sprung before *Candlemas*."—T.R.

[3] full a hand. 1577.

[4] "This remedy still is in Practice. . . . The first indication of corrupt blood is from the staring Hairs on the Tail near the Rump. Some instead of Soot and Garlick put a Dock Root, or the Root of a Bears Foot, which they call a Gargat Root, others flay the Dewlaps to the very Shoulders."—T.R.

Ewes vpon eaning.

21 By brembles and bushes, in pasture too full,
poore sheepe be in danger and loseth their wull.[1]
Now therefore thine ewe, vpon lamming so neere,
desireth in pasture that all may be cleere.

22 Leaue grubbing or pulling of bushes (my sonne)
till timely thy fences require to be donne.
Then take of the best, for to furnish thy turne,
and home with the rest, for the fier to burne.

Stubbing of gréenes.

23 In euerie greene,[2] if the fence be not thine,
now stub vp the bushes, the grasse to be fine.
Least neighbour doo dailie so hack[3] them beliue,
that neither thy bushes nor pasture can thriue.

24 In ridding[4] of pasture with turfes that lie by,[5]
fill euerie hole vp, as close as a dy.
The labour is little, the profit is gay,
what euer the loitering labourers say.

25 The sticks and the stones go and gather vp cleene,
for hurting of sieth or for harming of greene.[6]
For feare of Hew prowler, get home with the rest,
when frost is at hardest, then carriage is best.

Yoong lambes.

26 Yoong broome or good pasture thy ewes doo require,
warme barth and in safetie their lambes doo desire.
Looke often well to them, for foxes and dogs,
for pits and for brembles, for vermin and hogs.

[1] "Large Ant-Hills is much the best shelter for Ewes and Lambs." —T.R.

[2] "This is understood of Hedge Greens . . . . a space next the Hedge of a Rod or more in breadth."—T.R.

[3] make. 1577.

[4] "When you rid it of Bushes or Ant Hills."—T.R.

[5] with turnes so bye. 1577.

[6] "Hedge Greens."—T.R.

27 More daintie[1] the lambe, the more woorth to be sold,
the sooner the better for eaw that is old.
But if ye doo minde to haue milke of the dame,
till Maie doo not seuer the lambe fro the same.

28 Ewes yeerly by twinning rich maisters doo make, Rearing of lambs.
the lamb of such twinners for breeders go take.
For twinlings be twiggers, encrease for to bring,
though som for their twigging *Peccantem* may sing.

29 Calues likely that come between Christmas and Lent, Rearing of calues.
take huswife to reare, or else after repent:
Of such as doo fall betweene change and the prime,[2]
no rearing, but sell or go kill them in time.

30 Howse calfe, and go sockle it twise in a day, Howsing of cattel.
and after a while, set it water and hay.
Stake ragged to rub on, no such as will bend,
then weane it well tended, at fiftie daies end.[3]

31 The senior weaned his yoonger shall teach,
how both to drinke water and hay for to reach.[4]
More stroken and made of when ought it doo aile,
more gentle ye make it, for yoke or the paile.

32 Geld bulcalfe and ramlamb, as soone as they fall, Of gelding.
for therein is lightly no danger at all.
Some spareth the ton for to pleasure the eie,
to haue him shew greater when butcher shall bie.

33 Sowes readie to farrow this time of the yeere ¶
are for to be made of and counted full deere.
For now is the losse of a fare of the sow
more great then the losse of two calues of thy cow.

[1] "Likely, or thriving, such as will soon require more Milk than his old Dam can afford him."—T.R.

[2] "The first three days after the new moon or change."—T.R.

[3] "At present we rarely wean under twelve weeks."—T.R. 1710.

[4] "The hay is given them stuck in cleft sticks."—T.R.

6

¶ Rearing of pigs.

34 Of one sow togither reare few aboue fiue,
and those of the fairest and likest to thriue.
Ungelt of the best keepe a couple for store,
one bore pig and sow pig, that sucketh before.

¶ A way to haue large brēed of hogs.

35 Who hath a desire to haue store verie large,
at Whitsontide let him giue huswife a charge,
To reare of a sow at once onely but three,
and one of them also a bore let it bee.

¶ Gelding time.

36 Geld vnder the dam, within fortnight at least,
and saue both thy monie and life of the beast.
Geld later with gelders as many one do,
and looke of a doozen to geld away two.

Gelding of horse coltes.

37 Thy colts for thy saddle geld yoong to be light,
for cart doo not so, if thou iudgest aright.
Nor geld not but when they be lustie and fat:
for there is a point, to be learned in that.

Gelding of fillies.

38 Geld fillies (but tits) er an nine daies of age,
they die else of gelding (or gelders doo rage).
Yoong fils so likelie of bulke and of bone:
keepe such to be breeders, let gelding alone.

Reare the fairest of al things.

39 For gaining a trifle, sell neuer thy store,
what ioy to acquaintance, what pleasureth more?
The larger of bodie, the better for breede:
more forward of growing, the better they speede.

¶ Of cow and sow.

40 Good milchcow, well fed, that is faire and sound,
is yeerely for profit as good as a pound:
And yet by the yeere, I haue prooued er[1] now,
as good to the purse is a sow as a cow.

[1] or. 1577.

41 Keepe one and keepe both, with as little a cost, ¶
then all shall be saued and nothing be lost.
Both hauing togither what profit is caught,
good huswifes (I warrant ye) need not be taught.

42[1] For lamb, pig and calfe, and for other the like, ¶
tithe so as thy cattle the Lord doo not strike.
Or if yee deale guilefully, parson will dreue,
and so to your selfe a worse turne ye may geue.

43 Thy garden plot latelie well trenched and muckt,
would now be twifallowd, the mallowes out pluckt,[2]
Well clensed and purged of roote and of stone,
that falt therein afterward found may be none.

44 Remember thy hopyard, if season be drie, Weeding of hopyard.
now dig it and weed it, and so let it lie.
More fennie the laier the better his lust,
more apt to beare hops when it crumbles like dust.

45 To arbor begun, and quick setted[3] about, Trimming up arbors.
no poling nor wadling[4] till set be far out.
For rotten and aged may stand for a shew,
but hold to their tackling there doe but a few.[5]

46 In Ianiuere[6] husband that poucheth the grotes Sowing of otes. Late sowing not good.
will break vp his laie, or be sowing of otes,
Otes sowen in Ianiuere, laie[7] by the wheat,
in May by the hay for the cattle to eat.[8]

[1] St. 42 is not in 1577.
[2] "In trenching, bury no Mallow, Nettle-dock, or Briony Roots."—T.R.
[3] "Quick setted Arbors are now out of use, as agreeing very ill with the Ladies Muslins."—T.R. 1710.
[4] "Wattles are wood slit."—T.R.
[5] they cannot but feaw. 1577.
[6] January. 1577.
[7] "lay them by thy wheate" in 100 *Good Points.*
[8] "Such early sown Oats it is likely may be clearer of weeds; and if I buy my Hay in *May*, that is, before my Chapman knows what Quantity he shall have, he is rul'd by his Necessity for some ready money in Hand."—T.R.

47 Let seruant be readie, with mattock in hand,
to stub out the bushes that noieth the land :
And cumbersome rootes, so annoieng the plough,
turne vpward their arses with sorrow inough.

Breaking up lay in som countrie.

48 Who breaketh vp timelie his fallow or lay,
sets forward his husbandrie many a way.
This trimlie well ended doth forwardly bring,[1]
not onelie thy tillage, but all other thing.

49[2] Though lay land ye breke vp when Christmas is gon,
for sowing of barlie[3] or otes therevpon,
Yet hast[e] not to fallow til March be begun,
least afterward wishing it had ben vndun.

50[2] Such land as ye breake vp for barlie to sowe,
two earthes at the least er ye sowe it bestowe.[4]
If land be thereafter, set oting apart,
and follow this lesson, to comfort thine hart.

51 Some breaking vp laie soweth otes to begin,[5]
to suck out the moisture so sower therein.
Yet otes with hir sucking a peeler is found,
both ill to the maister and worse to som ground.

52 Land arable driuen or worne to the proofe,
and[6] craueth some rest for thy profits behoofe.
With otes ye may sowe it, the sooner to grasse,
more soone to be pasture to bring it to passe.

Thus endeth Januaries husbandrie.

[1] This tilth is a tilture, well forward doth bring. 1577.
[2] Sts. 49 and 50 are not in 1577.
[3] "Barley is now very rarely, if at all, sown on lay land. The fallow he speaks of I take to be the second ploughing for Barley."—T.R. 1710. Gervase Markham, in his *English Husbandman*, directs a digging in May, another, with manuring, in October, and "the last time of your digging and setting shall be at the beginning of April."
[4] "Barley-Ground ought to be as fine as an Ash-heap."—T.R.
[5] "Where the Ground is over rich, it fines and sweetens it."—T.R.
[6] "It" in *Tusser Redivivus*. "and." 1577.

36.

¶ Februaries abstract.

Chap. 33.

LAY compas ynow,
er euer ye plow.

2 Place doong heapes alowe,
more barlie to growe.

3 Eat etch er ye plow,
with hog, shéepe and cow.
Sowe lintels ye may,
and peason gray.
Kéepe white vnsowne,
till more be knowne.

4 Sow pease (good trull)
the Moone past full.
Fine séedes then sowe,
whilst Moone doth growe.

5 Boy, follow the plough,
and harrow inough.
So harrow ye shall,
till couerd be all.

6 Sowe pease not too thin,
er plough ye set in.

7 Late sowen sore noieth,
late ripe, hog stroieth.

8 Some prouender saue,
for plowhorse to haue.
To oxen that drawe,
giue hay and not strawe.
To stéeres ye may
mixe strawe with hay.

9 Much carting, ill tillage,
makes som to flie village.

10 Use cattle aright,
to kéepe them in plight.

11 Good quickset bie,
old gatherd will die.

12[1] Stick bows a rowe,
where runciuals growe.

13 Sowe kirnels and hawe,
where ridge ye did drawe.

14 Sowe mustard séed,
and helpe to kill wéed.
Where sets doo growe,
sée nothing ye sowe.

*** Februaries Abstract and Februaries Husbandry in the edition of 1577 differ much from that of 1580.

[1] Stanza 12 is 4, and st. 22 is 1 in 1577.

15 Cut vines and osier,
plash hedge of enclosier.
Féed highly thy swan,
to loue hir good man.
Nest high I aduise,
least floud doe arise.

16 Land meadow spare,
there doong is good ware.

17 Go strike off the nowles
of deluing mowles.
Such hillocks in vaine
lay leauelled plaine.

18 To wet the land,
let mowle hill stand.

19 Poore cattle craue
some shift to haue.

20 Cow little giueth
that hardly liueth.

21 Rid barlie al now,
cleane out of thy mow.
Choice séed out drawe,
saue cattle the strawe.

22 To coast man ride
Lent stuffe to prouide.

Thus endeth Februaries abstract, agréeing with Februaries husbandrie.

¶ Other short remembrances.

[23] Trench medow and redge,
dike, quickset, and hedge.
To plots not full,
ad bremble and hull.

[24] Let wheat and the rie
for thresher still lie.
Such strawe some saue,
for thacker to haue.

[25] Poore cunnie, so bagged,
is soone ouer lagged.
Plash burrow, set clapper,
for dog is a snapper.

[26] Good flight who loues,
must féed their doues.
Bid hauking adew,
cast hauke into mew.

[27] Kéepe shéepe out of briers,
kéepe beast out of miers.
Kéepe lambes from fox,
else shepherd go box.

[28] Good neighbour mine,
now yoke thy swine.
Now euerie day,
set hops ye may.

[29] Now set for thy pot,
best herbes to be got.

For flowers go set,
all sorts ye can get.

[30] As winter doth prooue,
so may ye remooue.
Now all things reare,
for all the yeare.

[31] Watch ponds, go looke
to wéeles and hooke.
Knaues seld repent
to steale in Lent.

[32] Alls fish they get
that commeth to net.
Who muck regards
makes hillocks in yards.

Here ends Februaries short remembrances.

37.

¶ Februaries husbandrie.

Chap. 34.

Feb, fill the dike
With what thou dost like.[1]

Forgotten month past,
Doe now at the last.

1 WHO laieth on doong er he laieth on plow,
such husbandrie vseth as thrift doth alow.
One month er ye spred it, so still let it stand,
er euer to plow it, ye take it in hand.

2 Place doong heape a low by the furrough along,
where water all winter time did it such wrong.
So make ye the land to be lustie and fat,
and corne thereon sowen to be better for that.

3 Go plow in the stubble, for now is the season,
for sowing of fitchis, of beanes, and of peason.
Sowe runciuals timelie, and all that be gray,
but sowe not the white till S. Gregories day.[2]

[1] with what ye like. 1577.

[2] 12th of March.

4 Sowe peason and beanes in the wane of the Moone,[1]
who soweth them sooner, he soweth too soone.
That they with the planet may rest and arise,
and flourish with bearing most plentifull wise.

5 Friend, harrow in time, by some maner of meanes,
not onely thy peason, but also thy beanes.
Unharrowed die, being buried in clay,
where harrowed florish, as flowers in May.

6 Both peason and beanes sowe afore ye doo plow,[2]
the sooner ye harrow, the better for yow.[3]
White peason so good for the purse and the pot:
let them be well vsed else well doo ye not.

7 Haue eie vnto haruest what euer ye sowe,
for feare of mischances, by riping too slowe.
Least corne be destroied, contrarie to right,
by hogs or by cattel, by day or by night.[4]

8 Good prouender labouring horses would haue,
good haie and good plentie, plow oxen doo craue.
To hale out the muck and to plow vp thy ground:
or else it may hinder thee many a pound.

9 Who slacketh his tillage, a carter to bee,
for grote got abrode, at home lose shall three.
And so by his dooing he brings out of hart
both land for the corne and horse for the cart.

[1] "Pease and Beans sown during the Increase do run more to Hawm or Straw, and during the Declension more to Cod, according to the common consent of country men. And I must own I have experienced it; but I will not aver it so as that it is not lyable to exceptions."—T.R.

[2] "This is called sowing under furrow, just before the second ploughing, which if neatly done lays them in rows."—T.R.

[3] "Because if they lye until they are swell'd the horse-footing is apt to endanger them."—T.R.

[4] "This regards Field Land; for in our Author's time Enclosures were not so frequent as now."—T.R. 1710.

10 Who abuseth his cattle and sterues them for meat,
  by carting or plowing, his gaine is not great.
Where he that with labour can vse them aright,
  hath gaine to his comfort, and cattle in plight.

11 Buie quickset at market, new gatherd and small,
  buie bushes or willow, to fence it withall.
Set willowes to growe, in the steede of a stake,
  for cattel in sommer, a shadow to make.

12 Stick plentie of bows among runciuall pease[1] ¶
  to climber thereon, and to branch at their ease. Runciual peason.
So dooing, more tender and greater they wex,
  if peacock[2] and turkey leaue iobbing their bex.

13 Now sowe and go harrow (where redge ye did draw[3])
  the seed of the bremble, with kernell and haw.
Which couered ouerlie, soone to shut out,
  goe see it be ditched and fenced about.

14 Where banks be amended and newly vp cast, Sowe mustard seede.
  sow mustard seed,[4] after a shower be past.
Where plots full of nettles be noisome to eie,
  sowe therevpon hempseed, and nettle will die.

15 The vines[5] and the osiers cut and go set, Cut or set vines.
  if grape be vnpleasant, a better go get.
Feed swan, and go make hir vp strongly a nest,
  for feare of a floud, good and high is the best.

[1] "Runcival pease find now very little Entertainment in Gentlemen's Gardens. . . . . In their room are got the Egg pea, the Sugar pea, Dutch admirals, etc."—T.R., 1710.

[2] "A Peacock, altho' a lovely Fowl to look on, ... is a very ill-natured Bird."—T.R.

[3] "A way of quicksetting or fencing Enclosures out of the common Field they had in the days of our Author."—T.R.

[4] "This is most in practice in Marshy Countreys."—T.R.

[5] "Those that thrive best with us are the small black Grape, the white Muscadine, and the Parsley grape."—T.R.

Catching of mowls.

16 Land meadow that yeerly is spared for hay,
now fence it and spare it, and doong it ye may.
Get mowle catcher cunninglie mowle for to kill,
and harrow and cast abrode euerie hill.

17 Where meadow or pasture to mowe ye doo laie,
let mowle be dispatched some maner of waie.
Then cast abrode mowlhill, as flat as ye can,
for many commodities following than.

18 If pasture by nature is giuen to be wet,
then bare with the mowlhill, though thick it be set.
That lambe may sit on it, and so to sit drie,
or else to lie by it, the warmer to lie.

Looke well to thy fence

19 Friend, alway let this be a part of thy care,
for shift of good pasture, lay pasture to spare.
So haue you good feeding, in bushets and lease,
and quickly safe finding of cattel at ease.

20 Where cattel may run about, rouing at wil,
from pasture to pasture, poor bellie to fil,
There pasture and cattel both hungrie and bare,
for want of good husbandrie worser doo fare.

21 Now thresh out thy barlie, for malt or for seed,
for bread corne (if need be) to serue as shall need.
If worke for the thresher ye mind for to haue,
of wheat and of mestlen vnthreshed go saue.

22 Now timelie for Lent stuffe[1] thy monie disburse,
the longer ye tarie for profit the wurse,
If one penie vantage be therein to saue,
of coast man or fleming be sure to haue.

Thus endeth Februaries husbandrie.

[1] "This Article is very much unregarded by Farmers at present, for fear, I suppose, of falling into Popery and Superstition; but lay that quite aside, and let us consult our Interest, Health, and Gratitude."—T.R. The writer of *Tusser Redivivus* here enlarges on the advantages, personal and national, of fish diet. Under Marches Husbandry, stanza 3, he mentions "Salt Fish, Furmity, Gruel, Wigs, Milk, Parsnips, Hasty-pudding, Pancakes, and twice a week Eggs," as the Farmer's Lenten Diet.

38.

¶ Marches abstract.

Chap. 35.

WHITE peason sowe,
scare hungry crow.

2 Spare meadow for hay,
spare marshes at May.

3[1] Kéepe shéepe from dog,
kéepe lambes from hog.
If foxes mowse[2] them,
then watch or howse them.

4 March drie or wet,
hop ground go set.
Yoong rootes well drest
prooue euer[3] best.
Grant hop great hill
to growe at will.
From hop long gut
away go cut.

5 Here learne the way
hop rootes to lay.

6 Rootes best to prooue,
thus set I looue.

7 Leaue space and roome,
to hillock to coome.

8 Of hedge and willow
hop makes his[4] pillow.
Good bearing hop
climes vp to the top.
Kéepe hop from sunne,
and hop is vndunne.

9 Hop tooles procure
that may endure.
Iron crowe like a stake,
déepe hole to make.
A scraper to pare
the earth about bare.
A hone to raise roote,
like sole of a boote.
Sharpe knife to cut
superfluous gut.

10 Who graffing looues,
now graffing prooues.
Of euerie suite,
graffe daintie fruite.
Graffe good fruite all,
or graffe not at all.

[1] St. 3, first couplet, What champion useth
woodland refuseth. 1577.
[2] mouth them. 1573 (M.); mowse. 1577.
[3] the. 1573, 1577.
[4] her. 1577.

11 Graffe soone may be lost,
both graffing and cost.
Learne here[1] take héed
what counsell doth béed.[2]

12 Sowe barlie that can,
too soone ye shall ban.
Let horse kéepe his owne,
till barlie be sowne.
Sowe euen thy land,
with plentifull hand.
Sowe ouer and vnder,
in claie is no woonder.

13[3] By sowing in wet,
is little to get.

14 Straight folow the plough,
and harrow inough.
With sling go throwe,[4]
to scare away crowe.

15 Rowle after a deaw,
when barlie doth sheaw.
More handsom to make it,
to mowe and to rake it.

16 Learne here ye may
best harrowing way.

17[5] Now rowle thy wheat,
where clods be too great.

18 Make readie a plot,
for séeds for the pot.

19 Best searching minds
the best waie finds.

20 For garden best
is south southwest.

21 Good tilth brings séedes,
euill tilture, wéedes.

22 For sommer sowe now,
for winter sée how.

23 Learne time to knowe,
to set or sowe.[6]

24 Yoong plants soone die,
that growes too drie.

25 In countrie doth rest,
what season is best.

26[5] Good peason and léekes
makes pottage for créekes.

27[5] Haue spoone meat inough,
for cart and the plough.
Good poore mans fare,
is poore mans care.
And not to boast,
of sod and roast.

28 Cause rooke and rauen
to séeke a new hauen.

Thus endeth Marches abstract, agréeing with Marches husbandrie.

[1] to. 1577. [2] bid, 1577; beed, 1585; breed, 1614.
[3] St. 13 is not in 1577. [4] sling or bowe. 1577.
[5] Stanzas 17, 26, and first couplet of 27 are not in 1577.
[6] Lines transposed in 1577.

¶ Other short remem-
brances.

[29] Geld lambes now all,
straight as they fall.
Looke twise a day,
least lambes decay.

[30] Where horse did harrow,
put stones in barrow,
And[1] laie them by,
in heapes on hy.

[31] Let oxe once fat
lose nothing of that.
Now hunt with dog,
vnyoked hog.

[32] With Doues good luck,
reare[2] goose and duck.
To spare aright
spare March his flight.

[33] The following additional
couplets are in 1577.

Saue chikins poore buttocks
from pye, crowe, & puttocks.

Some loue now best
yong rabbets nest.

Now knaues will steale
pig, lamb, and veale.

Here learne to knowe
what seedes to sowe.

And such to plant
whose seedes do want.

39.

Seedes and herbes for the
Kitchen.

1 Auens.
2 Betanie.
3 Bléets or béets, white or yellow.
4 Bloodwoort [Bloodwoorth, 1577].
5 Buglas.
6 Burnet.
7 Burrage.
8 Cabage remoue in June.
9 Clarie.
10 Coleworts.
11 Cresses.
12 Endiue.
13 Fenell.
14 French Malows.
15 French Saffron set in August.
16 Langdebiefe.
17 Léekes remoue in June.
18 Lettis remoue in May.
19 Longwort.
20 Liuerwort.
21 Marigolds often cut.
22 Mercurie.
23 Mints at all times.
24 Nep.
25 Onions [Oyneons, 1577] from December to March.
26 Orach or arach, redde and white.
27 Patience.

[1] or. 1577.

[2] hen. 1577.

28 Perceley.
29 Peneriall.
30 Primerose.
31 Poret.
32 Rosemary in the spring time [to growe south or west].[1]
33 Sage red and white.
34 [English][2] Saffron set in August.
35 Summer sauerie.
36 Sorell.
37 Spinage.
38 Suckerie.
39 Siethes.
40 Tanzie.
41 Time.
42 Violets of all sorts.
43 Winter sauerie.

40.

Herbes and rootes for sallets and sauce.

1 Alexanders, at all times.
2 Artichoks.
3 Blessed thistle, or *Carduus benedictus.*
4 Cucumbers in April and May.
5 Cresies, sowe with Lettice in the spring.
6 Endiue.
7 Mustard séede, sowe in the spring and at Mihelmas.
8 Musk million, in April and May.
9 Mints.
10 Purslane.
11 Radish, and after remoue them.
12 Rampions.
13 Rokat, in April.
14 Sage.
15 Sorell.
16 Spinage, for the sommer.
17 Sea holie.
18 Sperage, let growe two yeares, and then remoue.
19 Skirrets, set these plants in March.
20 Suckerie.
21 Tarragon, set in slippes in March.[3]
22 Violets [of all coulors].[4]

These buie with the penie,
Or looke not for anie.

1 Capers.
2 Lemmans.
3 Olives.
4 Orengis.
5 Rise.
6 Sampire.

[1] Omitted in 1577.
[2] Omitted in 1577.
[3] Tarragon, April, 1577.
[4] Omitted in 1577.

41.

Herbes and rootes to boile or to butter.

1 Beanes, set in winter.
2 Cabbegis, sowe in March, and after remooue.
3 Carrets.
4 Citrons, sowe in May.
5 Goordes in May.
6 Nauewes sowe in June.
7 Pompions in May.
8 Perseneps in winter.
9 Runciuall pease set in winter.
10 Rapes sowe in June.
11 Turneps in March & April.

42.

Strowing herbes of all sortes.

1 Bassel, fine and busht, sowe in May.
2 Baulme, set in March.
3 Camamel.
4 Costmarie.
5 Cousleps and paggles.
6 Daisies of all sorts.
7 Swéete fennell.
8 Garmander.
9 Isop, set in Februarie.
10 Lauender.
11 Lauender spike.
12 Lauender cotten.
13 Maierom knotted, sowe or set at the spring.
14 Mawdelin.
15 Penal riall.
16 Roses of all sorts, in Januarie and September.
17 Red mints.
18 Sage.
19 Tanzie.
20 Violets.
21 Winter sauerie.

43.

Herbes, branches, and flowers, for windowes and pots.

1 Baies, sowe or set in plants in Januarie.
2 Batchelers buttons.
3 Botles, blew, red, and tawnie.
4 Collembines.
5 Campions.
6 Cousleps.[1]
7 Daffadondillies.
8 Eglantine, or swéet brier.
9 Fetherfew.
10 Flower armor[2] sowe in May.
11 Flower de luce.
12 Flower gentle, white and red.
13 Flower nice.

[1] Omitted in 1577.

[2] armour. 1577; amour. 1614.

14 Gileflowers, red white and carnations, set in spring, and at Haruest in pots, pailes or tubs, or for sommer in beds.
15 Holiokes, red, white and carnations.
16 Indian eie, sowe in May, or set in slips in March.
17 Lauender of all sorts.
18 Larkes foot.
19 Laus tibi.
20 Lillium cum valium.[1]
21 Lillies, red and white, sowe or set in March and September.
22 Marigolds double.
23 Nigella Romana.
24 Pauncies or hartesease.
25 Paggles, gréene and yelow.
26 Pinkes of all sorts.
27 Quéenes gilleflowers.
28 Rosemarie.
29 Roses of all sorts.
30 Snag[2] dragons.
31 Sops in wine.
32 Swéete Williams.
33 Swéete Johns.
34 Star of Bethelem.
35 Star of Jerusalem.
36 Stocke gilleflowers of all sorts.
37 Tuft gilleflowers.
38 Veluet flowers, or french Marigolds.
39 Violets, yellow and white.
40 Wall gilleflowers of all sorts.

44.

Herbes to still in Sommer.

1 Blessed thistle.
2 Betanie [Betonye, 1577].
3 Dill.
4 Endiue.
5 Eiebright.
6 Fennell.
7 Fumetorie.
8 Isop.
9 Mints.
10 Plantine.
11 Roses red and damaske.
12 Respies.
13 Saxefrage.
14 Strawberies.
15 Sorell.
16 Suckerie.
17 Woodrofe for swéete waters and cakes.

45.

Necessarie herbes to growe in the garden for Physick, not rehersed before.

1 Annis.
2 Archangel.

[1] convallium. 1614.

[2] Snap. 1577.

3 Betanie.
4 Charuiel.
5 Cinqfile.
6 Cummin.
7 Dragons.
8 Detanie,[1] or garden ginger.
9 Gromel séed, for the stone.
10 Hartstong.
11 Horehound.
12 Louage for the stone.
13 Licoras.
14 Mandrake.
15 Mogwort [Mogworth, 1577].
16 Pionées.
17 Poppie.
18 Rew.
19 Rubarb.
20 Smalach, for swellings.
21 Saxefrage, for the stone.
22 Sauin, for the bots.
23 Stitchwort.
24 Valerian.
25 Woodbine.

[26] Thus ends in bréefe,
Of herbes the chéefe,
To get more skill,
Read whom ye will,
Such mo to haue,
Of field go craue.

46.

¶ Marches husbandrie.

Chap. 36.

March dust to be sold,
Worth ransome of gold.

Forgotten month past,
Doe now at the last.

1 WHITE peason, both good for the pot and the purse,[2] [Sowing of white peason. 1577.]
by sowing too timelie, prooue often the wurse.
Bicause they be tender and hateth the cold,
prooue March er ye sowe them, for being too bold.

2 Spare meadow at Gregorie, marshes at Pask, Spare eating of meadowe.
for feare of drie Sommer, no longer time ask.
Then hedge them and ditch them, bestow thereon pence:
corne, meadow and pasture, aske alway good fence.

[1] Betany, in 1577. Thus mistakes in synonyms arise.
[2] "The Retailer now sells them for 2¾*d.* the Quart."—T.R. 1710.

3 Of mastiues and mungrels, that manie we see,
a number of thousands too manie there bee.
In Lent haue an ey to sheep biters.
Watch therefore in Lent, to thy sheepe go and looke,
for dogs will haue vittles,[1] by hooke or by crooke.

Setting of hops.
4 In March at the furdest, drie season or wet,
hop rootes so well chosen, let skilfull go set.
The goeler[2] and yonger the better I loue;
well gutted[3] and pared, the better they proue.

5 Some laieth them croswise, along in the ground,
as high as the knee they doo couer vp round.
Some prick vp a stick in the mids of the same,
that little round hillock the better to frame.

6 Some maketh a hollownes, halfe a foot deepe,
with fower sets in it, set slant wise a steepe:
One foot from another, in order to lie,
and thereon a hillock, as round as a pie.

7 Fiue foot from another ech hillock would stand,
as straight as a leaueled line with the hand.
Let euerie hillock be fower foot wide,
the better to come to on euerie side.

8 By willowes that groweth thy hopyard without,
and also by hedges thy meadowes about.
Good hop hath a pleasure to climbe and to spred,
if Sunne may haue passage to comfort hir hed.

Hop tools.
9 Get crowe made of iron, deepe hole for to make,
with crosse ouerthwart it, as sharpe as a stake.
A hone[4] and a parer, like sole of a boote,[5]
to pare away grasse and to raise vp the roote.

[1] In Lent, dog's meat was scarce, and "a mort Lamb now and then was very apt to whet their appetite for Mutton."—T.R.

[2] goeler. 1577. goodlier. 1614. "The goeler is the yellower, which are the best setts, old roots being red."—T.R.

[3] "Well taken off from the old Roots."—T.R.

[4] "A common Rubber or Whetstone."—T.R.

[5] "The best, in my minde, are those triangular ones used by the Fen men and Bankers."—T.R. 1710.

10 In March is good graffing, the skilfull doo knowe, — Graffing.
so long as the wind in the East doo not blowe.
From Moone being changed til past be the prime,[1]
for graffing and cropping is verie good time.

11 Things graffed or planted,[2] the greatest and least,
defend against tempest, the bird[3] and the beast.
Defended shall prosper, the tother is lost,
the thing with the labour, the time and the cost.

12 Sowe barlie in March, in April and Maie, — Sowing of barlie.
the latter[4] in sand, and the sooner in claie.[5]
What worser for barlie than wetnes and cold ?
what better to skilfull than time to be bold ?

13[6] Who soweth his barlie too soone or in raine,
of otes[7] and of thistles shall after complaine.
I speake not of Maie weed, cockle and such,
that noieth the barlie, so often and much.

14 Let barlie be harrowed, finelie as dust,
then workmanly trench it and fence it ye must.
This season well plied, set sowing an end,
and praise and praie God a good haruest to send.

15 Some rowleth their barlie straight after a raine, — Rowling of barlie.
when first it appeareth to leauell it plaine.
The barlie so vsed, the better doth growe,
and handsome ye make it at haruest to mowe.

[1] cf. *ante*, p. 85, st. 4.
[2] plainted. 1577.
[3] "That impudent bird, a Tomtit, is not easily frighted."—T.R.
[4] "later."—T.R.
[5] "Barley is rarely sown in Clay, at present."—T.R. 1710.
[6] St. 13 is not in 1577.
[7] Gervase Markham says: "You shall take care that in your seede Barly there be not any Oates, for although they be in this case amongst Husbandmen accounted the best of weede, yet are they such a disgrace," etc. ; . . . . and he adds that "some grounds will . . . . bring forth naturally a certaine kinde of wilde Oates."—*English Husbandman*, Pt. I. ch. v.

16 Otes, barlie and pease, harrow after you sowe,[1]
for rie harrow first, as alreadie ye knowe.
Leaue wheat little clod, for to couer the head,
that after a frost, it may out and go spread.

17[2] If clod in thy wheat wil not breake with the frost,
if now ye doo rowle it, it quiteth the cost.
But see when ye rowle it, the weather be drie,
or else it were better vnrowled to lie.

¶ Gardening.

18 In March and in April,[3] from morning to night,
in sowing and setting, good huswiues delight:
To haue in a garden, or other like plot,
to turn vp their house, and to furnish their pot.

¶ 19 The nature of flowers dame Physick doth shew,
she teacheth them all to be knowne to a few.
To set or to sowe, or else sowne to remoue,
how that should be practised, learne if ye loue.

To know good land.

20 Land falling or lieng full South or southwest,
for profit by tillage is lightly the best.
So garden with orchard and hopyard I finde,
that want the like benefit, growe out of kinde.

¶ 21 If field to beare corne a good tillage doth craue,
what thinke ye of garden, what garden would haue?
In field without cost be assured of weedes,
in garden be suer thou loosest thy seedes.

¶ 22 At spring (for the sommer) sowe garden ye shall,
at haruest (for winter) or sowe not at all.
Oft digging, remoouing, and weeding (ye see),
makes herbe the more holesome and greater to bee.

[1] "That is, in our Countryman's Phrase, ... above furrow, that is upon land after the last ploughing."—T.R. Cf. *ante*, p. 88, st. 6.
[2] St. 17 is not in 1577.
[3] In March, April, and May. 1577.

23 Time faire, to sowe or to gather be bold, ¶
but set or remooue when the weather is cold.[1]
Cut all thing or gather, the Moone in the wane,
but sowe in encreasing, or giue it his bane.

24 Now set doo aske watering with pot or with dish, ¶
new sowne doo not so, if ye doo as I wish.
Through cunning with dible, rake, mattock, and spade,
by line and by leauell, trim garden is made.

25 Who soweth too lateward, hath seldome good seed,
who soweth too soone, little better shall speed.
Apt time and the season so diuers to hit,
let aier and laier[2] helpe practise and wit.

26[3] Now leekes are in season, for pottage full good, ¶
and spareth the milchcow and purgeth the blood.
These hauing, with peason for pottage in Lent,
thou sparest both otemell and bread to be spent.

27[3] Though neuer so much a good huswife doth care, ¶
that such as doe labour haue husbandlie fare.
Yet feed them and cram them til purse doe lack chinke,
no spoone meat, no bellifull, labourers thinke.

28 Kill crowe, pie and cadow, rooke, buzard and rauen, Destroie pie, rooks, and rauens nest, etc.
or else go desire them to seeke a new hauen.
In scaling the yoongest, to pluck off his beck,
beware how ye climber, for breaking your neck.

Thus endeth Marches husbandrie.

[1] "There is an old Sawe to this purpose:
'In Gard'ning never this Rule forget,
To Sow dry, and Set wet.'"—T.R.

[2] "By *Aier* I understand Situation, Weather, etc. . . . . By *Laier*, Composition, the Nature of the Soil, Heart of the Land, etc."—T.R.

[3] Sts. 26 and 27 are not in 1577; but instead—
Good peason and leekes, to make porredge in lent,
and pescods in July, saue fish to be spent.
Those hauing with other things plentifull than,
thou winnest the hart of the labouring man.

47.

¶ Aprils abstract.

Chap. 37.

1[1] SOME champions laie
to fallow in Maie.

2 When tilth plows breake,
poore cattle cries creake.

3 One daie er ye plow,
spred compas ynow.

4 Some fodder buieth,
in fen where it lieth.

5[1] Thou champion wight,
haue cow meat for night.

6 Set hop his pole,
make déepe the hole.

7 First, bark go and sell,
er timber ye fell.

8 Fence copie in,
er heawers begin.

9 The straightest ye knowe,
for staddles let growe.

10 Crab trée preserue,
for plough to serue.

11 Get timber out,
er yéere go about.

12 Som cuntries lack plowmeat,
and som doe want cowmeat.

13 Small commons and bare,
yéelds cattell ill fare.

14 Som common with géese,
and shéepe without fléese.
Som tits thither bring,
and hogs without ring.

15 Some champions agrée
as waspe doth with bée.

[1] Sts. 1–5 are not in 1577.

16 Get swineherd for hog,
but kill not with dog.
Wher swineherd doth lack,
corne goeth to wrack.

17 All goes to the Deuill,
where shepherd is euill.

18 Come home from land,
with stone in hand.

19 Man cow prouides,
wife dairie guides.

20 Slut Cisley vntaught
hath whitemeat naught.

21 Some bringeth in gaines,
some losse beside paines.

22 Run Cisse, fault known,[1]
with more than thine own.
Such Mistris, such Nan,
such Maister, such Man.

Thus endeth Aprils abstract,
agréeing with Aprils husbandrie.

*** In 1577 st. 11 is followed by sts. 20, 21, 22; then follows—

Such Mistres such Nan,
such master such man.
By such ill gestes,
poore Cis il restes.
Such fautes as thease
good dame will ease.
These faultes all ten,
abhorreth all men.
A warning for Cysse
for doing amysse.

48.

¶ Aprils husbandrie.

Chap. 38.

Swéete April showers,
Doo spring Maie flowers.

Forgotten month past,
Doe now at the last.

1[2] IN Cambridge shire forward to Lincolne shire way,
the champion maketh his fallow in May.
Then thinking so dooing one tillage woorth twaine,
by forcing of weede, by that meanes to refraine.

[1] cf. *post*, ch. 48, st. 21.
[2] Sts. 1–5 are not in 1577.

2 If April be dripping, then doo I not hate,
(for him that hath little) his fallowing late,
Else otherwise fallowing timelie is best,
for sauing of cattel, of plough and the rest.

3 Be suer of plough to be readie at hand,
er compas ye spred that on hillocks did stand:
Least drieing so lieing, doo make it decaie,
er euer much water doo wash it awaie.

4 Looke now to prouide ye of meadow for hay,
if fennes be vndrowned, there cheapest ye may.[1]
In fen for the bullock, for horse not so well,
count best the best cheape, wheresoeuer ye dwell.

5 Prouide ye of cowmeate, for cattel at night,
and chiefly where commons lie far out of sight:
Where cattel lie tied without any meat,
that profit by dairie can neuer be great.

Put poles to your hophils.

6 Get into thy hopyard with plentie of poles,
amongst those same hillocks deuide them by doles.
Three poles to a hillock[2] (I pas not how long)[3]
shall yeeld thee more profit, set deeplie and strong.

Felling of timber.

7 Sell barke to the tanner er timber yee fell,
cut lowe by the ground[4] or else doo ye not well.
In breaking[5] saue crooked, for mill and for ships,
and euer in hewing saue carpenters chips.

[1] "Now ye may see what medows are well laid up, and what not, and accordingly chuse your ground."—T.R.

[2] "I suppose in our Author's time they made the Hills less than they do now."—T.R. 1710.

[3] "Overpoling (especially in height) is worse than underpoling."—T.R.

[4] "Six inches at the but may be more worth than two foot in another part."—T.R.

[5] "Sawing out; it being called breaking-up by workmen in those parts near where our Author lived."—T.R.

8 First see it well fenced er hewers begin,
then see it well stadled,[1] without and within;
Thus being preserued and husbandlie donne,
shall sooner raise profit, to thee or thy sonne.

9 Leaue growing for stadles the likest and best,
though seller and buier dispatched the rest.
In bushes, in hedgerowe, in groue, and in wood,
this lesson obserued is needfull and good.

Stadling of woods.

10 Saue elme, ash and crabtree, for cart and for plough,
saue step for a stile, of the crotch of the bough.
Saue hazel for forks, saue sallow for rake,
saue huluer[2] and thorne, thereof flaile for to make.

11 Make riddance of carriage, er yeere go about,
for spoiling of plant that is newlie come out.
To carter (with oxen) this message I bring,
leaue oxen abrode[3] for anoieng the spring.

Discharge thy woods.

12[4] Allowance of fodder some countries doo yeeld,
as good for the cattel as haie in the feeld.
Some mowe vp their hedlonds[5] and plots among corne,
and driuen to leaue nothing, vnmowne, or vnshorne.

13 Some commons are barren, the nature is such,
and some ouer laieth the common too much.
The pestered commons small profit doth geeue,
and profit as little some reape I beleeue.

[1] "To stadle a Wood is to leave at certain distances a sufficient number of young Trees to replenish it."—T.R.

[2] "or Holly . . . . heavy enough for flail swingels."—T.R.

[3] T.R. reads "leave not oxe abroad," and explains spring to mean the young buds of felled underwood.

[4] Sts. 12 to 18 are not in 1577.

[5] "The laying of headlands for grass is frequently used in Norfolk to this day."—T.R. 1710.

14 Some pester the commons, with iades and with geese,
with hog without ring and with sheepe without fleese.
Some lose a daie labour with seeking their owne,
some meet with a bootie they would not haue knowne.

15 Great troubles and losses the champion sees,[1]
and euer in brauling, as wasps among bees:
As charitie that waie appeereth but small,
so lesse be their winnings, or nothing at all.

16 Where champion wanteth a swineherd for hog,
there many complaineth of naughtie mans dog.
Where ech his owne keeper appoints without care,
there corne is destroied er men be aware.

17 The land is well harted with helpe of the fold,
for one or two crops, if so long it will hold.
If shepherd would keepe them from stroieng of corne,
the walke of his sheepe might the better be borne.

18 Where stones be too manie, annoieng thy land,
make seruant come home with a stone in his hand.
By daily so dooing, haue plentie yee shall,
both handsome for pauing and good for a wall.

¶ Dairie matters.

19 From April beginning, till Andrew be past,
so long with good huswife, hir dairie doth last.
Good milchcow and pasture, good husbands prouide,
the resdue good huswiues knowes best how to guide.

¶ Ill huswiferie.

20 Ill huswife vnskilful to make hir owne chees,
through trusting of others hath this for hir fees.
Her milke pan and creame pot, so slabbered and sost,
that butter is wanting and cheese is halfe lost.

[1] "Our Author liv'd in the Reigns of King Henry the Eighth, King Edward the Sixth, Queen Mary and Queen Elizabeth: during which time there were several commotions about the taking in of Common Field Land. . . . The greatest part of the privileges of Common Fields, etc., are but so many privileges to wrong and quarrel with their neighbours."—T.R.

21 Where some of a cow doo raise yeerelie a pound, ¶
with such seelie huswiues no penie is found.
Then dairie maid (Cisley) hir fault being knowne,
away apace trudgeth, with more than hir owne.

22 Then neighbour, for Gods sake, if any you see, ¶
good seruant for dairie house, waine[1] her to mee.
Such maister such man, and such mistris such maid,
such husband and huswife, such houses araid.[2]

Ill huswiues saiengs.

49.

ℵ *A lesson for dairie maid Cisley, of ten* toppings gests.

(*a*) AS wife that will
good husband plese,
Must shun with skill
such gests as these.

(*b*) So Cisse that serues
must marke this note,
What fault deserues
a brushed cote.

(*c*) Gehezie, Lots wife, and Argusses eies, ¶
Tom piper, poore Cobler, and Lazarus thies,
Rough Esau, with Mawdlin, and Gentils that scrall,
With Bishop that burneth, thus knowe ye them all.[3]

Ten toppings gests vnsent for.

(*d*) *These toppingly gests be in number but ten,*
As welcome in dairie as Beares among men.
Which being descried, take heede of[4] *you shall,*
For danger of after claps, after that fall.

[1] waynes. 1573 (M.); wayne. 1577.
[2] and house is araid. 1573 (M.); "such houses arayde." 1577.
[3] With bishop that turneth and burneth up all. 1573 (M.) and 1577.
[4] if. 1577.

¶

White and drie. 1 Gehezie his sicknes was whitish and drie,
such cheeses, good Cisley, ye floted[1] too nie.

Too salt. 2 Leaue Lot with her piller (good Cisley) alone,
much saltnes in whitemeat is ill for the stone.

Full of eies. 3 If cheeses in dairie haue Argusses eies,
tell Cisley the fault in hir huswiferie lies.[2]

Houen. 4 Tom Piper hath houen and puffed vp cheekes,
if cheese be so houen, make Cisse to seeke creekes.

Tough. 5 Poore Cobler he taggeth his leatherlie trash,
if cheese abide tugging, tug Cisley a crash.

Full of spots. 6 If Lazer[3] so lothsome in cheese be espied,
let baies amend Cisley, or shift hir aside.

Full of heares. 7 Rough Esau was hearie from top to the fut,
if cheese so appeareth, call Cisley a slut.

Full of whey. 8 As Mawdlin wept, so would Cisley be drest,
for whey in hir cheeses, not halfe inough prest.

Full of gentils. 9 If gentils be scrauling, call magget the py,
if cheeses haue gentils, at Cisse by and by.

Burnt to the pan. 10 Blesse Cisley (good mistris) that Bishop doth ban
for burning the milke of hir cheese to the pan.

[11] *If thou (so oft beaten)*[4] *I will no more threaten,*
amendest by this: *I promise thee Cis.*

[12] Thus dairie maid Cisley, rehearsed ye see,
what faults with ill huswife, in dairie house bee.
Of market abhorred, to houshold a griefe,
to maister and mistris, as ill as a thiefe.

Thus endeth Aprils husbandrie.

[1] "Floting is taking off the Cream."—T. R.

[2] "Because she did not work the Curd well together."—T. R.

[3] "An inner corruption. . . . Chiefly occasioned from their using milk soon after calving."—T. R.

[4] Amend so oft beaten
for doing amisse. 1577.

50.

¶ Maies abstract.

Chap. 39.

1 PUT lambe from eawe,
to milke a feawe.

2 Be not too bold,
to milke and to fold.

3 Fiue eawes alow,
to euerie cow.

4 Shéepe wrigling taile
hath mads without faile.

5 Beat hard in the réede
where house hath néede.

6 Leaue cropping from May
to Mihelmas day.
Let Iuie be killed,
else trée will be spilled.

7 Now threshers warne
to rid the barne.

8 Be suer of hay
till thend of May.

9 Let shéepe fill flanke,
where corne is too ranke.
In woodland leuer,[1]
in champion neuer.

10 To wéeding away,
as soone as yée may.

11 For corne here réede,
what naughtie wéede.

12 Who wéeding slacketh,
good husbandrie lacketh.

13 Sowe buck or branke,
that smels so ranke.

14 Thy branke go and sowe,
where barlie did growe.
The next crop wheat
is husbandrie neat.

15 Sowe pescods some,
for haruest to come.

16 Sowe hemp and flacks,
that spinning lacks.

17 Teach hop to clime,
for now it is time.

18 Through fowles & wéedes
poore hop ill spéedes.
Cut off or crop
superfluous hop:
The titters or tine
makes hop to pine.[2]

19 Some raketh their wheat,
with rake that is great.
So titters and tine
be gotten out fine.

[1] euer. 1577.

[2] now take out fine. 1577.

20 Now[1] sets doe craue
some wéeding to haue.

21 Now draine as ye like
both fen and dike.

22 Watch bées in May,
for swarming away.
Both now and in June,
marke maister bées tune.

23 Twifallow thy land,
least plough else stand.

24 No longer tarrie,
out compas to carrie.

25 Where néede doth pray it,
there sée ye lay it.

26 Set Jack and Jone
to gather vp stone.

27 To grasse with thy calues,
take nothing to halues.

28 Be suer thy neat
haue water and meat.

29 By tainting of ground,
destruction is found.

30 Now carrege get
home fewell to fet.
Tell fagot and billet
for filching gillet.

31 In sommer for firing
let citie be buying.
Marke colliers packing
least coles be lacking.
(Sée opened sack)
for two in a pack.

32 Let nodding patch
go sléepe a snatch.

33 Wife as[2] you will,
now plie your still.

34 Fine bazell[3] sowe,
in a pot to growe.
Fine séedes sowe now,
before ye sawe how.

35 Kéepe ox from cow,
for causes ynow.

Thus endeth Maies abstract,
agréeing with Maies husbandrie.

¶ Two other short remem-
brances.

[36] From bull cow fast
till Crowchmas[4] be past.
From heifer bul hid thée
till Lammas[5] doth bid thée.

Here ends Maies short remembrances.

*** Sts. 14, 15, 19, are not in 1577.

[1] New. 1577. [2] yf. 1577. [3] Bezell. 1577.
[4] Saint Helens daie (*side note*). [5] August (*side note*).

51.

¶ Maies husbandrie.

Chap. 40.

Cold Maie and windie,
Barne filleth vp finelie.

Forgotten month past,
Doe now at the last.

1 AT Philip and Jacob, away with the lams Essex and Suffolke.
that thinkest to haue any milke of their dams.
At Lammas leaue milking, for feare of a thing:
least (*requiem æternam*) in winter they sing.

2 To milke and to fold them is much to require, Milking of eawes.
except yee haue pasture to fil their desire.
Yet manie by milking (such heede they doo take),
not hurting their bodies much profit doo make.

3 Fiue eawes to a cow, make a proofe by a score, ¶
shall double thy dairie, else trust me no more.
Yet may a good huswife that knoweth the skill,
haue mixt and vnmixt at hir pleasure and will.

4 If sheepe or thy lambe fall a wrigling with taile,
go by and by search it, whiles helpe may preuaile:
That barberlie handled I dare thee assure,
cast dust in his arse, thou hast finisht thy cure.

5 Where houses be reeded[1] (as houses haue neede),
now pare off the mosse, and go beat in the reed.
The iuster ye driue it, the smoother and plaine,
more handsome ye make it to shut off the raine.

6 From Maie til October leaue cropping, for why? Leaue off cropping.
in wood sere, whatsoeuer thou croppest wil dy.
Where Iuie imbraceth the tree verie sore, Destroie Iuie.
kill Iuie, or else tree wil addle no more.

1 "Reeding is no where so well done as in Norfolk and Suffolk. . . . It will bear a better slope than any other thatch."—T.R.

7 Keepe threshing for thresher, til Maie be come in,
to haue to be suer fresh chaffe in the bin.
And somewhat to scamble, for hog and for hen,
and worke when it raineth for loitering men.

Count store no sore.

8 Be sure of haie and of prouender some,
for labouring cattel til pasture be come.
And if ye doo mind to haue nothing to sterue,
haue one thing or other, for all thing to serue.

9 Ground compassed wel and a following[1] yeare,
(if wheat or thy barlie too ranke doo appeare)
Now eat it with sheepe or else mowe it ye may,
for ledging, and so, to the birds for a pray.

¶ Weeding.

10 In Maie get a weede hooke, a crotch and a gloue,
and weed out such weedes as the corne doth not loue:
For weeding of winter corne now it is best,
but June is the better for weeding the rest.

Il wéeds.

11 The May weed doth burn and the thistle doth freat,
the fitchis[2] pul downward, both rie and the wheat.
The brake and the cockle be noisome too much,
yet like vnto boddle no weede there is such.

¶

12 Slack neuer thy weeding, for dearth nor for cheape,
the corne shall reward it er euer ye reape.
And specially where ye doo trust for to seede,[3]
let that be well vsed, the better to speede.

Sowing of branke.

13 In Maie is good sowing, thy buck or thy branke,
that black is as pepper, and smelleth so ranke.
It is to thy land, as a comfort or muck,
and al thing it maketh as fat as a buck.

1 See note 3, p. 114.
2 "or, as some call it, the Tine-tare."—T.R.
3 to for seed. 1577.

14[1] Sowe buck after barlie, or after thy wheat,
a peck to a roode (if the measure be great);
Three earthes see ye giue it, and sowe it aboue,
and harrow it finelie if buck ye doo loue.

15[1] Who pescods would gather, to haue with the last,
to serue for his houshold till haruest be past,
Must sowe them in Maie, in a corner ye shal,
where through so late growing no hindrance may fal.

16 Good flax and good hemp for to haue of hir owne,
in Maie a good huswife will see it be sowne.
And afterward trim it, to serue at a neede,
the fimble to spin and the karl for hir seede.

¶ Sowing of flax and hempe.

17 Get into the hopyard, for now it is time,[2]
to teach Robin hop on his pole how to clime:
To follow the Sunne, as his propertie is,
and weede him and trim him, if aught go amis.

18 Grasse, thistle and mustard seede, hemlock and bur,
tine, mallow and nettle, that keepe such a stur.
With peacock and turkie, that nibbles off top,
are verie ill neighbors to seelie poore hop.

Il neighbours to the hop.

19 From wheat go and rake out the titters or tine,
if eare be not foorth, it will rise againe fine.
Use now in thy rie, little raking or none,
breake tine[3] from his roote, and so let it alone.

20 Bankes newly quicksetted, some weeding doo craue,
the kindlier nourishment thereby to haue.
Then after a shower to weeding a snatch,
more easilie weede with the roote to dispatch.

Weeding of quickset.

[1] Sts. 14 and 15 are not in 1577.
[2] "I am told that 20*s*. an acre is the common Price for looking after a hop ground."—T.R.
[3] Misprinted "time."

Now draine ditches.

21 The fen and the quamire,[1] so marrish be kind,
and are to be drained, now wine to thy mind:
Which yeerelie vndrained and suffered vncut,
annoieth the meadowes that thereon doo but.

¶ Swarming of bées.

22 Take heede to thy bees, that are readie to swarme,
the losse thereof now is a crownes worth of harme:[2]
Let skilfull be readie and diligence seene,
least being too careles, thou losest thy beene.

Twifallowing.

23 In Maie at the furthest, twifallow thy land,
much drout may else after cause plough for to stand:
This tilth being done, ye haue passed the wurst,
then after who ploweth, plow thou with the furst.

Carie out compas.

24 Twifallow once ended, get tumbrell and man,
and compas that fallow as soone as ye can.
Let skilfull bestow it, where neede is vpon,
more profit the sooner to follow[3] thereon.

25 Hide hedlonds with muck, if ye will to the knees,
so dripped and shadowd with bushes and trees:
Bare plots full of galles,[4] if ye plow ouerthwart,
and compas it then, is a husbandlie part.

26 Let children be hired, to lay to their bones,
from fallow as needeth to gather vp stones.
What wisedome for profit aduiseth vnto,
that husband and huswife must willingly do.

Forth to grasse with thy calues.

27 To gras with thy calues in some medow plot nere,
where neither their mothers may see them nor here.
Where water is plentie and barth to sit warme,
and looke well vnto them, for taking of harme.

[1] quamer. 1577.
[2] "The Proverb says, 'A Swarm in May is worth a Load of Hay.'"—T.R. 1710. Mavor says a swarm might fetch 15*s*. in his time (1812).
[3] The author of *Tusser Redivivus* and Mavor prefer *fallow*; though M. says that all standard editions read *follow*. Cf. st. 9.
[4] gales. 1577.

28 Pinch neuer thy wennels of water or meat,
if euer ye hope for to haue them good neat:
In Sommer time dailie, in Winter in frost,
if cattel lack drinke, they be vtterly lost.

Let not cattel want water.

29 For coueting much ouerlay not thy ground,
and then shall thy cattel be lustie and sound.
But pinch them of pasture, while Sommer doth last,
and lift at their tailes er an Winter be past.

Ouerlay not thy pastures.

30 Get home with thy fewell, made readie to fet,
the sooner the easier carrege to get:
Or otherwise linger the carrege thereon,
till (where as ye left it) a quarter be gon.

Get home thy fewel.

31 His firing in Sommer, let Citizen buie,
least buieng in Winter make purse for to crie.
For carman and collier harps both on a string,
in Winter they cast to be with thee to bring.[1]

Husbandrie for Citizens.

32 From Maie to mid August, an hower or two,
let patch sleepe a snatch, how soeuer ye do,
Though sleeping one hower refresheth his song,
yet trust not hob growthed for sleeping too long.

Sléeping time.

33 The knowledge of stilling is one pretie feat,
The waters be holesome, the charges not great.
What timelie thou gettest, while Sommer doth last,
thinke Winter will helpe thee, to spend it as fast.

¶ Stilling of herbes.

34 Fine bazell desireth it may be hir lot,
to growe as the gilloflower, trim in a pot,
That ladies and gentils, for whom she doth serue,
may helpe hir as needeth, poore life to preserue.[2]

¶

[1] "In our Author's time, and not long since, the Yarmouth and Ipswich Colliers were laid up in the Winter, and then the Spring Market was always dearest."—T.R.

[2] "Most people stroak Garden Basil, which leaves a grateful Smell on the Hand; and he will have it, that such stroaking from a fair lady preserves the life of the Basil."—T.R.

35 Keepe oxe fro thy cow that to profit would go,
least cow be deceiued by oxe dooing so:
And thou recompenced for suffering the same,
with want of a calfe and a cow to wax lame.

Thus endeth Maies husbandrie.

52.

¶ Iunes abstract.

Chap. 41.

1 WASH shéep for to share,
that shéepe may go bare.

2 Though fléese ye take,
no patches make.

3 Share lambes no whit,
or share not yit.

4 If meadow be growne,
let meadow be mowne.

5 Plough early ye may,
and then carrie hay.

6 Tis good to be knowne,
to háue all of thine owne.
Who goeth a borrowing,
goeth a sorrowing.

7 Sée cart in plight,
and all things right.

8 Make drie ouer hed,
both houell and shed.

9 Of houell make stack,
for pease on his back.

10[1] In champion some,
wants elbow rome.

11[1] Let wheat and rie,
in house lie drie.

12[1] Buie turfe and sedge,
or else breake hedge.

13 Good store howse néedfull
well ordred spéedfull.

[1] Sts. 10-12 are omitted in 1577.

14 Thy barnes repaire,
make flower[1] faire.

15 Such shrubs as noie,
in sommer destroie.

16 Swinge brembles & brakes,
get forkes and rakes.

17 Spare hedlonds[2] some,
till haruest come.

18 Cast ditch and pond,
to lay vpon lond.

A lesson of hopyard.

19 Where hops will growe,
here learne to knowe.
Hops many will coome,
in a roode of roome.

20 Hops hate the land,
with grauell and sand.

21 The rotten mold
for hop is worth gold.

22 The sunne southwest
for hopyard is best.

23 Hop plot once found,
now dig the ground.

24 Hops fauoreth malt,
hops thrift doth exalt:
Of hops more réede,
as time shall néede.

Thus endeth Junes abstract,
agréeing with Junes husbandrie.

53.

¶ Junes husbandrie.

Chap. 42.

Calme weather in June
Corne sets in time.

Forgotten month past,
Doe now at the last.

1 WASH sheepe (for the better) where water doth run, Shéepe sharing.
and let him go cleanly and drie in the sun.
Then share him and spare not, at two daies an end,
The sooner the better his corps will amend.

[1] *Query*, floor.

[2] hedlong. 1577.

Beware of euill shéepe shearers.

2 Reward not thy sheepe (when ye take off his cote)
with twitchis and patches, as brode as a grote.
Let not such vngentlenesse happen to thine,
least flie with hir gentils doo make it to pine.

Sheare lambes in Julie.

3 Let lambes go vnclipped, till June be halfe worne,
the better the fleeses will growe to be shorne.
The Pie will discharge thee for pulling the rest:
the lighter the sheepe is, then feedeth it best.

Mowing time.

4 If meadow be forward, be mowing of some;
but mowe as the makers may well ouercome:
Take heede to the weather, the wind and the skie,
if danger approcheth, then cock apace crie.

5 Plough earlie till ten a clock, then to thy hay,
in plowing and carting, so profit ye may.
By little and little, thus dooing ye win:
that plough shall not hinder when haruest comes in.

6 Prouide of thine owne to haue all things at hand,
least worke and the workman vnoccupide stand.
Loue seldome to borowe that thinkest to saue,
for he that once lendeth twise looketh to haue.

Trim well thy carts.

7 Let cart be well searched without and within,
well clouted and greased, er hay time begin.
Thy hay being carried, though carter had sworne,
carts bottome well boorded is sauing of corne.

8 Good husbands that laie to saue all things vpright,
for tumbrels and cart, haue a shed readie dight.
Where vnder the hog may in winter lie warme:
to stand so enclosed, as wind doo no harme.

9 So likewise a houell will serue for a roome,
to stack on the peason, when haruest shall coome.
And serue thee in winter, more ouer than that,
to shut vp thy porklings thou mindest to fat.

A houell is set vpon crotches[1] and couered with poles and strawe.

10[2] Some barnroome haue little, and yardroome as much,
yet corne in the field appertaineth to such:
Then houels and rikes they are forced to make,
abrode or at home for necessities sake.

11[2] Make sure of breadcorne (of all other graine),
lie drie and well looked to, for mouse and for raine.
Though fitchis and pease, and such other as they,
(for pestring too much) on a houell ye ley.

12[2] With whinnes or with furzes thy houell renew,
for turfe or for sedge, for to bake and to brew:
For charcole and sea cole, as also for thacke,
for tallwood and billet, as yeerlie ye lacke.

13 What husbandlie husbands, except they be fooles,
but handsome haue storehouse, for trinkets and tooles:
And all in good order, fast locked to ly,
what euer is needfull, to find by and by.

The husbandlie storhouse.

14 Thy houses and barnes would be looked vpon,
and all things amended er haruest come on.
Things thus set in order, in quiet and rest,
shall further thy haruest and pleasure thee best.

15 The bushes and thorne with the shrubs that do noy,
in woodsere[3] or sommer cut downe to destroy:
But where as decay to the tree ye will none,
for danger in woodsere, let hacking alone.

1 "forked posts."—T.R.
2 Sts. 10–12 are omitted in 1577.
3 goodsere. 1577.

Mowe downe brakes and meadow.

16 At Midsommer, downe with the brembles and brakes,
and after, abrode with thy forks and thy rakes:
Set mowers a mowing, where meadow is growne,
the longer now standing the worse to be mowne.

Mowe hedlonds at haruest or after in the seueral fields.

17 Now downe with the grasse vpon hedlonds about,
that groweth in shadow, so ranke and so stout.
But grasse vpon hedlond of barlie and pease,
when haruest is ended, go mowe if ye please.

18 Such muddie deepe ditches, and pits in the feeld,
that all a drie sommer no water will yeeld,
By fieing and casting that mud vpon heapes,
commodities many the husbandman reapes.

A lesson where and when to plant good Hopyard.

19 Whome fancie persuadeth, among other crops,
to haue for his spending, sufficient of hops,
Must willinglie follow, of choises to chuse,
such lessons approoued, as skilfull doo vse.

Naught for hops.

20 Ground grauellie, sandie, and mixed with clay,
is naughtie for hops any maner of way;
Or if it be mingled with rubbish and stone,
for drines and barrennes, let it alone.

Good for hops.

21 Choose soile for the hop of the rottenest mould,
well doonged and wrought, as a garden plot should:
Not far from the water (but not ouerflowne)
this lesson well noted is meete to be knowne.

22 The Sunne in the south, or else southly and west,
is ioy to the hop, as a welcomed gest;
But wind in the north, or else northly east,
to hop is as ill as a fraie in a feast.

23 Meete plot for a hopyard once found as is told,
make thereof account, as of iewell of gold.
Now dig it and leaue it, the Sunne for to burne,
and afterward fence it, to serue for that turne.

Now dig thy new hop ground.

24 The hop for his profit I thus doo exalt,
it strengtheneth drinke, and it fauoreth malt.
And being well brewed, long kept it will last,
and drawing abide, if ye drawe not too fast.

The praise of hops.

54.

¶ Julies abstract.

Chap. 43.

1 GO sirs and away,
to ted and make hay.
If stormes drawes nie,
then cock apace crie.

2 Let hay still bide,
till well it be dride.
(Hay made) away carrie,
no longer then tarrie.

3 Who best way titheth,
he best way thriueth.

4 Two good hay makers
woorth twentie crakers.

5 Let dallops[1] about
be mowne and had out.
Sée hay doo looke gréene,
sée féeld ye rake cléene.

6 Thry fallow I pray thée,
least thistles bewray thée.

7 Cut off, good wife,
ripe beane with a knife.

8 Ripe hempe out cull,
from karle to pull.
Let séede hempe growe,
till more ye knowe.

[1] dalors. 1577.

9 Drie flax get in,
for spinners[1] to spin.
Now mowe[2] or pluck
thy branke or buck.

10 Some wormewood saue,
for March to haue.

11 Mark Physick true,
of wormewood and rue.[3]
Get grist to the mill,
for wanting at will.

Thus endeth Julies abstract, agréeing with Julies husbandrie.

55.

¶ Julies husbandrie.

Chap. 44.

No tempest, good Julie,
Least corne lookes rulie.

Forgotten month past,
Doe now at the last.

Hay haruest.

1 GO muster thy seruants, be captaine thy selfe,
prouiding them weapon and other like pelfe.
Get bottles and walletts, keepe field in the heat,
the feare is as much, as the danger is great.

2 With tossing and raking and setting on cox,
grasse latelie in swathes is hay for an ox:
That done, go and cart it and haue it away,
the battel is fought, ye haue gotten the day.

Pay thy tithes.

3 Pay iustly thy tithes whatsoeuer thou bee,
that God may in blessing send foison to thee.
Though Vicar[4] be bad, or the Parson as euill,
go not for thy tithing thy selfe to the Deuill.

4 Let hay be well made, or auise else auouse,
for molding in goef,[5] or of firing the house.
Lay coursest aside for the ox and the cow,
the finest for sheepe and thy gelding alow.

[1] mayde. 1577.
[2] Go reape. 1577.
[3] Some woormwood saue
for March to haue. 1577.
[4] curat. 1577.
[5] mow. 1614.

5 Then downe with the hedlonds, that groweth about,
leaue neuer a dallop vnmowne and had out.
Though grasse be but thin, about barlie and pease,
yet picked vp cleane ye shall find therein ease.

6 Thry fallow betime, for destroieng of weede, Thry fal-lowing.
least thistle and duck[1] fall a blooming and seede,
Such season may chance, it shall stand thee vpon,
to till it againe, er an Sommer be gon.

7 Not rent[2] off, but cut off, ripe beane with a knife, ¶
for hindering stalke of hir vegetiue life. Gathering of garden beanes.
So gather the lowest, and leauing the top,
shall teach thee a trick, for to double thy crop.

8 Wife, pluck fro thy seed hemp the fiemble hemp clene, ¶
this looketh more yellow, the other more grene: Gather yellow hempe.
Vse ton for thy spinning, leaue Mihel the tother,
for shoo thred and halter, for rope and such other.

9[3] Now pluck vp thy flax, for the maidens to spin, ¶
first see it dried, and timelie got in.
And mowe vp thy branke, and away with it drie,
and howse it vp close, out of danger to lie.

10 While wormwood hath seed, get a handful or twaine, ¶
to saue against March to make flea to refraine: Wormewood get against fleas and infection.
Where chamber is sweeped, and wormwood is strowne,
no flea for his life dare abide to be knowne.

11[4] What sauer is better (if physick be true),
for places infected, than wormwood and rue.
It is as a comfort for hart and the braine,
and therefore to haue it, it is not in vaine.

[1] dock. 1577.
[2] rend. 1573 (M.), 1577.
[3] St. 9 wanting in 1577.
[4] St. 11 wanting in 1577.

¶ Be sure of bread and drinke for haruest.

12 Get grist to the mill, to haue plentie in store,
least miller lack water, as many doo more.
The meale the more yeeldeth, if seruant be true,
and miller that tolleth, take none but his due.

Thus endeth Julies husbandrie.

56.

¶ Augusts abstract.

Chap. 45.

1 THRY fallowing won,
get compassing don.

2 In June and in Awe
swinge brakes (for a lawe).

3 Pare saffron plot,
forget it not.
His dwelling made trim,
looke shortly for him:
When haruest is gon,
then saffron comes on.

4 A little of ground
brings saffron a pound.
The pleasure is fine,
the profit is thine.
Kéepe colour in drieng,
well vsed woorth buieng.

5[1] Maids, mustard séed reape,
and laie on a heape.

6[1] Good neighbors in déede,
change séede for séede.

7 Now strike vp drum,[2]
cum haruest man cum.
take paine for a gaine,
one knaue mars twaine.

8 Reape corne by the day,[3]
least corne doo decay.
By great is the cheaper,
if trustie were reaper.

9 Blowe horne for sleapers,
and chéere vp thy reapers.[4]

[1] Sts. 5, 6 are wanting in 1577.
[2] droom. 1577.
[3] Get reapers by day. 1577.
[4] giue gloues to, etc. 1573 (M.) and 1577.

10 Well dooings who loueth,
thes haruest points proueth.

11 Paie Gods part furst,
and not of the wurst.

12 Now Parson (I say),[1]
tith carrie away.

13 Kéepe cart gap wéele,
scare hog from whéele.

14[2] Mowe hawme to burne,
to serue thy turne:
To bake thy bread,
to burne vnder lead.

15[2] Mowne hawme being dry,
no longer let ly.
Get home thy hawme,
whilst weather is cawme.

16 Mowne barlie lesse cost,
ill mowne much lost.

17 Reape barlie with sickle,
that lies in ill pickle.[3]
Let gréenest stand,
for making of band.
Bands made without dew,
will hold but a few.

18 Laie band[4] to find her,
two rakes[5] to a binder.

19 Rake after sieth,
and pay thy tieth.
Corne carried all,
then rake it ye shall.

20 Let shock take sweate,
least gofe take heate.
Yet it is best reason,
to take it in season.

21 More often ye turne,
more pease ye out spurne.
Yet winnow them in,
er carrege begin.

22 Thy carting plie,
while weather is drie.

23 Bid gouing (clim)[6]
goue iust and trim.
Laie wheat for séede,
to come by at néede.
Séede barelie cast,
to thresh out last.

24 Lay pease vpon stacke,
if houell ye lack.
And couer it straight,
from doues that waight.

[1] That parson may. 1577.

[2] Sts. 14, 15, are wanting in 1577.

[3] Reape barley with hand,
that will not stand. 1577.

[4] hand. 1577.

[5] rakers. 1577.

[6] In 1577, Bid goeuing clim. *Query*, abbreviation for Clement.

25 Let gleaners gleane,
(the poore I meane).
Which euer ye sowe,
that first eate lowe.
The other forbare,
for rowen[1] to spare.

26 Come home lord singing,
com home[2] corne bringing.
Tis merie in hall,
when[3] beards wag all.

27 Once had thy desire,
pay workman his hire.
Let none be beguilde,
man, woman, nor childe.

28 Thanke God[4] ye shall,
and adue for all.

Works after haruest.[5]

29 Get tumbrell in hand,
for barlie land.

30 The better the muck,
the better good luck.

31 Still carrege is good,
for timber and wood.
No longer delaies,
to mend the high waies.

32 Some loue as a iewell,
well placing of fewell.

33 In piling of logs,
make houell for hogs.

34 Wife, plow doth crie,
to picking of rie.

35 Such séede as ye sowe,
such reape or else mowe.

36 Take shipping or ride.
Lent stuffe to prouide.

37 Let haberden lie,
in peasestraw drie.

38 When out ye ride,
leaue a good guide.

39 Some profit spie out,
by riding about.
Marke now, thorow yéere,
what cheape, what déere.

40 Some skill doth well
to buie and to sell.

[1] rewen. 1577.
[2] cart. 1573 (M.), 1577.
[3] let. 1577.
[4] so. 1577.
[5] The Works after Haruest are not in editions previous to 1580 (M.). But stanzas 47 and 48 are in Septembers Abstract. 1577.—Ed.

Of théefe who bieth,
in danger lieth.

41 Commoditie knowne,
abrode is blowne.

42 At first hand bie,
at third let lie.

43 Haue monie prest,
to buie at the best.

44 Some cattle home bring,
for Mihelmas spring.
By hauke and hound,
small profit is found.

45 Dispatch, looke home,
to loitring mome.
Prouide or repent,
milch cow for Lent.

46 Now crone[1] your shéepe,
fat those ye kéepe.
Leaue milking old cow,
fat aged vp now.

47 Sell butter and chéese,
good Faires few léese.
At Faires go bie,
home wants to supplie.

48 If hops looke browne,
go gather them downe.
But not in the deaw,
for piddling with feaw.

49 Of hops this knack,
a meanie doo lack.[2]
Once had thy will,[3]
go couer his hill.

50 Take hop to thy dole,
but breake not his pole.

51 Learne here (thou stranger)
to frame hop manger.

52 Hop poles preserue,
againe to serue.
Hop poles by and by,
long safe vp to dry.
Least poles wax scant,
new poles go plant.[4]

53 The hop kell dride,
will best abide.

*** Stanza 47 is st. 49 in Septembers Abstract in 1577; st. 48 is 50, second couplet reads—But not in a deawe,
nor pidling with feawe. 1577.

[1] *i.e.* pick out the crones.—T.R., but cf. Glossary.
[2] put in thy pack. 1577.
[3] fyll. 1577.
[4] ley new to plant. 1577.

Hops dried in loft,
aske tendance oft.
And shed their séedes,
much more than néedes.[1]

54 Hops dride small cost,
ill kept halfe lost.

Hops quickly[2] be spilt,
take héede if thou wilt.

55 Some come, some go,
This life is so.

Thus endeth Augusts abstract, agréeing with Augusts husbandrie.

57.

¶ Augusts husbandrie.

Chap. 46.

Dry August and warme,
Doth haruest no harme.

Forgotten month past,
Doe now at the last.

Thry fallowing.

1 THRY fallow once ended, go strike by and by,
both wheat land and barlie, and so let it ly.
And as ye haue leisure, go compas the same,
when vp ye doo lay it, more fruitfull to frame.

Mowing of brakes.

2 Get downe with thy brakes, er an showers doo come,
that cattle the better may pasture haue some.
In June and in August, as well doth appeere,
is best to mowe brakes, of all times in the yeere.

Paring of saffron.

3 Pare saffron betweene the two S. Maries daies,
or set or go shift it, that knowest the waies.
What yeere shall I doo it (more profit to yeeld ?)
the fourth in garden, the third in the feeld.

[1] The third couplet is omitted in 1577.
[2] soone. 1577.

4 In hauing but fortie foote workmanly dight,
take saffron ynough for a Lord and a knight.
All winter time alter[1] as practise doth teach,
what plot haue ye better, for linnen to bleach.[2] ¶ Huswiferie.

5[3] Maides, mustard seede gather, for being too ripe,
and weather it well, er ye giue it a stripe:[4]
Then dresse it and laie it in soller vp sweete,
least foistines make it for table vnmeete. ¶

6[5] Good huswifes in sommer will saue their owne seedes,
against the next yeere, as occasion needes.
One seede for another, to make an exchange,
with fellowlie neighbourhood seemeth not strange. ¶

7 Make sure of reapers, get haruest in hand,
the corne that is ripe, doo[6] but shed as it stand.
Be thankfull to God, for his benefits sent,
and willing to saue it with earnest intent. Corne haruest.

8 To let out thy haruest, by great[7] or by day,
let this by experience leade thee a way.
By great will deceiue thee, with lingring it out,
by day will dispatch, and put all out of dout. Champion by great, the other by day.

9 Grant haruest lord[8] more by a penie or twoo,
to call on his fellowes the better to doo:
Giue gloues to thy reapers,[9] a larges to crie,
and dailie to loiterers haue a good eie.

[1] after. 1577.

[2] "Saffron makes a very good Sward, whereon Linnen may lye hollow and bleach well enough."—T.R.

[3] Stanza 5 is wanting in 1573 (M.) and 1577.

[4] "Beating it upon a Hurdle or some other rough thing."—T.R.

[5] St. 6 is wanting in 1573 (M.) and 1577.

[6] doth. 1614.

[7] "Our Author is justly against letting Harvest by the great, for whoever does will certainly find himself cheated or slighted."—T.R.

[8] "Some stay'd sober working man, who understands all sorts of Harvest Work."—T.R. Cf. Matt. ix. 38.

[9] "Where the Wheat is thistly."—T.R.

Good haruest points.

10 Reape wel, scatter not, gather cleane that is shorne,
binde fast, shock apace, haue an eie to thy corne.
Lode safe, carrie home, follow time being faire,
goue iust in the barne, it is out of despaire.

11[1] Tithe dulie and trulie, with hartie good will,
that God and his blessing may dwell with thee still:
Though Parson neglecteth his dutie for this,
thanke thou thy Lord God, and giue erie man his.

Parson looke to thy tithe.

12 Corne tithed (sir Parson) to gather go get,
and cause it on shocks to be by and by set:
Not leauing it scattering abrode on the ground,
nor long in the field, but away with it round.

Kéepe hog from cart whéele.

13 To cart gap and barne, set a guide to looke weele,
and hoy out (sir carter) the hog fro thy wheele:
Least greedie of feeding, in following cart,
it noieth or perisheth, spight of thy hart.

14[1] In champion countrie a pleasure they take,
to mowe vp their hawme, for to brew and to bake.
And also it stands them in steade of their thack,
which being well inned, they cannot well lack.

15[1] The hawme is the strawe of the wheat or the rie,
which once being reaped, they mowe by and bie:
For feare of destroieng with cattle or raine,
the sooner ye lode it, more profit ye gaine.

Mowing of barlie.

16 The mowing of barlie, if barlie doo stand,
is cheapest and best, for to rid out of hand:
Some mowe it and rake it, and sets it on cocks,
some mowe it and binds it, and sets it on shocks.

[1] Stanzas 11, 14, and 15 are not in 1577.

Binding of barlie.

17 Of barlie the longest and greenest ye find,
leaue standing by dallops, till time ye doo bind:
Then early in morning (while deaw is thereon),
to making of bands till the deaw be all gon.

Spreading of barlie bands.

18 One spreadeth those bands, so in order to ly,
as barlie (in swatches) may fill it thereby:
Which gathered vp, with the rake and the hand,
the follower after them bindeth in band. ¶

Tithe of rakings.

19 Where barlie is raked (if dealing be true),
the tenth of such raking to Parson is due:
Where scatring of barlie is seene to be much,
there custome nor conscience tithing should gruch.[1]

20 Corne being had downe (any way ye alow),
should wither as needeth, for burning in mow:
Such skill appertaineth to haruest mans art,
and taken in time is a husbandly part.

Usage of peason.

21 No turning of peason till carrege ye make,
nor turne in no more, than ye mind for to take:
Least beaten with showers so turned to drie,
by turning and tossing they shed as they lie.

Lingring lubbers.

22 If weather be faire, and tidie[2] thy graine,
make speedily carrege, for feare of a raine:
For tempest and showers deceiueth a menie,
and lingering lubbers loose many a penie.

Best maner of gouing corn in the barn.

23 In gouing at haruest, learne skilfully how
ech graine for to laie, by it selfe on a mow:
Seede barlie the purest, goue out of the way,
all other nigh hand goue as just as ye may.

[1] "This alludes to the custom of Norfolk, where the Parson takes his Tyth in the Swarth, the Farmer also clears the Swarths, and afterwards with a Drag-Rake rakes his ground all over."—T. R.

[2] "Tidy is an old Word signifying neat, proper, or in Season, from the word Tide."—T. R.

Pease stack.

24 Stack pease vpon houell abrode in the yard,
to couer it quicklie, let owner regard:
Least Doue and the cadow, there finding a smack,
with ill stormie weather doo perish thy stack.

Leaue gleaning for the poore.

25 Corne carred, let such as be poore go and gleane,
and after, thy cattle to mowth it vp cleane.
Then spare it for rowen, till Mihel be past,
to lengthen thy dairie no better thou hast.

26 In haruest time, haruest folke, seruants and all,
should make all togither good cheere in the hall:
And fill out the black boule of bleith to their song,
and let them be merie all haruest time long.

Pay trulie haruest folke.

27 Once ended thy haruest, let none be begilde,
please such as did helpe thee, man, woman, and childe.
Thus dooing, with alway such helpe as they can,
thou winnest the praise of the labouring man.

Thanke God for all.

28 Now looke vp to Godward, let tong neuer cease
in thanking of him, for his mightie encrease:
Accept my good will, for a proofe go and trie:
the better thou thriuest, the gladder am I.

[End of Augusts Husbandry in 1577.]

Works after Haruest.[1]

29 Now carrie out compas, when haruest is donne,
where barlie thou sowest, my champion sonne:
Or laie it on heape, in the field as ye may,
till carriage be faire, to haue it away.

[1] Not in editions previous to 1580 (M.). Portions are in Septembers Husbandry 1577.—Ed.

30 Whose compas is rotten and carried in time,
and spred as it should be, thrifts ladder may clime.
Whose compas is paltrie and carried too late,
such husbandrie vseth that many doo hate.

31[1] Er winter preuenteth, while weather is good, Carriage of fewell.
for galling of pasture get home with thy wood.
And carrie out grauell to fill vp a hole:
both timber and furzen, the turfe and the cole.

32 Howse charcole and sedge, chip and cole[2] of the land, Well placing of fewell.
pile tallwood and billet, stacke all that hath band.
Blocks, rootes,[3] pole and bough, set vpright to the thetch:
the neerer more handsome in winter to fetch.

33 In stacking of bauen, and piling of logs, Houell for hogs.
make vnder thy bauen a houell for hogs,
And warmelie enclose it, all sauing the mouth,
and that to stand open, and full to the south.

34 Once haruest dispatched, get wenches and boies,
and into the barne, afore all other toies.
Choised seede to be picked and trimlie well fide,
for seede may no longer from threshing abide.

35 Get seede aforehand, in a readines had,
or better prouide, if thine owne be too bad.
Be carefull of seede, or else such as ye sowe,
be sure at haruest, to reape or to mowe.

36[4] When haruest is ended, take shipping or ride, Provision for Lent.
Ling, Saltfish and Herring, for Lent to prouide.
To buie it at first, as it commeth to rode,
shall paie for thy charges thou spendest abrode.

[1] Stanzas 31-33 are in Septembers Husbandry. 1577.
[2] turfe. 1577.
[3] Block rootes. 1577.
[4] Sts. 36-46 appear as sts. 25-35 in Septembers Husbandry. 1577.

37 Choose skilfullie Saltfish, not burnt at the stone,[1]
buie such as be good, or else let it alone.
Get home that is bought, and goe stack it vp drie,
with peasestrawe betweene it, the safer to lie.

Compassing of barlie land.

38 Er euer ye iornie, cause seruant with speede
to compas thy barlie land where it is neede.
One aker well compassed, passeth some three,
thy barne shall at haruest declare it to thee.

39 This lesson is learned by riding about,
the prices of vittels, the yeere thorough out.
Both what to be selling and what to refraine,
and what to be buieng, to bring in againe.

40 Though buieng and selling doth woonderfull well,
to such as haue skill how to buie and to sell:
Yet chopping and changing I cannot commend,
with theefe[2] and his marrow, for feare of ill end.

41 The rich in his bargaining needes not be tought,
of buier and seller full far is he sought.
Yet herein consisteth a part of my text,
who buieth at first hand, and who at the next.

Buieng at first hand.

42 At first hand he buieth that paieth all downe,
at second, that hath not so much in the towne,
At third hand he buieth that buieth of trust,
at his hand who buieth shall paie for his lust.

Realie monie bieth best cheape.

43 As oft as ye bargaine, for better or wurse,
to buie it the cheaper, haue chinkes in thy purse:
Touch kept is commended, yet credit to keepe,
is paie and dispatch him, er euer ye sleepe.

[1] "Such Fish as is dry'd on the Beach in too hot Weather."—T. R.
[2] knaue. 1577.

44 Be mindfull abrode of Mihelmas[1] spring,
for thereon dependeth a husbandlie thing:
Though some haue a pleasure, with hauke vpon hand,
good husbands get treasure, to purchase their land.

Hauking.

45 Thy market dispatched, turne home againe round,
least gaping for penie, thou loosest[2] a pound:
Prouide for thy wife, or else looke to be shent,
good milch cow for winter, another for Lent.

Winter milch cow.

46 In traueling homeward, buie fortie good crones,
and fat vp the bodies of those seelie bones.
Leaue milking and drie vp old mulley thy cow,
the crooked and aged, to fatting put now.

Old ewes.

47[3] At Bartilmewtide, or at Sturbridge faire,
buie that as is needfull, thy house to repaire:
Then sell to thy profit, both butter and cheese,
who buieth it sooner, the more he shall leese.

Buieng or selling of butter and chéese.

48 If hops doo looke brownish, then are ye too slowe,
if longer ye suffer those hops for to growe.
Now sooner ye gather, more profit is found,
if weather be faire and deaw of a ground.

Hops gathering.

49 Not breake off, but cut off, from hop the hop string,
leaue growing a little againe for to spring.
Whose hill about pared, and therewith new clad,
shall nourish more sets against March to be had.

Increasing of hops.

50 Hop hillock discharged of euerie let,
see then without breaking, ech pole ye out get.
Which being vntangled aboue in the tops,
go carrie to such as are plucking of hops.

The order of hops gathering.

[1] Mighelmas. 1577. [2] lossest. 1577.
[3] Sts. 47–54 occur as sts. 49–56 of Septembers Husbandry. 1577.

Hop manger.

51 Take soutage or haier (that couers the kell),
set like to a manger and fastened well:
With poles vpon crotchis as high as thy brest,
for sauing and[1] riddance is husbandrie best.

Saue hop poles.

52 Hops had, the hop poles that are likelie preserue,
(from breaking and rotting) againe for to serue:
And plant ye with alders or willowes a[2] plot,
where yeerelie as needeth mo poles may be got.

Drieng of hops.

53 Some skilfullie drieth their hops on a kell,
and some on a soller, oft turning them well.
Kell dried will abide, foule weather or faire,
where drieng and lieng in loft doo dispaire.

Kéeping of hops.

54 Some close them vp drie in a hogshed or fat,
yet canuas or soutage is better than that:
By drieng and lieng they quickly be spilt:
thus much haue I shewed, doo now as thou wilt.

55 Old fermer is forced long August to make,
his goodes at more leisure away for to take.
New fermer he thinketh ech houre a day,
vntill the old fermer be packing away.

Thus endeth and holdeth out Augusts husbandrie,
till Mihelmas Eue.

Tho. Tusser.

58.

¶ *Corne Haruest equally deuided* into ten partes.

Chap. 47.[3]

1 One part cast forth, for rent due out of hand,
2 One other part, for seede to sowe thy land.
3 Another part, leaue Parson for his tieth.
4 Another part for haruest, sickle and sieth.

[1] of. 1577. [2] some. 1577.
[3] This chapter is wanting in 1573 (M.); but is in 1577.

5 One part for plowwrite, cartwrite, knacker and smith,
6 One part to vphold thy teemes that drawe therewith.
7 One part for seruant and workmans wages lay.
8 One part likewise for filbellie day by day.
9 One part thy wife for needfull things doth craue.
10 Thy selfe and childe, the last one part would haue.

For naperie sope and candle, salt and sauce, tinker[1] and cooper, brasse and pewter.

[1] timber. 1577.

[11] Who minds to cote,
vpon this note,
may easily find ynough:
What charge and paine,
to litle gaine,
doth follow toiling plough.

[12] Yet fermer may
thanke God and say,
for yeerlie such good hap:
Well fare the plough,
that sends ynough
to stop so many a gap.

59.

¶ *A briefe conclusion, where you may see, Ech word in the verse, to begin with a T.*

Chap. 48.

1 THE thriftie that teacheth the thriuing to thriue,
Teach timelie to trauerse the thing that thou triue.
Transferring thy toiling, to timelines tought.
This teacheth thee temprance, to temper thy thought.

Triue for contriue.

5 Take trustie (to trust to) that thinkest to thee,
That trustily thriftines trowleth to thee.
Then temper thy trauell to tarie the tide,
This teacheth thee thriftines twentie times tride.

9 Take thankfull thy talent, thanke thankfully those
That thriftilie teacheth thy time to transpose.
Troth twise to thee teached, teach twentie times ten.
This trade thou that takest, take thrift to thee then.

[Thomas Tusser (1577).]

60.

[*Mans age deuided into twelue seauens.* 1614].

❡ Mans age deuided here ye haue,
By prentiships, from birth to his graue.

Chap. 49.

7 *The first seuen yeers bring vp as a childe,*
14 *The next to learning, for waxing too wilde.*
21 *The next keepe vnder sir hobbard de hoy,*
28 *The next a man no longer a boy.*
35 *The next, let lustie laie wisely to wiue,*
42 *The next, laie now or else neuer to thriue.*
49 *The next, make sure for terme of thy life,*
56 *The next, saue somewhat for children and wife.*
63 *The next, be staied, giue ouer thy lust,*
70 *The next, thinke hourely whither thou must.*
77 *The next, get chaire and crotches to stay,*
84 *The next, to heauen God send vs the way.*

Who looseth their youth, shall rue it in age:
Who hateth the truth, in sorowe shall rage.

61.

❡ *Another diuision of the nature* of mans age.

Chap. 50.

The Ape, the Lion, the Foxe, the Asse,
Thus sets foorth man, as in a glasse.

Ape *Like Apes we be toieng, till twentie and one,*
Lyon *Then hastie as Lions till fortie be gone:*
Foxe *Then wilie as Foxes, till threescore and three,*
Asse *Then after for Asses accounted*[1] *we bee.*

[1] accompted. 1577.

[2] Who plaies with his better, this lesson must knowe,
what humblenes Foxe to the Lion doth owe.
Foxe, Ape with his toieng and rudenes of Asse,
brings (out of good hower) displeasure to passe.

62.

Comparing good husband with vnthrift his brother, The better discerneth the tone from the tother.

Chap. 51.

1 ILL husbandrie braggeth,
to go with the best:
Good husbandrie baggeth
vp gold in his chest.

2 Ill husbandry trudgeth,
with vnthrifts about:
Good husbandry snudgeth,
for fear of a dout.

3 Ill husbandrie spendeth
abrode like a mome:
Good husbandrie tendeth
his charges at home.

4 Ill husbandrie selleth
his corne on the ground:
Good husbandrie smelleth
no gain that way found.

5 Ill husbandrie loseth,
for lack of good fence:
Good husbandrie closeth,
and gaineth the pence.

6 Ill husbandrie trusteth
to him and to hur:
Good husbandrie lusteth
himselfe for to stur.

7 Ill husbandrie eateth
himselfe out a doore:
Good husbandrie meateth
his friend and the poore.

8 Ill husbandrie daieth,
or letteth it lie:
Good husbandrie paieth,
the cheaper to bie.

9 Ill husbandrie lurketh,
and stealeth a sleepe:
Good husbandrie worketh,
his houshold to kéepe.

10 Ill husbandrie liueth,
by that and by this:
Good husbandrie giueth
to erie man his.

11 Ill husbandrie taketh,
and spendeth vp all:
Good husbandrie maketh
good shift with a small.

12 Ill husbandry praieth
his wife to make shift:
Good husbandrie saieth
take this of my gift.

13 Ill husbandry drowseth
at fortune so auke:
Good husbandrie rowseth
himselfe as a hauke.

14 Ill husbandrie lieth
in prison for debt:
Good husbandrie spieth
where profit to get.

15 Ill husbandrie waies
has to fraud what he can:
Good husbandrie praies
hath of euerie man.

16 Ill husbandrie neuer
hath welth to keep touch:
Good husbandrie euer
hath penie in pouch.

[17] Good husband his boone,
Or request hath a far.
Ill husband assoone
Hath a tode with an R.

63.

¶ *A comparison betweene Champion* countrie and seuerall.

Chap. 52.

1 THE countrie[1] enclosed I praise,
the tother delighteth not me,
For nothing the wealth it doth raise,
to such as inferior be.
How both of them partly I knowe,
here somewhat I mind for to showe.[2]

[1] countery. 1577.
[2] Because of them both I do know
I mind thereof somewhat to show. 1577.

2 There swineherd that keepeth the hog, Champion.
there neatherd, with cur and his horne,
There shepherd with whistle and dog,
be fence to the medowe and corne.
There horse being tide on a balke,
is readie with theefe for to walke.

3 Where all thing in common doth rest,
corne field with the pasture and meade,
Though common ye doo for the best,
yet what doth it stand ye in steade?
There common as commoners vse,
for otherwise shalt thou not chuse.[1]

4 What laier much better then there,
or cheaper (thereon to doo well?)
What drudgerie more any where
lesse good thereof where can ye tell?
What gotten by Sommer is seene:
in Winter is eaten vp cleene.

5 Example by Leicester shire,
what soile can be better than that?
For any thing hart can desire,
and yet doth it want ye see what.
Mast, couert, close pasture, and wood,
and other things needfull as good.

6 All these doo enclosure bring, Enclosure.
experience teacheth no lesse,
I speake not to boast of the thing,
but onely a troth to expresse.
Example (if doubt ye doo make):
by Suffolke and Essex go take.

[1] There common as commoners do,
As good else to cobble a shoe. 1573 (M.) and 1577.

Seuerall.

7 More plentie of mutton and biefe,
corne, butter, and cheese of the best,
More wealth any where (to be briefe),
more people, more handsome and prest,
Where find ye? (go search any coast)
than there where enclosure is most.

8 More worke for the labouring man,
as well in the towne as the feeld:
Or thereof (deuise if ye can)
more profit what countries doo yeeld?
More seldome where see ye the poore,
go begging from doore vnto doore?

Champion countrie.

9 In Norfolke behold the dispaire
of tillage too much to be borne:
By drouers from faire to faire,
and others destroieng the corne.
By custome and couetous pates,
by gaps, and by opening of gates.[1]

10 What speake I of commoners by,
with drawing all after a line:
So noieng the corne, as it ly,
with cattle, with conies,[2] and swine.
When thou[3] hast bestowed thy cost,
looke halfe of the same to be lost.

11 The flocks of the Lords of the soile
do yeerly the winter corne wrong:
The same in a manner they spoile,
with feeding so lowe and so long.
And therefore that champion feeld
doth seldome good winter corne yeeld.

[1] "In Norfolk (in our Author's time) there was a considerable Rebellion, call'd Ket's Rebellion against Inclosures, and to this day they take the Liberty of throwing open all Enclosures out of the Common Field, these are commonly call'd Lammas Lands, and half Year Lands."—T. R.

[2] sheep and with swine. 1577.

[3] one. 1577.

Champion noiances.

12[1] By Cambridge a towne I doo knowe,
where many good husbands doo dwell;
Whose losses by losels doth showe,
more here than is needfull to tell:
Determine at court what they shall,
performed is nothing at all.

13 The champion robbeth by night,
and prowleth and filcheth by day:
Himselfe and his beast out of sight,
both spoileth and maketh away
Not onely thy grasse, but thy corne,
both after, and er it be shorne.

14 Pease bolt with thy pease he will haue,
his houshold to feede and his hog:
Now stealeth he, now will he craue,
and now will he coosen and cog.
In Bridewell a number be stript,
lesse woorthie than theefe to be whipt.

15 The oxboy, as ill is as hee,
or worser, if worse may be found:
For spoiling from thine and from thee,
of grasse and of corne on the ground.
Laie neuer so well for to saue it,
by night or by daie he will haue it.

16 What orchard vnrobbed escapes?
or pullet dare walke in their jet?
But homeward or outward (like apes)
they count it their owne they can get.
Lord, if ye doo take them, what sturs!
how hold they togither like burs!

[1] Stanzas 12–21 are not in 1577.

17 For commons these commoners crie,
enclosing they may not abide:
Yet some be not able to bie
a cow with hir calfe by hir side.
Nor laie not to liue by their wurke,
but theeuishlie loiter and lurke.

18 The Lord of the towne is to blame,
for these and for many faults mo.
For that he doth knowe of the same,
yet lets it vnpunished go.
Such Lords ill example doth giue,
where verlets and drabs so may liue.

19 What footpathes are made, and how brode!
annoiance too much to be borne:
With horse and with cattle what rode
is made thorow erie mans corne!
Where champions ruleth the roste,
there dailie disorder is moste.

20 Their sheepe when they driue for to wash,
how careles such sheepe they doo guide!
The fermer they leaue in the lash,
with losses on euerie side.
Though any mans corne they doo bite,
they will not alow him a mite.

21 What hunting and hauking is there!
corne looking for sickle at hand:
Actes lawles to doo without feare,
how yeerlie[1] togither they band.
More harme to another to doo,
than they would be done so vntoo.

[1] *Query*, yarely.

22 More profit is quieter found
(where pastures in seuerall bee:)
Of one seelie aker of ground,
than champion maketh of three.
Againe what a ioie is it knowne,
when men may be bold of their owne!

23 The tone is commended for graine, Champion.
yet bread made of beanes they doo eate:
The tother for one loafe haue twaine, Seuerall.
of mastlin, of rie, or of wheate.
The champion liueth full bare,
when woodland full merie doth fare.

24 Tone giueth his corne in a darth, Champion.
to horse, sheepe, and hog euery daie;
The tother giue cattle warme barth, Seuerall.
and feede them with strawe and with haie.
Corne spent of the tone so in vaine:
the tother doth sell to his gaine.

25 Tone barefoote and ragged doth go, Champion.
and readie in winter to sterue:
When tother ye see doo not so, Seuerall.
but hath that is needfull to serue.
Tone paine in a cotage doth take,
when tother trim bowers doo make.

26 Tone laieth for turfe and for sedge, Champion.
and hath it with woonderfull suit:
When tother in euerie hedge, Seuerall.
hath plentie of fewell and fruit.
Euils twentie times worser than thease,
enclosure quickly would ease.

Seuerall.

27 In woodland the poore men that haue
scarse fully two akers of land,
More merily liue and doo saue,
than tother with twentie in hand.
Yet paie they as much for the twoo
as tother for twentie must doo.

28 The labourer comming from thence,
in woodland to worke any where:
(I warrant you) goeth not hence,
to worke anie more againe there.
If this same be true (as it is:)
why gather they nothing of this?

29 The poore at enclosing doo grutch,
because of abuses that fall,
Least some man should haue but too much,
and some againe nothing at all.
If order might therein be found,
what were to the seuerall ground?

Thus endeth Husbandry. 1577.
Here followeth Huswifery. 1573.

*** "It is likely this was wrote soon after Ket's rebellion, as a dissuasive from the like, and to persuade the poorer sort quietly to endure Enclosures."—T. R.

64.

¶ *The description of an enuious and* naughtie neighbour.

Chap. 53.[1]

[1] An enuious neighbour is easie to finde,
His cumbersome fetches are seldome[2] behinde.
His hatred procureth from naughtie to wurse,
His friendship like Iudas that carried the purse.

[1] This chapter precedes the Author's Life in 1577 edition.
[2] sieldome. 1614.

His head is a storehouse, with quarrels full fraught,
His braine is vnquiet, till all come to naught.
His memorie pregnant, old euils to recite,
His mind euer fixed each euill to requite.
His mouth full of venim, his lips out of frame,
His tongue a false witnes, his friend to defame.
His eies be promooters, some trespas to spie,
His eares be as spials, alarum to crie.
His hands be as tyrants, reuenging ech thing,
His feete at thine elbow, as serpent to sting.
His breast full of rancor, like Canker[1] to freat,
His hart like a Lion, his neighbour to eat.
His gate like a sheepebiter, fleering aside,
His looke like a coxcombe, vp puffed with pride.
His face made of brasse, like a vice in a game,
His iesture like Dauus, whom Terence doth name.
His brag as Thersites, with elbowes abrode.
His cheekes in his furie shall swell like a tode.
His colour like ashes, his cap in his eies,
His nose in the aire, his snout in the skies.
His promise to trust to as slipprie[2] as ice,
His credit much like to the chance of the dice.
His knowledge or skill is in prating[3] too much,
His companie shunned,[4] and so be all such.
His friendship is counterfait, seldome to trust,
His dooings vnluckie and euer vniust.
His fetch is to flatter, to get what he can,
His purpose once gotten, a pin[5] for thee than.

[1] Coprus. 1577.
[2] slipper. 1577.
[3] parting. 1577.
[4] shenned. 1577.
[5] penny. 1577.

[In the edition of 1577 the following piece is inserted here.]

64.*

To light a candell before the Deuill.

To beard thy foes shews forth thy witt,
but helpes the matter nere a whit.

MY sonne, were it not worst
to frame thy nature so,
That as thine vse is to thy friend,
likewise to greet thy foe:
Though not for hope of good,
yet for the feare of euill,
Thou maist find ease so proffering vp
a candell to the deuill.

This knowne, the surest way
thine enemies wrath to swage;
If thou canst currey fauour thus,
thou shalt be counted sage.
Of truth I tell no lye,
by proofe to well I knowe,
The stubborne want of only this
hath brought full many lowe.

And yet to speak the trouth
the Deuill is worse then naught,
That no good turne will once deserue,
yet looketh vp so haught.
Exalt him how we please,
and giue him what we can,
Yet skarcely shall we find such Deuill
a truly honest man.

But where the mighty may
  of force the weake constraine,
It shal be wysely doone to bow
  to voyd a farther payne,
Like as in tempest great,
  where wind doth beare the stroke,
Much safer stands the bowing reede
  then doth the stubborne oke.

And chiefly when of all
  thy selfe art one of those
That fortune needes, will haue to dwell
  fast by the Deuils nose:
Then (though against thine hart)
  thy tongue thou must so charme
That tongue may say, where ere thou come,
  the Deuill doth no man harme.

For where as no reuenge
  may stand a man in steede,
As good is then an humble speech,
  as otherwise to bleede.
Like as ye see by him
  that hath a shrew to wife,
As good it is to speak her faire
  as still to liue in strife.

Put thou no Deuill in boote
  as once did master Shorne:
Take heede as from madde bayted bull
  to keepe thee fro his horne.
And where ye see the Deuill
  so bold to wrest with lawe,
Make *congé* oft, and crouch aloofe,
  but come not in his clawe.

The scholer forth of schoole
  may boldlier take his mind,
The fields haue eyes, the bushes eares,
  false birds can fetch the wind.
The further from the gone
  the safer may ye skippe,
The nerer to the carters hand
  the nerer to the whippe.

The neerer to the whippe
  the sooner comes the jerke,
The sooner that poore beast is strucke
  the sooner doth he yerke.
Some loueth for to whippe,
  to see how ierkes will smart,
In wofull taking is that horse
  that nedes must drawe in cart.

Such fellow is the Deuell,
  that doth euen what he list,
Yet thinketh he what ere he doth
  none ought dare say, but whist.
Take therefore heed, my sonne,
  and marke full well this song,
Learne thus with craft to claw the deuell,
  else liue in rest not long.

65.

¶ *A sonet against a slanderous tongue.*

¶ Chap. 54.

[1] DOTH darnell good, among the flowrie wheat?
  Doo thistles good, so thick in fallow spide?
Doo taint wormes good, that lurke where ox should eat?
Or sucking drones, in hiue where bees abide?

Doo hornets good, or these same biting gnats ?
Foule swelling toades, what good by them is seene ?
In house well deckt, what good doth gnawing rats ?
Or casting mowles, among the meadowes greene ?
Doth heauie newes make glad the hart of man ?
Or noisome smels, what good doth that to health ?
Now once for all, what good (shew who so can ?)
Doo stinging[1] snakes, to this our Commonwealth ?

No more doth good a peeuish slanderous toung,
But hurts it selfe, and noies both old and young.

66.

¶ *A sonet vpon the Authors first seuen* yeeres seruice.

Chap. 55.

SEUEN times hath Janus tane new yéere by hand,
Seuen times hath blustring March blowne forth his powre :
To driue out Aprils buds, by sea and land,
For minion Maie, to deck most trim with flowre.
Seuen times hath temperate Ver, like pageant plaide,
And pleasant Æstas eke hir flowers told :
Seuen times Autumnes heate hath béene delaide,
With Hyems boistrous blasts, and bitter cold.
Seuen times the thirtéene Moones haue changed hew,
Seuen times the Sunne his course hath gone about :
Seuen times ech bird hir nest hath built anew,
Since first time you to serue, I choosed out.

Still yours am I, though thus the time hath past,
And trust to be, as[2] long as life shall last.

[1] stinking. 1577. [2] so. 1577.

67.

Man minded for to thriue
must wisely lay to wiue.
What hap may thereby fall
here argued find ye shall.

¶ *The Authours Dialogue betweene two* Bachelers, of wiuing and thriuing by Affir-*mation and Obiection.*

Chap. 56.

Affirmation.

[1] FREND, where we met this other day,
We heard one make his mone and say,
Good Lord, how might I thriue?
We heard an other answere him,
Then make thee handsome, trick and trim,
And lay in time to wiue.

Obiection.

[2] And what of that, say you to mee?
Do you your selfe thinke that to be
The best way for to thriue?
If truth were truely bolted out,
As touching thrift, I stand in dout,
If men were best to wiue.

Affirmation.

[3] There is no doubt, for proue I can,
I haue but seldome seene that man
Which could the way to thriue:
Vntill it was his happie lot,
To stay himselfe in some good plot,
And wisely then to wiue.

Obiection.

[4] And I am of an other minde,
For by no reason can I finde,
How that way I should thriue:
For where as now I spend a pennie,
I should not then be quit with mennie,
Through bondage for to wiue.

Affirmation.

[5] Not so, for now where thou dost spend,
Of this and that, to no good end,
Which hindereth thee to thriue:
Such vaine expences thou shouldst saue,
And daily then lay more to haue,
As others do that wiue.

Obiection.

[6] Why then do folke this prouerbe put,
The blacke oxe neare trod on thy fut,
If that way were to thriue?
Hereout a man may soone picke forth,
Few feeleth what a pennie is worth,
Till such time as they wiue.

Affirmation.

[7] It may so chaunce as thou doest say,
This lesson therefore beare away,
If thereby thou wilt thriue:
Looke ere thou leape, see ere thou go,
It may be for thy profite so,
For thee to lay to wiue.

Obiection.

[8] It is too much we dailie heare,
To wiue and thriue both in a yeare,
As touching now to thriue:

I know not herein what to spie,
But that there doth small profite lie,
  To fansie for to wiue.

Affirmation.

[9] In deede the first yeare oft is such,
That fondly some bestoweth much,
  A let to them to thriue:
Yet other moe may soone be founde,
Which getteth many a faire pounde,
  The same day that they wiue.

Obiection.

[10] I graunt some getteth more that day,
Than they can easily beare away,
  Nowe needes then must they thriue:
What gaineth such thinke you by that?
A little burden, you wote what,
  Through fondnesse for to wiue.

Affirmation.

[11] Thou seemest blinde as mo haue bin,
It is not beautie bringeth in
  The thing to make thee thriue:
In womankinde, see that ye do
Require of hir no gift but two,
  When ere ye minde to wiue.

Obiection.

[12] But two, say you? I pray you than
Shew those as briefly as you can,
  If that may helpe to thriue:
I weene we must conclude anon,
Of those same twaine to want the ton,
  When ere we chance to wiue.

Affirmation.

[13] An honest huswife, trust to mee,
Be those same twaine, I say to thee,
That helpe so much to thriue:
As honestie farre passeth golde,
So huswiferie in yong and olde,
Do pleasure such as wiue.

Honestie and huswiferie.

Obiection.

[14] The honestie in deede I graunt,
Is one good point the wife should haunt,
To make hir husband thriue:
But now faine would I haue you show,
How should a man good huswife know,
If once he hap to wiue?

Affirmation.

[15] A huswife good betimes will rise,
And order things in comelie wise,
Hir minde is set to thriue:
Vpon hir distaffe she will spinne,
And with hir needle she will winne,
If such ye hap to wiue.

Obiection.

[16] It is not idle going about,
Nor all day pricking on a clout,
Can make a man to thriue:
Or if there be no other winning,
But that the wife gets by hir spinning,
Small thrift it is to wiue.

Affirmation.

[17] Some more than this yet do shee[1] shall,
Although thy stocke be verie small,
Yet will shee helpe thee thriue:

[1] they. 1577.

Lay thou[1] to saue, as well as she,
And then thou shalt[2] enriched be,
When such thou hapst[3] to wiue.

Obiection.

[18] If she were mine, I tell thee troth,
Too much to trouble hir I were loth,
For greedines to thriue:
Least some should talke, as is the speech,
The good wiues husband weares no breech,
If such I hap to wiue.

Affirmation.

[19] What hurts it thee what some do say,
If honestlie she take the way
To helpe thee for to thriue?
For honestie will make hir prest,
To doo the thing that shall be best,
If such ye hap to wiue.

Obiection.

[20] Why did *Diogenes* say than,
To one that askt of him time whan,
Were best to wiue to thriue?
Not yet (quoth[4] he) if thou be yong,
If thou waxe old, then holde thy tong,
It is too late to wiue.

Affirmation.

[21] Belike he knew some shrewish wife,
Which with hir husband made such strife,
That hindered him to thriue:

[1] you. 1577.
[2] you shall. 1577.
[3] you hap. 1577.
[4] quod. 1577.

Who then may blame him for that clause,
Though then he spake as some had cause,
As touching for to wiue?

Obiection.

[22] Why then I see to take a shrew,
(As seldome other there be few)
Is not the way to thriue:
So hard a thing I spie it is,
The good to chuse, the shrew to mis,
That feareth me to wiue.

Affirmation.

[23] She may in something seeme a shrew,
Yet such a huswife as but few,
To helpe thee for to thriue:
This prouerbe looke in mind ye keepe,
As good a shrew is as a sheepe,
For you to take to wiue.

Obiection.

[24] Now be she lambe or be she eaw,
Giue me the sheepe, take thou the shreaw,
See which of vs shall thriue:
If she be shrewish thinke for troth,
For all her thrift I would be loth
To match with such to wiue.

Affirmation.

[25] Tush, farewell then, I leaue you off,
Such fooles as you that loue to scoff,
Shall seldome wiue to thriue:
Contrarie hir, as you do me,
And then ye shall, I warrant ye,
Repent ye if ye wiue.

Obiection.

[26] Friend, let vs both giue iustly place,
To wedded man to iudge this cace,
Which best way is to thriue:
For both our talke as seemeth plaine,
Is but as hapneth in our braine,
To will or not to wiue.

¶ *Wedded mans iudgement*
Vpon the former argument.

Moderator. [27] As Cock that wants his mate, goes rouing all about,
With crowing early and late, to find his louer out:
And as poore sillie hen, long wanting cock to guide,
Soone droopes and shortly then beginnes to peake aside:
Euen so it is with man and wife, where gouernment is found,
The want of ton the others life doth shortly soone confound.

[28] In iest and in earnest, here argued ye finde,
That husband and huswife togither must dwell,
And thereto the iudgement of wedded mans minde,
That husbandrie otherwise speedeth not well:
So somewhat more nowe I intende for to tell,
Of huswiferie like as of husbandrie tolde,
How huswifelie huswife helpes bring in the golde.

Thus endeth the booke of
Husbandrie.

[Finis (1577).]

The points of Huswiferie, vnited to *the comfort of Husbandrie, newly cor-* rected and amplified, with diuers good *lessons for housholders to recreate the* Reader, as by the Table at the end *hereof more plainlie may* appeere.

Set forth by Thomas Tusser Gentleman.

68.

To the right Honorable and my especiall *good Ladie and Maistres, the* Ladie Paget.

1 Though danger be mickle,
and fauour so fickle,
Yet dutie doth tickle
my fansie to wright:
Concerning how prettie,
how fine and how nettie,
Good huswife should iettie,[1]
from morning to night.

2 Not minding[2] by writing,
to kindle a spiting,
But shew by enditing,
as afterward told:
How husbandrie easeth,
to huswiferie pleaseth,
And manie purse greaseth
with siluer and gold.

[1] yettie. 1557.

[2] minded. 1577.

3 For husbandrie wéepeth,
where huswiferie sléepeth,
And hardly he créepeth,
vp ladder to thrift:
That wanteth to bold him,
thrifts ladder to hold him,
Before it be told him,
he falles without shift.

4 Least many should feare me,
and others forsweare me,
Of troth I doo beare me
vpright as ye sée:
Full minded to looue all,
and not to reprooue all,
But onely to mooue all,
good huswiues to bée.

5 For if I should mind some,
or descant behind some,
And missing to find some,
displease so I mought:
Or if I should blend them,
and so to offend them,
What stur I should send them
I stand in a dought.

6 Though harmles ye[1] make it
and some doo well take it,
If others forsake it,
what pleasure were that?
Naught else but to paine me,
and nothing to gaine me,
But make them disdaine me
I wot ner for what.

7 Least some make a triall,
as clocke by the diall,
Some stand to deniall,
some murmur and grudge:
Giue iudgement I pray you,
for iustlie so may you,
So fansie, so say you,
I make you my iudge.

8 In time, ye shall try me,
by troth, ye shall spy me,
So finde, so set by me,
according to skill:
How euer trée groweth,
the fruit the trée showeth,
Your Ladiship knoweth,
my hart and good will.

9 Thogh fortune doth measure,
and I doo lacke treasure,
Yet if I may pleasure
your Honour with this:
Then will me to mend it,
or mend er ye send it,
Or any where lend it,
if ought be amis.

Your Ladiships Seruant,

Thomas Tusser.

[1] I. 1577.

69.

¶ *To the Reader.*[1]

1 NOW listen, good huswiues, what dooings are here
set foorth for a daie, as it should for a yere.
Both easie to follow, and soone to atchiue,
for such as by huswiferie looketh to thriue.

2 The forenoone affaires, till dinner (with some,)
then after noone dooings, till supper time come.
With breakfast and dinner time, sup, and to bed,
standes orderlie placed, to quiet thine hed.

3 The meaning is this, for a daie what ye see,
that monthlie and yeerlie continued must bee.
And hereby to gather (as prooue I intend),
that huswiuelie matters haue neuer an end.

4 I haue not, by heare say, nor reading in booke,
set out (peraduenture) that some cannot brooke,
Nor yet of a spite, to be dooing with enie,
but such as haue skared me many a penie.

5 If widow, both huswife and husband may be,
what cause hath a widower lesser than she?
Tis needfull that both of them looke well about:
too careles within, and too lasie without.

6 Now therefore, if well ye consider of this,
what losses and crosses comes dailie amis.
Then beare with a widowers pen as ye may:
though husband of huswiferie somewhat doth say.

[1] "First introduced in the edition of 1580" (M.).

70.

¶ The Preface to the booke of *Huswiferie.*

1 TAKE weapon away, of what force is a man?
Take huswife from husband, and what is he than?

2 As louers desireth together to dwell,
So husbandrie loueth good huswiferie well.

3 Though husbandrie seemeth to bring in the gaines,
Yet huswiferie labours seeme equall in paines.

4 Some respit to husbands the weather may send,
But huswiues affaires haue neuer an end.

71.

As true as thy faith,
Thus huswiferie saith.

The praise of huswiferie.

I SERUE for a daie, for a weeke, for a yere,
For life time, for euer, while man dwelleth here.
For richer, for poorer, from North to the South,
For honest, for hardhead, or daintie of mouth.
For wed and vnwedded, in sicknes and health,
For all that well liueth, in good Commonwealth.
For citie, for countrie, for Court, and for cart,
To quiet the head, and to comfort the hart.

72.

¶ A description of Huswife and *Huswiferie.*

1 OF huswife doth huswiferie challenge that name,
of huswiferie huswife doth likewise the same,
Where husband and husbandrie ioineth with thease,
there wealthines gotten is holden with ease.

2 The name of a huswife what is it to say?
the wife of the house, to the husband a stay.
If huswife doth that, as belongeth to hur:
if husband be godlie,[1] there needeth no stur.

3 The huswife is she that to labour doth fall,
the labour of hir I doo huswiferie call.
If thrift by that labour be honestlie[2] got:
then is it good huswiferie, else is it not.

4 The woman the name of a huswife doth win,
by keeping hir house, and of dooings therein.
And she that with husband will quietly dwell,
must thinke on this lesson, and follow it well.

[Finis (1577).]

73.

Instructions to Huswiferie.

Serue God is the furst,
True loue is not wurst.

1 A DAILIE good lesson, of huswife in deede,
is God to remember, the better to speede.

2 An other good lesson, of huswiferie thought,
is huswife with husband to liue as she ought.

[1] wittie. 1577. Cf. *post*, ch. 100, st. 6. [2] be sued or got. 1577.

Wife comely no griefe,
Man out, huswife chiefe.

3 Though trickly to see to, be gallant to wiue,
yet comely and wise is the huswife to thriue.

4 When husband is absent, let huswife be chiefe,
and looke to their labour that eateth hir biefe.

Both out not allow,
Keepe house huswife thow.

5 Where husband and huswife be both out of place,
there seruants doo loiter, and reason their cace.

6 The huswife so named (of keeping the house,)
must tend on hir profit, as cat on the mouse.

Seeke home for rest,
For home is best.

7 As huswiues keepe home, and be stirrers about,
so speedeth their winnings, the yeere thorow out.

8 Though home be but homely, yet huswife is taught,
that home hath no fellow to such as haue aught.

¶ Vse all with skill,
Aske what ye will.

9 Good vsage with knowledge, and quiet withall,
make huswife to shine, as the sunne on the wall.

10 What husband refuseth all comely to haue,
that hath a good huswife, all willing to saue.

Be readie at neede,
All thine to feede.

11 The case of good huswiues, thus daily doth stand,
what euer shall chance, to be readie at hand.

12 This care hath a huswife all daie in hir hed,
that all thing in season be huswifelie fed.

By practise go muse,
How houshold to vse.

13 Dame practise is she that to huswife doth tell,
which way for to gouerne hir familie well.

14 Vse labourers gently, keepe this as a lawe,
make childe to be ciuill, keepe seruant in awe.

Who careles doe liue,
Occasion doe giue.

15 Haue euerie where a respect to thy waies,
that none of thy life any slander may raies.

16 What many doo knowe, though a time it be hid,
at length will abrode, when a mischiefe shall bid.

No neighbour reprooue,
Doe so to haue looue.

17 The loue of thy neighbour shall stand thee in steede,
the poorer, the gladder, to helpe at a neede.

18 Vse friendly thy neighbour, else trust him in this,
as he hath thy friendship, so trust vnto his.

¶ Strike nothing vnknowne,
Take heede to thine owne.

19 Reuenge not thy wrath vpon any mans beast,
least thine by like malice be bid to like feast.

20 What husband prouideth with monie his drudge,
the huswife must looke to, which waie it doth trudge.

74.

A digression.

[1] NOW, out of the matter, this lesson I ad,
concerning cock crowing, what profit is had.
Experience teacheth, as true as a clock:
how winter night passeth, by marking the cock.

[2] Cock croweth at midnight, times few aboue six,
with pause to his neighbour, to answere betwix.
At three a clock thicker, and then as ye knowe,
like all in to Mattens, neere daie they doo crowe.

[3] At midnight, at three, and an hower ere day, Cocke crowing.
they vtter their language, as well as they may.
Which who so regardeth what counsell they giue,
will better loue crowing, as long as they liue.

For being afraid,
Take heede good maid:
Marke crowing of cock,
For feare of a knock.

[4] ¶ *The first cock croweth.*

Ho, Dame it is midnight: what rumbling is that?

The next cock croweth.[1]

Take heede to false harlots, and more, ye wot what.

If noise ye heare,
Looke all be cleare:
Least drabs doe noie thee,
And theeues destroie thee.

[5] ¶ *The first cock croweth.*

Maides, three a clock, knede, lay your bucks, or go brew,

The next cock croweth.[1]

And cobble and botch, ye that cannot buie new.

Till cock crow agen,
Both maidens and men:
Amend now with speede,
That mending doth neede.[2]

[6] ¶ *The first cock croweth.*

Past fiue a clock, Holla: maid, sleeping beware,

The next cock croweth.[1]

Least quickly your Mistres vncouer your bare.

Maides, vp I beseech yee,
Least Mistres doe breech yee:
To worke and away,
As fast as ye may.

[1] showeth. 1577.

[2] Both mayden and man
mend now what ye can.
Leave gibber gabber
mend slibber slabber. 1577.

75.

¶ Huswiferie.

[Now listen, good huswiues, what doings are here
set out for a day as it should for a yere. 1577.]

¶ *Morning workes.*[1]

No sooner some vp,
But nose is in cup.

1 GET vp in the morning as soone as thou wilt,
with ouerlong slugging good seruant is spilt.

2 Some slouens from sleeping no sooner get vp,
but hand is in aumbrie, and nose in the cup.

That early is donne,
Count huswifely wonne.

3 Some worke in the morning may trimly be donne, Morning workes.
that all the day after can hardly be wonne.

4 Good husband without it is needfull there be,
good huswife within as needfull as he.

Cast dust into yard,
And spin and go card.

5 Sluts corners auoided shall further thy health,
much time about trifles shall hinder thy wealth.

6 Set some to peele hempe or else rishes to twine,
to spin and to card, or to seething of brine.

Grind mault for drinke,
See meate do not stinke.

7 Set some about cattle, some pasture to vewe,
some mault to be grinding against ye do brewe.

8 Some corneth, some brineth, some will not be taught,
where meate is attainted, there cookrie is naught.

[1] This and other sub-titles are not in 1577.

76.

¶ *Breakefast doings.*

To breakefast that come,
Giue erie one some.

Breakefast.

1 CALL seruants to breakefast by day starre appere,
a snatch and to worke, fellowes tarrie not here.

2 Let huswife be caruer, let[1] pottage be heate,
a messe to eche one, with a morsell of meate.

No more tittle tattle,
Go serue your cattle.

3 What tacke in a pudding, saith greedie gut wringer,
giue such ye wote what, ere a pudding he finger.

4 Let seruants once serued, thy cattle go serue,
least often ill seruing make cattle to sterue.

77.

¶ *Huswifely admonitions.*

Thée for thriue.

Learne you that will thee,
This lesson of mee.[2]

1 NO breakefast of custome prouide for to saue,
but onely for such as deserueth to haue.

2 No shewing of seruant what vittles in store,
shew seruant his labour, and shew him no more.

Of hauocke beware,
Cat nothing will spare.

3 Where all thing is common, what needeth a hutch?
where wanteth a sauer, there hauocke is mutch.

4 Where window is open, cat maketh a fray,
yet wilde cat with two legs is worse by my fay.

[1] see. 1577.
[2] How daintie some be. 1573.

Looke well vnto thine,
Slut slouthfull must whine.

5 An eie in a corner who vseth to haue,
reuealeth a drab, and preuenteth a knaue.

6 Make maide to be clenly, or make hir crie creake,
and teach hir to stirre, when hir mistresse doth speake.

Let hollie wand threate,
Let fisgig be beate.

7 A wand in thy hand, though ye fight not at all,
makes youth to their businesse better to fall.

8 For feare of foole had I wist[1] cause thee to waile,
let fisgig be taught to shut doore after taile.

Too easie the wicket,
Will still appease clicket.

9 With hir that will clicket make daunger to cope,
least quickly hir wicket seeme easie to ope.

10 As rod little mendeth where maners be spilt,
so naught will be naught say and do what thou wilt.

Fight seldome ye shall
But vse not to brall.

11 Much bralling with seruant, what man can abide?
pay home when thou fightest, but loue not to chide.

12 As order is heauenly where quiet is had,
so error is hell, or a mischiefe as bad.

What better a lawe.
Than subjects in awe?

13 Such awe as a warning will cause to beware,
doth make the whole houshold the better to fare.

14 The lesse of thy counsell thy seruants doe knowe,
Their dutie the better such seruants shall showe.

[1] "A wise man saith not, had I wist."—Uncertain Author in *Tottel's Miscellany* (p. 244, Arber's ed.).

Good musicke regard,
Good seruants reward.

15 Such seruants are oftenest painfull and good,
that sing in their labour, as birdes in the wood.

16 Good seruants hope iustly some friendship to feele,
and looke to haue fauour what time they do weele.

By once or twise
Tis time to be wise.

17 Take runagate Robin, to pitie his neede,
and looke to be filched, as sure as thy creede.

18 Take warning by once, that a worse do not hap,
foresight is the stopper of many a gap.

Some change for a shift,
Oft change, small thrift.

19 Make fewe of thy counsell to change for the best,
least one that is trudging infecteth the rest.

20 The stone that is rolling can gather no mosse,
for maister and seruant, oft changing is losse.

Both liberall sticketh,
Some prouender pricketh.

One liberall. 21 One dog for a hog, and one cat for a mouse,
one readie to giue is ynough in a house:

22 One gift ill accepted, keepe next in thy purse,
whom prouender pricketh are often the wurse.

78.

¶ *Brewing.*

Brew somewhat for thine,
Else bring vp no swine.

Brewing. 1 WHERE brewing is needfull, be brewer thy selfe,
what filleth the roofe will helpe furnish the shelfe:

2 In buieng of drinke, by the firkin or pot,
the tallie ariseth, but hog amendes not.[1]

[1] Score quickely ariseth, hog profiteth not. 1577.

Well brewed, worth cost,
Ill vsed, halfe lost.

3 One bushell well brewed, outlasteth some twaine,
and saueth both mault, and expences in vaine.[1]

4 Too new is no profite, too stale is as bad,
drinke dead or else sower makes laborer sad.

Remember good Gill,
Take paine with thy swill.

5 Seeth grains in more water, while grains be yet hot, Séething of graines.
and stirre them in copper, as poredge in pot.

6 Such heating with straw, to haue offall good store,
both pleaseth and easeth, what would ye haue more?

79.

¶ *Baking.*

Newe bread is a driuell.
Much crust is as euill.

1 NEW bread is a waster, but mouldie is wurse, Baking.
what that way dog catcheth, that loseth the purse.

2 Much dowebake I praise not, much crust is as ill,
the meane is the Huswife, say nay if ye will.

80.

¶ *Cookerie.*

Good cookerie craueth,
Good turnebroch saueth.

1 GOOD cooke to dresse dinner, to bake and to brewe, Cookerie.
deserues a rewarde, being honest and trewe.

2 Good diligent turnebroch and trustie withall,
is sometime as needfull as some in the hall.

[1] Two troubles for nothing, is cost to no gaine. 1577.

81.

¶ *Dairie.*

Good dairie doth pleasure,
Ill dairie spendes treasure.

Dairie.

1 GOOD huswife in dairie, that needes not be tolde,
deserueth hir fee to be paid hir in golde.

2 Ill seruant neglecting what huswiferie saies,
deserueth hir fee to be paid hir with baies.

Good droie woorth much.[1]
Marke sluts and such.

3 Good droie to serue hog, to helpe wash, and to milke,
more needfull is truelie than some in their silke.

4 Though homelie be milker, let cleanlie be cooke,
for a slut and a slouen be knowne by their looke.

In dairie no cat,
Laie bane for a rat.

Traps for rats.

5 Though cat (a good mouser) doth dwell in a house,
yet euer in dairie haue trap for a mouse.

6 Take heede how thou laiest the bane for the rats,
for poisoning seruant, thy selfe and thy brats.

82.

¶ *Scouring.*

No scouring for pride,
Spare kettle whole side.

Scouring.

1 THOUGH scouring be needfull, yet scouring too mutch,
is pride without profit, and robbeth[2] thine hutch.

2 Keepe kettles from knocks, set tubs out of Sun,
for mending is costlie, and crackt is soone dun.

[1] Though droy be, etc. 1577.

[2] rubbeth. 1573, 1577.

83.

Washing.

Take heede when ye wash,
Else run in the lash.

1 MAIDS, wash well and wring well, but beat ye wot how, Washing.
if any lack beating, I feare it be yow.

2 In washing by hand, haue an eie to thy boll,
for launders and millers, be quick of their toll.

Drie sunne, drie winde,
Safe binde, safe finde.

3 Go wash well, saith Sommer, with sunne I shall drie,
go wring well, saith Winter, with winde so shall I.

4 To trust without heede is to venter a ioint,
giue tale and take count, is a huswifelie point.

Where many be packing,
Are manie things lacking.

5 Where hens fall a cackling, take heede to their nest,
where drabs fall a whispring, take heede to the rest.

6 Through negligent huswifes, are many things lacking,
and Gillet suspected will quickly be packing.

84.

Malting.

Ill malting is theft,
Wood dride hath a weft.

1 HOUSE may be so handsome, and skilfulnes such, Malting.
to make thy owne malt, it shall profit thee much.

2 Som drieth with strawe, and some drieth with wood,
wood asketh more charge, and nothing so good.

Take heede to the kell,
Sing out as a bell.

3 Be suer no chances to fier can drawe,
the wood, or the furzen, the brake or the strawe.

4 Let Gillet be singing, it doth verie well,
to keepe hir from sleeping and burning the kell.

Best dride best speedes,
Ill kept, bowd breedes.

5 Malt being well speered, the more it will cast,
malt being well dried, the longer will last.

6 Long kept in ill soller, (vndoubted thou shalt,)
through bowds without number loose quickly thy malt.

85.

¶ *Dinner matters.*

For hunger or thirst,
Serue cattle well first.

Dinner time.

1 BY noone see your dinner, be readie and neate,
let meate tarrie seruant, not seruant his meate.

2 Plough cattle a baiting, call seruant to dinner,
the thicker togither, the charges the thinner.

Togither is best,
For hostis and gest.

3[1] Due season is best, altogither is gay,
dispatch hath no fellow, make short and away.

4 Beware of Gill laggoose, disordring thy house,
mo dainties who catcheth, than craftie fed mouse!

Let such haue ynough,
That follow the plough.

5 Giue seruant no dainties, but giue him ynough,
too many chaps walking, do begger the plough.

6 Poore seggons halfe starued worke faintly and dull,
and lubbers doo loiter, their bellies too full.

Giue neuer too much,
To lazie and such.

7 Feede lazie that thresheth a flap and a tap,
like slothfull, that all day be stopping a gap.

8 Some litherly lubber more eateth than twoo,
yet leaueth vndone that another will doo.

[1] Stanzas 3-12 are not in 1577.

Where nothing will last,
Spare such as thou hast.

9 Some cutteth thy linnen, some spoileth[1] their broth,
bare table to some doth as well as a cloth.

10 Treene dishes be homely, and yet not to lack,
where stone is no laster take tankard and iack.

Knap boy on the thums,
And saue him his crums.

11 That pewter is neuer for manerly feastes,
that daily doth serue so vnmanerly beastes.

12 Some gnaweth and leaueth, some crusts and some crums,
eat such their own leuings, or gnaw their own thums.

Serue God euer furst,
Take nothing at wurst.

13 At Dinner, at Supper, at morning, at night,
giue thankes vnto God, for his gifts so in[2] sight. Grace before and after meate.

14 Good husband and huswife, will sometime alone,
make shift with a morsell and picke of a bone.

Inough thou art tolde,
Too much will not holde.

15 Three dishes well dressed, and welcome withall,
both pleaseth thy friend and becommeth thine hall.

16 Enough is a plentie, too much is a pride,
the plough with ill holding, goes quicklie aside.

86.

¶ *Afternoone workes.*

Make companie breake,
Go cherish the weake.

1 WHEN Dinner is ended, set seruants to wurke,
and follow such fellowes[3] as loueth to lurke. Afternoone workes.

2 To seruant in sicknesse see nothing ye grutch,
a thing of a trifle shall comfort him mutch.

[1] spilleth. 1577. [2] in thy. 1577. [3] marchants. 1577.

Who manie do feede,
Saue much they had neede.

3 Put chippings in dippings, vse parings to saue,
fat capons or chickens that lookest to haue.

4 Saue droppings and skimmings, how euer ye doo,
for medcine for cattell, for cart and for shoo.

Leane capon vnmeete,
Deere fed is vnsweete.

5 Such ofcorne as commeth giue wife to hir fee,
feede willingly such as do helpe to feede thee.

6 Though fat fed is daintie, yet this I thee warne,
be cunning in fatting for robbing thy barne.

Peece hole to defende.
Things timely amende.

7 Good semsters be sowing of fine pretie knackes,
good huswifes be mending and peecing their sackes.

8 Though making and mending be huswifely waies,
yet mending in time is the huswife to praies.

Buie newe as is meete,
Marke blanket and sheete.

9 Though Ladies may rend and buie new ery day,
good huswifes must mend and buie new as they may.

10 Call quarterly seruants to court and to leete,
write euerie Couerlet, Blanket, and Sheete.

Shift slouenly elfe,
Be gayler thy selfe.

11 Though shifting too oft be a theefe in a house,
yet shift slut and slouen for feare of a louse.

12 Graunt doubtfull no key of his chamber in purse,
least chamber doore lockt be to theeuerie a nurse.

Saue feathers for gest,
These other rob chest.

Saue feathers.

13 Saue wing for a thresher, when Gander doth die,
saue feather of all thing, the softer to lie.

14 Much spice is a theefe, so is candle and fier,
sweete sauce is as craftie as euer was frier.

Wife make thine owne candle,
Spare pennie to handle.

15 Prouide for thy tallow, ere frost commeth in, Candle making.
and make thine owne candle, ere winter begin.

16 If pennie for all thing be suffred to trudge,
trust long, not to pennie, to haue him thy drudge.

87.

¶ *Euening workes.*

Time drawing to night,
See all things go right.

1 WHEN hennes go to roost go in hand to dresse meate, Euening workes.
serue hogs and to milking and some to serue neate.

2 Where twaine be ynow, be not serued with three,
more knaues in a companie worser they bee.

Make lackey to trudge,
Make seruant thy drudge.

3 For euerie trifle leaue ianting thy nag,
but rather make lackey of Jack boie thy wag.

4 Make seruant at night lug in wood or a log,
let none come in emptie but slut and thy dog.

False knaue readie prest,
All safe is the best.

5 Where pullen vse nightly to pearch in the yard,
there two legged foxes keepe watches and ward.

6 See cattle well serued, without and within,
and all thing at quiet ere supper begin.

Take heede it is needeful,
True pittie is meedeful.

7 No clothes in garden, no trinkets without,
no doore leaue vnbolted, for feare of a dout.

8 Thou woman whom pitie becommeth the best,
graunt all that hath laboured time to take rest.

88.

¶ *Supper matters.*

Vse mirth and good woorde,
At bed and at boorde.

Supper time huswiferie.

1 PROUIDE for thy husband, to make him good cheere,
make merrie togither, while time ye be heere.

2 At bed and at boord, howsoeuer befall,
what euer God sendeth be merrie withall.

No brawling make,
No ielousie take,

3 No taunts before seruants, for hindring of fame,
no iarring too loude for auoyding of shame.

4 As fransie and heresie roueth togither,
so iealousie leadeth a foole ye wot whither.

Tend such as ye haue,
Stop talkatiue knaue.

5 Yong children and chickens would euer be eating,
good seruants looke dulie for gentle intreating.

6 No seruant at table vse sausly to talke,
least tongue set at large out of measure do walke.

No snatching at all,
Sirs, hearken now all.

7 No lurching, no snatching, no striuing at all,
least one go without and another haue all.

8 Declare after Supper, take heede thereunto,
what worke in the morning ech seruant shall do.

89.

After supper matters.

Thy soule hath a clog,
Forget not thy dog.

1 REMEMBER those children whose parents be poore, Workes after supper.
which hunger, yet dare not craue[1] at thy doore.

2 Thy Bandog that serueth for diuerse mishaps,
forget not to giue him thy bones and thy scraps.

Make keies to be keepers,
To bed ye sleepers.

3 Where mouthes be many, to spend that thou hast,
set keies to be keepers, for spending too fast.

4 To bed after supper let drousie go sleepe,
least knaue in the darke to his marrow do creepe.

Keepe keies as thy life,
Feare candle good wife.

5 Such keies lay vp safe, ere ye take ye to rest,
of dairie, of buttrie, of cubboord and chest.

6 Feare candle in hailoft, in barne, and in shed,
feare flea smocke and mendbreech, for burning their bed.

See doore lockt fast,
Two keies make wast.

7 A doore without locke is a baite for a knaue,
a locke without key is a foole that will haue.

8 One key to two locks, if it breake is a greefe,
two keies to one locke in the ende is a theefe.

Night workes troubles hed,
Locke doores and to bed.

9 The day willeth done whatsoeuer ye bid,
the night is a theefe, if ye take not good hid.

10 Wash dishes, lay leauens, saue fire and away,
locke doores and to bed, a good huswife will say.

[1] to. 1577.

To bed know thy guise,
To rise do likewise.

Bed time. 11 In winter at nine, and in sommer at ten,
to bed after supper both maidens and men.

Time to rise. 12 In winter at fiue a clocke, seruant arise,
in sommer at foure is verie good guise.

Loue so as ye may
Loue many a day.

13 Be lowly not sollen, if ought go amisse,
what wresting may loose thee, that winne with a kisse.

14 Both beare and forebeare now and then as ye may,
then, wench God a mercie, thy husband will say.

90.

¶ *The ploughmans feasting daies.*

This would not be slept,
Old guise must be kept.

1 GOOD huswiues, whom God hath enriched ynough,
forget not the feastes that belong to the plough.
The meaning is onelie to ioie and be glad,
for comfort with labour is fit to be had.

Plough Monday.

Leicestershire. 2 Plough Monday, next after that Twelftide is past,
bids out with the plough, the woorst husband is last.
If ploughman get hatchet or whip to the skreene,
maides loseth their cock if no water be seene.

Shroftide.

Essex and Suffolke. 3 At Shroftide to shrouing, go thresh the fat hen,
if blindfild can kill hir, then giue it thy men.
Maides, fritters and pancakes ynow see ye make:
let slut haue one pancake, for companie sake.

Sheepe shearing.

4 Wife make vs a dinner, spare flesh neither corne, Northamptonshire.
make wafers and cakes, for our sheepe must be shorne.
At sheepe shearing neighbours none other thing craue,
but good cheere and welcome like neighbours to haue.

The wake day.

5 Fill ouen full of flawnes, Ginnie passe not for sleepe, Leicestershire.
to morow thy father his wake day will keepe.
Then euerie wanton may daunce at hir will,
both Tomkin with Tomlin, and Jankin with Gill.

Haruest home.

6 For all this good feasting, yet art thou not loose,
till ploughman thou giuest his haruest home goose.
Though goose go in stubble, I passe not for that,
let goose haue a goose, be she leane, be she fat.

Seede cake.

7 Wife, some time this weeke, if the wether hold cleere, Essex and Suffolke.
an end of wheat sowing we make for this yeere.
Remember you therefore though I doo it not:
the seede Cake, the Pasties, and Furmentie pot.

Twise a week roast.

8 Good ploughmen looke weekly, of custome and right,
for roast meat on Sundaies and Thursdaies at night.
This dooing and keeping such custome and guise,
they call thee good huswife, they loue thee likewise.

91.

¶ The good huswifelie *Physicke.*

[1] GOOD huswiues prouides, ere an sicknes doo come,
of sundrie good things in hir house to haue some.
Good Aqua composita, Vineger tart,
Rose water and treakle, to comfort the hart.

[2] Cold herbes in hir garden for agues that burne,
that ouer strong heat to good temper may turne.
While Endiue and Suckerie, with Spinnage ynough,
all such with good pot herbes should follow the plough.

[3] Get water of Fumentorie, Liuer to coole,
and others the like, or els lie like a foole.
Conserue of the Barberie, Quinces and such,
with Sirops that easeth the sickly so much.

Physition. [4] Aske *Medicus* counsell, ere medcine ye make,
and honour that man, for necessities sake.
Though thousands hate physick, because of the cost,
yet thousands it helpeth, that else should be lost.

Good diet. [5] Good broth and good kéeping do much now and than,
good diet with wisedome best comforteth man.
In health to be stirring shall profit thée best,
in sicknes hate trouble, séeke quiet and rest.

Thinke on thy soule and haue a good hope. [6] Remember thy soule, let no fansie preuaile,
make readie to Godward, let faith neuer quaile.
The sooner thy selfe thou submittest to God,
the sooner he ceaseth to scourge with his rod.

92.

¶ The good motherlie *nurserie.*

[1] GOOD huswiues take paine, and doo count it good luck,
to make their owne brest their owne childe to giue suck.
Though wrauling and rocking be noisome so neare,
yet lost by ill nursing is woorser to heare.

[2] But one thing I warne thee, let huswife be nurse,
least husband doo find thée too franke with his purse.
What hilback and filbellie maketh away,
that helpe to make good, or else looke for a fraie.

[3] Giue childe that is fitly, giue babie the big,
giue hardnes to youth and to roperipe a twig.
Wee find it not spoken so often for naught,
that children were better vnborne than vntaught,

[4] Some cockneies with cocking are made verie fooles,
fit neither for prentise, for plough, nor for schooles.
Teach childe to aske blessing, serue God, and to church,
then blesse as a mother, else blesse him with burch.
Thou huswife thus dooing, what further shall néede?
but all men to call thée good mother in déede.

93.

¶ Thinke on the poore.

REMEMBER the poore, that for Gods sake doo call,
for God both rewardeth and blesseth withall.
Take this in good part, whatsoeuer thou bee:
and wish me no woorse than I wish vnto thee.

94.

¶ A comparison betweene good *huswiferie and euill.*

Comparing togither, good huswife with bad,
The knowledge of either, the better is had.

1 ILL huswiferie lieth
till nine of the clock.
Good huswiferie trieth
to rise with the cock.

2 Ill huswiferie tooteth,
to make hir selfe braue.
Good huswiferie looketh
what houshold must haue.

3 Ill huswiferie trusteth
to him and to hir.
Good huswiferie lusteth
hir selfe for to stir.

4 Ill huswiferie careth
for this nor for that.
Good huswiferie spareth
for feare ye wot what.

5 Ill huswiferie pricketh
hir selfe vp in pride.
Good huswiferie tricketh
hir house as a bride.

6 Ill huswiferie othing
or other must craue.
Good huswiferie nothing.
but needfull will haue.

7 Ill huswiferie mooueth
with gossep to spend.
Good huswiferie loueth
hir houshold to tend.

8 Ill huswiferie wanteth
with spending too fast.
Good huswiferie canteth[1]
the lenger to last.

9 Ill huswiferie easeth
hir selfe with vnknowne.
Good huswiferie pleaseth
hir selfe with hir owne.

10 Ill huswiferie brooketh
mad toies in hir hed.
Good huswiferie looketh
that all things be fed.

11 Ill huswiferie bringeth
a shilling to naught.
Good huswiferie singeth,
hir cofers full fraught.

12 Ill huswiferie rendeth,
and casteth aside.
Good huswiferie mendeth,
else would it go wide.

[1] scanteth. 1577.

13 Ill huswiferie sweepeth
her linnen to gage.
Good huswiferie keepeth,
to serue hir in age.

14 Ill huswiferie craueth
in secret to borow.
Good huswiferie saueth
to day for to morow.

15 Ill huswiferie pineth,
not hauing to eate.
Good huswiferie dineth,
with plentie of meate.

16 Ill huswiferie letteth
the Diuell take all.
Good huswiferie setteth
good brag of a small.

Good huswife good fame hath of best in the towne,
Ill huswife ill name hath of euerie clowne.

Thus endeth the booke of
Huswiferie.

95.

For men a perfect warning
How childe shall come by larning.

1 ALL you that faine would learne the perfect waie,
To haue your childe in Musick something séene,
Aske nature first what thereto she doth saie,
Ere further suite ye make to such a Quéene.
For doubtlesse *Grossum caput* is not he
Of whom the learned Muses séene will be.

2 Once tride that nature trim hath done hir part,
And Ladie Musick farre[1] in loue withall,
Be wise who first doth teach thy childe that Art,
Least homelie breaker mar fine ambling ball.
Not rod in mad braines hand is that can helpe,
But gentle skill doth make the proper whelpe.

[1] ? faire [1614].

3 Where choise is hard, count good for well a fine,
Skill mixt with will, is he that teacheth best:
Let this suffice for teaching childe of thine,
Choose quickly well for all the lingring rest.
Mistaught at first how seldome prooueth well!
Trim taught, O God, how shortly doth excell!

4 Although as ships must tarrie winde and tide,
And perfect howers abide their stinted time;
So likewise, though of learning dailie tride,
Space must be had ere wit may thereto clime.
Yet easie steps, and perfect way to trust,
Doth cause good spéede, confesse of force we must.

5 Thus in the childe though wit ynough we finde,
And teacher good néere hand or óther where,
And time as apt as may be thought with minde,
Nor cause in such thing much to doubt or feare.
Yet cocking Mams, and shifting Dads from schoóles,
Make pregnant wits to prooue vnlearned fooles.

6 Ere learning come, to haue first art thou taught,
Apt learning childe, apt time that thing to frame,
Apt cunning man to teach, else all is naught,
Apt parents, glad to bring to passe the same.
On such apt ground the Muses loue to bilde,
This lesson learne; adue else learned child.

[In the edition of 1573, The Sonnet to Lady Paget, which follows the Posies, is placed here.]

96.

¶ *The description of a womans age by vi.* times xiiij yeeres prentiship, with *a lesson to the same.*

14 TWO first seuen yeeres, for a rod they doe whine,
28 Two next, as a perle in the world they doe shine,
42 Two next, trim beautie beginneth to swerue,
56 Two next, for matrones or drudges they serue,
70 Two next, doth craue a staffe for a stay,
84 Two next, a beere to fetch them away.

A Lesson {
Then purchase some pelfe,
by fiftie and thrée:
or buckle thy selfe,
a drudge for to bée.

97.

¶ The Inholders posie.[1]

[1] AT meales my friend who vitleth here, and sitteth with his host,
Shall both be sure of better chere, and scape with lesser cost.

[2] But he that will attendance haue, a chamber by himselfe,
Must more regard what pains do craue than passe of worldly pelfe.

[1] Not in edition of 1573.

[3] Let no man looke to purchase linne with pinching by
the waie,
But laie before he takes his Inne to make his purse to paie.

[4] For nothing paie and nothing praie, in Inne it is the gise,
Where no point gain, there no point pain, think this if
you be wise.

[5] For toiling much and spoiling more, great charge smal
gains or none,
Soone sets thine host at needams shore,[1] to craue the
beggers bone.

[6] Foreséeing this, come day or night, take vp what place
ye please.
Vse mine as thine, let fortune spight, and boldly take
thine ease.

98.

¶ Certaine Table Lessons.

1 FRIEND, eat lesse, and drinke lesse,[2] and buie thee a knife,
else looke for a caruer not alway too rife.
Some kniueles their daggers for brauerie weare,
that often for surfetting neede not to feare.

2 At dinner and supper the table doth craue
good fellowly neighbour good manner to haue.
Aduise thee well therefore, ere tongue be too free,
or slapsauce be noted too saucie to bee.

3 If anything wanteth or seemeth amis,
to call for or shew it, good maner it is.
But busie fault finder, and saucie withall,
is roister like ruffen, no manner at all.

[1] A pun recorded by Ray. Needham is in Suffolk (M.).
[2] eateles and drinkles. 1577.

4 Some cutteth the napkin, some trencher will nick,
some sheweth like follie, in many a trick.
Let such apish[1] bodie so toieng at meate,
go toie with his nodie, like ape in the streate.

5 Some commeth vnsent for, not for thy good cheere,
but sent[2] as a spiall, to listen and heere.
Which being once knowne, for a knaue let him go,
for knaue will be knauish, his nature is so.

99.

¶ *Lessons for waiting seruants.*

1 ONE diligent seruiture, skilfull to waight,
more comelieth thy table than other some eight,
That stand for to listen, or gasing about,
not minding their dutie, within nor without.

2 Such waiter is fautie that standeth so by,
vnmindful of seruice, forgetting his ey.
If maister to such giue a bone for to gnaw,
he doth but his office, to teach such a daw.

3 Such seruiture also deserueth a check,
that runneth out fisging with meat in his beck.
Such rauening puttocks for vittles so trim,
would haue a good maister to puttock with him.

4 Who daily can suffer, or else can afoord,
his meat so vp snatched that comes from his boord?
So tossed[3] with cormorants, here and there some,
and others to want it that orderlie come?

5 Good seruiture waieth (once dinner begon,)
what asketh attendance and what to be don.
So purchasing maister a praise with the best,
gets praise to himselfe, both of maister and gest.

[1] Let apishle. 1577. [2] bent. 1577. [3] toesed. 1577.

100.

¶ *Husbandly posies for the hall.*

1 FRIEND, here I dwell, and here I haue a little worldly pelfe,
Which on my friend I kéepe to spend, as well as on my selfe.

2 What euer fare you hap to finde, take welcome for the best,
That hauing then disdaine thou not, for wanting of the rest.

3 Backbiting talk that flattering blabs know wily how to blenge,
The wise doth note, the friend doth hate, the enmie will reuenge.

4 The wise will spend or giue or lend, yet kéepe to haue in store,
If fooles may haue from hand to mouth, they passe vpon no more.

5 Where ease is sought, at length we sée, there plentie waxeth scant,
Who careles liues go borow must, or else full often want.

6 The world doth think the welthy man is he that least shall néed,
But true it is the godlie[1] man is he that best shall spéed.

101.

¶ *Posies for the parler.*

1 AS hatred is the serpents noisome rod,
So friendship is the louing gift of God.

2 The dronken friend is friendship very euill,
The frantike friend is friendship for the Deuill.

3 The quiet friend all one in word and déede
Great comfort is, like ready gold at néede.

[1] Cf. *ante*, ch. 72, st. 2.

4 With bralling fooles that wrall for euerie wrong,
Firme friendship neuer can continue long.

5 In time that man shall seldome friendship mis,
That waith what thing touch kept in friendship is.

6 Oft times a friend is got with easie cost,
Which vsed euill is oft as quickly lost.

7 Hast thou a friend, as hart may wish at will?
Then vse him so to haue his friendship still.

8 Wouldst haue a friend, wouldst knowe what friend is best?
Haue God thy friend, who passeth all the rest.

102.

¶ *Posies for the gests chamber.*

1 THE slouen and the careles man, the roinish nothing nice,
To lodge in chamber comely deckt, are seldome suffred twice.

2 With curteine som make scaberd clene, with couerlet their shoo,
All dirt and mire some wallow bed, as spanniels vse to doo.

3 Though bootes and spurs be nere so foule, what passeth some thereon?
What place they foule, what thing they teare, by tumbling thervpon.

4 Foule male some cast on faire boord, be carpet nere so cléene,
what maners careles maister hath, by knaue his man is séene.

5 Some make the chimnie chamber pot to smell like filthie sink,
Yet who so bold, so soone to say, fough, how these houses stink?

6 They therefore such as make no force what comly thing they spil,
Must haue a cabben like themselues, although against their wil.

7 But gentlemen will gently doe where gentlenes is sheawd,
Obseruing this, with loue abide, or else hence all beshreawd.

103.

¶ *Posies for thine owne bed chamber.*

1 WHAT wisdom more, what better life, than pleseth God to send?
what worldly goods, what longer vse, than pleseth God to lend?

2 What better fare than well content, agréeing with thy wealth?[1]
what better gest, than trustie friend, in sicknes and in health?

3 What better bed than conscience good,[2] to passe the night with sléepe?
what better worke than daily care fro sinne thy selfe to kéepe?

4 What better thought, than think on God and daily him to serue?
What better gift than to the poore that ready be to sterue?

5 What greater praise of God and man, than mercie for to shew?[3]
who merciles shall mercie finde, that mercie shewes to few?

6 What worse despaire, than loth to die for feare to go to hell?
what greater faith than trust in God, through Christ in heauen to dwell?

[1] what mirth to godly welth. 1577. [2] quiet rest. 1577.
[3] . . . . . than hatred to forsake
What merciles shall mercy get, that mercy none will take. 1577. [1573 M.].

104.

¶ A Sonet to the Ladie Paget.

[1] SOME pleasures take,
and cannot giue,
but onely make
poore thanks their shift:
Some meaning well,
in debt doo liue,
and cannot tell
how else to shift.

[2] Some knock and faine
would ope the doore,
to learne the vaine
good turne to praise:
Some shew good face,
and be but poore,
yet haue a grace,
good fame to raise.

[3] Some owe and giue,
yet still in det,
and so must liue,
for aught I knowe:
Some wish to pay,
and cannot get,
but night and day
still more must owe.

[4] Euen so must I, for seruice past,
Still wish you good while life doth last.

105.

¶ Principall points of Religion.

1 TO praie to God continually,
To learne to know him rightfully.
2 To honour God in Trinitie,
3 The Trinitie in vnitie.
The Father in his maiestie,
The Sonne in his humanitie,
The holie Ghosts benignitie,
Three persons, one in Deitie.
4 To serue him alway holily,
5 To aske him all thing needfully,

6 To praise him in all companie,[1]
7 To loue him alway hartilie,[2]
8 To dread him alway christianlie,[3]
9 To aske him mercie penitently,[4]
10 To trust him alway faithfully,
11 To obey him alway willingly,
12 To abide him alway patiently,
13 To thanke him alway thankfully,
14 To liue here alway vertuously,
15 To vse thy neighbour honestly,
16 To looke for death still presently,
17 To helpe the poore in miserie,
18 To hope for heauens felicitie,
19 To haue faith hope and charitie,
20 To count this life but vanitie:
be points of Christianitie.

106.

¶ The Authors beleefe.

God the Father.

1 THIS is my stedfast Créede, my faith, and all my trust,
That in the heauens there is a God, most mightie, milde and iust.
A God aboue all gods, a King aboue all kings,
The Lord of lords, chiefe gouernour of heauen and earthly things.

2 That power hath of life, of death, of heauen and hell,

Maker of Heauen.

That all thing made as pleaseth him, so woonderfull to tell:
That made the hanging Skies, so deckt with diuers lights,
Of darknes made the chéerfull daies, and all our restfull nights.

[1] alway worthely. 1577.
[2] steadfastlie. 1573 (M.), 1577.
[3] fearfullie. 1573 (M.), 1577.
[4] heartilie. 1573 (M.), 1577.

3 That clad this earth with herbe, with trées, and sundrie fruites, The earth.
With beast, with bird, both wild and tame, of strange and sundrie suites:
That intermixt the same with mines like veines of Ore,
Of siluer, golde, of precious stones, and treasures many more.

4 That ioyned brookes to dales, to hilles fresh water springs, The waters, frost and snowe.
With riuers swéete along the méedes, to profit many things:
That made the hoarie frosts, the flakie snowes so trim,
The honie deawes, the blustering windes, to serue as pleaseth him.

5 That made the surging seas, in course to ebbe and flo, The seas.
That skilfull man with sailing ship, mought trauell to and fro:
And stored so the same, for mans vnthankfull sake,
That euery nation vnder heauen mought thereby profit take.

6 That gaue to man a soule, with reason how to liue, The soul of man.
That doth to him and all things else, his blessing dailie giue:
That is not séene, yet séeth how man doth runne his race,
Whose dailie workes both good and bad, stand knowne before his face.

7 That sendeth thundring claps, like terrours out of hell, Thunder and plagues.
That man may know a God there is, that in the heauens doth dwel:
That sendeth threatning plagues, to kéepe our liues in awe,
His benefites if we forget, or do contemne his lawe.

8 That dailie hateth sinne, and loueth vertue well, Full of mercie.
And is the God of Abraham, Isac, and Israell,
That doth displeasure take, when we his lawes offend,
And yet amids his heauie wrath, his mercie doth extend.

Christ the Sonne.

9 This is that Lord of hostes, the father of vs all,
The maker of what ere was made, my God on whom I call:
Which for the loue of man, sent downe his onelie sonne,
Begot of him before the worldes were any whit begonne.

Christes birth. Christ, God and man.

10 This entred Maries wombe, as faith affirmeth sure,
Conceiued by the holy Ghost, borne of that virgine pure;
This was both God and man, of Jewes the hoped king,
And liued here, saue onely sinne, like man in euerie thing.

Christ, our Messias.

11 This is that virgins childe, that same most holie Preist,
The lamb of God, the prophet great, whom scripture calleth Christ,
This that Messias was, of whom the Prophet spake,
That should tread down the serpents head and our attonement make.

Christes passion.

12 This Judas did betray, to false dissembling Jewes,
Which vnto Pilat being Judge, did falsely him accuse:
Who (through that wicked Judge) and of those Jewes despight,
Condemned and tormented was, with all the force they might.

13 To liuing wight more euill, what could such wretches do?
More pearcing wounds, more bitter pains, than they did put him to?
They crowned him with thorne, that was the king of kings,
That sought to saue the soule of man, aboue all worldly things.

Christes death.

14 This was that Pascall lambe whose loue for vs so stood,
That on the mount of Caluerie,[1] for vs did shed his blood:
Where hanging on the Crosse, no shame he did forsake,
Till death giuen him by pearcing speare, an ende of life did make.

[1] Caluerine. 1577.

15 This Ioseph séeing dead, the bodie thence did craue, Christes buriall.
And tooke it forthwith from the crosse, and laid it in his graue,
Downe thence he went to hell, in vsing there his will, Christes descension.
His power[1] I meane, his slained corps in tumb remaining still.

16 From death to life againe, the third day this did rise, Christes resurrection.
And séene on earth to his elect, times oft in sundrie wise:
And after into heauen, ascend he did in sight, Christes ascension.
And sitteth on the right hand there, of God the father of might.

17 Where for vs wretches all, his father he doth pray,
To haue respect vnto his death, and put our sinnes away:
From thence with sounded trump, which noise all flesh shall dread, Christ shall be our iudge.
He shall returne with glorie againe, to iudge the quicke and dead.

18 Then shall that voice be heard, Come, come, ye good to mée, The Iudges sentence.
Hence, hence to hell you workers euill, where paine shall euer bée:
This is that louing Christ, whom I my Sauiour call,
And onely put my trust in him, and in none else at all.

19 In God the holy Ghost, I firmely do belieue, God the holy Ghost.
Which from the father and the sonne a blessed[2] life doth giue,
Which by the Prophets spake, which doth all comfort send,
Which I do trust shall be my guide, when this my life shall ende.

20 A holy catholike Church, on earth I graunt there is, The Catholike Church.
And those which frame their liues by that, shall neuer do[3] amis:
The head whereof is Christ, his word the chiefest post:
Preseruer of this temple great, is God the holy Ghost.

[1] soule. 1577. [2] proceeding. 1577. [3] speede. 1577.

The Communion of Saints.

21 I do not doubt there is a multitude of Saints,
More good is don resembling them, than shewing them our plaints:
Their faith and workes in Christ, that glorie them did giue,
Which glorie we shall likewise haue, if likewise we do liue.

Forgiuenesse of sinnes.

22 At God of heauen there is, forgiuenesse of our sinnes,
Through Christes death, through faith in it, and through none other ginnes:
If we repentant here, his mercie dailie craue,
Through stedfast hope and faith in Christ, forgiuenes we shall haue.

Mans resurrection.

23 I hope and trust vpon the rising of the flesh,
This corps of mine that first must die, shall rise againe afresh:
The soule and bodie euen then, in one shall ioyned bée,
As Christ did rise from death to life, euen so through Christ shall wée.

Life euerlasting.

24 As Christ is glorified, and neuer more shall die,
As Christ ascended into heauen, through Christ euen so shall I:
As Christ I count my head, and I a member of his,
So God I trust for Christes sake, shall settle me in blis.

[25] Thus here we learne of God, that there be persons thrée,
The Father, Sonne, the holy Ghost, one God in trinitée,
In substance all like one, one God, one Lord, one might,
Whose persons yet we do diuide, and so we may by right.

[26] As God the Father is the maker of vs all,
So God the Sonne redéemer is, to whom for helpe we call,
And God the holy Ghost, the soule of man doth winne,
By moouing hir to waile for grace, ashamed of hir sinne.

[27] This is that God of gods, whom euerie soule should loue,
Whom all mens hearts should quake for feare his wrath on them to moue:
That this same mightie God, aboue all others chiefe,
Shall saue my soule from dolefull Hell, is all my whole beliefe.

107.

Of the omnipotencie of God, *and debilitie of man.*

1 O GOD thou glorious God, what god is like to thée?
What life, what strength is like to thine, as al the world may see?
The heauens, the earth, the seas, and all thy workes therein,
Do shew (to who thou wouldst to know) what thou hast euer bin.

2 But all the thoughts of man, are bent to wretched euill,
Man doth commit idolatrie bewitched of the Deuill.
What euill is left vndone, where man may haue his will,
Man euer was an hypocrite, and so continues still.

3 What daily watch is made, the soule of man to slea, What these 4 principal diuels do signifie.
By Lucifer, by Belzabub, Mammon, and Asmodea?
In diuelish pride, in wrath, in coueting too much,
In fleshly lust the time is spent, the life of man is such.

4 The ioy that man hath here, is as a sparke of fier,
His acts be like the smoldring smoke, himselfe like dirt and mier.
His strength euen as a réede, his age much like a flower,
His breth or life is but a puffe, vncertaine euerie hower.

5 But for the holy Ghost, and for his giftes of grace,
The death of Christ, thy mercie great, man were in wofull case.
O graunt us therefore Lord, to amend that is amisse,
And when from hence we do depart, to rest with thee in blisse.

108.

Eleemosyna prodest homini in vita, in morte, & post mortem.

Out of S. Augustine.

Of almes déedes.

[1] FOR onely loue to God, more Christian like to liue,
And for a zeale to helpe the poore, thine almes daily giue.
Let gift no glorie looke, nor euill possesse thy minde:
And for a truth these profites thrée, through almes shalt thou finde.

[2] 1 First here the holy Ghost shall daily through his grace,
Prouoke thée to repentant life, Gods mercie to embrace.

2 Of goods and friends (by death) when thou thy leaue must take,
Thine almes déedes shall claspe thy soule, and neuer it forsake.

[3] 3 When God shall after death, call soone for thine account,
thine alms then through faith in Christ, shal al things els surmount.
But yet for any déede, put thou no trust therein,
but put thy trust in God (through Christ) to pardon thée thy sin.

[4] For else as cackling hen with noise bewraies hir nest,
Euen so go thou and blaze thy déeds, and lose thou all the rest.

109.

Malus homo, out of S. Augustine.

OF naughtie man, I read, two sundrie things are ment,
The ton is man, the other naught, which ought him to repent.
The man we ought to loue, bicause of much therein,
The euill in him we ought to hate, euen as a filthie sin.
So doth thy daily sinnes the heauenly Lord offend,
But when thou dost repent the same, his wrath is at an end.

110.

Of two sorts of men, the tone good, and tother bad, out of S. Augustine.

SINCE first the world began, there was and shall be still,
Of humane kind two sundrie sorts, thon good and thother ill:
Which till the iudgement day, shall here togither dwell,
But then the good shall vp to heauen, the bad shall downe to hell.

Diabolo cùm resistitur, est vt formica: Cùm verò eius suggestio recipitur, fortis est vt leo.

Out of S. Augustine.

WHEN Sathan we resist, a Pismier shall he be,
But when we séeme to giue him place, a Lion then is he.

111.

❡ *Eight of S. Barnards verses, both in Latine* and English with one note to *them both.*[1]

1 *CUR mundus militat, sub vana gloria,*
Cuius prosperitas, est transitoria?
Tam citò labitur, eius potentia,
Quàm vasa figuli, quæ sunt fragilia?

1 Why[2] so triumphes the world, in pompe and glorie vaine,
Whose state so happie thought, so fickle[3] doth remaine?
Whose brauerie slipprie stands, and doth so soone decaie,
As doth the potters pan, compact of brittle claie?

2 *Plus crede literis, scriptis in glacie,*
Quàm mundi fragilis, vanæ fallaciæ,
Fallax in præmijs, virtutis specie,
Quæ nunquam habuit tempus fiduciæ.

2 More credite sée thou giue, to letters wrote in ise,
Than vnto vaine deceits, of brittle worlds deuise.
In gifts to vertue due, beguiling many one,
Yet those same neuer haue long time to hope vpon.

3 *Magis credendum est, viris fallacibus,*
Quàm mundi miseris prosperitatibus,
Falsis insanijs et voluptatibus,
Falsis quoque studijs et vanitatibus.

3 To false dissembling men more trust is to be had,
Than to the prosperous state of wretched world so bad:
What with voluptuousnes, and other maddish toies,
False studies won with paine, false vanities and ioies.

[1] "These eight verses of St. Bernard seem to have been extremely popular at one period. . . . In the 'Paradise of Dainty Devices,' first printed in 1576, we find translations of the same words" (Mason).

[2] Who. 1577. [3] unsteady. 1577.

4 *Dic vbi Salomon, olim tam nobilis?*
Vel vbi Samson est, dux invincibilis?
Vel dulcis Ionathas, multùm amabilis?
Vel pulcher Absolon, vultu mirabilis?

4 Tell where is *Salomon*, that once so noble was?
Or where now *Samson* is, in strength whome none could pas?
Or woorthie *Ionathas*, that prince so louely bold?
Or faier *Absolon*, so goodlie to behold?

5 *Quò Cæsar abijt, celsus imperio?*
Vel Diues splendidus, totus in prandio?
Dic vbi Tullius, clarus eloquio?
Vel Aristoteles, summus ingenio?

5 Shew whither is *Cesar* gone, which conquered far and néere?
Or that rich famous *Carle*, so giuen to bellie chéere:
Shew where is *Tullie* now, for eloquence so fit?
Or *Aristoteles*, of such a pregnant wit?

6 *O esca vermium! ô massa pulueris!*
O ros! ô vanitas! cùr sic extolleris,
Ignoras penitùs vtrùm cras vixeris,
Fac bonum omnibus, quàm diu poteris.

6 O thou fit bait for wormes! O thou great heape of dust!
O dewe! O vanitie! why so extolst thy lust?
Thou therefore ignorant, what time thou hast to liue,
Doe good to erie man, while here thou hast to giue.

7 *Quàm breue festum est, hæc mundi gloria?*
Vt umbra hominis, sic eius gaudia,
Quæ semper subtrahit, æterna præmia,
Et ducunt hominem, ad dura deuia.

7 How short a feast (to count) is this same worlds renowne?
Such as mens shadowes be, such ioies it brings to towne.
Which alway plucketh vs from Gods eternall blis:
And leadeth man to hell, a iust reward of his.

8 *Hæc mundi gloria, quæ magni penditur,*
Sacris in literis, flos fœni dicitur,
Vt leue folium, quod vento rapitur,
Sic vita hominum, hac vita tollitur.

8 The brauerie of this world, estéemed here so much,
In Scripture likened is, to flowre of grasse and such:
Like as the leafe so light, through winde abrode is blowne,
So life in this our life, full soone is ouerthrowne.[1]

112.

¶ *Of the Authors linked Verses departing* from Court to the Country.[2]

1 Muse not my friend to finde me here,
Contented with this meane estate:
And séeme to doo with willing chéere,
That courtier doth so deadly hate.

For fortunes looke,
Hath changed hew:
And I my booke,
Must learne anew.

2 And yet of force, to learne anew,
Would much abash the dulled braine:
I craue to iudge if this be trew,
The truant child that knowth the paine.

But where a spight,
Of force must bée:
What is that wight,
May disagrée?

3 No, no, God wot, to disagrée,
Is ventring all to make or mar:
If fortune frowne we dailie sée,
It is not best to striue too far.

For lordlie bent,
Must learne to spare:
And be content
With countrie fare.

4 From daintie Court to countrie fare,
Too daintie fed is diet strange:
From cities ioy, to countrie care,
To skillesse folke is homelie change.

Where néede yet can,
None other skill:
Somtime poore man
Must breake his will.

[1] . . . . which wind abrod doth blowe,
So doth this worldly life, the life of man bestow. 1577.

[2] "In the edition of 1573 this piece is entitled 'Of the Author's departing from the Court to the Country,' and the verses are printed consecutively—four long lines and then four short lines."—M. So, in 1577.

5 If courtlie change so breaketh will
That countrie life must serue the turne :
What profit then in striuing still,
Against the prick to séeme to spurne?

If court with cart
Must be content,
What ease to hart,
Though mind repent?

6 What gaine I though I doo repent,
My crotches[1] all are broke and gon :
My woonted friends are careles bent,
They feare no chance I chance vpon.

As néede doth make
Old age to trot :
So must I take,
In woorth my lot.

7 Now if I take in woorth my lot,
That fatall chance doth force me to,
If ye be friends embraid[2] me not,
But vse a friend as friends should do.

Behold the horse
Must trudge for pelfe,
And yet of forse,
Content it selfe.

113.

The Authors life.[3]

1 NOW gentle friend, if thou be kinde, Epodium.
Disdaine thou not, although the lot
Will now with me no better be,
than doth appere :
Nor let it grieue, that thus I liue,
But rather gesse, for quietnesse,
As others do, so do I to,
content me here.

2 By leaue and loue, of God aboue,
I minde to shew, in verses few,
How through the breers, my youthfull yeeres,
haue runne their race :
And further say, why thus I stay,
And minde to liue, as Bee in hiue,
Full bent to spend my life to an end,
in this same place.[4]

[1] chrotches. 1577. [2] upbraid. 1614.
[3] First added to the 1573 edition.—M.
[4] "The author means London ; but though it is believed he died there, it is evident from the sequel, that he left it on account of the plague."—M.

Borne at Riuenhall in Essex.

3 It came to pas, that borne I was
Of linage good, of gentle blood,
In Essex laier, in village faier,
that Riuenhall hight:
Which village lide by Banketree side,
There spend did I mine infancie,
There then my name, in honest fame,
remaind in sight.

4 I yet but yong, no speech of tong,
Nor teares withall, that often fall
Set to song schoole.
From mothers eies, when childe out cries,
to part hir fro:
Could pitie make, good father take,
But out I must, to song be thrust,
Say what I would, do what I could,
his minde was so.

Queristers miserie.

5 O painfull time, for euerie crime,
What toesed eares, like baited beares!
What bobbed lips, what ierks, what nips!
what hellish toies!
What robes, how bare! what colledge fare!
What bread, how stale! what pennie Ale!
Wallingford Colledge.
Then Wallingford, how wart thou abhord
of sillie boies!

6 Thence for my voice, I must (no choice)
Away of forse, like posting horse,
Singing mens commissions.
For sundrie men, had plagards then,
such childe to take:
The better brest,[1] the lesser rest,
To serue the Queere, now there now heere,
For time so spent, I may repent,
and sorrow make.

[1] Cf. Shakespere's Twelfth Night, ii. 3.

7 But marke the chance, my self to vance,
By friendships lot, to Paules I got,
So found I grace, a certaine space,
still to remaine:
With Redford there, the like no where,
For cunning such, and vertue much,
By whom some part of Musicke art,
so did I gaine.

Iohn Redford an excellent Musician [organist of St. Paul's. M.]

8 From Paules I went, to Eaton sent,
To learn streight waies, the latin phraies,
Where fiftie three stripes giuen to mee,
at once I had:
For fault but small, or none at all,
It came to pas, thus beat I was,
See Udall see, the mercie of thee,
to me poore lad.

Nicholas Vdall school-master at Eaton.

9 From London hence, to Cambridge thence,
With thanks to thee, O Trinitee,
That to thy hall, so passing all,[1]
I got at last:
There ioy I felt, there trim I dwelt,
There heauen from hell, I shifted well,
With learned men, a number then,
the time I past.

Trinitie hall in Cambridge.

10 Long sicknes had, then was I glad
To leaue my booke, to proue and looke,
In Court what gaine, by taking paine,
mought well be found:
Lord Paget than, that noble man,
Whose soule I trust is with the iust,
That same was hee enriched mee,
with many a pound.

Quartan ague.

Lord Paget good to his seruants.

[1] "Till it was repaired, between 1740 and 1750, it is said to have been but a poor-looking place; and which is reported to have been characterized by Dr. Mar, the Vice-Chancellor, when speaking of it to the King of Denmark, as *le petit coigne.*"—M.

11 When[1] this betide, good parents dide,
One after one, till both were gone,
Whose petigree, who list may see,
in Harolds Booke:
Whose soules in blis be long ere this,
For hope we must, as God is iust,
So here that craue shall mercie haue,
that mercie looke.

The hope we haue of the dead.

The vices of the Court.

12 By Court I spide, and ten yeres tride
That Cards and Dice, with Venus vice,
And peeuish pride, from vertue wide,
with some so wraught:
That Tiburne play made them away,
Or beggers state as euill to hate,
By such like euils, I saw such dreuils,
to come to naught.

13 Yet is it not to be forgot,
In Court that some to worship come,
And some in time to honour clime,
and speede full well:
Some haue such gift, that trim they shift,
Some profite make, by paines they take,
In perill much, though oft are such,
in Court that dwell.

The Court commended.

The no-bilitie at variance in Edward the 6 daies.

Katewade.

14 When court gan frowne and strife in towne,
And lords and knights, saw heauie sights,
Then tooke I wife, and led my life
in Suffolke soile.
There was I faine my selfe to traine,
To learne too long the fermers song,
For hope of pelfe, like worldly elfe,
to moile and toile.

[1] While. 1577.

15 As in this booke, who list to looke,
Of husbandrie, and huswiferie,
There may he finde more of my minde,
concerning this:
To carke[1] and care, and euer bare,
With losse and paine, to little gaine,
All this to haue, to cram sir knaue,
what life it is.

At Katewade in Suffolke this booke first deuised.

16 When wife could not, through sicknes got,
More toile abide, so nigh Sea side,
Then thought I best, from toile to rest,
and Ipswich trie:
A towne of price, like paradice,
For quiet then, and honest men,
There was I glad, much friendship had,
a time to lie.

Ipswich commended.

17 There left good wife this present life,
And there left I, house charges lie,
For glad was he, mought send for me,
good lucke so stood:
In Suffolke there, were euerie where,
Euen of the best, besides the rest,
That neuer did their friendship hid,
to doo me good.

The deth of his first wife.

18 O Suffolke thow, content thee now,
That hadst the praies in those same daies,
For Squiers and Knights, that well delights
good house to keepe:
For Norfolke wiles, so full of giles,
Haue caught my toe, by wiuing so,
That out to thee, I see for mee,
no waie to creepe.

Newe maried in Norfolk.

[1] carp. 1573.

Mistres Amie Moone.

19 For lo, through gile, what haps the while,
Through Venus toies, in hope of ioies,
I chanced soone to find a Moone,[1]
  of cheerfull hew:
Which well a fine me thought did shine,
Did neuer change, a thing most strange,
Yet kept in sight, hir course aright,
  and compas trew.

The charges following a yoong wife.

20 Behold of truth, with wife in youth,
For ioie at large, what daily charge,
Through childrens hap, what opened gap,
  to more begun.
The childe at nurse, to rob the purse,
The same to wed, to trouble hed.
For pleasure rare, such endlesse care,
  hath husband wun.

West Diram Abbie.

21 Then did I dwell in Diram sell,
A place for wood, that trimlie stood,
With flesh and fish, as heart would wish:
  but when I spide

Land-lordes at variance.

That Lord with Lord could not accord,
But now pound he, and now pound we,
Then left I all, bicause such brall,
  I list not bide.

Sir Richarde Soothwell.

22 O Soothwell, what meanst thou by that,
Thou worthie wight, thou famous knight,
So me to craue, and to thy graue,
  go by and by?
O death thou fo, why didst thou so
Ungently treat that Iewell great,
Which opte his doore to rich and poore,
  so bounteously?

[1] His second wife.

23 There thus bestad, when leaue I had,
By death of him, to sinke or swim,
And rauens I saw togither draw,
in such a sort: His vij executors.
Then waies I saught, by wisdome taught,
To beare low saile, least stock should quaile,
Till ship mought finde, with prosperous winde,
some safer port.

24 At length by vew, to shore I drew,
Discharging straight both ship and fraight,
At Norwich fine, for me and mine, Norwich Citie.
a citie trim:
Where strangers wel may seeme to dwel, Norwich qualities.
That pitch and pay, or keepe their day,
But who that want, shall find it scant
so good for him.

25 But Salisburie how were kept my vow, Maister Salisburie deane of Norwich.
If praise from thee were kept by mee,
Thou gentle deane, mine onely meane,
there then to liue?
Though churles such some to craue can come,
And pray once got, regard thee not,
Yet liue or die, so will not I,
example giue.

26 When learned men could there nor then, In 138 houres I neuer made drop of water.
Deuise to swage the stormie rage,
Nor yet the furie of my dissurie,
that long I had:
From Norwich aire, in great despaire,
Away to flie, or else to die,
To seeke more helth, to seeke more welth,
then was I glad.

27 From thence so sent, away I went,
With sicknes worne, as one forlorne,
To house my hed, at Faiersted,
where whiles I dwelt:
The tithing life, the tithing strife,
Through tithing ill, of Jacke and Gill,
The dailie paies, the mierie waies,
too long I felt.

Faiersted parsonage in Essex.

28 When charges grew, still new and new,
And that I spide, if parson dide,
(All hope in vaine) to hope for gaine,
I might go daunce:
Once rid my hand of parsonage land,
Thence by and by, away went I,
To London streight, to hope and waight,
for better chaunce.

Lease for parsons life.

London commended.

29 Well London well, that bearst the bell
Of praise about, England throughout,
And dost in deede, to such as neede,
much kindnes shew:
Who that with thee can hardly agree,
Nor can well prais thy friendly wais,
Shall friendship find, to please his mind,
in places few.

Vnthrifts order.

30 As for such mates, as vertue hates,
Or he or thay, that go so gay,
That needes he must take all of trust,
for him and his:
Though such for wo by Lothburie go,
For being spide about Cheapeside,
Least Mercers bookes for monie lookes,
small matter it is.

31 When gaines was gon, and yeres grew on,
And death did crie, from London flie,
In Cambridge then, I found agen,
  a resting plot:
In Colledge best of all the rest,
With thanks to thee, O Trinitee,[1]
Through thee and thine, for me and mine,
  some stay I got.

The plague at London [1574, 1575].

Trinitie College in Cambridge.

32 Since hap haps so, let toiling go,
Let seruing paines yeeld forth hir gaines,
Let courtly giftes, with wedding shiftes,
  helpe now to liue:
Let Musicke win, let stocke come in,
Let wisedome kerue, let reason serue,
For here I craue such end to haue,
  as God shall giue.

Youth ill spent makes age repent.

33 Thus friends, by me perceiue may ye,
That gentrie standes, not all by landes,
Nor all so feft, or plentie left
  by parents gift:
But now and then, of gentlemen,
The yonger sonne is driuen to ronne,
And glad to seeke from creeke to creeke,
  to come by thrift.

A lesson for yonger brothers.

34 And more by this, to conster is,
In world is set, ynough to get,
But where and whan, that scarsely can,
  the wisest tell:
By learning some to riches come,
By ship and plough some get ynough,
And some so wiue that trim they thriue,
  and speede full well.

A true lesson.

[1] Founded in 1546.

Hardnes in youth not the worst.

35 To this before, adde one thing more,
Youth hardnes taught, with knowledge wraught,
Most apt do prooue, to shift and shooue,
among the best:
Where cocking Dads make sawsie lads,
In youth so rage, to beg in age,
Or else to fetch a Tibourne stretch,
among the rest.

Cocking of youth not the best.

36 Not rampish toie, of girle and boie,
Nor garment trim, of hir or him,
In childhoode spent, to fond intent,
good end doth frame:
If marke we shall, the summe of all,
The end it is, that noted is,
Which if it bide, with vertue tride,
deserueth fame.

Not pride in youth, but welth in age needfull.

37 When all is done, lerne this my sonne,
Not friend, nor skill, nor wit at will,
Nor ship nor clod, but onelie God,
doth all in all:
Man taketh paine, God giueth gaine,
Man doth his best, God doth the rest,
Man well intendes, God foizon sendes,
else want he shall.

Man doth labour and God doth blesse.

38 Some seeke for welth, I seeke my helth,
Some seeke to please, I seeke mine ease,
Some seeke to saue, I seeke to haue
to liue vpright:
More than to ride, with pompe and pride,
Or for to iet,[1] in others det,
Such is my skill, and shall be still,
for any wight.

A contented minde is worth all.

[1] set. 1573.

39 Too fond were I, here thus to lie,
Unles that welth mought further helth,
And profit some should thereby come,
to helpe withall:
This causeth mee well pleasde to bee,
Such drift to make, such life to take,
Enforsing minde remorse to finde,
as neede neede shall.

40 Friend, al thing waid, that here is said, Happie that liues well, vnhappie dies euill.
And being got, that paies the shot,
Me thinke of right haue leaue I might,
(death drawing neere:)
To seeke some waies, my God to praies,
And mercy craue, in time to haue,
And for the rest, what he thinkes best,
to suffer heere.

FINIS.

[Of edition of 1580, but see over.]

[114.]

The following poem is not to be found after the edition of 1573 and its reprint of 1577.—M.

Fortuna non est semper amica,
Superbiam igitur semper devita.

1 Though Fortune smiles, and fawnes vpon thy side,
Thyself extol for that no whit the more ;
Though Fortune frownes and wresteth al thing wide,
Let fancy stay, keepe courage still in store ;
For chance may change as chance hath don before :
Thus shalt thou holde more safe then honour got,
Or lose the losse,[1] though Fortune will or not.

2 Thy friend at this shall dayly comfort haue,
When warely thus, thou bearest thy selfe vpright,
Thy foes at this shall gladly friendship craue,
When hope so small is left to wrecke their spight,
For lowly liefe withstandeth enuy quight :
As floeting ship, by bearing sayl alowe,
Withstandeth stormes when boistrous winds do blowe.

3 Thy vsage thus in time shall win the gole,
Though doughtful haps, dame fortune sendes betweene,
And thou shalt see thine enemies blow the cole,
To ease thine hart much more then thou dost weene,
Ye though a change most strangely should be seene,
Yet friend at neede shall secret friendship make,
When foe in deede shal want his part to take.

[1] lesse. M.

A Table of the points of Huswiferie *mentioned in this Booke.*

FINIS.

¶ Imprinted at London,
by Henrie Denham, dwel-
ling at Paternoster Row,
at the figure of the Starre,
being the assigne of
William Seres.

Cum priuilegio Regiæ Maiestatis.

¶ A hundreth good pointes of husbandrie.

(.˙.)

A hundreth good pointes, of good husbandry,
maintaineth good household, with huswifry.
Housekeping and husbandry, if it be good:
must loue one another, as cousinnes in blood.
The wife to, must husband as well as the man:
or farewel thy husbandry, doe what thou can.

¶ *To the right honorable and my speciall good lord* and maister, the lord Paget, Lord priuie seale.

THOMAS TUSSER MADE ME

The trouth doth teache, that tyme must serue.
(How euer man, doth blase hys mynde)
(Of thynges most lyke, to thryue or sterue :)
Much apt to iudge, is often blynde.
And therfore, tyme it doth behoofe :
Shall make of trouth, a perfit proofe.

Take you my lord, and mayster than,
(Unlesse mischaunce mischaunseth me :)
Such homely gyft, of your own man,
Synce more in court, I may not be :
and let your praise, wonne here tofore,
Remayne abrode, for euermore.

My seruyng you, thus vnderstande,
And god his helpe, and yours withall :
Dyd cause good lucke, to take myne hande
Erecting one, most lyke to fall :
My seruing you, I know it was,
Enforced this, to come to passe.

So synce I was, at Cambridge tought,
Of court ten yeres, I made a say ;
No musike than, was left vnsought,
A care I had, to serue that way,
My ioye gan slake, then made I chaunge,
Expulsed myrth, for musike straunge.

My musike synce, hath been the plough,
Entangled with, some care among :
The gayn not great, the payn enough,
Hath made me syng, another song.
And if I may, my song auowe ;
No man I craue, to iudge but you.

¶ Your seruant,

Thomas Tusser.

¶ *Concordia paruæ res crescunt*
Discordia maximæ dilabuntur.

1. Where couples agree not, is rancor and poysen,
where they two kepe house, than is neuer no foysen:
But contrary lightly, where couples agree,
what chaunseth by wisdom, looke after to see.

2. Good husbandes, that loueth good housholdes to kepe,
be sometime full carefull, when others do slepe:
To spend as they may, or to stop at the furst,
for running behinde hand, or feare of the wurst.

3. Then count with thy purse, when thy haruest is in,
thy cardes being tolde, how to saue or to win:
But win or els saue, or els passe not to farre,
For hoping to make, least thou happen to marre.

4. Make money thy drudge, for to folow thy warke,
and Wisdom thy steward, good Order thy clarke:
Prouision thy cator, and all shall goe well,
for foysen is there, where prouision doth dwell.

5. With some folke on sundayes, their tables do reke:
and halfe the weke after, their diners to seke.
At no tyme to much, but haue alway ynough:
is housholdy fare, and the guyse of the plough.

6. For what shal it profet, ynough to prouide,
and then haue it spoiled, or filched aside:
As twenty lode busshes, cut downe at a clappe,
such hede may be taken, shall stoppe but a gappe.

7. Good labouring threshers, are worthy to eate,
Good husbandly ploughmen, deserueth their meate,
Good huswiuely huswiues, that let for no rest,
should eate when they list, and should drinke of the best.

8. Beware raskabilia, slouthfull to wurke,
proloiners and filchers, that loue for to lurke:
And cherishe well willers, that serueth thy nede,
take time to thy Tutor, God sende the good spede.

¶ August.

9. When haruest is done, all thing placed and set,
for saultfishe and herring, then laie for to get:
The byeng of them, comming first vnto rode,
shal pay for thy charges, thou spendest abrode.

10. Thy saultfishe well chosen, not burnt at the stone,
or drye them thyselfe, (hauing skill is a lone:)
Brought salfe to thy house, would be packed vp drie,
with pease strawe betweene, least it rot as it lie.

11. Or euer thou ride, with thy seruauntes compound,
to carry thy muckhilles, on thy barley ground:
One aker wel compast, is worth akers three,
at haruest, thy barne shall declare it to thee.

12. This good shalt thou learne, with thy riding about,
the prises of thinges, all the yere thoroughout:
And what time is best, for to sell that thou haue,
and how for to bye, to be likely to saue.

13. For bying and selling, doth wonderfull well,
to him that hath wit, how to by and to sell:
But chopping and chaungeing, may make such a breck,
that gone is thy winninges, for sauing thy neck.

14. The riche man, his bargaines are neuer vnsought,
the seller will fynde him, he nede not take thought:
But herein consisteth, a part of our text,
who byeth at first hand, and who at the next.

15. He byeth at first hand, that ventreth his golde,
he byeth at second, that dare not be bolde:
He byeth at third hand, that nedes borrow must,
who byeth of him, than shall pay for his lust.

16. When euer thou bargain, for better or wurse,
let alway one bargain, remain in thy purse:
Good credit doth well, but good credit to kepe,
is pay and dispatche him, or euer thou slepe.

17. Be mindeful abrode, of thy Mighelmas spring,
for theron dependeth, a marueilous thing:
When gentiles vse walking, with hawkes on their handes,
Good husbandes, with grasing doe purchase their landes.

18. And as thou come homeward, bye xl. good crones,
and fatte me the bodies, of those sely bones:
With those and thy swine, or and shrouetyde be past,
thy folke shal fare well, where as others shal fast.

19. Thy saffron plot, pared in saint mary daies,
for pleasure and profit, shal serue many waies:
With twenty foote square, knowing how for to doo,
shal stede both thine own house, and next neighbour too.

¶ September.

20. Threshe sede and goe fanne, for the plough may not lye,
September doth bid, to be sowing of rye:
The redges well harrowde, or euer thou strike,
is one poynt of husbandry, rye land do like.

21. Geue winter corne leaue, for to haue full his lust,
sowe wheate as thou mayst, but sowe rye in the dust:
Be carefull for sede, for such sede as thou sowe,
as true as thou liuest, loke iustly to mowe.

22. The sede being sowne, waterforow thy ground,
that rain, when it cummeth, may runne away round:
The diches kept skowred, the hedge clad with thorne,
doth well to drayne water, and saueth thy corne.

23. Then furth with thy slinges, and thine arowes & bowes,
till ridges be grene, kepe the corne from the crowes:
A good boye abrode, by the day starre appere,
shall skare good man crowe, that he dare not come nere.

24. At Mihelmas, mast would be loked vpon,
and lay to get some, or the mast time be gon:
It saueth thy corne well, it fatteth thy swyne;
In frost it doth helpe them, where els they should pine.

¶ October.

25. The rye in the ground, while September doth last:
October for wheate sowing, calleth as fast.
What euer it cost thee, what euer thou geue,
have done sowing wheate, before halowmas eve.

26. The mone in the wane, gather fruit on the tree,
the riper, the better for graffe and for thee.
But michers, that loue not to bie nor to craue:
make some gather sooner, els fewe should they haue.

27. Or winter doe come, while the weather is good:
for gutting thy grounde, get the home with thy wood.
Set bauen alone, lay the bowghes from the blockes:
the drier, the les maidens dablith their dockes.

28. For rooting thy grounde, ring thy hogges thou hast nede:
the better thou ring them, the better they fede.
Most times with their elders, the yong ones kepe best:
then yoke well the great knaues, and fauour the rest.

29. But yoke not thy swine, while thine akorne time last:
for diuers misfortunes, that happen to fast.
Or if thou loue eared, and vnmaimed hogges:
giue eie to thy neighbour, and eare to his dogges.

¶ Nouembre.

30. Get vp with thy barley lande, dry as thou can:
at March (as thou layest it) so loke for it than.
Get euer before hande, drag neuer behinde:
least winter beclip thee, and breake of thy minde.

31. At Hallowmas, slaughter time sone commeth in:
and than doth the husbande mans feasting begin.
From that time, to Candlemas weekely kill some:
their offal for household, the better shal come.

32. All soules that be thursty, bid threshe out for mawlt:
well handled and tended, or els thou dost nawlt.
Thencrease of one strike is a pek for thy store:
the maker is bad els, or pilfreth the more.

33. For Easter, at Martilmas hange vp a biefe:
for pease fed and stall fed, play pickpurse the thiefe.
With that and fat bakon, till grasse biefe come in:
thy folke shall loke cherely, when others loke thin.

34. Set gardeine beanes, after saint Edmonde the king:
the Moone in the wane, theron hangeth a thing.
Thencrease of one gallonde, well proued of some:
shall pleasure thy householde, ere peskod time come.

35. Except thou take good hede, when first they apere,
the crowes will be halfe, grow they neuer so nere.
Thinges sowne, set or graft, in good memory haue:
from beast, birde and weather to cherishe and saue.

¶ Decembre.

36. Abrode for the raine, when thou canst do no good;
then go let thy flayles, as the threshers were wood.
Beware they threshe clene, though the lesser they yarne:
and if thou wilt thriue, loke thy selfe to thy barne.

37. If barne rome will serue, lay thy stoouer vp drye
and eche kinde of strawe, by hitselfe let it lie.
Thy chaffe, housed sweete, kept from pullein and dust:
shall serue well thy horses, when labour they must.

38. When pasture is gone, and the fildes mier and weate:
then stable thy plough horse, and there giue them meate.
The better thou vse them, in place where they stande:
more strength shall they haue, for to breake vp thy lande.

39. Giue cattell their fodder, the plot drie and warme:
and count them, for miring or other like harme.
Trust neuer to boyes, if thou trust well to spede:
be serued with those, that may helpe at a nede.

40. Serue first out thy rie strawe, then wheate & then pease,
then otestrawe then barley, then hay if you please.
But serue them with haye, while thy straw stoouer last,
they loue no more strawe, they had rather to fast.

41. Kepe neuer such seruantes, as doth thee no good,
for making thy heare, growing thorrough thy hood.
For nestling of verlettes, of brothels and hoores:
make many a rich man, to shet vp his doores.

¶ Christmas.

42. Get Iuye and hull, woman deck vp thyne house:
and take this same brawne, for to seeth and to souse.
Prouide vs good chere, for thou knowst the old guise:
olde customes, that good be, let no man dispise.

43. At Christmas be mery, and thanke god of all:
and feast thy pore neighbours, the great with the small.
yea al the yere long, haue an eie to the poore:
and god shall sende luck, to kepe open thy doore.

44. Good fruite and good plenty, doth well in thy loft:
then lay for an orcharde, and cherishe it oft.
The profet is mickell, the pleasure is mutch;
at pleasure with profet, few wise men will grutch.

45. For plantes and for stockes, lay afore hand to cast:
but set or remoue them, while twelue tide doe last.
Set one from another, full twenty fote square:
the better and greater, they yerely will bare.

¶ January.

46. When Christmas is done, kepe not Christmas time still:
be mindefull of rering, and loth for to kill.
For then, what thou rerist thou nede not to dout:
will double thy gaine, ere the yere come about.

47. Be gredy to spende all, and careles to saue:
and shortly be nedy, and redy to craue.
be wilfull to kill, and vnskilfull to store:
and sone giue vp houskeping, longe any more.

48. Thy calues then, that come betwene new yere and lent:
saue gladly for store, lest thou after repent.
For all thing at that time, that colde feleth some:
shall better beare colde, when the next winter come.

49. Weane no time thy calfe, vnder xl daies olde:
and lay for to saue it, as thou sauest golde.
yet calues that doe fal, betwene change and the prime:
pas seldome to rere them, but kill them in time.

50. For stores of thy swine, be thou carefull betwix:
of one sow at one time, rere seldome past six.
The fewe that she kepe, much the better shal bee:
of all thing, one good is worth steruelinges three.

51. Geld vnder the dame, within fornight at least:
and saue both thy money, and life of the beast.
But gelde with the gelder, as many one doe:
and of halfe a dosen, go geld away two.

52. Thy coltes for the sadle, geld yong to be light:
for cart doe not so, if thou iudgest a right.
Nor geld not, but when they be lusty and fat:
for there is a point, to be learned in that.

53. Geld marefoles, but titts ere and nine dayes of age:
they die els of gelding, some gelders wil gage.
But marefoles, both likely of bulke and of bone:
kepe such to bring coltes, let their gelding alone.

54. For gaining a trifle, sell neuer thy store:
for chaunsing on worse, then thine owne were before.
More larger of body, the better for brede:
more forward of growing, the better they spede.

55. Thy sowes, great with fare, that come best for to rere:
loke dayly thou seest them, and count them full dere.
For that time, the losse of one fare of thy sowe:
is greater, then losse of two calues of thy kowe.

56. A kow good of milk, big of bulke, hayle and sounde,
is yerely for profet, as good as a pounde.
And yet, by the yere haue I proued ere now:
as good to the purse, is a sow as a kow.

57. Kepe one and kepe both, so thou maist if thou wilt.
then all shall be saued, and nothing be spilt.
Kepe two bease, and one sow, and liue at thine ease:
and no time for nede, bye thy meate but thou please.

58. Who both by his calues, and his lambes will be knowne:
may well kill a neate, and a shepe of his owne.
And he, that will rere vp a pig in his house:
shall eate sweter bakon, and cheaper fed sowse.

59. But eate vp thy veale, pig and lambe being froth:
and twise in a weeke, go to bed without broth.
As that man that pas not, but sell away sell:
shall neuer kepe good house, where euer he dwell.

60. Spende none but thyne owne, howsoeuer thou spende:
nor haft not to god ward, for that he doth sende.
Tythe truly for al thing, let pas of the rest:
the iust man, his dealinges god prospereth best.

61. In January, husbandes that powcheth the grotes:
will breake vp their lay, or be sowing of otes.
Sow Jauiuer Otes, and lay them by thy wheate;
in May, bye thy hay for thy cattel to eate.

¶ Februarij.

62. In Feuerell, rest not for taking thine ease:
get into the grounde with thy beanes, and thy pease.
Sow peason betimes, and betimes they will come:
the sooner, the better they fill vp a rome.

63. In euery grene, where the fence is not thine:
the thornes stub out cleane, that the grasse may be fine.
Thy neighbours wil borow, els hack them beliue:
so neither thy grasse, nor the bushes shall thriue.

64. Thy seruant, in walking thy pastures aboute:
for yokes, forkes and rakes, let him loke to finde oute.
And after at leyser let this be his hier:
to trimme them and make them at home by the fier.

65. When frostes will not suffer to ditche nor to hedge:
then get the an heate, with thy betill and wedge.
A blocke at the harthe, cowched close for thy life:
shall helpe to saue fier bote, and please well thy wife.

66. Then lop for thy fewel, the powlinges well growen:
that hindreth the corne, or the grasse to be mowen.
In lopping, and cropping, saue Edder and stake
thyne hedges, where nede is to mende or to make.

67. No stick, nor no stone, leaue vnpicked vp clene:
for hurting thy sieth, or for harming thy grene.
For sauing of al thing, get home with the rest.
the snow frozen hardest, thy cart may goe best.

68. Spare meddowes at shroftide, spare marshes at paske:
for feare of a drougth, neuer longer time aske.
Then hedge them, and ditche them, bestow thereon pence:
for meddow and corne, craueth euer good fence.

69. And alway, let this be a part of thy care:
for shift of good pasture, lay pasture to spare.
Then seauer thy groundes, and so keping them still:
finde cattel at ease, and haue pasture at will.

¶ Marche.

70. In Marche, sow thy barley thy londe not to colde:
the drier the better, a hundreth times tolde.
That tilth harrowde finely, set sede time an ende:
and praise, and pray God a good haruest to sende.

71. Sow wheate in a meane, sow thy Rie not to thin;
let peason and beanes, here and there, take therein.
Sow barley and otes, good and thick doe not spare:
giue lande leaue, her sede or her wede for to bare.

72. For barley and pease, harrow after thou sowe:
for rye, harrow first seldome after I trowe.
Let wheat haue a clodde, for to couer the hedde:
that after a frost, it may out and goe spredde.

¶ A digression from husbandrie: to a poynt or two of huswifrie.

[72a] Now here I think nedeful, a pawse for to make;
to treate of some paines, a good huswife must take.
For huswifes must husbande, as wel as the man:
or farewel thy husbandrie, do what thou can.

[72b] In Marche, and in Aprill, from morning to night:
in sowing and setting, good huswiues delight.
To haue in their gardein, or some other plot:
to trim vp their house, and to furnish their pot.

[72c] Haue millons at Mihelmas, parsneps in lent:
in June, buttred beanes, saueth fish to be spent.
With those, and good pottage inough hauing than:
thou winnest the heart, of thy laboring man.

¶ Aprill.

[72d] From Aprill begin, til saint Andrew be past:
so long with good huswiues, their dairies doe last.
Good milche bease and pasture, good husbandes prouide:
good huswiues know best, all the rest how to guide.

[72e] But huswiues, that learne not to make their owne cheese:
with trusting of others, haue this for their feese.
Their milke slapt in corners, their creame al to sost:
their milk pannes so flotte, that their cheeses be lost.

[72f] Where some of a kowe, maketh yerely a pounde :
these huswiues crye creake, for their voice will not sounde.
The seruauntes, suspecting their dame lye in waighte :
with one thing or other, they trudge away straight.

[72g] Then neighbour (for gods sake) if any such bee ;
if you know a good seruant, waine her to mee.
Such maister, suche man, and such mistres suche mayde :
such husbandes and huswiues, suche houses araide.

[72h] For flax and for hemp, for to haue of her owne :
the wife must in May, take good hede it be sowne.
And trimme it, and kepe it to serue at a nede :
the femble to spin, and the karle for her sede.

[72i] Good husbandes, abrode seketh al well to haue :
good huswiues, at home seketh al well to saue.
Thus hauing and sauing, in place where they meete :
make profit with pleasure, suche couples to greete.

¶ May.

73. Both Philip and Jacob, bid put of thy lammes :
that thinkest to haue any milke of their dammes.
But Lammas aduiseth thee, milke not to long :
for hardnes make pouerty, skabbed among.

74. To milke and to folde them, is much to require :
except thou haue pasture, to fill their desire.
But nightes being shorte, and such hede thou mayst take :
not hurting their bodies, much profit to make.

75. Milke six ewes, for one kowe, well chosen therefore :
and double thy dayrie, els trust me no more.
And yet may good huswiues, that knoweth the skill :
haue mixt or vnmixt, at their pleasure and will.

76. For gredy of gaine, ouerlay not thy grownde :
and then shall thy cattell, be lusty and sownde.
But pinche them of pasture, while sommer time last :
and plucke at their tailes, ere & winter be past.

77. Pinche weannels at no time, of water nor meate :
if euer thou hope to have them good neate.
In sommer at al times, in winter in frost :
if cattell lacke drinke, they be vtterly lost.

78. In May at the furdest, twy fallow thy lande:
much drougth may cause after, thy plough els to stande.
That tilth being done, thou hast passed the wurste:
then after, who plowgheth, plowgh thou with the furste.

¶ June.

79. In June get thy wedehoke, thy knife and thy gloue:
and wede out such wede, as the corne doth not loue.
Slack no time thy weding, for darth nor for cheape:
thy corne shall reward it, or euer thou reape.

80. The maywede doth burne, and the thistle doth freate:
the Tine pulleth downe, both the rie and the wheate.
The dock and the brake, noieth corne very much:
but bodle for barley, no weede there is such.

81. In June washe thy shepe, where the water doth runne:
and kepe them from dust, but not kepe them from sunne
Then share them and spare not, at two daies anende,
the sooner, the better their bodies amende.

82. Rewarde not the shepe, when thou takest his cote:
with two or three patches, as brode as a grote:
The flie than and wormes, will compel it to pine:
more paine to thy cattell, more trouble is thine.

83. But share not thy lammes, till mid July be worne:
the better their cotes will be growne to be shorne.
The pie will discharge thee, for pulling the reste:
the lighter the shepe is, then fedeth it beste.

84. Saint Mihel byd bees, to be brent out of strife:
sajnt John bid take honey, with fauour of life.
For one sely cottage, set south good and warme:
take body and goodes, and twise yerely a swarme.

85. At Christmas take hede, if their hiues be to light:
take honey and water, together wel dight.
That mixed with strawes, in a dish in their hiues:
they drowne not, they fight not, thou sauest their lyues.

86. At midsommer downe with thy brimbles and brakes:
and after abrode, with thy forkes and thy rakes.
Set mowers a worke, while the meddowes be growne;
the lenger they stande, so much worse to be mowne.

87. Prouide of thine owne, to haue all thing at hande:
els worke and the workman, shall oftentimes stande.
Loue seldome to borow, that thinkest to saue;
who lendeth the one, will loke two thinges to haue.

88. Good husbandes that laye, to saue all thing vpright:
for Tumbrels and cartes, haue a shed redy dight.
A store house for trinkets kept close as a iayle:
that nothing be wanting, the worthe of a nayle.

89. Thy cartes would be searched, withoute and within;
well cloughted and greased, or hay time begin.
Thy hay being caried, though carters had sworne:
the cartes bottome borded, is sauing of corne.

¶ Julii.

90. Then muster thy folke, play the captaine thyselfe:
prouiding them weapon, and suche kinde of pelfe.
Get bottels and bagges, kepe the fielde in the heate:
the feare is not muche, but the daunger is great.

91. With tossing and raking, and setting on cox:
the grasse that was grene, is now hay for an ox.
That done, leaue the tieth, lode thy cart and awaye:
the battell is fought, thou hast gotten the daye.

92. Then doune with thy hedlondes, thy corne rounde about:
leaue neuer a dalop, vnmoune or had out.
Though grasse be but thinne, about barley and pease:
yet picked vp clene, it shall do thee good ease.

93. Thryfallowe betime, for destroing of weede:
least thistle and dock, fall a bloming and seede.
Such season may hap, it shall stande the vpon:
to till it againe, or the somer be gone.

94. And better thou warte, so to doe for thy hast:
then (hardnes) for slougth make thy lande to lie wast.
A redy good forehorse, is dainty to finde:
be hindred at first, and come alway behinde.

95. Thy houses and barnes, would be loked vpon:
and all thing amended, or haruest come on.
Thinges thus set in ordre, at quiet and rest:
thy haruest goeth forwarde and prospereth best.

96. Sainct James willeth husbandes, get reapers at hande:
the corne, being ripe doe but shead as it stande.
Be sauing and thankfull, for that god hath sent:
he sendeth it thee, for the selfe same entent.

97. Reape well, scatter not, gather cleane that is shorne:
binde fast, shock a pase, pay the tenth of thy corne.
Lode salfe, carry home, lose no time, being faier:
golfe iust, in the barne, it is out of dispaier.

98. This done, set the pore ouer all for to gleane:
and after thy cattel, to eate it vp cleane.
Then spare it for pasture, till rowen be past:
to lengthen thy dayrey, no better thou hast.

99. Then welcome thy haruest folke, seruauntes and all:
with mirth and good chere, let them furnish thine hall.
The haruest lorde nightly, must geue the a song:
fill him then the blacke boll, or els he hath wrong.

100. Thy haruest thus ended, in myrth and in ioye:
please euery one gently, man woman and boye.
Thus doing, with alway, such helpe as they can:
thou winnest the name, of a right husband man.

Finis.

Nowe thinke vpon god, let thy tonge neuer cease:
from thanking of him, for his myghty encrease.
Accept my good wil, finde no fault tyll thou trye:
the better thou thryuest, the gladder am I.

¶ *A sonet or brief rehersall of the properties of the twelue monethes afore rehersed.*

As Janeuer fryse pot, bidth corne kepe hym lowe:
And feuerell fill dyke, doth good with his snowe:
A bushel of Marche dust, worth raunsomes of gold
And Aprill his stormes, be to good to be solde:
As May with his flowers, geue ladies their lust:
And June after blooming, set carnels so iust:
As July bid all thing, in order to ripe:
And August bid reapers, to take full their gripe.
September his fruit, biddeth gather as fast:
October bid hogges, to come eate vp his mast:
As dirtie Nouember, bid threshe at thine ease:

December bid Christmas, to spende what he please:
So wisdom bid kepe, and prouide while we may:
For age crepeth on as the time passeth away.

Finis.

Thinges thriftie, that teacheth the thriuing to thriue;
teache timely to trauas, the thing that thou triue.
Transferring thy toyle, to the times truely tought:
that teacheth the temperaunce, to temper thy thought.
To temper thy trauaile, to tarrye the tide:
this teacheth the thriftines, twenty times tride.
Thinke truely to trauaile, that thinkest to thee:
the trade that thy teacher taught truely to the.
Take thankfully thinges, thanking tenderly those:
that teacheth thee thriftly, thy time to transpose.
The trouth teached two times, teache thou two times ten:
this trade thou that takest, take thrift to the then.

¶ Imprinted at London in flete strete
within Temple barre, at the sygne of the
hand and starre, by Richard Tottel,
the third day of February, An. 1557.
*Cum priuilegio ad impri-
mendum solum.*

NOTES AND ILLUSTRATIONS.

*** *With the exception of the first five Notes, the references are to Chapters and Stanzas; thus* "**1.** 1." *means Chapter* I. *Stanza* 1.

(Notes signed M. are from Dr. Mavor's edition of 1812, and those signed T. R. are from Hilman's *Tusser Redivivus*, 1710.)

Page 2, stanza 1. "Er in aught be begun;" that is, before a beginning be made in anything, the verb being used impersonally.

2. The directions which are stated briefly in the Abstract will be found in the Month's Husbandry in the stanza bearing the same number.

3. "Pilcrowe," the mark of a new paragraph in printing (¶). A corruption of *paragraph*, through *parcraft*, *pilcraft*, to *pilcrow*. "Paragrapha, *pylcraft* in wrytynge."—Medulla Gramm. "*Paragraphus, Anglice* a pargrafte in wrytynge."—Ortus. "Paragraphe or *Pillcrow*, a full sentence, head or title."—Cotgrave. "A *Pilkcrow*, vide Paragraph."—Gouldman.

Page 3, col. 2, line 2 from bottom. "Crosserowe." "Shee that knowes where Christes crosse stands, will neuer forget where great A dwells."—Tom Tell-Trothe's New Year's Gift (New Shakspere Soc. ed. Furnivall), p. 33. "The Christs-crosse-row or Hornebooke, wherein a child learnes it."—Cotgrave. The alphabet was called the *Christ-cross-row*, some say because a cross was prefixed to the alphabet in the old primers; but as probably from a superstitious custom of writing the alphabet in the form of a cross as a charm. This was even solemnly practised by the Bishop in the consecration of a church. See Picart's Relig. Ceremonies, vol. i. p. 131.—Nares.

Page 4, col. 2, line 45. "A medicine for the cowlaske." In Sloane MS. 1585, f. 152, will be found a recipe for the cure of diarrhœa, the components of which appear to be the yolk of a new-laid egg, honey, and fine salt.

1. 1. In the edition of 1557, the first stanza of the Epistle reads somewhat differently; see p. 220.

1. 1. "Time trieth the troth," in Latin "Veritas temporis filia," occurs in Tottel's Miscellany, 1557, repr. 1867, p. 221.—Hazlitt's English Proverbs.

1. 2. "Vnlesse mischance mischanceth me"=unless fortune is unkind to me. "Remaine abrode for euermore," *i.e.* be given to the writings of others.

It is noticeable that though in the Author's Epistle he spells his name, most probably for convenience sake, as Tuss*a*r, he on all other occasions spells it Tuss*e*r, which is no doubt correct. In the edition of 1557 the name is spelt correctly, although the corresponding line of the stanza commences with the letter *a*. See p. 220.

2. 6. "Like Iugurth, Prince of Numid." Jugurtha, an illegitimate son of Mastanabal, after the death of Micipsa murdered his two sons and seized on the sovereignty of Numidia. War was declared against him by the Romans, and after some time Metellus drove him to such extremes that he was obliged to take refuge with his father-in-law, Bocchus, by whom he was given up to Marius, was carried in triumph to Rome, and finally starved to death. The history of the war against him is related in Sallust's *Bellum Jugurthinum.*

"With losses so perfumid;" *i.e.* pervaded, thoroughly imbued; we use *imbued* nearly in the same way.

2. 7. Harrison, in his Description of England (E.E.T. Soc. ed. Furnivall, part i. p. 241), gives a very bad character to the landlords of his day: "What stocke of monie soeuer he [the farmer] gathereth and laieth vp in all his yeares, it is often seene, that the landlord will take such order with him for the same, when he renueth his lease, which is commonlie eight or six yeares before the old be expired (sith it is now growen almost to a custome, that if he come not to his lord so long before, another shall step in for a reuersion, and so defeat him out right) that it shall neuer trouble him more than the haire of his beard, when the barber hath washed and shaued it from his skin. And as they commend these, so (beside the decaie of house-keeping whereby the poore haue beene relieued) they speake also of three things that are growen to be verie grieuous vnto them, to wit, the inhansing of rents, latelie mentioned; the dailie oppression of copiholders, whose lords seeke to bring their poore tenants almost into plaine seruitude and miserie, dailie deuising new meanes, and seeking vp all the old, how to cut them shorter and shorter, *doubling, trebling, and now and then seuen times increasing their fines;* driuing them also for euerie trifle to loose and forfeit their tenures, (by whom the greatest part of the realme dooth stand and is mainteined,) to the end they may fleece them yet more." See also Norden's Surveyor's Dialogue, ed. 1607, p. 51.

The following curious prayer is in Edward the Sixth's Liturgies:—"The earth is Thine, O Lord, and all that is contained therein, notwithstanding Thou hast given possession of it to the children of men, to pass over the time of their short pilgrimage in this vale of misery. We heartily pray Thee to send Thy Holy Spirit into the hearts of those that possess the grounds, pastures, and dwelling-places of the earth, that they, remembering themselves to be Thy tenants, may not rack nor stretch out the rents of their houses and lands, nor yet take unreasonable fines and incomes after the manner of covetous worldlings, but so let them out to others, that the inhabitants thereof may both be able to pay the rents, and also honestly to live and nourish their families, and relieve the poor. Give them grace also to consider that they are but strangers and pilgrims in this world, having here no dwelling-place, but seeking one to come; that they, remembering the short continuance of their life, may be contented with that which is sufficient, and not join house to house and land to land, to the impoverishment of others; but so behave themselves in letting out their lands, tenements, and pastures, that after this life they may be received into everlasting dwelling-places, through, etc."

"Fleeces"=fleecings, frauds, impositions. It *may*, perhaps, be used literally, of selling wool at a loss.

2. 8. "Ictus sapit." This corresponds to our proverb, "The burnt child dreads the fire," or perhaps more nearly to "Once bit, twice shy." In the "Proverbs of Hendyng" we find it as: "The burnt child fire dreadeth, quoth Hendyng." Ray, in his "Collection of Proverbs," edit. 1737, says: "Piscator ictus sapit; struck by the scorpion fish, or pastinaca, whose prickles are esteemed venomous."

3. 4. If Tusser is here writing literally, the price of his book, in "the golden days of good Queen Bess," was only a groat or two at the utmost.—M.

3. 7. "Shere"=shire; the construction is—don't think that *every* bit of land (or county) can profit by following my directions, for soils differ. Compare chapter 19, stanza 8, p. 48.

4. 1. "Must keepe such coile;" must bustle about, exert themselves. Cf. Scott's "Lord of the Isles," canto v. stanza 1: "For wake where'er he may, man wakes to care and *coil*." And Shakspere: "I pray you watch about Signor Leonata's door; for the wedding being there to-morrow, there is a great *coil* to-night."

5. 1. In the edition of 1570 the first stanza of the "Preface to the Buier" reads as follows:

> "What lookest thou herein to haue?
> Trim verses thy fansie to please?
> Of Surry so famous that craue,
> Looke nothing but rudenes in these."

The reference in the third line being to Henry Howard, Earl of Surrey, author of the Translation of the second and fourth Books of the Æneid of Virgil, and of numerous other poems, who was executed in 1547. In the footnote to this Preface it is stated that the metre is peculiar to Shenstone, but this is incorrect, as it is also used by Prior: "Despairing beside a clear stream."

7. line 5. "The sea for my fish," *i.e.* for my fishpond.

9. 1. With "The Ladder to Thrift" we may compare the following "Maxims in *-ly*," from the Lansdowne MS. 762, f. 16*b* (see Babees Book, ed. Furnivall, p. 247):

"Aryse erly,
Serue God devowtely,
And the worlde besely,
Doo thy werk wisely,
Yeue thyne almes secretly,
Goo by the waye sadly,
Answer the people demuerly,
Goo to thy mete appetitely,
Sit therat discretely,
Of thy tunge be not to liberally,
Arise therfrom temperally,
Go to thy supper soberly,
And to thy bed merely,
Be in thyn Inne jocundely,
Please thy loue duely,
And slepe suerly."

9. 12. "Familie," here used in the sense of the Latin original *familia*=household, servants. Compare chap. 73, st. 13.

9. 29. Compare Shakspere, Richard II. Act ii. sc. 4, 24: "And crossly to the good all fortune goes."

9. 30, note. "To bridle wild otes fantasie," *i.e.* to restrain the excesses of youth.

10. 4. "Well to account of which honest is not;" never think highly of that which is not honourable, or honestly come by.

10. 5. Cf. Hebrews xiii. 4: "Marriage is honourable in all, and the bed undefiled." Tusser evidently does not appreciate "love in a cottage."

10. 8. "Giue ouer to sudgerne, that thinkest to thee;" *i.e.* make up your mind to settle down in one place and to give up roaming about, if you hope to prosper, lest the grumbling of your hosts and the wants of the nurses prove too expensive for you. Compare "The Dialogue of Wiving and Thriving," stanza 3, p. 152.

10. 10. Dr. Mavor suggests that the third line of this stanza should read: "Of tone *or* them both," "meaning, if we smell the savour of saving or winning or them both."

10. 11. A fool and his money are soon parted.

10. 12. "Good bargaine a dooing," etc. When you have a chance of making a good bargain, don't let every one know; but when you want to sell anything, then let it be published abroad as widely as possible. In the first case don't hesitate or haggle about it, but "take the ball on the hop;" in the second, don't be in a hurry to take the first offer, if you are not ashamed of what you wish to sell.

10. 14. "Of the complaint of such poore tenants as paie *rent corne* vnto their landlords, I speake not, who are often dealt withall very hardlie. For beside that in the measuring of ten quarters, for the most part they lose one through the iniquitie of the bushell (such is the greedinesse of the appointed receiuers thereof), fault is found also with the goodnesse and cleannesse of the graine. Wherby some peece of monie must needs passe vnto their purses to stop their mouths withall, or else my lord will not like of the corne: 'Thou are worthie to loose thy lease, etc.' Or if it be cheaper in the market, than the rate allowed for it is in their rents, then must they paie monie, and no corne, which is no small extremitie."—Harrison, part i. p. 301.

10. 15. "In this quatrain all the later editions of our author read uniformly *misers* for *michers* (thieves or pilferers). What kind of *misers* 'unthriftiness' would make never seems to have been considered. 'Careless and rash' is a gallicism for carelessness and rashness."—M. "Mychare, *capax*, *cleps*, *furunculus*."—Prompt. Parv.

"*Mychers*, hedge crepers, fylloks and lushes,
That all the somer kepe dyches and bushes."—The Hyeway to the Spytell House, ed. Atterson, ii. 11. See also Townley Mysteries, pp. 216, 308. "*Caqueraffe*, a base *micher*, scurvie hagler, lowsie dodger, etc. *Caqueduc*, a niggard, *micher*, etc."—Cotgrave.

10. 17. "Make hunger thy sauce." This is the proverb "hunger is the best sauce," which is reckoned amongst the aphorisms of Socrates: "Optimum cibi condimentum fames, sitis potus."—Cicero, De Finibus, Bk. II.

10. 19. "Mastive, *Bandog*, *Molossus*."—Baret's Alvearie, 1580. "The tie-dog or band-dog, so called bicause manie of them are tied up in chaines and strong bonds, in the daie time, for dooing hurt abroad, which is an huge dog, stubborne, ouglie, eager, burthenous of bodie (and therefore but of little swiftnesse), terrible and fearfull to behold, and oftentimes more fierce and fell than anie Archadian or Corsican cur. . . . . They take also their name of the word 'mase' and 'theefe' (or 'master theefe' if you will), bicause they often stound and put such persons to their shifts in townes and villages, and are the principall causes of their apprehension and taking."—Harrison, Descrip. of England, part ii. pp. 44–5. "We han great *Bandogs* will teare their skins."—Spenser, Shep. Cal. September.

10. 20. "The credite of maister," etc. If servants are allowed the credit or trust, which should only be allowed to their master and mistress, much trouble will be the result.

10. 21. "Be to count ye wote what," that is, nothing to signify, of little importance.

10. 22. "So, twentie lode bushes," etc. So, without proper management, twenty loads of bushes may be so wasted as only to serve for the stopping of a single gap.

"A"=one, a single: a very common use in Early English; cf. William of Nassington's "Myrrour of Lyfe," lines 2, 3;

"Fader and Sonne and Haly Gaste
That er *a* God als we trowe maste"—that is, *one* God.

10. 24. Some, upon Sundays, have their tables covered with smoking dishes, and then have to seek, *i.e.* do without dinners for the rest of the week.

10. 28. "Skarborow warning." Grose says it means, "A word and a blow and the blow first." R. J. S. in Notes and Queries, 1st Ser. i. 170, adds that it is a common proverb in Yorkshire. Fuller states that the saying arose from "Thomas Stafford, who in the reign of Mary, A.D. 1557, with a small company, seized on Scarborough Castle, and before the townspeople had the least notice of their approach." Another explanation is that, if ships passed the castle without saluting it, a shotted gun was fired at them. In a ballad by Heywood another derivation is given:

"This term *Scarborow warning* grew (some say)
By hasty hanging for rank robbery theare.
Who that was met, but suspect in that way,
Strait he was trust up, whatever he were."

This implies that Scarborough imitated the Halifax gibbet law.—N. & Q. 1st Ser. i. 138. In a letter by Toby Matthew, Bishop of Durham, to the Archbishop of York, Jan. 19, 1603, he writes: "When I was in the midst of this discourse I received a message from my Lord Chamberlain that it was his Majesty's pleasure that I should preach before him on Sunday next, which *Scarborough warning* did not only perplex me, but so puzzel me as no mervail if somewhat be prætermitted, which otherwise I might have better remembered."—N. & Q. 4th Ser. xii. 408. "*Scarborough warning.* The antiquity of the phrase is shown by its occurrence in Puttenham's 'Arte of English Poetrie,' ed. 1589. The following is the passage, from p. 199 of Arber's reprint: [We have] 'many such prouerbiall speeches: as, *Totnesse is turned French*, for a strange alteration: *Skarborow warning*, for a sodaine commandement, allowing no respect or delay to bethinke a man of his busines.'"—Note by Rev. W. Skeat. See also Ray's Proverbs.

10. 28. "Sir I arest yee;" that is, the Sheriff's officer, who, touching your arm, would use these words.

10. 29. "Legem pone," a curious old proverbial or cant term for *ready money*.

"There are so manie Danaes now a dayes,
That love for lucre, paine for gaine is sold;
No true affection can their fancie please,
Except it be a Iove, to raine downe gold
Into their laps, which they wyde open hold;
If *legem pone* comes, he is receav'd,
When *vix haud habes* is of hope bereav'd."—
The Affectionate Shepheard, 1594.

"But in this there is nothing to bee abated, all their speech is *legem pone*, or else with their ill custome they will detaine thee."—G. Minshul, Essays in Prison.

"*Oremus*," from Lat. *orare*=to beg, here means making excuses for non-payment of debts.

"*Præsta quæsumus*"=lend me, I pray. Compare *Preste*=a loan, *Pretoes*=loans, in Halliwell. A lender hates to hear a man say *Præsta*.

The word "collects" is used here in its original meaning of short prayers; thus the prayers before the Epistle and Gospel in the Prayer Book are called Collects, as containing briefly the lessons of the Epistle and Gospel.

10. 30. "Nor put to thy hand," etc.; that is, do not meddle in the business of other people, and be careful whom you assist, lest by being too free and generous you yourself may be put to inconvenience. Ray gives: "Put not thy hand between the bark and the tree," that is, do not meddle in family affairs.

10. 32. *et seq.* Tusser here, while acknowledging the necessity and advantages of the practice of "giving credit" in business, impresses strongly upon his readers the dishonesty and danger of promiscuous borrowing and lending, either to relations or friends, winding up with the advice never to trust a man who has once broken his engagements, without a surety, and never to lend a second time to a man who is angry with you for asking for payment of what he already owes.

10. 35. "The foole at the bottom, the wise at the brim;" referring to the proverb, "Better spare at brim than at bottom," that is, "Better be frugal in youth, than be reduced to the necessity of being saving in age." Ray also gives another proverb of a similar character, "'Tis too late to spare when the bottom is dry." "Sera in fundo parsimonia."—Seneca, Epist. i.

10. 36. "Felix quem faciunt aliena pericula cautum." Cf. Barbour's Bruce, ed. Skeat, p. 612.

10. 39. "Stands thee vpon." Compare Shakspere, King Richard II. Act ii. sc. 3, 138: "*It stands* your grace *upon* to do him right;" and, "*It stands* me much *upon*,
To stop all hopes whose growth may damage me."—Richard III. Act iv. sc. 2, 59.

10. 45. "Jankin and Jenikin" are only names for servants in general.

10. 46. "The proverb says, and who'd a proverb cross?
That stones, when rolling, gather little moss."—Vade Mecum for Malt Worms, 1720, p. 6 (part 2). See also Ray's Proverbs. Cf. "On the stone that styll doth turne about,
There groweth no mosse."—Sir T. Wiat, "How to use the Court," l. 4. A similar proverb occurs in Piers Plowman, A Text, Passus x. l. 101: "Selden moseth the marbel-ston that men ofte treden." Cf. also, "Syldon mossyth the stone þat oftyn

ys tornyd and wende."—"How the good wife taught her daughter," pr. in Q. Elizabeth's Achademy, ed. Furnivall, p. 39. In the Verses on Lord Burghley's Crest (printed in Thynne's Animaduersions, Chaucer Soc. ed. Furnivall), stanza 32, we read:

> "And prouerbe olde was not deuis'd in veyne,
> That 'roolinge stone doth neuer gather mosse';
> Who lightly leaves in myddest of all his peine,
> His former labor frustrates with his losse;
> But who continues as he did begynne,
> Withe equall course the pointed goale doth wynne."

See also chapt. 77. 20, p. 170.

10. 48. "Of all [the lawyers] that euer I knew in Essex, Denis and Mainford excelled, till John of Ludlow, alias Mason, came in place, vnto whome in comparison they two were but children: for this last in lesse than three or foure yeares, did bring one man (among manie else-where in other places) almost to extreame miserie (if beggerie be the vttermost) that before he had the shauing of his beard, was valued at two hundred pounds (I speake with the least) and finallie feeling that he had not sufficient wher-with to susteine himselfe and his familie, and also to satisfie that greedie rauenour, which still called vpon him for new fees, he went to bed, and within foure daies made an end of his wofull life, euen with care and pensiuenesse. After his death also he so handled his sonne, that there was neuer sheepe shorne in Maie, so neere clipped of his fleece present, as he was of manie to come: so that he was compelled to let awaie his land, bicause his cattell and stocke were consumed, and he no longer able to occupie the ground."—Harrison, Descript. of Eng. part i. pp. 206–7.

"Daw"=a chattering fool. See Peacock's Glossary (Eng. Dial. Soc.).

10. 49. From this stanza it would seem that sportsmen did not hesitate to trespass on the lands of others in former days any more than at present, but in such cases Tusser recommends the "mild answer which turneth away wrath," and sets out the advantages of courteousness and respect to one's superiors.

10. 51. "That flesh might be more plentifull and better cheaper, two daies in the weeke, that is Fryday and Saturday, are specially appointed to fish, and now of late yeares, by the prouidence of our prudent Princesse, Elizabeth, the Wednesday also is in a manner re-strained to the same order, not for any religion or holinesse sup-posed to be in the eating of fish rather than of flesh, but onely for the ciuill policie as I haue said. That as God hath created both for man's use, so both being used or refrained at certaine seasons, might by that entercourse be more abundant. And no doubt, if all daies appointed for that purpose were duly obserued, but that flesh and fish both would be much more plentifull, and beare lesse price than they doe. For accounting the Lent season, and all fasting daies in the yeare together with Wednesday and Friday and Saturday, you shall see that the one halfe of the yeare is ordeined to eate fish in."—Cogan's Haven of Health, ed. 1612, p. 138.

"It is lawfull for euerie man to feed vpon what soeuer he is able to purchase, except it be vpon those daies whereon eating of flesh is especiallie forbidden by the lawes of the realme, which order is taken onelie to the end our numbers of cattell may be the better increased, and that aboundance of fish which the sea yeeldeth, more generallie receiued. Beside this, there is great consideration had in making of this law for the preseruation of the nauie, and maintenance of conuenient numbers of sea faring men, both which would otherwise greatlie decaie, if some meanes were not found whereby they might be increased."—Harrison, Descript. of Eng. part i. p. 144.

The following menu for a fish day is given in the Liber Cure Cocorum, p. 54, ed. Morris:

"For a servise on fysshe day.

Fyrst white pese and porray þou take,
Cover þy white heryng for goddys sake;
þen cover red heryng, and set abufe,
And mustard on heghe, for goddys lufe;
þen cover salt salmon on hast,
Salt ele þer wyth on þis course last.
For þe secunde course, so god me glad,
Take ryse and fletande fignade,
þan salt fysshe and stok fysshe take þou schalle,
For last of þis course, so fayre me falle.
For þe iii cours sowpys done fyne,
And also lamprouns in galentyne,
Bakun turbut and sawmon ibake
Alle fresshe, and smalle fysshe þou take
þerwith, als trouȝte, sperlynges, and menwus with al,
And loches to horn sawce versance shal."

See also the Babees Book, ed. Furnivall, p. 50.

10. 60. "Setteth his soule vpon sixe or on seauen," that is, risks his life on the cast of a die.

11. "Sit downe Robin and rest thee." I was inclined to think that this was the burden of some ballad, but Mr. Chappell, to whom I applied, is of opinion that it was not.

"An habitation inforced," etc., *i.e.* it is better to settle down, even late in life, than not at all. Comp. chap. 10, stanza 8, p. 19.

12. 1. For a great portion of the year the only animal food eaten was in a salted state. In the autumn as much meat was cured as would last the winter; and until the pastures had been for some time abundant, that is, not until Midsummer, there were no means of fattening cattle. After the winter months, veal and bacon were welcomed as the precursors of fresh beef; and those who lived near the sea-coast enjoyed the addition of fresh fish; but the state of the roads prevented the inland parts of the country partaking of this benefit. The consumption of fish during Lent and on other fast-days, comprising a great part of the year, being expressly directed by statute, the people, even after the abolition of the old religion, provided themselves at several large fairs held almost expressly for the sale and distribution of salt-fish.

12. 3. "Veale and Bakon is the man," *i.e.* is the proper food, or is in season.

"Martilmas beef," beef killed at Martinmas, and dried for winter use. "Biefe salted, dried up in the chimney, Martlemas biefe."—Hollyband's Dict. 1593. See note to l. 383 of Wallace, in Specimens of Eng. Literature, ed. Skeat, p. 391.

"Beefe is a good meate for an Englysshe man, so be it the beest be yonge, and that it be not kowe-flesshe; for olde beefe and kowe-flesshe doth ingender melancolye and leporouse humoures. Yf it be moderatly powderyd, that the groose blode by salte may be exhaustyd, it doth make an Englysshe man stro*n*ge, the educacion of hym with it co*n*syderyd. Martylmas beef, whiche is called 'hanged beef' in the rofe of the smoky howse, is not laudable; it maye fyll the bely, and cause a man to drynke, but it is euyll for the stone, and euyll of dygestyon, and maketh no good iuce. If a man haue a peace hangynge by his syde, and another in his bely, that the whiche doth hange by the syde shall do hym more good, yf a showre of rayne do chaunse, than that the which is in his bely, the appetyde of mans sensualyte notwithstandynge."—Andrew Boorde's Dyetary, E. E. Text Soc. edit. F. J. Furnivall, chap. xvi.

"In a hole in the same Rock was three Barrels of nappy liquour; thither the Keeper brought a good Red-Deere Pye, cold Roast Mutton, and an excellent shooing-horn of hang'd *Martimas* Biefe."—1639, John Taylor, Part of this Summers Travels, p. 26.

"*Bacon* is good for carters, and plowe men, the which be euer labouryng in the earth or dunge; but and yf they haue the stone and vse to eate it, they shall synge 'wo be to the pye!' Wherefore I do say that coloppes and egges is as holsome for them as a talowe candell is good for a horse mouth, or a peece of powdred Beefe is good for a blere eyed mare."—A. Boorde, Regyment, fo. K iii. b.

"As for *bacon* it is in no wise commended as wholsome, especially for students, or such as haue feeble stomacks. But for labouring men it is conuenient according to that Latine prouerbe, grosse meate for grosse men."—Cogan's Haven of Health, p. 116.

12. 4. The farmers in old times were greater economists than now. "Old crones and such old things," it seems, fell commonly to their own share, while the best meat was probably sold.—M. Compare also 21. 1.

12. 5. "All Saints doe laie," etc. All Saints' Day expects or lays itself out for pork and souse, sprats and smelts for the household.

"When it [the bore] is killed, scalded, and cut out, of his former parts is our brawne made, the rest is nothing so fat, and therefore it beareth the name of sowse onelie, and is commonly reserved for the serving-man and hind, except it please the owner to have anie part ther of baked, which are then handed of custome after this manner. The hinder parts being cut off, they are first drawne with lard, and then sodden; being sodden, they are sowsed in claret wine and vineger a certeine space and afterward baked in pasties, and eaten of manie in steed of the wild bore, and trulie it is very good meat. The pestles[1] may be hanged up a while to drie before they be drawne with lard if you will, and thereby prove the better."—Harrison, Descrip. of Eng. part ii. p. 11.

"*Spurlings* are but broad *Sprats*, taken chiefly on our Northern coast; which being drest and pickled as Anchovaes be in Provence, rather surpass them than come behind them in taste and goodness. . . . . As for Red Sprats and *Spurlings*, I vouchsafe them not the name of any wholesome nourishment, or rather of no nourishment at all; commending them for nothing, but that they are bawdes to enforce appetite and serve well the poor man's turn to quench hunger."—Muffett, p. 169, quoted in The Babees Book, ed. Furnivall. "Smelt=Spirling or Sparling in Scotland, Salmo Sperlanus."—Yarrell, Names of British Fishes. "A Sperlynge, *ipimera, sperlingus*."—Catholicon Anglicum. See also Glossary to Specimens of Early Eng., ed. Morris and Skeat.

12. 6. "Embrings." Ember days or weeks, set apart for consecrating to God the four seasons of the year, and for imploring his blessing by fasting and prayer. They were settled by the Council of Placentia A.D. 1095.—M. *Embring* is a more correct form, being nearer to A.S. *ymbren*. A connexion with Ger. *quatember* is out of the question.

12. 7. See as to the law relating to fasting and fish days, the note on 10. 51.

13. 5. "It is an ill winde turnes none to good," *i.e.* turns to good for none.

"An yll wynd that blowth no man good,
The blower of whych blast is she;
The lyther lustes bred of her broode
Can no way brede good propertye."—Song against Idleness, by John Heywood, *circa* 1540.

"Ah! Sirra! it is an old proverb and a true
I sware by the roode!
It is an il wind that bloues no man to good."—Marriage of Wit and Wisdom, 1570. Quoted in Hazlitt's Handbook of Proverbs, p. 240.

[1] legs.

"Leaue anker in mud," *i.e.* drift, and break away from their anchorage.

14. 3. "If great she appereth," *i.e.* if seen through a dense atmosphere, which causes her to appear much larger, it is an indication of approaching rain. The reverse is the case when the atmosphere is rare, and the orb of the moon appears small.

14. 4. "Tyde flowing is feared," etc. "The Spaniards think that all who die of chronic diseases breathe their last during the ebb."—The Doctor, p. 207. Compare also in David Copperfield, "Mr. Barkis going out with the tide." Tusser, however, seems to mean that it was the flow and not the ebb which was dangerous to sick persons.

15. 8. "He that fast spendeth must need borrow,
But when he must pay again, then is all the sorrow."—
MS. of 15th cent. in Rel. Antiqua, vol. i. p. 316.

16. 1. September is the month when the annual labours of agriculture begin their round, and it is therefore, justly, put first in the Calendar of farming. Some, indeed, take their bargains from Lady-day; but this is by no means so convenient as Michaelmas.—M.

16. 2. The off-going tenant of champion or open field, as is still customary, allows the in-coming tenant to summer fallow that portion of the ground which is destined for wheat. But the occupier of woodland or inclosures holds the whole till the expiration of his term, unless certain stipulations are made by lease; and without a lease, neither the real interest of the tenant nor the landowner can be consulted.—M.

16. 3. "Buieng or selling of pig in a poke," *i.e.* making a blind bargain.

"A good cochnay coke,
Though ye loue not to bye the pyg in the poke,
Yet snatche ye at the poke, that the pyg is in,
Not for the poke, but the pyg good chepe to wyn."—Heywood's Dialogue (1546), ed. 1562, part ii. cap. 9. See also Hazlitt's Handbook of English Proverbs, p. 413.

17. 1. A *gofe* is a *mow* (rick); and the *gofe*-ladder is for the thresher to ascend and descend, in order to throw down the sheaves with the assistance of the *short pitch-fork*, while the *long* was probably for pitching the straw. The *straw-fork* and *rake* were to turn the straw from off the threshed corn, and the *fan* and *wing* to clean it. A *cartnave* might be required to stand on in this operation. A *casting shovel*, such as maltmen use, enables the farmer to select the best and heaviest grain for seed, as they always fly farthest if thrown with equal force.—M.

17. 3. A *skep* is a small basket or wooden vessel with a handle, to fetch corn in and for other purposes.—M.

17. 4. "*Aperne* is an old provincial pronunciation, adopted from a still older *napern* or *nappern;* and Halliwell observes, that *nappern* is still the pronunciation in the North of England. This word is interesting as illustrating two points: (1) the shifting of *r*, so that the various pronunciations of *apern* and *apron* correspond to the variations *brid* for *bird*, and *burd* for *bride;* and (2) the loss of the initial *n;* for *apron* is for Fr. *naperon*, a large napkin; see Roquefort and Wedgwood. *Naperon*, without *n* and *e*, is *apron;* without *n* and *o*, it is *apern*."—Rev. Walter W. Skeat in N. & Q. 1869.

"To make whyte lethyre. Take halfe an unce of whyte coperose and di. ȝ. of alome, and salle-peter the mowntance of the yolke of an egge, and yf thou wolle have thy skynne thykke, take of whetmele ij handfulle, and that is sufficient for a galone of water; and if thou wolle have thy skynne rynnyng, take of ry mele ij handfulle, and grynd alle thyes saltes smale, and caste hem into lewke warme water, and let heme melt togedyre, and so alle in ewene warme water put therein thy skynne. And if hit be a velome skynne, lett hit be thereinne ix days and ix nyȝtes . . . and if hit be a parchement skyne, let hit ly thereinne iv days and iv nyȝtes; . . . thanne take coperose of the whyttest the quantité of ij benys for j skynne and the yolke of j egge, and breke hit into a dysse, and than put water over the fyre, and put thereinne thy coperas, and than put thy yolke in thy skyne, and rub hit alle abowte, and thanne ley thy skynne in the seyde water, and let hit ly, ut dictum est."—From the Porkington MS. 15th cent.

17. 5. A Pannel and Ped have this difference, the one is much shorter than the other, and raised before and behind, and serves for small burdens; the other is longer and made for Burdens of Corn. These are fastened with a leathern Girt, called a Wantye. —T. R. Miss Mitford, in her "Recollections," writes that her father, who used to ride a favourite gentle blood-mare, had a *pad* constructed, perched and strapped upon which, and encircled by his arm, she used to accompany him.

17. 6. A cart or wagon whose wheels are hooped and clouted with iron is called in Lincoln a *shod-cart* or *shod-wain.* In the Paston Letters, ed. Gairdner, vol. ii. p. 245, we have "*clot shon*"=boots tipped with iron. "Clowte of a shoo, *pictasium.*"—Prompt. Parv. Cf. Milton, Comus, l. 634:

"The dull swain
Treads on it daily with his clouted shoon."

In Lancashire a "Clout-nail" is a large nail used for fixing iron *clouts* on the wooden axle-trees of carts.

17. 7. "Ten sacks," each holding a coome or four bushels, are only sufficient for a single load of wheat; but farms were not so large, nor the produce so great when Tusser wrote.

A *pulling hook* is a barbed iron for drawing firing from the wood stack.—M.

17. 9. "A nads"=an adze, an instance (like a nall=an awl, above) of the *n* of the article being joined to the following vowel.

Similarly we have "atte nale"=at the ale-house, a corruption of A.S. æt þan ale.—See Piers Plowman, ed. Skeat, B. Text, Prologue, l. 43. So in Sir Thomas More's Workes, 1557, p. 709, we have "A verye nodypoll *nydyote*" for *idiot*. Other instances of the prefixed *n* are "nonce, a nother, nagares (=augers)." Cf. "One axe, a bill, iiij *nagares*, ij hatchettes, an ades," etc.—Shakspereana Genealogica, 1869, p. 472.

"A Douercourt beetle" is explained by Dr. Mavor as "one that is large (like the rood of Dover once so celebrated) and capable of making a great noise," and he adds that "there is an old proverb 'A Dover Court: all speakers and no hearers.'" But this explanation is entirely erroneous: there is no reference whatever to *Dover*, but, as the following extract will show, a Dovercourt beetle simply means one made of the wood of the elms of Dovercourt in Essex, which were celebrated for their soundness and lasting qualities: "Of all the elms that euer I saw, those in the south side of *Douer court*, in Essex neere Harwich, are the most notable, for they growe, I meane, in crooked maner, that they are almost apt for nothing else but nauie timber, great ordinance, and *beetels;* and such thereto is their naturall qualitie, that being vsed in the said behalfe, they continue longer, and more long than anie the like trees in whatsoeuer parcell else of this land, without cuphar,[1] shaking or cleauing, as I find."—Harrison, Descr. of Eng. part i. p. 341.

17. 10. In the Hist. of Hawsted, Suffolk, by Sir J. Cullum, 2nd ed. p. 216, we are told that there, in the 14th century, oxen were as much used as horses; and, in ploughing heavy land, would go forward where horses would stop. "A horse kept for labour ought to have every night the 6th part of a bushel of oats; for an ox, 3½ measures of oats, 10 of which make a bushel, are sufficient for a week."

17. 11. "The ploughstaff is alluded to by Strutt (Manners and Customs, ii. 12): 'The ploughman yoketh oxen to the plough, and he holdeth the plough-stilt [*i.e.* principal hale or handle] in his left hand, and in his right hand the *ploughstaff* to break the clods.' See plate 32 (vol. i.) in Strutt, and the picture of a plough at work prefixed to Mr. Wright's edition of Piers the Plowman, copied from MS. T. [MS. R. 3. 14, Trin. Coll. Camb.]."—Piers Plowman, ed. Skeat, B. vi. 105.

17. 13. "Hoigh de la roy," that is, excellent or proper; but why, I cannot say.

17. 14. A *cradle* is a three-forked instrument of wood, on which the corn is caught as it falls from the scythe, and thus is laid in regular order. It is heavy to work with; but is extremely useful for cutting barley or oats, which are intended to be put into sheaves.—M.

17. 17. Tar was the common salve for all sores in cattle. "Two

[1] Cracking.

pounds of tar to a pound of pitch," is a good composition for sheep marks.—M. "Every shepherd used to carry a *tar-box*, called a *tarre-boyste* in the Chester Plays, p. 121, or a *terre-powghe* (=tar pouch) in P. Pl. Crede, l. 618. It held a salve containing tar which was used for anointing sores in sheep. Compare

"Heare is tarre in a potte
To heale from the rotte."—Chester Plays, p. 120.

See also History of Agriculture and Prices in England, by J. E. Thorold Rogers, vol. i. p. 31. Note to P. Plowman, ed. Skeat, C. x. 262–264.

17. 18. "Sealed and true," *i.e.* certified and stamped as correct. In Liber Albus, ed. Riley, p. 233, we read: "No brewster or taverner shall sell from henceforth by any measure but the gallon, pottle, and quart; and that these shall be *sealed* with the seal of the Alderman," etc. See also the Statute of Sealed Measures, *id.* p. 290.

16. 9. *Striking* is the last ploughing before the seed is committed to the ground; previously to which the ridges are to be harrowed.

16. 13. "Sowe barlie and dredge." In the 13th century the grain crops chiefly cultivated in England were wheat, "berecorn," *dragg*, or a mixture of vetches and oats, beans and pease. The regulations for the brewers of Paris in 1254 prescribe that they shall brew only "de grains, c'est à savoir d'orge de mestuel, et de *dragèe*." "*Dredge* mault, malt made of oats, mixed with barley malt, of which they make an excellent quick sort of drink."—Bp. Kennett's Gloss. "A mixture of oates and barley; and at present used very seldom in malting."—T. R. "*Dragée* aux chevaux, provender of divers sorts of pulse mixed together."—Cotgrave. From Way's Notes in Prompt. Parv. s. v. Dragge.

16. 14. **17.** 13. "Mother, moether." This word is derived by Sir H. Spelman from Danish *moer*=an unmarried girl. "*Puera*, a woman chylde, callyd in Cambrydgeshyre a *modder*." "*Pupa*, a yonge wenche, a gyrle, a *modder*."—Elyot's Lat. Dict. 1538. "*Fille*, a maid, girle, *modder*, lasse."—Cotgrave. Ben Jonson uses the word in his "Alchymist": "Away, you talk like a foolish *mauther*."—Act iv. sc. 7. Richard Brome also has it in the Eng. Moor, Act iii. sc. i.:

P. "I am a *mother*, that do want a service.
Qu. O, thou'rt a Norfolk woman (cry thee mercy,)
Where maids are *mothers*, and *mothers* are maids."

"I have been informed by an intelligent friend, who is a native of Norfolk, that on a certain trial in that county, it was asked who was the evidence of what had been stated. The answer was, 'A *mather* playing on a planchard.' The Judge was nonplussed, till the meaning was explained, namely, 'A girl playing on the floor.'"—M.

16. 14. Forby (Vocab. 1830) says: "Crow-keeper, a boy employed to scare crows from new sown land. Lear, in his madness, says: 'That fellow handles his bow like a crow-keeper.' Besides lustily whooping, he carries an old gun, from which he cracks a little powder, and sometimes puts in a few stones, but seldom hits, and still seldomer kills a crow." Cf. Romeo and Juliet, Act i. sc. 4: "Scaring the ladies like a crow-keeper."

16. 16. A Marsh Wall is a Sea bank, made with considerable slope to sea-ward, which is called a Break or Breck; it is faced with Turf which sometimes is worn by the sea, or Holes made in it by Crabs, etc. The Foreland is a piece of Land that lies from the foot of the Bank to Sea-ward, and must be well look'd after, that it wear not away or come too near the Bank (as the Workmen term it).—T. R.

16. 22. A brawner should be kept cool and hard, which encreaseth his shield, as the skin of the shoulder is called.—M.

16. 23. Measles in hogs are small round globules or pustules that lie along the muscles; and are occasioned by uncleanness and want of water.—M.

16. 24. The retting of hemp, as it is called, should be done with care. It should be taken out of the water as soon as it begins to swim. The smell left by hemp and flax is extremely unpleasant, as travellers in the flax districts of the North of Ireland well know.

16. 28. "In time of plenty of mast, our red and fallow deere will not let to participat thereof with our hogs, more than our nete: yea, our common pultrie also, if they may come vnto them. But as this abundance dooth prooue verie pernicious vnto the first, so the egs which these latter doo bring foorth (beside blackenesse in color and bitternesse of tast,) haue not seldome beene found to breed diuerse diseases vnto such persons as haue eaten of the same."—Harrison, Descrip. of Eng. part i. p. 339.

16. 31. If your dog sets chaunting (crying) these lawless hogs, haunting (or frequenting) your fields so often, he does you a benefit.

16. 34. *Shaken* timber is such as is full of clefts and cracks. *Bestowe* and *stick* it, is to lay the boards neatly on each other, with sticks between, to admit the air.

16. 37. The *hook and line* is a cord with a hook at its end to bind up anything with, and carry it away.—M.

18. 3. "Flaies," probably a misprint in the edition of 1580 for *flails*, which is the reading of the other editions.

18. 32. Cotgrave has: "Hastiveau, a *hasting* apple or peare;" and "Hastivel, as Hastiveau; or a soon-ripe apple, called the St. John's apple." Lacroix (Manners, Customs, etc., during the Middle Ages, p. 116) mentions "hastiveau, an early sort of pear."

18. 48. "Vergis and perie." "Verjuice is well known to be the juice of Crabs, but it is not so much taken notice of, that for strength and flavour it comes little short if not exceeds lime-juice." —T. R. "Verjuice, or green juice, which, with vinegar, formed the essential basis of sauces, and is now extracted from a species of green grape, which never ripens, was originally the juice of sorrel; another sort was extracted by pounding the green blades of wheat."—Lacroix, Manners, Customs and Dress, during the Middle Ages, p. 167.

18. 51. Make up your hedges with brambles and holly. "Set no bar"=put no limit, do not leave off planting quicksets while the months have an R in their names. See chap. 35, stanza 6, p. 77, and note to 19. 33.

19. 1. Laying up here signifies the first plowing, for Barley it is often plow'd, so as that a Ridge-balk in the middle is covered by two opposite furrows.—T. R.

19. 2. By Fallow is understood a Winter-fallow, or bringing Ground to a Barley Season.—T. R.

19. 9. "Brantham" parish, in Essex, in which Cattiwade is situated, and the place where Tusser first commenced farming. The average yield of corn in his time was, on each acre well tilled and dressed, twenty bushels of wheat, thirty-two of barley, and forty of oats and pulse.

19. 12. Wheat does not thrive well either on very poor or very rich land. If the land is *peeled* or poor, the grain is *burnt* or *steelie*, and if *proud* (too heavily manured), the grain is apt to run to straw.

19. 17. "There grows in several parts of Africa, Asia, and America, a kind of corn called Mays, and such as we commonly name *Turkey wheat*. They make bread of it, which is hard of digestion, heavy in the stomach, and does not agree with any but such as are of a robust and hail constitution."—A Treatise on Foods, by Mons. L. Lemery, London, 1704, p. 71.

19. 20. *Breadcorne* and *drinkcorn* mean wheat and barley, the first being used for the making of bread, the second for malting purposes. Mr. Peacock, in his Glossary of Manley, etc., has: "*Breadcorn*, corn to be ground into *breadmeal* (*i.e.* flour with only a portion of the bran taken out, from which brown bread is made); not to be used for finer purposes. It is a common custom of farmers, when they engage a bailiff, to give him a certain sum of money per annum, and to allow him also his *breadcorn* at 40*s.* per quarter." Cf. Piers Plowman, C. Text, Passus ix. 61: "A boussel of *bredcorne*."

19. 30. Hazlitt gives as a proverb: "To play the devil in the bulmong." An acre of bullimong land was worth 33*s.* 4*d.*; see 57. 39.

19. 33. According to Norden (Surveyor's Dialogue, 1607, p. 239) the best mode of making a quickset hedge is as follows: "The plants of whitethorne, mixed here and there with oke and ash"; if the plants are not easily procured, then "the berries of the white or hawthorne, acornes, ash keyes mixed together, and these wrought or wound up in a rope of straw, wil serve, but they will be somewhat longer in growing. Make a trench at the top or in the edge of the ditch, and lay into it some fat soyle, and then lay the rope all along the ditch, and cover it with good soile also, then cover it with the earth, and ever as any weedes or grasse begins to grow, pull it off and keepe it as cleane as may be from all hindrances, and when the seeds begin to come, keepe cattle from bruising them, and after some two or three yeares, cut the yong spring by the earth, and so will they branch and grow thick, and if occasion serve, cut them so again alwayes, preserving the oake and ashe to become trees." The best time to lay the berries in this manner is "in *September* or *October*, if the berries be fully ripe."

19. 34. A "porkling" was worth 28*d.* at the time. See 57. 39.

19. 37. With reference to the "daintiness" of the Flemings, many of whom were settled on the East coast, compare the following:

> "Now bere and *bacon* bene fro Pruse ibrought
> Into Flaundres, as loved and fere isoughte;
> Osmonde,[1] coppre, bowstaffes, stile,[2] and wex,
> Peltre-ware,[3] and grey, pych, terre, borde, and flex,
> And Coleyne threde, fustiane, and canvase,
> Corde, bokeram; of olde tyme thus it wase.
> But the *Flemmyngis*, amonge these thinges dere,
> In comen lowen[4] beste *bacon* and bere.
> Thus arre they hogges; and drynkyn wele ataunt;[5]
> Farewel, Flemynge! hay, harys, hay, avaunt!"—
>
> Wright's Political Songs, ii. 171.

19. 38. *Light fire*, as it is termed, is still used in Norfolk.—M.

19. 39. "Bowd eaten malt." "The more it be dried (yet must it be doone with soft fire) the sweeter and better the malt is, and the longer it will continue, whereas if it be not dried downe (as they call it), but slackelie handled, it will breed a kind of worme, called a *wiuell*, which groweth in the floure of the corne, and in processe of time will so eat out it selfe, that nothing shall remaine of the graine but euen the verie rind or huske." — Harrison, Description of England, part i. pp. 156–7. R. Holme says that "the Wievell eateth and devoureth corn in the garners; they are of some people called *bowds*."—Acad. of Arm. Bk. ii. p. 467. "Bruk is a maner of flye, short and brodissh, and in a sad husc, blak hed, in shap mykel toward a golde *bowde*, and mykhede[6] of twyis and þryis atte moste of a gold *bowde*, a chouere, oþer vulgal can y non þerfore."—Arundel MS. 42, f. 64. The name *gold bowde* probably denotes a species of *Chrysomela*, Linn. Way, in Prompt. Parv.

19. 40. See note on "A Medicine for the Cowlaske," p. 4. Sloes gently baked in an oven are best preserved. They are an

[1] A kind of iron. [2] Steel. [3] Hides.
[4] Love. [5] So much. [6] Size.

excellent and cheap remedy for laxity of the bowels, in men or cattle, if judiciously used.—M.

20. 2. Dr. Mavor suggests that as Tusser is pretty correct in his rhymes, he probably wrote *beasty* originally. In Pegge's Forme of Cury, 1780, p. 111, are given two recipes for the prevention of *Restyng* in Venisoun.

20. 16. "Stouer." *Stover* is the term now applied to the coarser hay made of clover and artificial grasses, which is kept for the winter feed of cattle. But in Shakespeare's time the artificial grasses were not known in England, and were not introduced till about the middle of the seventeenth century. In Cambridgeshire I am informed that hay made in this manner is not called "stover" till the seeds have been threshed out. In the sixteenth century the word was apparently used to denote any kind of winter fodder except grass hay. Compare

"Thy turfy mountains, where live nibbling sheep,
And flat meads thatch'd with *stover*, them to keep."—Shakspere, Tempest, Act iv. sc. 1; and Drayton, Polyolbion, xxv. 145,

"And others from their Carres, are busily about,
To draw out Sedge and Reed, for Thatch and *Stover* fit."

"Stover" is enumerated by Ray among the South- and East-Country words as used in Essex, and is to be found in Moor's Suffolk Words and Forby's Vocabulary of East Anglia.

21. 1. See note on 12. 4.

21. 3. In cleaning corn for *seed*, *casting* or throwing it with a *casting shovel* (see 17. 1) from one heap to another, in order to select the heaviest grains, which will always go farthest, is an excellent practice: but in *malting*, this is not necessary, as the light grains and seeds of weeds may be skimmed off in the cistern.—M.

21. 5. Wheat is well known to work better in grinding and baking after it has undergone a natural heat in the rick or mow. Wheat that is threshed early keeps with difficulty.—M.

21. 10. "Rauening curres" seem to have been as great a nuisance in Tusser's time as at present, in spite of what Dr. Mavor terms one of the "few patriotic taxes which we have to boast of."

21. 12. St. Edmund's Day (20th November) may probably be the proper time for planting garlic and beans; but why the moon should be "in the wane" we are not informed, though, according to Tusser, "thereon hangeth a thing." The moon was formerly supposed to extend her power over all nature, and not over the tides and weather only.

21. 13. The farmer who "looks to thrive" must "have an eye," not only to his barn, but also to the cruel habits or tricks of his servants; otherwise he may find his cattle maimed or otherwise injured, and his poultry made "to plaie tapple vp taile," a cant expression, meaning to tumble head over heels. Cf. the Scotch phrase, "coup your creels."

21. 15. The leathern bottle, from its size, must have been a most convenient vehicle for the removal of corn and other stolen property.

21. 22. Our author does not appear to have had any idea of the use of soot as a top-dressing to land, but its value is now well understood, as one of the greatest improvers of cold, mossy grass-lands.

21. 23. It is leanness and ill-dressing that occasion nits and lice, not the state of the weather when they are taken to house.

22. 25. l. 7. There is a mistake in the printing of this line: there should be no parenthesis, and the word *er* should be omitted. Thus the lines will read:

"Fat hog or ye kill it,
Or else ye doo spill it."

23. 4. The rack ought to be accessible on all sides, and perhaps high enough for small cattle to escape under it from their more powerful adversaries.—M.

"*Barth.*" Wedgwood includes this under *berth*, the seaman's term for snug anchorage for themselves or their vessels. See Glossary.

23. 7. Cf. "*A fires-bird*, for that she sat continually by the fire side."—Tom Tell-Trothe's New Yeare's Gift, New Shakspere Soc. ed. Furnivall, p. 12.

23. 9. "Beath." Bathing at the Fire, as it is commonly called, when the wood is yet unseasoned, sets it to what purpose you think fit.—T. R.

23. 24. "Camping." "Goals were pitched 150 or 200 yards apart, formed of the thrown-off clothes of the competitors." Each party had two goals 10 or 15 yards apart. The parties, 10 to 15 aside, stand in line facing their own goals and each other, at 10 yards distance, midway between the goals and nearest that of their adversaries. An indifferent spectator throws up the ball—the size of a cricket ball—midway between the confronted players, whose object is to seize and convey it between their own goals. The shock of the first onset to catch the falling ball is very great, and the player who seizes it speeds home pursued by his opponents, through whom he has to make his way, aided by the jostlings of his own sidesmen. If caught and held, or in imminent danger of it, he *throws* the ball, but must in no case *give* it, to a comrade, who, if it be not arrested in its course, or he be jostled away by his eager foes, catches it, and hurries home, winning the game or *snotch* if he contrive to *carry, not throw*, it between the goals. A holder of the ball caught with it in his possession loses a *snotch*. At the loss of each of these the game recommences after a breathing time. Seven or nine *snotches* are the game, and these it will sometimes take two or three hours to win. Sometimes a large football was used, and the game was then called "*kicking camp*," and if played with the shoes on, "*savage camp*."—Abridged from Major Moor's Description.

Ray says it prevailed, in his time, most in Norfolk, Suffolk, and Essex. It was new to Sir T. Browne on his settling in Norfolk, and is not mentioned by Strutt amongst the "Sports and Pastimes of the English People."

Mr. Spurdens, in his Supplement to Forby's Vocabulary, remarks: "The contests were not unfrequently fatal to many of the combatants. I have heard old persons speak of a celebrated *Camping*, Norfolk against Suffolk, on Diss Common, with 300 on each side. Before the ball was thrown up, the Norfolk men inquired tauntingly of the Suffolk men if they had brought their coffins. The Suffolk men after fourteen hours were the victors. Nine deaths were the result of the contest within a fortnight. These were called *fighting camps*, for much boxing was practised in them." Cf.

"This faire floure of womanheed
Hath two pappys also smalle,
Bolsteryd out of lenghth and breed,
Lyche a large *Campyng ball.*"—Lydgate.

Camping Land was a piece of ground set apart for the game. A field abutting on the churchyard at Swaffham was willed for the purpose by the Rector in 1472. At East Bilney and Stowmarket are pieces of ground still called *Camping land.* Sir John Cullum, in his "History of Hawstead, Suffolk," describes the *Camping-pightle* as mentioned A.D. 1466. "*Campar* or pleyar at foott balle, *campyon* or *champyon.*"—Prompt. Parv. "Camping is Foot Ball playing, at which they are very dextrous in Norfolk; and so many People running up and down a piece of ground, without doubt evens and saddens it, so that the Root of the Grass lies firm. . . . The trampling of so many People drives also the Mole away."—T. R.

25. 3. "All quickly forgot as a play on a stage." Comp. Shakspere, As you Like it, Act ii. sc. 7: "All the world's a stage," etc., and Merchant of Venice, Act i. sc. 1, where Antonio calls the world "A stage where every man must play a part." "Totus mundus agit histrionem," from a fragment of Petronius, is said to have been the motto on the Globe Theatre. Calderon wrote a play called El Teatro del Mundo (The Theatre of the World). It is remarkable for containing the lines:

"En el teatro del mundo
Todos son representantes," *i.e.* in the stage of the world all men are players.—W. W. S. In the old play of Damon and Pythias (Dodsley's Old Plays, ed. Hazlitt, iv. 31) the following occurs:

"Pythagoras said that this world was like a stage,
Where many play their parts: the lookers on, the sage
Philosophers are, said he, whose part is to learn
The manners of all nations, and the good from the bad to discern."

The same comparison occurs also in Don Quixote, part ii. cap. 12. See note to 60. 1.

26. 1. Psalm cxliv. 4.

26. 3. "Atrop." "The fatall sisters," Clotho, Lachesis, and Atropos, daughters of Erebus and the Night, were supposed to spin out the life of man as it were a long thread, which they drew out in length, till his fatal hour had arrived; but if by any other casualty his days were shortened, then *Atropos* was said to have cut the thread in two. Hence the old verse: "Clotho colum bajulat, Lachesis trahit, Atropos occat."

27. 4. "Euer among," an expression of frequent occurrence in Early English, meaning "constantly, continually." Compare the Mod. Eng. "all the while." In a Carol of the fifteenth century, we read:

> "Thys endus nyȝth
> I saw a syȝth,
> A stare as bryȝt as day;
> And *ever among*
> A mayden song
> Lullay, by by, lullay."

And in another:

> "Our der Lady she stod hym by,
> And wepe water ful bytterly,
> And terys of blod *ever among*."

28. 4. "As onely of whom our comfort is had." The expression is obscure, but the meaning is clear: as the only one from whom our comfort (or strength) is derived.

29. 2. "Good husbands," that is, good husbandmen or farmers.

29. 3. "Then lightly," an old form of expression. Tusser means that poor people are then *probably* or *generally* most sorely oppressed. Cf. "Short summer *lightly* has a forward spring."—Shakspere, Richard III. Act iii. sc. 1.

31. 3. "Few Capons are cut now except about Dorking in Surrey; they have been excluded by the turkey, a more magnificent, but perhaps not a better fowl."—Pegge's Forme of Cury, ed. 1780, p. 19.

32. 1. "Vpon the tune of King Salomon." Mar. 4, 1559, there is a receipt from Ralph Newberry for his licence for printing a ballad called "Kynge Saloman," Registr. Station. Comp. Lond. notat. A fol. 48a. Again in 1562, a licence to print "iij balletts, the one entituled 'Newes oute of Kent;' the other, a 'Newe ballat after the tune of Kynge Solomon;' and the third, 'Newes oute of Heaven and Hell.'"—*Ibid.* fol. 75a. Again, *ibid.* "Crestenmas Carowles auctorisshed by my lord of London." A ballad of Solomon and the Queen of Sheba is entered in 1567, *ibid.* fol. 166a.—Warton's Hist. of Eng. Poetry, ed. Hazlitt, vol. iii. p. 428.

32. 4, l. 7. There is some confusion here, although the sense is clear; probably we should read, "and *flies* from sinne," etc.

33. 32. "Michel cries," *i.e.* to delay the operation of cutting, and therefore the cries of the animals, till Michaelmas, will have the effect of getting them into such condition as better to please the butchers' eyes.

33. 36. "Bulchin," a double diminutive=*bull-ock-in*, cf. *man-ik-in*.

"For ten mark men sold a little *bulchin*;
Litille less men tolde a bouke of a motoun;
Men gaf fiveten schillynges for a goos or a hen."—R. de Brunne's Chronicle, ed. Hearne, i. 174. See also Langtoft, p. 174, and Middleton, iii. 524.

34. 2. "Apricot;" in Shakspere, and in other writers of that century, apricock; in older writers abricot and abrecocke; from L. *præcoqua* or *præcocia*=early, from the fruit having been considered to be an early peach. A passage in Pliny (Hist. Nat. xv. 12) explains its name: "Post autumnum maturescunt Persica, æstate *præcocia*, intra xxx annos reperta." Martial also refers to it in the following words:

"Vilia materius fueramus præcoqua ramis,
Nunc in adoptivis persica cara sumus."—Liber xiii. Ep. 46. The English, although they take their word from the French, at first restored the *k*, and afterwards adopted the French termination, *apricot*.—See a paper on the word in N. & Q. for November 23, 1850. "I account the *White peare-plum stocks* the best to *Inoculate Aprecock buds* upon, although they may be done upon other *Plum-stocks* with good successe, if they be good juycie stocks, able to give a good nourishment, for *Aprecock trees* require much nourishment."—Austen's Treatise on Fruit Trees, 1657, p. 57. Cotgrave (Fr. Dict.) gives, "Abricot: m. The Abricot, or Apricocke plum." Minsheu (Span. Dict. 1599) has, "Albarcoque, or Alvarcoque, m. an apricocke." Compare Midsummer Night's Dream, iii. 1. 169: "Feed him with apricocks and dewberries"; and Rich. II. Act iii. sc. 4, 29: "Go bind you up yon dangling apricocks."

34. 4. "Boollesse." In the Grete Herball *bolays*, in Prompt. Parv. *bolas*. Prunus communis, Huds.; var. insititia, L. In Bacon's Essays xlvi. the name is spelt "*bullises*."

34. 5. "Cheries." Austen, in his Treatise on Fruit Trees, Oxford, 1657, p. 56, enumerates the following kinds of cherries: "The *Flanders Cherry*, most generally planted, is a great bearing fruit. The *May Cherries* are tender, and the trees must be set in a warm place. The *Black-hart Cherry*, a very speciall fruit, and a great bearing fruit, and doubtlesse exceeding proper to presse for wine either to drink of itselfe, or to mix the juyce with *Cider* to give it a *colour* as *Clarret-wine*, it being of a deepe red, and a small quantity of it will colour a gallon of *Cider* or *White wine*. There is a *Cherry* we call the *great bearing Cherry* of M. Milleu. It may very well be called the *great bearer*, for the trees seldome fayle of great store of fruits, although in a cold and sharp spring."

34. 6. "Chestnuts." Often spelt, but improperly, *chesnut*, as though the *cheese*-like nut. From the O. Fr. *Chastaigne*, and the Ital. *Castagna*, we learn its true derivation, namely from *Castanea* in Thessaly, its native place.

34. 7. "Cornet plums."=cornel plums; called also cornel cherry. O. Fr. *cornille*, now *cornouille*, L. Lat. *cornolium*, from Lat. *cornus*=a cornel cherry tree.

34. 8. "The *Damasco-plum* is a good fruit and the trees beare well."—Austen's Treatise on Fruit Trees, 1657.

34. 9. Andrew Boorde, in his Introduction of Knowledge, ed. Furnivall, p. 283, says: "*Fylberdes* be better than hasell nuttes; yf they be newe, and taken from the tree, and the skyn or the pyth pulled of, they be nutrytyue, and doth increase fatnes."

34. 10. "Goose beries." Dr. R. A. Prior says: "From the Flemish *kroes* or *kruys berie*, Swed. *krusbär*, a word that bears the two meanings of 'cross-' and 'frizzle-berry,' but was given to this fruit with the first meaning, in reference to its triple spine, which not unfrequently presents the form of a cross. This equivocal word was misunderstood and taken in its other sense of 'frizzle-berry,' and translated into German and herbalist Latin as '*kraüsel-beere*,' and '*uva crispa*.' The Fr. *groseille* and Span. *grosella* are corruptions of Ger. *kraüsel*."

34. 11. "Some Authors affirme that there have been *Vine-yards* in England in former times, though they be all destroyed long since. Divers places retaine the name of Vine yards still, at *Bromwell Abby* in *Norfolke* and at Elie in Cambridgshiere which afforded *Wine;* what else is the meaning of these old Rimes?

> 'Quatuor sunt Elie, Lanterna, Capella Mariæ
> Et molendinum, nec non dans Vinea vinum.'

Englished thus:

> 'Foure things of Elie Towne much spoken are,
> The Leaden Lanthorn, Maries Chappell rare,
> The mighty Mil-hill in the Minstre field,
> And fruitful *Vine-yards* which sweet wine doe yeeld.'

And doubtlesse men might plant Vines with good successe, to make good wine even with us. There are many kinds of Vines, but I know none so good, and fit for our climate as the *Parsley Vine* or Canada Grape, we see by experience yearly it beares abundance of fruit unto perfection. And whosoever would plant Vines in England I think he cannot meet with a better kind than the *Parsley Vine* both for *bearing* and *goodnesse*. The *Fox grape* is a faire *large Fruit* and a very *great bearer* although not of so much esteem as divers others. The *Frantiniack Grape* is of great accompt with many, and is a speciall fruit where it comes to perfect ripenesse, which it hardly does, except the Vine be set upon the *South-wall* where it may have *much sun*. The *Red* and *White Muskadine Grape* are speciall fruits and beare very well, and come to perfect ripenesse if the Vine grow upon the *South-wall* or upon the *Easte-wall* which is best next. There is the *Curran Grape*, *Cluster Grape*, and many other kinds of good grapes, and the fruits are *better* or *worse* according to the *place* they grow in: If they have *much sun*, and be *well ordered*, the fruit will be *better* and *sooner ripe*."—Austen's Treatise of Fruit Trees, 1657.

34. 12. "There are very many kinds of *Plums*, many more than of Cherries. I esteeme the *Mustle Plum* one of the best, being a faire large black plum, and of an excellent rellish, and the *trees beare abundantly*. The Damazeene also is an excellent fruit. The *Violet* and *Premorden* Plum-trees are very *great bearing trees*, and the fruits pleasant and good. The *White Peare-plum-stocks* are accounted the best, and the *Damson-stocks* the worst for grafting upon."—*Ibid.* p. 57.

34. 13. "Hurtillberies (= Whortleberries) called 'Hurts' for shortness at Godalming. I suspect this may be connected with Hurtmoor, the name of a dale near Godalming."—Note by Rev. W. W. Skeat. "'Hurtilberries' for 'whortleberries,' itself a corruption for 'myrtleberries.'"—Dr. Prior, Popular Names of British Plants, 1870.

34. 14. "Medlars, called in Normandy and Anjou *meslier*, from Lat. *mespilus*, but as the verb *mesler* became in English *meddle*, so this fruit also, although a word of different origin, took a *d* for an *s* and became *medlar*."—*Ibid.*

"The Kernells [of medlers] bruised to dust, and drunk in liquor (especially where Parsly roots have been steeped), doe mightily drive out stones and gravell from the kidneyes."—Austen, Treatise on Fruit Trees, 1657, p. 84.

34. 15. "The *Juyce of Mulberries* is knowne by experience to be a good remedy for a sore mouth, or throat, such as are perfectly ripe relax the belly, but the unripe (especially dry'd) are said to bind exceedingly, and therefore are given to such as have *Lasks and Fluxes*."—*Ibid.* p. 84.

34. 16. "Peach, in old works spelt Peske, Peesk, Peshe, and Peche, O. Fr. *pesche*, L. *Persica*, formerly called *malum persicum* = Persian apple, from which the Arabs formed their name for it with the prefix *el* or *al*, and thence the Spanish *alberchigo*."—Dr. R. A. Prior.

Austen, in his work already quoted, says (p. 58): "Of *Peaches* there are divers kinds. I know by experience the *Nutmeg and Newington Peaches* to be excellent fruits, especially the *Nutmeg* Peach."

34. 18. Evidently a misprint for Peare-plums, which is the reading of all the later editions. Austen, in his Treatise on Fruit Trees, recommends that Peaches be grafted on plum stocks, such as the *White Peare-plum-stock*.

34. 19. The word "Quince" preserves only a single letter of its original form. A passage in the Romaunt of the Rose shows an early form of the word, and also exhibits *chestnut* and *cherry* in a transitional stage of adoption from the French. The author of the Romaunt writes :

> "And many homely trees there were,
> That peaches, *coines*, and apples bere ;
> Medlers, plummes, peeres, chesteines,
> Cherise, of which many one faine is."

It is evident that the English word is a corruption of the French *coing*, which we may trace through the Italian *cotogna* to Lat. *cotonium* or *cydonium malum*, the apple of Cydon, a town in Crete.—Taylor's Words and Places. In the Paston Letters, i. 245, occurs the word "chardequeyns," that is, a preserve made of quinces. See also the Babees Book, E.E.T. Soc. ed. Furnivall, p. 152. In the ordinances of the household of George, Duke of Clarence, p. 103, *charequynses* occur under the head of spices, their price being 5 shillings "the boke," or £2 10*s*. for 10 lbs., A.D. 1468.

34. 20. "Respis." In Turner's Herbal called *Raspis* or *Raspices*, the latter of which is apparently a double plural. Probably from *resp*, a word that in the Eastern counties means a shoot, a sucker, a young stem, and especially the fruit-bearing stem of raspberries (Forby). This name it may owe to the fact that the fruit grows on the young shoots of the previous year."

34. 21. "Reisons," most probably currants. "Raysouns of Coraunte."—Pegge's Forme of Cury, ed. 1780, p. 16.

34. 24. "Seruice trees." Dr. R. A. Prior, in his Popular Names of British Plants, 1870, p. 209, says: "Service-, or, as in Ph. Holland's Pliny more correctly spelt, Servise-tree, from L. *Cervisia*, its fruit having from ancient times been used for making a fermented liquor, a kind of beer:

> Et pocula læti
> Fermento atque acidis imitantur vitea *sorbis*.—Virg.

Georgics III. 379. Diefenbach remarks (Or. Eur. 102): 'bisweilen bedeutet cervisia einen nicht aus Getreide gebranten Trank;' and Evelyn tells us in his Sylva (ch. xv.), that 'ale and beer brewed with these berries, being ripe, is an incomparable drink.' The *Cerevisia* of the ancients was made from malt, and took its name, we are told by Isidore of Seville, from *Ceres, Cereris*, but this has come to be used in a secondary sense without regard to its etymological meaning, just as in *Balm-tea* we use *tea* in the sense of an infusion, without regard to its being properly the name of a different plant." Wild Service, the rowan tree ; *Pyrus aucuparia*, Gärt.

34. 25. "Wallnuts are usually eaten after meales to close up the stomach, and help digestion. And according to *Avicen* (Can. lib. 2, cap. 501), recentes sunt meliores stomacho (the newer the better for the stomach). Bread or Bisket may be made of the meale being dried. The young nuts peeled are preserved, and candied for Banquetting stuffe: and being ripe the Kernells may be crusted over with sugar, and kept long. *Avicen* says (Can. lib.

2, cap. 501): 'Iuglans ficubus et Rutâ medicina omnibus venenis': Wallnuts with Figs and Rue is a preservative against all poison. Schol. Salern. reckons *Wallnuts* for one of the six things that resist poyson: 'Allia, Nux, Ruta, Pyra, Raphanus cum Theriaca:

Hæc sunt Antidotum contra mortale venenum.'
Garlicke, Rue, Peares, Treacle and Nuts:
Take these and then no deadly poyson hurts.

Mithridates the great: his preservative was (as is recorded by Pliny, Nat. Hist. lib. 23, c. 18), '*Two Wallnuts*, two Figs, 20 leaves of Rue and a grain of salt stamped together,' which taken no poyson that day could hurt him. *Greene Wallnuts* about Midsommer distilled and drunk with vineger, are accounted a certain preservative against the Pestilence."—Austen's Treatise of Fruit Trees, 1657. "*Walnuts* be hurtful to the memory, and so are Onyons, because they annoy the eyes with dazeling dimnesse through a hoate vapour."—T. Newton, Touchstone, ed. 1581, f. 125*b*. The original prescription of the antidote of Mithridates, discovered by Pompey among the archives of the king, was very simple. Q. Serenus tells us that

"Magnus scrinia regis
Cum raperet victor, vilem deprehendit in illis
Synthesin, et vulgata satis medicamina risit:
Bis denum rutæ folium, salis et breve granum,
Juglandesque duas, terno cum corpore ficus."

Cf. Piers Plowman, C. Text, Pass. xiii. 143:

"As in a *walnote* withoute ys a byter barke,
And after þat biter barke be þe shele aweye,
Ys a curnel of comfort kynde to restorie." On which

see Mr. Skeat's note.

34. 26. "Warden appulles rosted, stued, or baken, be nutrytyue, and doth comfort the stomache, specyally yf they be eaten with comfettes."—Andrew Boorde's Dyetary, ed. Furnivall, E.E.T. Soc. p. 284. And again, *ibid.* p. 291, as a remedy for the Pestilence: "Let hym vse to eate stued or baken wardens, yf they can be goten; yf not, eate stued or baken peers, with comfettes: vse no grosse meates, but those the which be lyght of dygestyon."

35. 3. "Froth" refers here to veal and pig and lamb, all three. Halliwell suggests *tender* as the meaning. It seems to mean *pulpy* or *light*.

35. 4. "Be greedie in spending," that is, he who is eager to spend and careless in saving, will soon become a beggar, and he who is ready to kill, and unskilful in storing, need look for no plenty.

35. 5. There are certain wheels called Dredge Wheels, by the use of which loads may be carried thro' meadows, even if it be not a frost.—T. R.

35. 7. "Doue houses." The Norfolk and Suffolk rebels, under

Kett in 1549, say in their list of Grievances: "We p[r]ay that noman vnder the degre of a knyght or esquyer, kepe a *dowe-house*, except it hath byn of an ould au*n*chyent costome."—See Ballads from Manuscripts, ed. Furnivall, i. 149.

35. 9. "To buie at the stub," that is, to buy on the ground or on the spot, and do the carriage oneself. A.S. *styb*, Dutch *stobbe*= a stump; whence Eng. *stubborn*, *stubble*.

35. 13. "Edder and stake;" still in common use in Kent, Sussex, etc. See Ray's Glossary, s.v. Yeather.

35. 15. "So far as in lopping," etc., seems to imply that the tops will take root of themselves without planting.

35. 18. Spenser uses "Prime" in the sense of "Spring-time." See Fairy Queene, Canto ii. st. 40, iv. 17, and vi. 13.

35. 23. "Beliue"=in the night, according to Tusser Redivivus, but wrongly. See Mr. Skeat's note in Ray's Glossary, *s.v.* Beliue.

35. 25. Hugh Prowler is our Author's name for a night walker. —T. R.

35. 28. Harrison, ed. 1587, fo. 42, speaks of sheep, "such as bring foorth but one at a time," as *andlings*, from which it would seem that *twinlings* mean sheep such as *bring forth twins* and *not the twins* themselves. Dr. Mavor says: "Twin lambs are supposed to perpetuate their prolific quality, and are therefore kept for breeders." In some parts of Norfolk and Lincoln they will keep none but *twinlins*, but then it is in rich land as Mershland and Holland.—T. R.

"Peccantem" should be *peccavi*, which is the reading of the editions of 1573, 1585, and 1597.

35. 31. "For yoke or the paile:" whether intended for the yoke or for the dairy.

35. 34. The strongest pigs are observed to suck foremost, because there they find milk in the greatest abundance.—M.

35. 38. "Yoong fils." We should certainly read, as required by the rhythm of the line, *fillies*, which is found in the editions of 1573, 1577, and 1597.

35. 45. "As concerning *Arbors, Seats, etc., in Orchards and Gardens*, I advise men to make them of *Fruit trees*, rather then of *Privet*, or other rambling stuffe, which yeelds no profit, but only for shade. If you make them of *Cherry-trees*, *Plum-trees*, or the like, there will be the same advantage for *shade*, and all the *Fruits* superadded. All that can be objected is, that *Fruit-trees* are longer in growing up then *Privet*, *Virgine Bower*, or the like, whereof *arbors* are commonly made. It is answered. Though *Fruit-trees* are something longer in covering an *Arbor*, then some other things, yet they make sufficient amends in their *lasting and bearing fruits*."—Austen's Treatise of Fruit Trees, 1657, p. 61.

35. 46. Oats sown in January would be most likely to rise free from weeds, but it is not often that the season and the soil will admit of such early culture. The whole stanza is somewhat enigmatical. The earlier editions read uniformly: "by the hay," etc., but the more modern have: "buy thee hay," etc., which is probably the correct reading. The obvious meaning is, provide early what may be required, that you may escape risk of failure and dearth. If you buy your hay in May, you are prepared against the worst.

36. 25. *Plash* here means to pleach down a hedge over the burrows; *set* means plant over the place where the burrows are, not to stop the rabbits from coming out, but to give them a means of escape from the dogs who might otherwise *snap* them up before they reached their holes.

36. 26. A cage for moulting hawks was called a *mewe*. "For the better preservation of their health they strowed mint and sage about them; and for the speedier *mewing* of their feathers they gave them the slough of a snake, or a tortoise out of the shell, or a green lizard cut in pieces."—Aubrey's Wilts. MS. p. 341. Ducange (Glossary M. et I. Lat.) has "*Muta*, Accipitrum domuncula in qua includuntur falcones, cum plumas mutant; accipitres enim quotannis pennas mutant."

36. 31. "All's fish they get," etc. See Gascoyne's Steele Glass, Arber's Reprint, p. 57.

37. 1. "Feb. fill the dike." In Mr. Robinson's Whitby Glossary is given as a weather expression of Yorkshire: "February fill-dike, and March muck't out." Another form is in Hazlitt's Eng. Proverbs:

"February fill dike be it black or be it white:
But if it be white, it's better to like."

"Fevrier remplit les fosses: Mars les seche."—Fr. Provb.

37. 12. "Leaue iobbing," *i.e.* leave off jobbing, or pecking, with their beaks. See Prompt. Parv. p. 36. "Bollyn, or *jowin* wythe the bylle as byrdys (byllen or *iobbyn* as bryddys K. *iobbyn* with the byl H.P.). *Rostro*."

37. 13. See note to ch. 19, stanza 33.

37. 16. Moles, for the trapping of which each parish used to maintain a sapper and miner, are found to be excellent husbandmen, the little heaps of friable soil which they throw up furnishing, when spread abroad, the best of top dressings. "It may be novel to some to be informed that moles may be taken with dogs, properly trained. This may serve to diversify the life of a professed hunter." —M.

37. 18. As for *mole-hills* forming a warm and dry station for lambs, the same may be said with much greater propriety of *ant-hills;* yet neither would be suffered to remain on a well-managed farm.

37. 19. Lease, a small enclosure near the homestall.—M. A name used in some countries for a small piece of ground of 2 or 3 acres.—T. R.

37. 21. "Mestlen." "Years ago in Norfolk thousands of acres yeelded no better grain crop than rye, of which the bread of farm households was made. *Meslin* bread made of wheat and rye in equal quantity was for the master's table alone."—Forby. "And there at the manor of Marlingford, and at the mill loaded both carts with *Mestlyon* and Wheat."—Paston Letters, iii. p. 294. "For they were neither hogs nor devils, nor devilish hogs, nor hoggish devils, but a *mesling* of the two."—Fairfax. The mixed grain, meslin, was used in France in the concoction of beer, as appears by the regulations for the brewers of Paris, 1254, who were to use "*grains, c'est à savoir, d'orge, de* mestuel, *et de* dragée."—Reglements t. Louis IX. ed. Depping, p. 29. At a dinner given in 1561 to the Duke of Norfolk by the Mayor of Norwich, there were provided: "xvj loves white bread iv*d.*, xviij loves wheaten bread, ix*d.*, iij loves *mislin* bread iij*d.*"—Leland, Itin. vi. xvii. Plot (Hist. of Oxford, p. 242) says that the Oxfordshire land termed sour is good for wheat and "miscellan," namely wheat and rye mixed.

37. 22. It is to be regretted, both on the score of policy and health, that in reforming false principles, we renounced salutary practices. Days of abstinence from flesh-meat, if not prescribed by authority, should be voluntarily imposed on ourselves. If the fisherman purchases bread of the farmer, the farmer in his turn ought to encourage the fisherman, who in peace and war has the highest claims to support.—M.

39. 1. "Auens." "Avence herbe, Avancia, Sanamunda."—Prompt. Parv. By some called *harefoot.* It was used in cookery; see Pegge's Forme of Cury, ed. 1780, p. 13.

39. 2. "Betanie." Lat. *betonica*, said by Pliny to have been first called *Vettonica*, from the Vettones, a people of Spain.

39. 3. "Bleets." The name of some pot-herb which Evelyn in Acetaria takes to be the "Good Henry," and remarks of it that, "'tis insipid enough." Greek βλιτον=insipid. In Lyte's Dodoens, p. 547, are given three kinds of Blitte or Bleet, and the French name is said to be *Pourrée rouge.* "*Suæda maritima*, or sea-blite, belongs to the goose-foot tribe; the good-king-Henry, or *Chenopodium bonus-Henricus*, is of the same tribe. See Flowers of the Field, by C. A. Johns."—Note by Rev. W. W. Skeat.

39. 4. "Bloodwoort," called also Bloody-dock, from its red veins and stems. *Rumex sanguineus*, L. Called also *Walwort* and Danewort in Lyte's Dodoens, 1578, p. 380, who says that the "fumes of Walwort burned, drieth away Serpentes and other venemous beastes."

39. 5. "The rootes of Borage and *Buglosse* soden tender and made in a Succade, doth ingender good blode, and doth set a man in a temporaunce."—A. Boorde's Dyetary, E.E.T. Soc. ed. Furnivall, p. 278.

39. 6. "Burnet, a term formerly applied to a brown cloth, Fr. *brunette*, It. *brunetta*, and given to the plant so called from its brown flowers."—Dr. Prior, Popular Names of British Plants, 1870. Called also *Pimpinell.*—Lyte's Dodoens, 1578, p. 138.

39. 7. "Burrage." Fr. *bourache*, M. Lat. *borago*. Apuleius says that its original name was "*corrago*, quia cordis affectibus medetur," a word that the herbalists suppose to have become, by change of *c* to *b*, *borrago*. See A. Boorde's Dyetary, ed. Furnivall, pp. 278–280.

39. 9. "Clarie." M. Lat. *sclarea*, from *clarus*=clear, and prefix *ex*. Called by the apothecaries *clear-eye*, translated into *Oculus Christi*, *Godes-eie*, and *See-bright*, and eye-salves made of it. *Salvia Sclarea*, Linn. "Called in French *Ornale* or *Fonte-bonne;* it maketh men dronke and causeth headache, and therefore some Brewers do boyle it with their Bier in steede of Hoppes."—Lyte's Dodoens, ed. 1578, p. 253.

39. 10. "Coleworts." Dioscorides (quoted in Cogan's Haven of Health, p. 49) says (lib. 2, cap. 113) that "if they be eaten last after meats, they preserue the stomacke from surfetting, and the head from drunkennesse. Yea some write, that if one would drinke much wine for a wager, and not be drunke, but to haue also a good stomacke to meate, that he should eate before the banquet raw Cabage leaues with Vinegar so much as he list, and after the banquet to eate againe foure or fiue raw leaues, which practice is much vsed in Germanie. . . . The Vine and the Coleworts be so contrarie by nature that if you plant Coleworts neere to the rootes of the Vine, of it selfe it will flee from them. Therefore it is no maruaile if Colewortes be of such force against drunkennesse; But I trust no student will prooue this experiment, whether he may be drunken or not, if he eate Coleworte leaues before and after a feast."

39. 13. The numerous virtues of this herb are thus summed up in the King's Coll. MS. of the Promptorium:

"Bis duo dat maratrum, febres fugat atque venenum,
Et purgat stomacum, sic reddit lumen acutum."

Macer gives a detailed account, in which the following remarkable passages occur: "þe edderes wole ete fenel, when her yen dasnyþ, and so she getiþ ayene her clere sighte; and þer þoroghe it is founde and preved þat fenel doþ profit to mannis yene: þe yen þat ben dusked, and dasniþ, shul be anoynted with þe ius of fenelle rotis medeled with hony; and þis oynement shalle put a-way alle þe dasewenesse of hem, and make hem bryȝt." The virtue of fennel in restoring youth, was a discovery attributed by Macer to serpents; "þis prouiþ auctours and filisoferis, for serpentis whan men *(sic)* olde, and willeth to wexe stronge, myghty, and yongly a-yean, þei gon and eten ofte fenel, and þei become yongliche and myghty."—MS. in the possession of H. W. Diamond, Esq. This herb is called in German *Fenchel*, Dutch *Venckel*. In Piers Plowman mention occurs of: "A ferthyng worth of fynkel-sede for fastinge daies;" C. vii. 360; spelt *fenel* in the other texts. "Fenkylle or fenelle, *feniculum*."—Prompt. Parv. "Fenelle or fenkelle, *feniculum, maratrum*."—Catholicon Anglicum.

39. 16. "Andreas the Herborist writeth that the root of the Langdebeefe tyed or bounde to the diseased place, swageth the ache of the veynes (called *Varix*) being to muche opened or enlarged and fylled with grosse blood."—Lyte's Dodoens, 1578, p. 568. See also Gerard's Herbal, 1633.

39. 17. "Leek." A remnant of A.S. *porleac*, from Lat. *porrum* and *leac*=a plant, Ger. *lauch*.

39. 19. "Longwort," called in Lyte's Dodoens, p. 125, Sage of Jerusalem, "whiche herbe hath no particular vse in Physicke, but it is much vsed in Meates and Salades with egges, as is also Cowslippes and Prymeroses, whervnto in temperature it is much like." See also Gerard's Herbal, 1633, where it is called "Cowslips of Jerusalem."

39. 20. "Liuerwort," so called from the liver shape of the thallus, and its supposed effects in disease of the liver. O. L. Ger. *Steenleuerwuyt*. According to Lyte's Dodoens, p. 59, "a soueraigne medicine against the heate and inflammation of the Lyuer, and all hoate Feuers or Agues." *Anemone Hepatica*, Linn.

39. 21. "Marigolds are hote and dry, an herbe well knowen and as vsual in the kitchin as in the hal: the nature whereof is to open at the Sunne rising, and to close vp at the Sunne setting. It hath one good propertie and very profitable for Students, that is by the vse thereof the sight is sharpened. And againe the water distilled of Marigolds when it flowreth, doth help the rednesse and inflammation of the eyes if it be dropped into them, or if a linnen cloth wet in the water be laid upon them. Also the powder of Marigolds dried, being put into the hollownesse of the teeth, easeth toothach. And the juice of the herbe mingled with a little salt, and rubbed often times vpon Warts, at length weareth them away."—Cogan's Haven of Health, ch. 63. Called in the Grete Herbal *Mary Gowles*, a name that seems to have originated in the A.S. *merse-mear-gealla* =marsh-horse-gowl, the marsh marigold, or *caltha*, transferred to the exotic plant of our gardens and misunderstood as *Mary Gold*. It is often mentioned as *Gold* simply by our older poets:

"That she sprunge up out of the molde
Into a floure was named *golde*."—Gower, ed. 1554,

f. 120. "The yellow marigold, the sunne's own flower," says Heywood in Marriage Triumphe, and "so called," says Hyll (Art of Gard. ch. xxx.), "for that after the rising of the sun unto noon, this flower openeth larger and larger; but after the noontime unto the setting of the sun the flower closeth more and more, so that after the setting thereof it is wholly shut up."

"The marigold observes the sun,
More than my subjects me have done."—K. Charles I.

39. 22. "Mercurie." A name rather vaguely applied in old works, probably the "Good Henry, *Chenopodium Bonus Henricus*." Called also "Allgood," Dutch *algoede*, Ger. *allgut*, from Lat. *tota* *bona*, Cotgrave and Palsgrave *toutte bonne*, on account of its excellent qualities as a remedy and as an esculent; hence the proverb: "Be thou sick or whole, put *Mercury* in thy koale."—Cogan, Haven of Health, ch. 28. "The Barons Mercury, or male Phyllon dronken, causeth to engender male children, and the Mayden Mercurie, or gyrles Phyllon dronken, causeth to engender Gyrles or Daughters." —Lyte's Dodoens, p. 78.

39. 24. "Nep," common Cat-mint. "Dronken with honied water is good for them that haue fallen from a lofte, and haue some bruse or squat, and bursting, for it digesteth the congeled and clotted bloud, and is good for the payne of the bowels, the shortnesse of breath, the oppillation or stopping of the breast, and against the Jaundice."—Lyte, p. 148. See also Gerard's Herbal, 1633. "Nepe, herbe, *Coloquintida, cucurbita*."—Prompt Parv. "Neppe, an herbe, *herbe du chat*."—Palsgrave. Forby gives the Norfolk simile "as white as *nep*," in allusion to the white down which covers this plant.

39. 26. "Orach," *Atriplex hortensis*, or *sativa*, formerly *Arach*, Prompt. Parv. *Arage*, in MS. Harl. 979 *Arasches*, Fr. *arroche*, from Low Lat. *aurago* from *aurum*=gold, by the addition to it of *ago*=*wort*, as in plantago, lappago, etc. At the same time its use in the cure of jaundice, *aurugo*, may have fixed upon the plant the name of the disease.

> "*Atriplicem* tritam cum nitro, melle, et aceto,
> Dicunt appositam calidam sedare podagram:
> *Ictericis* dicitque Galenus tollere morbum
> Illius semen cum vino sæpius haustum."—Macer, cap.

xxviii. l. 7, quoted by Dr. Prior.

39. 27. "Patience," called in Lyte's Dodoens, p. 559, "Wild Docke," and stated to be a remedy for jaundice, the "bitinges and stinginges of Scorpions," and the tooth ache, and if "hanged about the necke it doth helpe the kinges euill or swelling in the throte."

39. 29. If the virtues of Penny Royal, as stated in Lyte's Dodoens, p. 232, be true, the use of it might now be advantageously adopted by the consumers of London drinking water. He says: "If at any time men be constrayned to drinke *corrupt, naughtie, stinking*, or salte water, throw Penny royall into it, or strow the pouder thereof into it, and it shall not hurte any bodie." It is sometimes called Pudding-grass, from its being used to make stuffings for meat, formerly called *puddings*. It is recommended by Andrew Boorde (Dyetary, ed. E.E.T. Soc. p. 281) as a remedy for melancholy, and to comfort the spirits of men.

39. 30. "Primerose," from *Pryme rolles*, the name it bears in old books and MSS. The Grete Herball, ch. cccl. says: "It is called *Pryme Rolles* of *pryme tyme*, because it beareth the first floure in *pryme tyme*." It is also so called in Frere Randolph's Catalogue.

Chaucer writes it in one word *primerole.* (See also MS. Addit. 11,307, f. 37:

> "He shal ben lyk the lytel bee
> That seketh the blosme on the tre,
> And souketh on the *prumorole.*")

Primerole is an abbreviation of Fr. *primeverole*, It. *primaverola*, dimin. of *prima vera*, from *fior di prima vera*=the first spring flower. Primerole, as an outlandish unintelligible word, was soon familiarized into *prime rolles*, and this into *primrose.* This is explained in popular works as meaning the first rose of the spring, a name that never could have been given to a plant that in form and colour is so unlike a rose. But the rightful claimant is, strange to say, the *daisy*, which in the South of Europe is a common and conspicuous flower in early spring, while the *primrose* is an extremely rare one, and it is the *daisy* that bears the name in all the old books. See Fuchs, Hist. Stirpium, 1542, p. 145, where there is an excellent figure of it, titled *primula veris*; and the Ortus Sanitatis, ed. Augsb. 1486, ch. cccxxxiii., where we have a very good woodcut of a daisy titled "masslieben, *Premula veris*, Latine." Brunfelsius, Novum Herbarium, ed. 1531, speaking of the Herba paralysis, the cowslip, says, p. 1590, expressly, "Sye würt von etlichen Doctores *Primula veris* genaunt, das doch falsch ist wann *Primula veris* ist matsomen oder zeitlosen." Brunschwygk (De Arte Distillandi, 1500, book ii. c. viii.) uses the same words. The Zeitlose is the daisy. Parkinson (Th. Bot. p. 531) assigns the name to both the daisy and the primrose. Matthioli (ed. Frankfort, 1586, p. 653) calls his Bellis Major "*Primo fiore maggiore*, seu *Fiore di prima vera*, nonnullis *Primula veris major*," and figures the moon-daisy. His Bellis minor, which seems to be our daisy, he calls "*Primo fiore minore*, *Fior di primavera*, Gallis *Marguerites*, Germanis *Masslieben*." At p. 883, he figures the cowslip, and calls that also "*Primula veris*, Italis *Fiore di primavera*, Gallis *primevere*."—Dr. Prior's Pop. Names of British Plants. "*Petie Mulleyn* (whiche we call *Cowslippe* and *Primerose*) is of two sortes. The smaller sorte, which we call Primerose, *Herbasculum minus*, is of diuers kindes, as yellow and greene, single and dubble."—Lyte's Dodoens, p. 122.

39. 32. "Rosemary," Lat. *rosmarinus*, sea-spray, from its usually growing on the sea-coast and its odour, is recommended by Lyte for fastening loose teeth. "Take of rewe a grete quantite, and sawge halfe als mekille, and *rosemaryne* the same quantitee."—MS. Linc. Med. f. 283. According to Andrew Boorde it is a remedy for "palses and for the fallynge syckenes, and for the cowghe, and good agaynst colde."

39. 34. "Safron," Sp. *azafran*, from Arabic *al zahafaran*. On the cultivation, etc., of Saffron in England, there is a long account in Harrison's Description of England, book iii. cap. 24. See note to 57. 3.

39. 37. "Spinage." "Called in Arabic *Hispanach*: 'Arabicæ factionis principes *Hispanach*, hoc est, Hispanicum olus nominant.'—Fuchs, Hist. Stirp. p. 668. Dodoens (bk. v. 1. 5) tells us, '*Spinachiam* nostra ætas appellat, nonnulli *spinacheum* olus. Ab Arabibus et Serapione *Hispanac* dicitur.' Brunfelsius (ed. 1531) says expressly at p. 16, 'Quæ vulgo *spinachia* hodie, Atriplex *Hispaniensis* dicta est quondam; eo quod ab Hispania primum allata est ad alias exteras nationes.' Tragus also calls it *Olus Hispanicum*; Cotgrave, *Herbe d'Espaigne*; and the modern Greeks σπαναχιον."—Dr. R. A. Prior.

39. 39. Lyte, p. 642, says: "*Cyues* or Rushe onions: this kinde of Leekes is called in English Cyues, and of Turner in Latine, *Cepa pallacana*, and in Greke Gethyun, which he Englisheth by al these names, a Cyue, a Civet, a Chyue, or *Sweth*."

39. 40. "Tanzie," Fr. *athanasie*, contracted to *tanacée* and *tanaisie*. Lyte says, p. 18, that it was sold in the shops under the name of *Athanasia*, the Greek word for immortality, and that it was so called, "quod non cito flos inarexat." A cake used to be made in which tansy was one of the ingredients, and which was called Tansay-Cake. The following recipe for it is given in MS. Sloane 1986, f. 100:

"Breke egges in bassyn, and swynge hem sone,
Do powder of peper therto anone,
Then grynde *tansay*, tho juse owte wrynge,
To blynde with tho egges, withowte lesynge.
In pan or skelet thou shalt hit frye,
In buttur well skymm et wyturly,
Or white grece thou may take therto,
Geder hit on acake, thenne hase thou do,
With platere of tre, and frye hit browne,
On brodeleches serve hit thou schalle,
With fraunche-mele[1] or other metis withalle."

In Halliwell's Dict. is also given a recipe for a dish called *Tansie*. Cogan, in his Haven of Health, p. 65, says: "It is much vsed among vs in England about Easter, with fried egs, not without good cause, to purge away the fleame engendred of fish in Lent season, whereof wormes are soone bred in them that be thereto disposed, though the common people vnderstand not the cause, why *Tansies* are more vsed after Lent, than at any other time of the yeare." "To prevent being Bug-bitten. Put a sprig or two of *Tansy* at the bed head, or as near the pillow as the smell may be agreeable."—T. Cosnett's Footman's Directory, p. 292. "For to dystroy a Wrang Nayle, othewyse callyd a Corne. Take wylde *tansey*, and grynde yt, and make yt neshe, and ley it therto, and it

[1] A dish composed chiefly of eggs and sheeps' fat.

wyl bryng yt owght."—Lambeth MS. 306, f. 65, quoted in Political, Relig. and Love Poems (E. E. Text Soc. ed. Furnivall), p. 36.

40. 3. "Blessed Thistle." "So worthily named for the singular vertues that it hath. . . . . . It sharpneth the wit and memorie, strengthneth all the principall parts of the bodie, quickneth all the senses, comforteth the stomacke, procureth appetite, and hath a speciall vertue against poyson, and preserueth from the Pestilence, and is excellent good against any kinde of Feuer, being vsed in this manner: Take a dramme of the powder, put it into a good draught of ale or wine, warme it and drink it a quarter of an hour before the fit doth come, then goe to bed, couer you well with clothes and procure sweate, which by the force of the herbe will easily come foorth, and so continue vntill the fit be past. . . . For which notable effects this herbe may worthily be called *Benedictus* or *Omnimorbia*, that is a salue for euery sore, not knowen to Physitians of old time, but lately reuealed by the speciall providence of Almighty God."—Cogan's Haven of Health, p. 545.

40. 10. "Purslane," in Turner's Herball *Purcellaine*, in the Grete Herball *Porcelayne*, in Dodoens *Purcelayne*. "It is good against St. Antonies fier, called *erysipelas*." — Lyte's Dodoens, p. 576. "Purslain in Latin is called *Portulaca*, *a portula*=a little gate, because they fancied it to be like one."—Lemery's Treatise on Foods, 1704, p. 92.

40. 12. "Rampions," Fr. *raiponce*, "a word mistaken as in the case of *cerise* and *pease*, for a plural, and the *m* inserted for euphony." —Dr. Prior, Popular Names of British Plants.

40. 13. "Men say that who so taketh the seede of Rockat before he be beaten or whipt, shalbe so hardened that he shall easily endure the payne, according as Plinie writeth."—Lyte's Dodoens, p. 622. What a pity Tusser did not know of this property of the Rocket! from his own account he had plenty of opportunities of testing it at Eton.

40. 14. "Sage causeth wemen to be fertill, wherefore in times past the people of Egypt, after a great mortalite and pestilence, constreyned their wemen to drinke the iuyce therof, to cause them the sooner to conceyue, and to bring foorth store of children."—Lyte's Dodoens, p. 252.

40. 6*. "Sampere is a weede growing neare the sea-side, and is very plentifull about the Ile of Man, from whence it is brought to diuers parts of England, preserved in Brine, and is no lesse wholesome than Capers."—Cogan's Haven of Health, p. 64. The Eng. Samphire is a corruption of the Fr. Herbe de *Saint Pierre*, from its growing on the rocks on the sea-shore. The leaves are used in the form of a pickle as an article of diet.

41. 2. "The *Ionians* had so much Veneration for them that they swore by *Cabbages*, and were therein as superstitious as the *Egyptians*, who gave divine Honours to *Leeks* and *Onions*, for the great Benefits which they said they received from them."—Lemery's "Treatise on Foods," 1704, p. 73.

41. 4. "Citrons," according to Lyte, p. 704, will cure "tremblynge of the hart and pensiue heavinesse, wamblynges, vomitinges, and lothsomnesse of the stomache." The citron was probably introduced into Europe with the orange by the Arab conquerors of Spain, and first received in England from that country. By a MS. in the Tower it appears that in 1290, 18 Edw. I., a large Spanish ship came to Portsmouth, and that from her cargo Queen Eleanor purchased Seville figs, dates, pomegranates, 15 *Citrons*, and 7 *poma de orenge*.—Way in Prompt. Parv.

42. 1. "The garden Basill is called in English *Basill Royall* or *Basill gentle*, and the smaller kinde is called *Bushse* (sic) *Basill*. The herbe brused with vineger and holden to the nose of suche as are faynt and falle*n* into a sound bringeth them againe to the*m*selues, and the seede therof giue*n* to be smelled upo*n* causeth the sternutation or niesing."—Lyte's Dodoens, p. 241. "One thing I read in Hollerius (Lib. i. cap. i.) of Basill, which is wonderfull. 'A certaine Italian, by often smelling to Basill, had a scorpion bred in his braine, and after vehement and long paines he died thereof.'"—Cogan's Haven of Health, p. 50. See also 51. 34.

42. 4. "Costmary, L. *Costus amarus*, Fr. *coste amere*, misunderstood as *Costus Mariæ*, an error that has very naturally arisen from this plant having been dedicated to St. Mary Magdalene, and called after her, *Maudlin*, either in allusion to her box of scented ointment, or to its use in the uterine affections over which she presided. In old authors it occurs as *Herba sanctæ* or *divæ Mariæ*." —Dr. R. Prior, Popular Names of Brit. Plants. Called also Alecost from its having formerly been esteemed an agreeable aromatic bitter, and much vsed for flavouring ale: "If you list to make a pleasant drinke, and comfortable to the stomache, put certaine handfuls of this herbe in the bottome of a vesselle, and tunne up new Ale vpon it."—Cogan, Haven of Health, ch. 69.

42. 5. "Paggles," spelt also Paigle, Pagle, Pagel, Peagle, Pegyll and Pygil, a name now confined to the Eastern Counties, and generally assigned to the Cowslip, but by Ray and Moor to the *Ranunculus bulbosus*. The derivation is uncertain. "Blake (yellow) as a paigle."—Ray. In Suffolk the name is applied to the Crowfoot, the *Cuckoo-flower*.

42. 8. "Our common germander or thistle benet is found and knowne to bee so wholesome and of so great power in medicine, as anie other hearbe, if they be vsed accordinglie."—Harrison, Descript. of Eng., ed. Furnivall, pt. i. p. 326. "The iuyce of the leaues mengled with oyle, and straked vpon the eyes, driueth away the white cloude, called the Hawe or Pearle in the eye, and all manner dimness of the same."—Lyte's Dodoens, p. 25.

42. 12. "That which is commonly called Sothernewood is the male kinde of this herbe, and that which we doe call *Lauender-cotten* is the female, named in Latine *Cypressus* or *Santolina*. The setting of *Lauender-cotten* within the house in floure pots must needes be very wholesome, for it driveth away venemous wormes, both by strawing, and by the sauour of it, and being drunke in wine it is a remedie against poyson."—Cogan's Haven of Health, p. 56.

42. 14. "Mawdelin," spelt also *Maudlin*, *Mawdeleyn* and *Maudeline*, appears to have derived its name similarly to *Costmary*, q.v., and to have been applied to the same uses.

43. 1. "Baies," Bays, from French *baie*, which is formed from Lat. *bacca*=a berry. In old writers *bay* is used for a *berry* generally, as "the bayes of ivyne," but in time the term came to be applied to the berries of the *sweet bay*, called by Virgil *lauri baccas*, from their being an article of commerce; from the berry the term was extended to the tree itself.

43. 2. "Bachelor's Buttons." So called, according to Johnson's Gerarde, p. 472, "from their similitude to the jagged cloathe buttons anciently worne in this kingdom," but according to others from "a habit of country fellows to carry them in their pockets to divine their success with their sweethearts." Called by Lyte (Dodoens, p. 421), *Goldcup* or *Gold knoppe*, and described as a double variety of the flower now known so well as the Butterflower, or Buttercup, the Fr. *bouton d'or*.

43. 4. "Columbine," called Colourbine in Lincoln, *Aquilegia vulgaris*, used for making stuffed chine.

43. 7. "Daffadowndilly, Daffodilly, Affodilly, and Daffodil, Lat. *asphodelus*, from which was formed *Affodilly*, the name of it in all the older writers, but subsequently confused with that of another flower, the so-called *sapharoun* or saffron *lily*:

'The thyrde *lylye* ȝyt there ys,
That ys called felde lylye, y wys,
Hys levys be lyke to *sapharoun*,
Men know yt therby many one.'—MS. Sloane, 1571.

With the taste for alliteration that is shown in popular names, the *Sapharoun-lily*, upon blending with *affodilly*, became, by a sort of mutual compromise, *daffadowndilly*, whence our *daffodilly* and *daffodil*."—Dr. R. A. Prior, Popular Names of British Plants. "Strew me the ground with daffadowndillies."—Spenser, Shep. Cal. 140.

43. 8. "Eglantine," a word of doubtful origin. Chaucer writes it *eglatere* and *eglentere*. Fr. *aiglantier*, Prov. *aiglentina*=wild rose. Diez derives it from Lat. *aculeus*=a prickle, through the adj. *aculentus*.

43. 9. Feverfew (*Pyrethrum parthenium*), a genus of Composite plants, common in our gardens, and deriving its name from having long been employed as a popular remedy in ague and other fevers, and as an emmenagogue. It appears to possess stimulant and tonic properties. It is a perennial plant, and may attain a height of one or two feet. Its leaves are flat and broad, its flowers small. It is nearly allied to Camomile. The variety grown in gardens is well known under the name of "golden feather."

43. 10. "Flower armor," evidently the ***Floramor***, Fr. ***fleur d'amour***, from a misconception of its Latin name *Amaranthus*, as though a compound of *Amor*, love, and *anthus*, a flower.

43. 11. "Flower de luce," the *flos deliciarum* of the Middle Ages. Ducange, quoting from the history of the Harcourts, says:— "Thomas, Dux Exoniæ habet comitatum de Harcourt . . . . per homagium ac reddendum *florem deliciarum* apud Castrum de Rouen," etc. (A.D. 1423). Another derivation is as follows:—"Louis VII. dit le Jeune, prit le premier des *fleurs de lis*, par allusion à son nom de Loys (comme on l'écrivait alors). On a dit dans ce temps-là *Fleur de Loys*, puis *Fleur de Louis*, enfin, *Fleur de Lis*." (Grandmaison, Dict. Heraldique.) The flower that he chose seems to have been a *white* one, for Chaucer says:

"His nekke was white as is the *flour de lis*."

In E. K.'s Glossary to Spenser's Shep. Cal. April, we read "*Flower delice*, that which they use to misterme *Flowre deluce* being in the Latine called *Flos delitiarum*."

43. 12. According to Lyte the Flower Gentle is identical with the Floramor (see above). Various species of *Amaranthus*, including the Flower amor (43. 10), and what we now call *Celosia cristata*, or Cockscomb, were included under this name. Parkinson (Paradisus, p. 370) says: "We have foure or five sorts of Flower-gentle to trimme up this our Garden withall."—Note by Mr. J. Britten.

43. 14. "Gilliflower, formerly spelt *gyllofer* and *gilofre* with the *o* long, from Fr. *giroflée*, Ital. *garofalo*, in Douglas's Virgil *jereflouris*, words formed from M. Lat. *garoffolum*, *gariofilum*, or, as in Albert Magn. (lib. vi. cap. 22), *gariofilus*, corrupted from Lat. *caryophyllum* =a clove, and referring to the spicy odour of the flower, which seems to have been used in flavouring wines to replace the more costly clove of India. The name was originally given in India to plants of the Pink tribe, especially the carnation, but has in England been transferred of late years to several Cruciferous plants. That of Chaucer, Spenser, and Shakspere was, as in Italy, *Dianthus caryophyllus*, Linn., that of later writers and gardeners *Matthiola* and *Cheiranthus*, Linn. Much of the confusion in the names of plants has arisen from the vague use of the French terms *Giroflée*, *Oeillet*, and *Violette*, which were, all three of them, applied to flowers of the Pink tribe, but subsequently extended, and finally restricted in English to very different plants. *Giroflée* has become *Gilliflower*, and passed over to the *Cruciferæ*, *Oeillet* has been restricted to the *Sweet Williams*, and *Violette* has been appropriated to one of the numerous claimants of its name, the genus to which the pansy belongs."—Dr. R. A. Prior.

43. 15. "Holiokes," in Huloet's Dict. Holy Hoke. Wedgwood (Etym. Dict.) derives it from A.S. *hoc*, Welsh *hocys*=a mallow, and says that it obtained the title of *Holy* from its being brought from the Holy Land, where it is indigenous.

43. 16. "Indian Eie." This was probably a *Dianthus* of some kind (French *œillet*), the same perhaps which is now grown in our gardens as Indian or Chinese Pink.

43. 19. *Laus tibi*, "a narcissus with white flowers. It groweth plenteously in my Lorde's garden in Syon and it is called of divers White Laus tibi."—Turner's Herball, pt. ii. b. 2. "It is very difficult to ascertain what plant was meant by this name, which is also mentioned by Turner in his 'Names of Herbes' (1548), and in his 'Libellus' (1538), where there is a long disquisition concerning it. It may be *Narcissus poeticus*, L., as Mr. B. D. Jackson supposes in his reprint of the 'Libellus' or possibly *N. biflorus*, L."—Note by Mr. J. Britten.

43. 20. "Lillium cum vallium," the "Lily of the Valley," in Lyte *Lyllie Conuall*, and also termed *May Blossoms*, *May Lyllies*, and *Lyrvconfancy*.

43. 23. "Nigella Romana." The *Nigella Damascena*, Linn., a favourite old-fashioned garden annual, still to be met with in gardens under the names of "Love-in-a-mist," or "Devil-in-a-bush."

43. 24. "Pansy," or Paunce, Fr. *pensée*, thought. According to Dr. Johnson the name is derived from Lat. *panacea*, but there is no evidence of the plant ever having been so called, or having been regarded as a panacea. It has received more popular names perhaps than any other plant, both in our own and in foreign languages. The following are some of the quaint titles given to it: "Cull me to you," or "Cuddle me to you," "Love and Idle," "Live in Idleness," "Love in Idleness" (originally "Love in idle," *i.e.* in vain); "Love in idle Pances," "Tittle my fancy," "Kiss me, ere I rise," "Jump up and kiss me," "Kiss me at the garden gate," "Pink of my John," "Herb Trinity," and "Three faces under one hood," from the three colours combined in one flower. It was also called "Hearts-ease," and "Flame flower" (M. Lat. *Viola flammea*).

Heartsease, a term meaning "*a cordial*," as in Sir W. Scott's Antiquary, ch. xi., "Buy a dram to be eilding and claise, and a supper and *hearts-ease* into the bargain," given to certain plants supposed to be cardiac: at present [applied] to the *pansy* alone, but by Lyte, Bulleyn, and W. Turner, to the *Wallflower* equally.—Dr. R. A. Prior's Popular Names of British Plants, which see for an account of the origin of the name.

43. 31. "Sops-in-Wine," the Clove Gilliflower, *Dianthus caryophyllus*, L., so called from the flowers being used to flavour wine or ale. Cf. Chaucer's Rime of Sir Thopas, B. 1950:

"Ther springen herbes grete and smale,
The lycorys and cetewale,
And many a clowe gilofre,
And notemuge to putte in ale,
Whether it be moyste or stale."

"Bring Coronations and *Sops in wine* worne of Paramoures."
Spenser, Shep. Cal. April.

"Garlands of Roses and *Sopps in Wine*."—Ibid. May. E. K., in his Glossary, says: "*Sops in Wine*, a flowre in colour much like a *coronation* (carnation), but differing in smel and quantitye."

43. 32. "Sweete Williams," from Fr. *oeillet*, Lat. *ocellus*, a little eye, corrupted to *Willy*, and thence to *William*, "in reference, perhaps, to a popular ballad, 'Fair Margaret and Sweet William,'[1] a name assigned by W. Bulleyn (f. 48) to the Wallflower, but by later herbalists and modern gardeners, as here, to a species of pink, *Dianthus barbatus*, Linn. According to an article in the Quarterly Review (No. 227), it formerly bore the name of 'Sweet Saint William'; but the writer gives no reference, and probably had no authority for saying so."—Dr. R. A. Prior, pp. 228 and 250.

43. 33. "Sweete Johns." Apparently a variety of Sweet William. See Parkinson's "Paradisus," pp. 319, 321, for descriptions and figures: "The chiefe differences betweene them are, that [Sweet Williams] have broader, and darker greene leaues, somewhat brownish, especially towards the points, and that the flowers stand thicker and closer, and more in number together, in the head or tuft."—Note by Mr. J. Britten.

43, 35. "Star of Jerusalem." This is usually *Tragopogon pratensis*, L., as in Gerard, p. 736, but some other plant is likely to be meant here.—Note by Mr. J. Britten.

43. 37. "Tuft gilleflowers." Probably some low-growing *Dianthus*, such as that figured as "Matted Pinkes" by Parkinson (Paradisus, p. 315).—Note by Mr. J. Britten.

43. 38. "Veluet flowers," according to Dr. Prior, the "love-lies-bleeding," *Amaranthus caudatus*, Linn., from its crimson velvety tassels; according to Lyte, the same as the Flower Gentle, or Floramor, Fr. *passevelours*, *A. tricolor*, Linn.

44. 5. "Eyebright." "Divers Authours write that goldfinches, linnets, and some other Birds make use of this Herb for the repairing of their own and their young ones sight."—Coles, "Adam in Eden," 1657, p. 46. It is the "Euphrasy" of Milton, P. L. xi. 414. A similar story is told of the Hawk-weed. See Pliny (lib. xx. c. 7).

44. 7. "Fumetorie," Fr. *fume terre*, Lat. *fumus terræ*, earth-smoke, it being believed to be produced without seed from vapours arising from the earth, as stated by Platearius: "Dicitur *fumus terræ*, quod generatur a quadam fumositate grossâ, a terrâ resolutâ, et circa

[1] Printed in Ritson's Early Songs and Ballads, ed. Hazlitt, 1877.

superficiem terræ adherente." Pliny (lib. xxv. c. 13) says that it takes its name from causing the eyes to water when applied to them, as smoke does;

> "Take youre laxatives
> Of lauriol, centaure, and *fumytere*."—
> Chaucer, Nonnes Prestes Tale, 143.

See Burton's Anat. of Melancholy, pp. 432–3 and 438, ed. 1845.

44. 17. "Woodrofe," spelt according to an old distich thus:

> "Double U, double O, double D, E,
> R, O, double U, double F, E."

It derives its name originally from the Fr. *roue*=a wheel, dimin. *rouelle*, the leaves being set on the stems so as to resemble the large *rowels* of ancient spurs.

45. 2. "Archangel." This is *Archangelica officinalis*, the stalks of which "were formerly blanched and eaten as Celeri. . . . . The gardeners near London, who have ditches of water running through their gardens, propagate great quantities of this plant, for which they have a great demand from the confectioners, who make a sweetmeat with the tender stalks of it cut in May."—Martyn's ed. of Miller's Gardener's Dictionary. It is still sometimes grown in gardens for use in the above-mentioned manner. According to Cogan (Haven of Health, p. 71), it will cure the bite of a mad dog.

45. 6. According to Cogan "Cummin" was extensively used for washing the face, it having the effect, if not used too often, of making the complexion clear; if used to excess, it caused paleness. He continues, "In Matthiolus (lib. 3, cap. 60) I reade a practise to be wrought with *Cummine* seedes, and (as I thinke) hath been vsed in time past of Monkes and Friers. They that counterfait holinesse and leannesse of bodie, doe often vse Cummine seedes in their meates, and be perfumed therewith."—Haven of Health, p. 47.

45. 8. "Detanie." Dittany (*Origanum onites*, Linn.) was commonly cultivated in gardens at this period. Gerard, p. 795, says it is "a hot and sharpe hearbe," and speaks of it as biting the tongue.

45. 9. Gromell, Grummel, or Graymyle, as Turner says it should be written, from *granum solis* and *milium solis* together. "That is al one," says the Grete Herbal, "*granum solis* and *milium solis*." The common *gromwell* or gray millet, *Lithospermum officinale*, Linn., was formerly esteemed as a remedy for the stone and other diseases. In a treatise on the virtues of plants, written in the 15th century, Roy. MS. 18 A. vi. f. 766, the following description is given: "*Granum solis* ys an herbe þat me clepyþ *gromel*, or lyþewale: thys herbe haþ leuys þat be euelong, and a lytyl white flour, and he haþ whyte seede ischape as a ston that me clepyþ margery perl." Cotgrave gives "Gremil, grenil, the hearb *gromill*, *grummell*, or *graymill*, peare-plant, lichewall." The word is derived by Skinner "*a granis sc. lapideis, quæ pro seminibus habet, q.d. granile*."—Way, in Prompt. Parv. "Grumelle, *milium, gramen solis*."—Catholicon Anglicum.

45. 12. "Louage," spelt in Prompt. Parv. and in Holland's Trans. of Pliny, *love-ache*, as though it were love-parsley. French *levesche*, A.S. *lufestice*, *Levisticum officinale*, Koch.

45. 14. "Mandrake." Matthioli (lib. iv. c. 61) tells us that Italian ladies in his own time had been known to pay as much as 25 and 30 ducats for one of the artificial mandrakes (common white bryony) of itinerant quacks, and describes the process of their manufacture. They were supposed to remove sterility; hence Rachel's anxiety to obtain them (Genesis xxx. 14). There were numerous other superstitions regarding this plant; amongst others it was said to shriek when torn up. See Gerard's Herbal, 1597, p. 280, and Peacock's Glossary of Manley, etc., E. D. Soc. Lupton (Book of Notable Things, iii. 39) gives instructions for the manufacture of Mandrakes from bryony roots. The true Mandrake is *Atropa Mandragora*, Linn.

45. 15. Mogwort. "Mugwort, a name that corresponds in meaning with its synonym *wyrmwyrt*, wormwood, from O.E. *mough*, *moghe*, or *moughte*, a maggot or moth.

'And wormes and *moghes* on þe same manere
Sal þat day be in wittenes broght;'—Hampole, Pricke of Conscience, l. 5572; and Wycliffe (Matt. vi. 20):

'Where neþer ruste ne *moughte* destruyeþ.'

The name was given to this plant from its having been recommended by Dioscorides to ward off the attacks of these insects. 'Mogwort, al on as seyn some, modirwort: lewed folk þat in manye wordes conne no rygt sownynge, but ofte shortyn wordys, and changyn lettrys and silablys, þey corruptyn þe *o* into *u*, and *d* into *g*, and syncopyn *i*, smytyn awey *i* and *r*, and seyn mugwort.' —MS. Arundel, 42, f. 35. It is unnecessary to have recourse to this singular process. The plant was known both as a *moth-wort* and as a *mother-wort*, but while it was used almost exclusively as a *mother-wort*, it still retained, at the same time, the name of *mugwort*, a synonym of *moth-wort*. In Ælfric's glossary it is called *matrum herba*."—Dr. R. A. Prior. See Brand's Pop. Antiq. for an account of the superstitious custom of seeking under the root of this plant on Midsummer-eve for a coal, to serve as a talisman against many disasters.

45. 18. "Rew." Shakspere, Hamlet, iv. 5. 181: "There's rue for you; and here's some for me: we may call it herb-grace o' Sundays." And Winter's Tale, iv. 4. 74:

"For you there's rosemary and rue; these keep
Seeming and savour all the winter long:
Grace and remembrance be to you both."

Some suppose it to have been called "herb of grace" on account of the many excellent properties it was held to possess, being a specific against poison, the bites of venomous creatures, etc.; but probably it was so called because "rue" means "repent." Cf. also Richard II. Act iii. sc. 4. 105:

"Here in this place
I'll set a bank of *rue*, sour herb of grace."

45. 22. "Bots." "Pease an beanes are as danke here as a dog, and this is the next way to give poor jades the *bottes*."—Shakspere King Henry IV. Act ii. sc. 1. "Begnawne with *bots*."—Taming of Shrew, Act iii. sc. 2.

"Sauin." "It is often put into horses' drenches, to helpe to cure them of the bots, and other diseases."—Parkinson, Paradisus, p. 607.

45. 23. "Stitchwort," spelt *Stich-wurt* in Mayer and Wright, Nat. Antiquities, 1857, and given from a thirteenth century MS. as the translation of "Valeriane." Supposed to possess the power of curing a pain or *stitch* in the sides.—See Gerard's Herbal, 1597, p. 43. *Stellaria Holostea*, Linn.

45. 25. "Woodbine," not a *bine* that *grows in woods*, but a creeper that binds or entwines trees, the honeysuckle. A.S. *wudu-winde* and *wudu-bind*, from *wudu*=a tree, and *windan*, *bindan*=to entwine. In Shakspere (Mids. Night Dr. Act iv. sc. 1) it seems to mean the bittersweet:

"So doth the woodbine the sweet honeysuckle
Gently entwist."

46. 2. "Gregorie." "This day (12th March) seems to have been much used as a date for agricultural observances: cf. 37. 3. In connexion with this it is worth while to note the Suabian saying, 'Säe Erbsen Gregori' (sow cabbage on St. Gregory's Day). See Swainson's Weather Folklore, p. 168."—Note by Mr. J. Britten.

46. 3. "Mastiues and Mungrels." Although the influence of a very patriotic sumptuary tax has diminished the number of dogs, we have still 'thousands too manie.' [This may with truth be said even still.] However, as Lent now makes little difference in the mode of living, which it certainly did in the earlier period of the Reformation, our dogs are not driven by our meagre fare to prey on the lambs; and therefore need not be particularly watched on this account.—M. Mastif is derived from O. Fr. *mestif* = a mongrel (Cotgrave). In the Craven dialect a great dog is still called a *masty*. See note to 10. 19.

By "hooke or by crooke" occurs in Spenser, Faery Queene, Bk. v. Canto 2, stanza 27; also in Heywood's Works, 1562, reprint 1867, p. 35.

46. 8. No trees appear preferable to willows for fencing hop grounds; and none are said to be worse than elms, as they attract mildews.—M.

46. 12. "What better to skilfull," etc., that is, what can be more profitable to the experienced farmer than to know when to be bold, that is, to venture the early sowing of barley?

46. 13. The Mayweed (*Anthemis cotula*) is common in corn-fields and hedgerows. "May-weed or stinking camomile."—T. R. "Resembling cammomil but of a stinking savour and odious to bees." Coles' Dict. 1676.

Cockle or *Cokyl* was used by Wycliffe and other old writers in the sense of a weed generally, but in later works has been confined to the *gith* or *corn-pink*.

46. 16. Our author's meaning is, sow barley, oats and pease above furrows and harrow them in; while rye is best ploughed in with a shallow furrow.

46. 21. "Without cost," that is, on which no expense has been incurred.

46. 24. Watering is necessary in dry seasons for what is fresh *set* or planted, but not for what is newly sown.

46. 26. It is to be lamented, both on account of the health and the finances of the poor, that they are so much attached, either to solid food, or to watery infusions of tea. Herbs, pulse and roots might often supersede more expensive articles of diet. Spoonmeat, in this part of the island at least, is in no high request at this period, though it appears to have been indispensable formerly.—M.

47. 20. "There remaineth yet a third kinde of meats, which is neither fish nor flesh, commonly called *white meats*, as egges, milk, butter, cheese, which notwithstanding proceede and come of flesh, as egges from the henne, and milk from the cowe. Yet because they are not plainely flesh, they are permitted to be eaten upon the fish daies."—Cogan's Haven of Health, ed. 1612, p. 149.

"But how soeuer this case standeth, *white meats*, as milke, butter and cheese, which were neuer so deere as in my time, and woont to be accounted of as one of the chiefe staies throughout the Iland, are now reputed as foods appertinent onelie to the inferiour sort, whilest such as are more wealthie, doo feed vpon the flesh of all kinds of cattell accustomed to be eaten, all sorts of fish taken vpon our coasts and in our fresh rivers, and such diuersitie of wild and tame foules as are either bred in our Iland or brought ouer vnto vs from other countries of the maine."—Harrison, Descript. of England, ed. Furnivall, Part I. p. 144. *White meats* in Lincoln now mean the flesh of lamb, veal, rabbits, chickens, pheasants, etc.

48. 4. "Count best the best cheape": "For it doth the buyer more credit and service."—Ray. We still say "Cheap and nasty;" and in the Towneley Mysteries, p. 102, there is the same sentiment:

"Men say lyght chepe
letherly for yeeldys,"

equivalent to our English proverb: "Light cheap, litter yield."

48. 7. It is always advisable to pay carpenters their fair wages, without any allowance of chips, which is a great temptation for them to waste timber.—M. In hewing timber, if the workman hews square, the seller of the timber loses all the gain of the *Wane* *edges*, which gain in short is a cheat, although a very customary one.—T.R.

48. 8. "Within these fortie yeeres we shall haue little great timber growing aboue fortie yeeres old; for it is commonlie seene that those yong *staddles* which we leaue standing at one and twentie yeeres fall, are vsuallie at the next sale cut downe without any danger of the statute, and serue for fire bote, if it please the owner to burne them."—Harrison, Part I. p. 345. "There is a Statute made, 35 Henry the 8, and the 1 Eliz. for the preseruation of timber trees, Oake, Ash, Elme, Aspe, and Beech: and that 12 storers and *standils* should bee left standing at euery fall, vpon an acre."—Norden's Surveyor's Dialogue, 1607, p. 213. On the decrease in woods, etc., in England, see Harrison's Description of England (New Shakspere Soc. edit. F. J. Furnivall, Part I. p. 344) and Norden's Surveyor's Dialogue, 1607, p. 214, in the latter of which one cause is stated to be the large number of hammers and furnaces for the manufacture of iron, and the quantity of charcoal used in the glass-houses; there being, as he says: "now or lately in Sussex, neere 140 hammers and furnaces for iron, and in it, and Surry adjoyning 3,400 glasse houses: the hammers and furnaces spend, each of them, in every 24 houres 2, 3 or foure loades of charrcoale."—p. 215. "There is a Law in Spaine, that he that cuts down *one Tree*, shall plant *three* for it."—A Treatise of Fruit Trees, R. A. Austin, Oxford, 1657, p. 128.

48. 11. "Leaue oxen abrode," etc. The Author of Tusser Redivivus is supported in his reading of this line by the edition of 1597, which has "leaue *not* oxe abrode." The sense, however, may possibly be, "keep oxen at a distance, for fear of injuring the young shoots. "*Springe* or ympe that commeth out of the rote." —Huloet's Abcedarium, 1552. "Keep from biting, treading underfoot, or damage of beasts . . . . . . whereby mischief may be done to the *Springs*, during the time limited by the statute for such kind of wood."—Brumby Lease, 1716, in Peacock's Glossary, E. Dial. Soc.

48. 14. "Meet with a bootie," etc., that is, as we say, find something which was never lost.

48. 16. Wanteth=is without, does not keep.

48. 22. "Waine her to mee." Perhaps=waggon, that is, drive, carry her to me," but it is a forced expression.

"Such maister such man." Another form of the proverb is, "Trim, Tram; like master, like man." "Tel maitre, tel valet" (Fr.).

49. Compare with Tusser's description of the faults to be avoided in the making of cheese the following extracts on the same subject:

"Now what cheese is well made or otherwise may partly be perceiued by this old Latine verse:

Non nix, non Argos, Methusalem, Magdaleneve,
Esaus, non Lazarus, caseus ille bonus.

That is to say, Cheese should not be white as Snowe is, nor full of eyes as Argos was, nor old as Methusalem was, nor full of whey or weeping as Marie Magdalen was, nor rough as Esau was, nor full of spots as Lazarus. Master Tusser in his Booke of husbandrie addeth other properties also of Cheese well made, which who so listeth may read. Of this sort for the most part is that which is made about Banbury in Oxfordshire: for of all cheese (in my iudgement) it is the best, though some preferre Cheshire Cheese made about Nantwich: and other also commend the Cheese of other countries: But Banbury Cheese shall goe for my money: for therein (if it be of the best sort) you shall neither tast the renet nor salt, which be two speciall properties of good Cheese. Now who so is desirous to eate Cheese, must eate it after other meat, and in little quantitie. A pennyweight, according to the old saying, is enough."—Cogan's Haven of Health, ed. 1612, pp. 158–9.

Andrew Boorde, in his Dyetary already referred to, p. 266, mentions 5 kinds of cheese, namely: "grene chese, softe chese, harde chese and spermyse. Besyde these iiij natures of chese, there is a chese called a rewene chese, the whiche, yf it be well orderyd, doth passe all other cheses, none excesse taken." . . . . "Chese that is good oughte not be to harde nor to softe, but betwyxt both; it shuld not be towgh nor brultell; it ought not to be swete, nor tarte, nor to salt, nor to fresshe; it must be of good savour and taledge, nor full of iyes, nor mytes, nor magottes."

"Yf a chees is drie,
Hit is a vyce, and so is many an eye
Yf it see with, that cometh yf sounyng brendde,
Or moche of salt, or lite of presse, it shende."—

Palladius on Husbondrie, E. E. Text Soc. ed. Lodge, p. 154.

With these extracts showing the essentials of good cheese, compare the following description of Suffolk Cheese, locally termed *Bang and Thump*, and made of milk several times skimmed:

"Unrivall'd stands thy county cheese, O Giles!
Whose very name alone engenders smiles;
Whose fame abroad by every tongue is spoke,
The well-known butt of many a flinty joke,
Its name derision and reproach pursue,
And strangers tell of "three times skimm'd skye blue."—
Blomfield.

Its toughness has given rise to a number of local illustrations. In one the cheese exclaims:

"Those that made me were uncivil,
For they made me harder than the devil;
Knives won't cut me; fire won't sweat me;
Dogs bark at me, but can't eat me."

"Hunger will break through stone walls, or anything except Suffolk cheese," is a proverb from Ray. Mowbray says "it is only fit to be cut up for gate latches, a use to which it is often applied." Other writers represent it as most suitable for making wheels for wheelbarrows.

49 *c.* "Argusses eies." The mythical Argus, surnamed Panoptes (the All-seer), had a hundred eyes; he was placed by Juno to guard Io, and at his death his eyes were transplanted to the peacock's tail.

49. 1. To fleet or skim the cream is a verb still in use in East Anglia, and the utensil used for the purpose is termed a *fleeting-dish.* "I flete mylke, take away the creame that lyeth above it whan it hath rested."—Palsgr. "*Esburrer,* to fleet the creame potte; *laict esburré,* fleeted milk; *maigne,* fleeted milke or whaye." —Hollyband's Treasurie. "Ye *floted* too nie" = you skimmed off too much of the cream.

49. 3. If cheeses are full of eyes, it is a proof that the curd was not properly worked.

49. 4. Hoven cheese is occasioned by negligence in breaking the curd; and therefore Cisley deserves to be driven to *creeks,* or holes and corners, for her idleness and inattention.—M.

49. 5. Tough or leathery cheese may arise from its being set too hot, or not worked up, and the curd broken in proper time.—M.

49. 6. Various causes may bring on corruption in cheese, such as the use of beastings, or milk immediately after calving, moisture, bruises and such like.

49. 7. Hairs in cheese can only arise from inexcusable carelessness, or from Cisley's combing and decking her hair in the dairy.

49. 9. Magget the py = the magpie, a pun on the word magget, in its two meanings of 1. a maggot, 2. a magpie, commonly called in Prov. Eng. *magot-pie, maggoty-pie,* from *mag, maggot* = *Meg, Maggie* = *Margery, Margaret,* and *pie*; Fr. *margot,* old dimin. of *Marguerite,* and common name of the magpie. The line, therefore, reads, "If maggots be crawling in the cheese, fetch magget the py." "*Pie,* meggatapie."—Cotgrave. Cf. Shakspere, Macbeth, Act iii. sc. 4, 125.

49. 10. "Cisley, in running after the Bishop in passing, as was the practice in former times, in order to obtain his blessing, might accidentally leave her milk on the fire; and on her return, finding it burnt to the pan, might probably curse the prelate for her mishap, which conduct deserved correction, or a left-handed blessing from her mistress." So Dr. Mavor. Mr. Skeat remarks in reference to it: "That stupid story makes me cross; it is such an evident invention, and no soul has ever adduced the faintest proof of any such practice. The allusion is far less circuitous, viz. to the bishops who burnt people for heresy. That they did so is too notorious." The following extract appears strongly to bear out Mr. Skeat's view: "When a thynge speadeth not well we borowe speach and say '*the byshope hath blessed it,*' because that nothynge speadeth well that they medyll withall. If the podech be burned to, or the meate over rosted, we say '*the byshope has put his fote in the potte*,' or '*the byshope hath played the coke*,' because the byshopes burn who they lust, and whosoever displeaseth them." — Quotation from Tyndale's Obedyence of a Chrystene Man, 1528, p. 166, in Brockett, North Country Glossary, 1825, page 16. If we consider that these verses were written while the memory of the numbers who had suffered death at the stake for their religion was still fresh in the minds of the people, Mr. Skeat's view, borne out, as it is, by the foregoing extract, certainly appears the more reasonable and probable.

50. 11. "Here reede": we may take this as meaning either "here read," or, adopting the older meaning of the word *reede* (A.S. *rǽd*=advice, warning), as "hear my advice or warning."

50. 27. "Take nothing to halues," that is, do nothing by halves.

50. 30. "Tell fagot and billet," etc.; count your faggots and fire-wood, to prevent the boys and girls from pilfering it, so that when you come to fetch it you find "a quarter be gone." So also in the next stanza, watch the coal men filling the sacks, lest you should get short weight; and, when the coals are delivered, see the sacks opened, for fear the coal dealer and the carman should be 'two in a pack,' or 'harp on one string,' and between them you be defrauded.

51. 1. "Philip and Jacob," that is, St. Philip and St. James' Day, May 1st. "When flocks were more uniform as to breed and management, lambs used to be separated from their dams on this day, for the purpose of tithing as well as milking."—M. "Requiem æternam," a portion of the Roman Catholic Service for the dead, hence "least *requiem æternam* in winter they sing"=lest they die in the winter from not having been allowed to become sufficiently strong before being taken from their dams, and thus being incapable of enduring the severity of the weather.

51. 4. "Barberlie handled," that is, "*secundum artem*, as a barber surgeon would do, by first cutting away extraneous substances, and then rubbing the part with dust."—M. Tusser Redivivus calls the lumps of dirt and worms which gather on the wool under a sheep's tail "*treddles*."

51. 6. During the summer season, hollow and decayed pollards in particular, or woodsere, cannot be lopped without danger. Ivy, however, is to be removed; or it will, by the closeness of its embraces, prevent trees from *addling*, that is, growing or increasing in size.—M.

51. 8. The Thrasher serves the Cattle with fresh Straw, the Hogs with Risk (offal, corn and weeds, and short knotty straw).—T.R. (May).

51. 10. "A weede hooke, a crotch, and a gloue." Fitzherbert (Boke of Husbandry, 1586) enumerates, as "y[e] chyef instrumentes for weeding, a paier of tonges made of wood and in the farther end it is nicked to hold ye wede faster . . . . yf it be drye wether then must ye have a *wedying hoke* with a socket set upon a lytle staffe a yard longe. And this hoke wolde be wel steled and grounde sharpe bothe behynde and before. And in his other hande he hath a *forked stycke* a yarde long." The whole account of weeding in the "Boke" is very quaint. In former days thistles were gathered from the corn for the feeding of cattle, and the left hand of the reaper was guarded with a leathern glove: there is an entry among the expenses of the Priory of Holy Island for 1344–5 of "gloves for 14 servants when they gathered the tythe corn, 2*s.* 8*d.*" See Johnston's "Botany of the Eastern Borders."—Note by Mr. J. Britten.

51. 11. "The May weed doth burn" (*Anthemis cotula*, L.). The juice of this plant is possessed of an acrid blistering property which renders it extremely noxious to reapers. The irritating effects are produced in a still greater degree by the seed when ripe, and are mostly manifested in the lower extremities, from the close adhesion of the seeds by their rough surface, aided by the friction of the shoe, causing first abrasion, then active inflammation, and even ulceration. Dr. Bromfield (Flora Vectensis) says: "I have been repeatedly assured by the peasantry that they have known men incapacitated for work, and laid up, from the injurious operation of this noxious weed, for days together in harvest time."

"The thistle doth fret." Fitzherbert (Boke of Husbandry) says: "The thystell is an yll wede rough and sharpe to handle, and *freateth away the cornes* nyghe it.

"The fitches pul downward." The hairy tare, *Vicia hirsuta*, L. Fitch=vetch.

"The cockle," *Lychnis Githago*, L. "*Cockole* hath a large smal [*sic*] leafe and wyll beare v or vi floures purple colloure as brode as a grote, and the sede is rounde and blacke."—Fitzherbert, Boke of Husbandry.

"Boddle." The corn marigold, *Chrysanthemum segetum*, L., more usually called boodle or buddle in the East of England; in Kent, yellow bottle; in Scotland, gools, gules, or goolds, in allusion to the colour of the flower. This is a very noxious weed, the non-extirpation of which in Scotland was formerly a punishable offence: certain persons (hence called "gool-riders") were appointed to ride through the fields on a certain day, and impose a fine of three shillings and fourpence, or a wether sheep, for every stalk of the plant found growing in the corn. The custom is of great antiquity, and exists in a modified form at the present day, the fine being reduced to a penny. Linnæus states that a similar law exists in Denmark.—Note by Mr. J. Britten.

51. 13. Buckwheat, Dutch *bockweit*, Ger. *buckwaitzen*, from the resemblance of its triangular seeds to beech-nuts, a name adopted with its culture from the Dutch.—It is a tender plant, and must be sown late.—M. It is also very proper to sow it (bucke) before wheat, the ground is made clean and fine by it, and it sufficing itself with a Froth leaves the solid Strength for the Wheat.—T.R. (May). *Polygonum Fagopyrum*, Linn.

"Brank"=buckwheat, from a Latin word, *brance*, that occurs in Pliny lib. xviii. cap. 7, where it seems rather to mean a barley. "Galliæ quoque suum genus farris dedere, quod illic *brance* vocant, apud nos sandalam, nitidissimi grani." The word will be identical with *blanc*, white, Port. *branco*, and equivalent to *wheat*, which properly means "white."—Popular Names of British Plants, Dr. R. A. Prior, 1870, p. 28. Pancakes are made of it in Holland.—T.R.

51. 15. Pidgeons, Rooks, and other Vermine, about that time begin to be scanted, and will certainly find them [peas] out, be they in never so by a Corner.—T.R. (May).

51. 16. Fimble, or Female Hemp, so called, I suppose, because it falls to the Female's share to *tew-taw* it, that is, to dress it and to spin it, etc. The Fimble Hemp is that which is ripe soonest and fittest for spinning, and is not worth above half as much as the *Carle* with its seed.—T.R. "The male is called *Charle Hempe*, and *Winter Hempe*; the Female *Barren Hempe* and *Sommer Hempe*."—Gerard's Herball, p. 572. "Hemp was much cultivated here until the end of the great war with France. The *Carl* or male hemp was used for ropes, sackcloth, and other coarse manufactures: the *fimble*, or female hemp, was applied to making sheets and other domestic purposes."—Peacock's Gloss. of Manley, etc., E. D. Soc.

It is curious that the Karl or male hemp should be in reality the female plant, but other authors use the names in the same way. "The femell hempe . . . . beareth no sede."—Fitzherbert, "Boke of Husbandry." See also 55. 8. Gerard says the female hemp is "barren and without seede, contrarie to the nature of that sexe."—Note by Mr. J. Britten.

51. 17. The fact of the Hop being one of the plants which twine from left to right had thus been observed as early as Tusser's time. —Note by Mr. J. Britten.

51. 19. The tine tare ["a tare that *tines* or encloses and imprisons other plants, *Vicia hirsuta*."—Prior] is now seldom attempted to be raked out, for fear of greater mischief from the practice than from its neglect. The safest way is certainly to cut the tine near the root, but the operation is extremely tedious.—M.

51. 21. "The Fawy riseth in Fawy moore in a verie *quaue mire*, on the side of an hill."—Harrison, ed. 1587, Bk. i. c. 12.

Cf. "The wal wagged and clef, and al the worlde *quaved*."—
Piers Plowman, ed. Skeat, B Text, Passus xviii. 61.

"Quave of a myre (quaue as of a myre), *Labina*. Quavyn, as myre, *Tremo*."—Prompt. Parv. Horman, in his chapter *de re edificatoriâ*, observes that "a *quauery* or a maris and unstable foundation must be holpe with great pylys of alder rammed downe, and with a frame of tymbre called a crossaundre (*fistucâ*)." In Caxton's Mirrour of the World, Part II. c. 22, it is said, "understande ye how the erthe quaueth and shaketh, that somme peple calle an erthe quaue, by cause they fele the erthe meue and quaue vnder their feet." "Quaue myre, *foundriere crouliere*." — Palsgrave. Forby gives Quavery-mavery = undecided, hesitating. — Way, Note in Prompt. Parv., *s.v.* Quave.

51. 25. The meaning is, make your dunghill on the headland, especially where shaded with trees and bushes, as they will prevent the moisture from exhaling.—M.

"I see in some meddowes *gaully* places where little or no grasse at al groweth, by reason (as I take it) of the too long standing of the water, for such places are commonly low, where the water standeth, not hauing vent to passe away, and therefore meanes must be first made for the evacuation of the water: for the continual standing of the water consumeth the grasse, and makes the place bare, and sinketh it. In such a place, therefore, sow in the Spring-time some hay-seed, especially the seed of the claver grasse,[1] or the grasse hony-suckle,[2] and other seeds that fall out of the finest and purest hay: and in the sowing of it, mingle with it some good earth; but sow not the hony-suckle grasse in too moist a ground, for it liketh it not."—Norden's Surveyor's Dialogue, 1607, pp. 201–2. Gauls are void spaces in Coppices which serve for nothing but to entice the Cattel into it, to its great Damage.—T.R.

51. 29. If the land is overstocked in summer, you may, perhaps, be obliged to assist your cattle to rise in winter; or, in other words, "to lift at their tails."—M. Cf. 21. 14.

51. 32. It appears to have been the custom formerly to allow, in warm weather, sleep for an hour or two. In Norfolk we are told the practice is not quite obsolete on churning days when the mistress and maids get up early; and likewise among the ploughmen, where two journies a day are performed with their teams, and an interval allowed for rest.—M.

"Patch." Cf. Shakspere, Mid. Night's Dr., Act iii. sc. 2; and Merchant of Venice, Act ii. sc. 5.

"Growthed"=grout-hed=thick head, fat head. Cf. *growtnoul*= a blockhead. "*Growte nowle* come to the King."—Promos and Cassandra, p. 81.

51. 33. Stilling, or distilling, may be a "pretty feat," but we doubt if it is very profitable, and if it does not furnish a temptation to dram-drinking, under the mask of simple and medicinal *waters*. —M.

52. 6. See note to 15. 8.

[1] Clover. [2] Trefoil.

52. 16. "Swinge brembles and brakes," this is, cut down with a sweeping instrument somewhat resembling a scythe.

53. 1. "Sheep-shearing takes place only once, viz. in the month of June; the heaviest wethers weigh sixty pounds, others from forty to fifty pounds: they bear at the most not more than six, others four or five pounds of wool; one of the best wethers (notwithstanding that they are very abundant) sells for about twenty shillings, that is, ten French francs or five thalers; the inferior sort about ten shillings, or five francs; and the worst about six or eight English shillings. The skin of the best wether and sheep is worth about twelve pence, that is, four and a half German batzen; the worst about eight pence or three batzen; a pound of wool about twelve pence, or four and a half batzen."—Rathgeb, 1602, Rye, p. 51 (quoted in Harrison's Description of England, ed. Furnivall, Part I. p. lxxxiii). "Running Water is best, . . . but then it is oft-times very sheer and cold."—T.R. (June).

53. 2. "Grote." "In this yere [1349] the kynge caused to be coyned grotes and half grotes, the whiche lacked of the weight of his former coyne, ii$^{s.}$ vi$^{d.}$ in a li [*libra*, pound] Troy."—Fabyan, p. 461. The *groat* was only equal to about three and a half silver pennies instead of four.

53. 3. "The Pie will discharge thee," etc., that is, the magpie will save you the trouble, etc., alluding to birds eating vermin on sheep's backs.

53. 4. "Ouercome"=overtake, or keep up with; don't mow more than you can easily make, not too much at once, lest part of it be spoiled for want of hands.

"Cock apace." Cf. Piers Plowman, C. Text, Passus vi. 12, 13 (ed. Skeat).

> "Canstow seruen, he seide, oþer syngen in a churche,
> Oþer *coke for my cokers*, oþer to þe cart picche?"

i.e. put hay into cocks for my harvest men. Mr. Skeat quotes in his note to this passage: "Bee it also prouided, that this act, nor anything therein contained, doe in any wise extende to any *cockers* or haruest folkes that trauaile into anie countrie of this realme for haruest worke, either corne haruest, or hay haruest, if they doe worke and labour accordingly."—Rastall, Statutes; Vagabonds, etc., p. 474.

53. 5. To employ your labourers in ploughing, or in performing other parts of husbandry, till the dew is off the grass, is unquestionably a saving of time, and essentially forwards the business of the farm.—M.

53. 6. He who is constantly borrowing tools and other things which he ought to have of his own, lays himself under obligation to the lender, who expects twice as much in return.

53. 15. "Woodsere" here means the proper season for felling wood.

53. 18. "Fieing." "Feigh, Fey, vb. to clean out a drain, gutter or cesspool. 'Paid to John Lavghton in haruest for *feighinge* the milne becke.'—Kirton in Lindsey Ch. Acc. 1582. George Todd's *feyin'* out the sink hole."—Peacock's Glossary, E. Dial. Soc. 1877. To *fey* a ditch or pond is to empty and clean it; and the mud taken from such places, if mixed with lime or chalk, forms an excellent compost for pasture grounds.—M. Cf. Icel. *fægja*, to cleanse, whence our word is derived.

53. 19. "Of late yeares also we haue found and taken vp a great trade in planting of *hops*, whereof our moorie hitherto and vnprofitable grounds doo yeeld such plentie and increase that there are few farmers or occupiers in the countrie, which haue not gardens and hops growing of their owne, and those farre better than doo come from Flanders vnto vs. Certes the corruptions vsed by the Flemings, and forgerie dailie practised in this kind of ware, gaue vs occasion to plant them here at home; so that now we may spare and send manie ouer vnto them. And this I know by experience that some one man by conuersion of his moorie grounds into hopyards, wherof before he had no commoditie, dooth raise yearelie by so little as twelue acres in compasse two hundred markes; all charges borne toward the maintenance of his familie. Which industrie God continue! Though some secret freends of Flemings let not to exclaime against this commoditie, as a spoile of wood, by reason of the poles, which neuerthelesse after three yeares doo also come to the fire, and spare their other fewell."—Harrison, Descript. of Eng., 1587, p. 110. "Lowe and spungie grounds trenched is good for hopps, as Suffolke, Essex, and Surrie, and other places doe find to their profit."—Norden, p. 206. Evelyn, Sylva, pp. 201, 469, ed. Hunter, asserts that there was a petition against them temp. Henry VI., but no record of it appears on the rolls of Parliament. Brewing with hops was not introduced here till the reign of King Henry VIII. (Stow, Hist. p. 1038.) *Bere*, however, is mentioned in 1504. (Leland, Coll. vi. p. 30, and see Dr. Percy on Northumberland Book, p. 414.) —Pegge's Forme of Cury, ed. 1780, p. xxiii. See a long note in Prompt. Parv., *s.v.* Hoppe; and also "Pharmacographia," p. 496.

54. 11. For wanting at will=for fear of having none when you really want it.

55. 2. Hay for neat cattle may be made with less labour, and more expeditiously than for horses; because, if it is a little mow burnt, it will not be the less acceptable to them; and besides, the fermentation it undergoes, if not carried too far, has a natural tendency to mellow coarse grass.—M.

55. 4. *Avise auouse* is French jargon for *take precautions.* Ill-made hay is apt to take fire; if much wetted with rain, to become mouldy. Hard and fine hay is best for horses; soft and coarse hay will be more acceptable to cattle; while short hay is coveted by sheep.—M.

55. 6. Thry fallowing, or the third plowing, should be performed pretty early in the summer, in order that the ground may acquire sufficient hardness to resist the seeds of thistles and other weeds, even at the risk of requiring another stirring.—M.

55. 7. This can only refer to garden beans, but the practice is now obsolete.

55. 8. See note to 51. 16.

55. 10. "Wormwood, a word corrupted from A.S. *wermod*, Ger. *wermuth*, O.S. *weremede*, words which seem to be compounded with Ger. *wehren*, A.S. *werian*=to keep off, and *mod* or *made*=*maggot*, but which, by an accidental coincidence of sound, have been understood as though the first syllable were *worm*. L. Diefenbach would prefer to derive it from a Celtic root that means "bitter," Welsh *chwerw*, Cornish *whcrow*. Be its origin what it may, it was understood in the Middle Ages as meaning a herb obnoxious to maggots, and used to preserve things from them, and was also given as an anthelmintic or worm medicine. *Artemisia Absinthium*, L."—Dr. R. A. Prior, Pop. Names of Brit. Plants. "Two sorts of *Wormewood* are well knowen of many, that is, our common Wormewood, and that which is called *Ponticum*, now sowen in many gardens, and commonly called French-wormewood. And while it is yong, it is eaten in Salats with other herbes, to the great commoditie of the stomacke and Liuer. For it strengthneth a weake stomacke, and openeth the Liuer and Splene. For which purpose there is to be had in the Stilliard at London a kind of wine named Worme-wood wine, which I would wish to be much used of all such Students as be weake of stomacke. They may easily haue a rundlet of three or foure gallons or lesse, which they may draw within their owne chambers as need requireth. I was woont when appetite failed to steepe a branch or two of common Wormewood in halfe a pint of good white wine, close couered in some pot all night, and in the morning to straine it through a clean linnen cloth, and put in a little sugar and warme it, and so drinke it. Or sometime to burne a little quantitie of wine with sugar, and a branch or two of Wormewood put into it. Wherein I have found many times marvellous commoditie, and who so shall vse it now and then, shal be sure of a good stomacke to meat, and be free from wormes."—Cogan's Haven of Health, p. 55. "*Wormwood*, centaury, pennyroyal, are likewise magnified and much prescribed, especially in hypochondrian melancholy, daily to be used, sod in whey."—Burton, Anat. of Melancholy, p. 432.

55. 12. "As many doo more," *i.e.* as many others do. Cf. 63. 18.

56. 7. There is a proverb: "One scabb'd sheep's enough to spoil a flock."

56. 11. In Lincolnshire corn affected by the smut is called *Parson corn*, the reason assigned being that when tithes were paid in kind, the sheaves that had the most smuts in them were always given to the *parson*, if he could be seduced into taking them.—See Peacock's Gloss. of Manley, etc., E. Dial. Soc. 1877.

56. 20. *Mow-burn* is occasioned by the Hay being stack'd too soon, before its own juice is thoroughly dried, and by Norfolk people is called the *Red Raw*; not such as is occasioned by stacking it when wet with Rain, which is a nasty musty and stinks.—T.R.

56. 26. Hentzner, p. 79 (quoted in Harrison's Description of England, ed. F. J. Furnivall, p. lxxxiv), says: "As we were returning to our inn (at Windsor, Sept. 14), we happened to meet some country people celebrating their Harvest-home; their last load of corn they crown with flowers, having besides an image richly dressed, by which, perhaps, they would signify Ceres; this they keep moving about, while men and women, men and maid servants, riding through the streets in the cart, shout as loud as they can till they arrive at the barn."

"Tis merie in hall,
When beards wag all."

This proverb is of great antiquity. It occurs in the Life of Alexander (formerly, but erroneously, attributed to Adam Davie), written in 1312, where the words are:

"Swithe mury hit is in halle,
When burdes wawen alle."—Weber's Met. Rom.

It occurs also in Shakspere, 2 Henry IV. Act v. sc. 3, and is quoted in the *Merie Tales of Skelton*, 1567. See also Ray's Proverbs.

57. 3. In Harrison's Descript. of England, Part II. p. 50 *et seq.*, there is a long chapter on the cultivation and uses of Saffron in England, from which I extract the following: "As the Saffron of England, which Platina reckneth among spices, is the most excellent of all other; for it giueth place neither to that of Cilicia, whereof Solinus speaketh, neither to anie that commeth from Cilicia, where it groweth upon the mount *Taurus*, *Tmolus*, *Italie*, *Ætolia*, *Sicilia* or *Licia*, in sweetnesse, tincture and continuance; so of that which is to be had amongst us, the same that grows about Saffron Walden, somtime called Waldenburg, in the edge of Essex, first of all planted there in the time of Edward the Third, and that of Glocestershire and those westerlie parts, which some thinke to be better than those of Walden, surmounteth all the rest, and therefore beareth worthilie the higher price, by sixpence or twelue pence most commonlie in the pound. . . . . The heads of saffron are raised in Julie, either with plough, raising or tined hooke; and being scowred from their rosse or filth, and seuered from such heads as are ingendred of them since the last setting, they are interred againe in Julie and August by ranks or rowes, and being couered with moulds, they rest in the earth, where they cast forth little fillets and small roots like vnto a scallion, until September, in the beginning of which moneth the ground is pared and all weeds and grasse that groweth vpon the same remooved, to the intent that nothing may annoie the floure when as his time dooth come to rise. These things being thus ordered in the latter end of the aforesaid moneth [of September], the floure beginneth to appeere of a whitish blew, fesse, or skie colour, and in the end shewing itselfe in the owne kind, it resembleth almost the *Leucotion* of *Theophrast*, sauing that it is longer, and hath in the middest thereof three chines verie red and pleasant to behold. These floures are gathered in the morning before the rising of the sunne, which otherwise would cause them to welke or flitter. And the chines being picked from the floures, these are throwne into the doong-hill; the other dried vpon little kelles couered with streined canuasses vpon a soft fire; wherby and by the weight that is laied vpon them, they are dried and pressed into cakes, and then bagged vp for the benefit of their owners. In good yeeres we gather foure score or an hundred pounds of wet saffron of an acre, which being dried dooth yeeld twentie pounds of drie and more. Whereby, and sith the price of saffron is commonlie about twentie shillings in monie, or not so little, it is easie to see what benefit is reaped by an acre of this commoditie. . . . . For admit that the triple tillage of an acre dooth cost 13 shillings foure pence before the saffron be set, the clodding sixteene pence, the taking of euerie load of stones from the same foure pence, the raising of euerie quarter of heads six pence, and so much for cleansing of them, besides the doong which is woorth six pence the load to be laid on the first yeere, for the setting three and twentie shillings and foure pence, for the paring fiue shillings, six pence for the picking of a pound wet, etc.; yea though he hire it readie set, and paie ten pounds for the same, yet shall he susteine no damage, if warme weather and open season doo happen at the gathering." Harrison then describes fully the culture of saffron, and the adulterations and tricks practised by the dealers, and afterwards describes the virtues of it: "Our saffron (beside the manifold vse that it hath in the kitchin and pastrie, also in our cakes at bridals, and thanksgivings of women) is verie profitably mingled with those medicines which we take for the diseases of the breast, of the lungs, of the liuer, and of the bladder; it is good also for the stomach if you take it in meat, for it comforteth the same, and maketh good digestion: being sodden also in wine, it not onelie keepeth a man from dronkennesse, but incorageth also unto procreation of issue. If you drinke it in sweet wine, it inlargeth the breath, and is good for those that are troubled with the tisike and shortnesse of the wind: mingled with the milke of a woman, and laied vpon the eies, it staieth such humors as descend into the same, and taketh away the red wheales and pearles that oft grow about them: it killeth moths if it be sowed in paper bags verie thin, and laid vp in presses among tapistrie or apparrell: also it is verie profitable laid vnto all inflammations, painefull aposthumes, and the shingles, and doth no small ease vnto deafnes. . . . . Three drams thereof taken at once, which is about the weight of one shilling nine pence halfe penie, is deadlie poison."

57. 3. "The two S. Maries daies," *i.e.* July 22nd, St. Mary Magdalene's Day, and August 15th, the feast of the Assumption of the Virgin Mary.—M. Mr. Skeat suggests that the days meant are August 15th and September 8th, the Nativity of the Virgin Mary.

57. 5. Mustard-seed is very apt to shed, and therefore should be gathered before it becomes too ripe. After dressing it is to be laid in a soller or garret. "Soller, a lofte, *garnier*."—Palsgrave. "Garytte, hay solere."—Prompt. Parv.

57. 8. Though all the editions which I have seen read as printed in the text, it is evident that Tusser meant exactly the opposite, viz.:

> "By day will deceiue thee, etc.
> By great will dispatch, etc."

Men who take work by the great, that is, by the job or contract, are, as experience tells us, naturally anxious to get the work done as soon as possible, while those who are engaged by the day as naturally try to spin out the work as long as they can. According to Carr's *Craven Glossary*, a Day-work is three roods of land. "Four perches make a day-worke; ten daysworks make a roode or quarter." (Twysden MS. quoted by Halliwell.) The latter agrees with Norden's statement: "You must know (says he), that there goe 160 perches to one acre; 80 perches to halfe an acre; 40 perches to one roode, which is ¼ of an acre; ten *daies worke* to a roode, foure perches to a daies worke; 16 foote and a halfe to a perche." (*Surveior's Dialogue*, 1610.) In Cowel's *Interpreter* we read "*Day-were of Land*, as much arable ground as could be ploughed up in one day's work, or one journey, as the farmers still call it."

57. 9. "Harvest lord," the principal reaper who goes first and regulates the movements of the rest; *Harvest-Lady*, the second reaper in the row, called in Cambridgeshire the *Harvest-Queen*. The rate at which the *Harvest-lord* reaped of course regulated that of the others, and therefore Tusser recommends that he should have a penny or two extra in order to encourage him to have an eye to the loiterers, and to keep all up to the mark. Cf.:

> "At heighe pryme Peres lete the plowe stonde,
> To oversen hem hymself, and who-so best wrouȝte
> He shulde be huyred therafter whan heruest tyme come."

Piers Plowman, ed. Skeat, E. E. Text Soc. B Text, Passus vi. 114. The following particulars as to the farmer's expenses at harvest time are quoted by Mr. Skeat in his notes to Piers Plowman, C. Text, Passus ix. 104, from Sir J. Cullum's Hist. of Hawsted, Suffolk, 2nd ed.: "The outgoings [in harvest] were called the costs of autumn, and are thus stated. In 1388, [we find] the expences of a ploughman, head reaper, baker, cook, brewer, *deye*, 244½ reapers (*sic*) hired for 1 day; 30 bedrepes (days of work performed in harvest-time by the customary tenants, at the *bidding* of their lord), the men [being] fed, according to custom, with bread and herring;

3 qrs. 3 bu. of wheat from the stock; 5 qrs. 3 bu. of malt from the stock; meat bought, 10*s.* 10*d.*; 5 sheep from the stock; fish and herrings bought, 5*s.*; herrings bought for the customary tenants, 7*d.*; cheese, milk, and butter bought (the dairy being let), 9*s.* 6*d.*; salt, 3*d.*; candles, 5*d.*; pepper, 3*d.*; spoons, dishes, and faucets, 5*d.* 30 bedrepes, as before; 19 reapers, hired for 1 day, at their own board, 4*d.* each; 80 men, for 1 day, and kept at the lady's board, 4*d.* each: 140½ men (*sic*) hired for 1 day, at 3*d.* each; the wages of the head reaper, 6*s.* 8*d.*; of the brewer, 3*s.* 4*d.*; of the cook, 3*s.* 4*d.* 30 acres of oats tied up by the job (*per taskam*), 1*s.* 8*d.*; 6 acres of bolymong cut and tied up by the job, 3*s.* 4*d.*; 16 acres of pease, cut by the job, 8*s.*; 5 acres of pease and bolymong, cut and tied up by the job, 2*s.* 6*d.*; 3 acres of wheat, cut and tied up by the job, 1*s.* 11*d.*" [Here follow similar details for 1389, including a mention of 5 pairs of harvest-gloves, 10*d.*] "What a scene of bustling industry was this! for, exclusive of the baker, cook, and brewer, who, we may presume, were fully engaged in their own offices, here were 553 persons employed in the first year; in the second, 520; and in a third, 538; yet the annual number of acres, of all sorts of corn, did not much exceed 200. From this prodigious number of hands, the whole business must have been soon finished. There were probably 2 principal days; for two large parties were hired, every year, for 1 day each. . . . . These ancient harvest-days must have exhibited one of the most cheerful spectacles in the world. One can hardly imagine a more animated scene than that of between 200 and 300 harvest-people all busily employed at once, and enlivened with the expectation of a festivity, which perhaps they experienced but this one season in the year. All the inhabitants of the village, of both sexes, and all ages, that could work, must have been assembled on the occasion; a muster that, in the present state of things, would be impossible. The success of thus compressing so much business into so short a time must have depended on the weather. But dispatch seems to have been the plan of agriculture at this time, at least in this village. We have seen before, that 60 persons were hired for 1 day, to weed the corn. These throngs of harvest-people were superintended by a person who was called the head-reaper (*supermessor* or *præpositus*), who was annually elected, and presented to the lord, by the inhabitants; and it should seem that, in this village at least, he was always one of the customary tenants. The year he was in office, he was exempt from all or half of his usual rents and services, according to his tenure; he was to have his victuals and drink at the lord's table, if the lord kept house (*si dominus hospitium tenuerit*); if he did not, he was to have a livery of corn, as other domestics had; and his horse was to be kept in the manor-stable. He was next in dignity to the steward and bailiff. The hay-harvest was an affair of no great importance. There were but 30 acres of grass annually

mown at this period. This was done or paid for by the customary tenants. The price of mowing an acre was 6*d*."

By an "Assessment of the Corporation of Canterbury," made in 1594, the following were the rates of wages declared payable:—"Every labourer from Easter to Michaelmas, with meat and drink, 4*d*. per day; finding himself, 10*d*.; and from Michaelmas to Easter, with meat and drink, 4*d*.; without, 8*d*. Mowers per day, with meat and drink, 8*d*.; finding themselves, 14*d*. By the acre, with meat and drink, 4*d*.; without, 8*d*. Reapers per day, with meat and drink, 6*d*.; finding themselves, 12*d*.; by the acre, with meat and drink, 14*d*.; without, 28*d*. Plashing and teeming of a quick hedge, 2*d*. per rod. Laying upon the band and binding and copping of oats, 8*d*., barley, 10*d*. Threshers by the quarter with meat and drink, for the quarter and making clean of wheat and rye, 5*d*., oats and barley, 3*d*.; without meat and drink, for the quarter and making clean of wheat and rye, 12*d*., oats and barley, 6*d*. Making talewood, the load, 4*d*.; billets, per 1000, 12*d*. A bailiff, with livery, £3 per annum; without livery, £3 6*s*. 8*d*."—Hasted's Antiquities of Canterbury, 1801, vol. ii. Appendix.

"Larges," "usually a shilling" (says Major Moor in his Suffolk Glossary). "For this the reapers will ask you if you 'chuse to have it hallered.' If answered, yes, they assemble in a ring, holding each other's hands, and inclining their heads to the centre. One of them, detached a few yards apart, calls loudly, thrice, 'Holla Lar!—Holla Lar!—Holla Lar!—j e e s.' Those in the ring lengthen out o-o-o-o with a low sonorous note and inclined heads, and then throwing the head up, vociferate 'a-a-a-ah.' This thrice repeated for a shilling is the established exchange in Suffolk." "*Largesse* bounty, handfuls of money cast among the people."—Cotgrave. "Crye a larges when a rewarde is geven to workemen, *stipem vociferare*."—Huloet's Dict. 1552. The phrase "crie a largesse" occurs in Piers Plowman, B Text, xiii. 449. As to the gloves given to harvest-men see above and note to 51. 10.

57. 16. Though barley is generally mown, it is a slovenly practice, unless when performed with a cradle scythe.—M. See note to 16. 14.

57. 17. "Dallops," patches of barley which have run to straw.—M.

57. 22. Tidie means *neat*, *proper*, and *in season*.—M.

57. 24. "There finding a smack," *i.e.* finding a pleasant repast.

"Doo perish," *i.e.* cause to perish, ruin: the use of "do" in this sense is very common in Early English.

57. 25. "Lengthen" here is equivalent to increase the extent or produce of.

57. 26. "Fill out the black boule," etc. I am quite unable to explain this line; the "boule of bleith" is evidently the "merry bowl," but the epithet *black* I do not understand.

57. 30. "Thrifts ladder may clime," *i.e.* may prosper. Cf. ch. 9.

"*That* many doo hate," in edd. of 1573, 1580, 1585, etc., the reading is "*as* many do hate."

57. 36. "Ling perhaps looks for great extolling, being counted the beefe of the sea, and standing every fish-day (as a cold supporter) at my Lord Maior's table: yet it is nothing but a long cod: whereof the greater sised is called Organe Ling, and the other Codling, because it is no longer then a Cod, and yet hath the taste of Ling: whilst it is new it is called green-fish: when it is salted it is called Ling, perhaps of lying, because the longer it lyeth . . . . the better it is, waxing in the end as yellow as a gold noble, at which time they are worth a noble a piece."—Muffett, pp. 154-5, quoted in the Babees Book, ed. Furnivall.

57. 39. The following prices of various articles in Suffolk will be interesting:—1566. A lode of straw IIIIs.—1582. A capon VI*d.*; a calfe V*s.*; a firkin of butter VII*s.* VII*d.*; a capon and a pullet VI*d.*; a cocke (to fight) IIII*d.* (5 cockes bought to fight); a pullett III*d.* 5 pullets, 5 capons, 5 cockes, 1 calfe, were provided on the reckninge day and "these are allowed in the Churchwardens' accompte to be paide by them."—1590. To Coke for IIII combes of w otes whh he served to the Quene VI*s.* VIII*d.*; 14 rod of ditching cost V*s.* IIII*d.*—1596. Makinge a surplis for the church was II*d.*; a payer of hoose was XII*d.* another XIII*d.*; makyng this boke of accts (a single sheet written on two sides) VI*d.*—1599. Three days work ditchynge 2*s.*; a hard day's work was therefore 8*d.* per day, and a usual day's 4*d.* or 6*d.*; three days thatchinge (Thos. Garrarde) II*s.* IIII*d.*; wode was II*s.* the lode.—1587 or 8. A capon vi*d.*; a calfe v*s.*; a firkin of butter vii*s.* viii*d.*: two capons and one pullett vi*d.*; a cocke iiii*d.*; one cocke and one pullett vi*d.*; one pullett iii*d.*—1583 No. 5. One short spurred cocke ii*d.*; one chycken ii*d.*; one hene ii*d.*—1583 No. 4. Fower combes and too bushell of ottes at iv*s.* iv*d.* the combe: thre henes att thre pence a pece; bowes and arrowes IIII*d.*; ten milch kine 30*s.* each; seven bullocks 7*s.* each; six calves 5*s.* each; six horses together £7; one acre of wheat, XX*s.*; one acre of Bullimong land 33*s.* 4*d.*; a new carte £11; a porkling 28*d.*

Increased facilities of communication, and the numerous means that farmers now possess, through the press, of obtaining information as to prices of produce, etc., render *riding about* almost unnecessary.

57. 41. Tusser again sets out the advantages of ready money transactions, and of *keeping touch*, that is, punctuality and faithful regard to engagements. He buys at first hand who pays ready money from his own pocket; at second hand who pays ready money, but who, in order to enable him to do so, has to borrow a portion of the amount, because he has not so much money as he requires with him; at third hand who buys on credit.

57. 47. "Stourbridge or Sturbich, the name of a common field extending between Chesterton and Cambridge, near the little brook Sture, for about half a mile square, is noted for its fair which is kept annually on September 19th, and continues a fortnight. It is surpassed by few fairs in Great Britain, or even in Europe, for traffic, though of late it is much lessened. The booths are placed in rows like streets, by the name[s] of which they are called, as Cheapside, etc., and are filled with all sorts of trades. The Duddery, an area of 80 or 100 yards square, resembles Blackwell Hall. Large commissions are negotiated here for all parts of England in cheese, woolen goods, wool, leather, hops, upholsterers' and ironmongers' ware, etc., etc. Sometimes 50 hackney coaches from London, ply morning and night, to and from Cambridge, as well as all the towns around, and the very barns and stables are turned into inns for the accommodation of the poorer people. After the wholesale business is over, the country gentry generally flock in, laying out their money in stage-plays, taverns, music-houses, toys, puppet-shows, etc., and the whole concludes with a day for the sale of horses. This fair is under the jurisdiction of the University of Cambridge."—Walker's Gazetteer, ed. 1801. See also index to Brand's Antiquities.

Camden says it was anciently called Steresbrigg, from the little river Stere or Sture that runs by it (in his Britannia, under Cambridgeshire). There have been many guesses at the name and origin of this fair, *e.g.* that of Fuller in his History of the University, p. 66, concerning the clothier of Kendal. The truth of the matter is this: King John granted Sturbridge fair for the benefit of the hospital of lepers which stood there (*v. decretum Hubert. Arch. Cantuar. in Concil. Londinen. An.* 1200. *Regn. Johann.*; Spelman, ii. 127): in the certificatorium we are told that the keeper of the hospital holds twenty-four and a half acres of land in the county of Cambridgeshire to maintain these lepers. The Vice Chancellor has the same power in this fair that he has in the town of Cambridge. The University is always to have ground assigned for a booth by the mayor. Midsummer Fair was granted to the Prior and Convent of Barnwell, for much the same reason that Sturbridge was to the Lepers,—*ad eorum sustentationem.* In the reign of Henry the Sixth the Nuns of St. Radegund had the grant of Garlick Fair for the same reason.

"Sturbridge Fair was formerly proclaimed by both the Corporation and the University authorities. Originally lasting six weeks, in 1785 it lasted only three weeks, and now it lasts but one week. A very amusing account of its proclamation by the Vice Chancellor will be found in Gunning's 'Reminiscences of Cambridge.'"—S. N. in Notes and Queries, Aug. 25, 1877.

"When th' fair is done, I to the Colledg come,
Or else I drinke with them at Trompington,
Craving their more acquaintance with my heart,
Till our next *Sturbridg Fair*; and so wee part."—
Brathwaite's Honest Ghost, 1658, p. 189.

57. 51. "When it [the malt] hath gone, or beene turned, so long [21 days] vpon the floore, they carrie it to a kill, couered with *haire cloth*, where they giue it gentle heats (after they haue spread it there verie thin abroad) till it be drie, and in the meane while they turne it often, that it may be vniformelie dried."—Harrison, Description of England, ed. F. J. Furnivall, Part I. p. 156.

57. 55. Cf. September's Husbandry, Stanza 1.

58. 1. One part in ten is far below the present average value of land. If the whole produce will clear *four* rents, the industrious farmer would have no reason to complain, though he is now subject to heavy taxes, which, it is to be remarked are not included in the list of outgoings.—M.

58. 12. "Well fare the plough." On a flyleaf of a MS. of Piers Plowman (MS. R. 3, 14, in Trinity Coll. Camb.) is written,

"God spede the plouȝ
& sende vs korne I-now."

See print in beginning of Wright's ed. of Piers Plowman.

59. The advice given in this short piece, the most difficult, perhaps, that Tusser had written, is very good, but he has strained alliteration to an extravagant pitch.

60. 1. In the reign of Elizabeth an Act was passed, requiring a seven years' apprenticeship to enable a person to set up in business or trade; and hence the idea arose of dividing human life into periods of seven years.—M. The idea is much older; for, in Arnold's Chronicle (edition 1811), page 157, we find:—"The vij Ages of Mā liuing ī the World. The furst age is infance and lastith from y[e] byrth vnto vij yere of age. The ij is childhod and endurith vnto xv yere age. The iij age is adholocencye and endurith vnto xxv yere age. The iiij age is youth and endurith vnto xxxv yere age. The v age is manhod and endurith vnto l yere age. The vj age is [elde] and lasteth vnto lxx yere age. The vij age of mā is crepill and endurith vnto dethe."

See Prompt. Parv. p. 7, for another version of the above, the limits assigned to the several stages being different, and the seventh stage beginning at the resurrection.

61. 2. "Foxe, Ape with his toieng," etc. Dr. Mavor's edition reads, "For Ape with his toieng," etc.

62. "The tone from the tother;" the tone=that one, the tother= that other; where the *t* is the sign of the neuter gender, as in tha-*t*, i-*t*; compare the Latin *d* in i-*d*, quo-*d*, illu-*d*.—In ch. 110, p. 201, we have the curious forms "*thon*" and "*thother*."

62. 6. "To him and to hur," that is, to every one, or to any one. Cf. 94, 3, and

"The white lambe þat hurte was with the spere
Flemere of feendes out of hym and here."
Chaucer, Man of Law's Tale, l. 460, Six-Text ed.

62. 8. "Daieth"=dayeth, that is, appoints a *day* on which he promises to pay.

Gervase Markham, in the First Part of the English Husbandman, ch. 6, remarks:—"You may by these usuall observations, and the helpe of a better judgement, imploy the fruits of your labours to the best profit, and sell everything at the highest price, except you take upon you to *give day* and sell upon trust, which if you doe, you may then sell at what unconscionable reckoning you will." Cf.

"When drapers draw no gaines by *giving day*."—
Gascoigne, The Steel Glass, 1094.

62. 10. "By that and by this;" that is, by anything, or by chance. Compare stanza 6, and chap. 67, stanza 5, p. 153.

62. 17. "A tode with an R" is an elegant euphemism for *torde*; the meaning being that a bad husbandman is more likely to receive insults and refusals, than compliance with his requests. Compare Wycliffe's translation of Luke xiii. 8, as given at p. 365 of Dr. Bosworth's edit. of the Gothic and Anglo-Saxon Gospels, with the Versions of Wycliffe and Tyndale, London, 1865.

63. 6. "Experience should seeme to proue playnely, that Inclosures should be profitable and not hurtfull to the common weale; for we see the countryes where most Inclosiers be, are most wealthy, as *Essex*, *Kent*, *Northamptonshyre*, etc. And I have hearde a Ciuilian once say, that it was taken for a Maxime in his lawe (this saying), 'that which is possessed of many in common, is neglected of all;' and experience sheweth that Tenaunts in common be not so good husbandes, as when euery man hath his parte in seueralty; also, I have heard say, that in the most countreyes beyonde the Sea, they knowe not what a common grounde meaneth."—Stafford's Examination of Complaints, New Shakspere Soc., ed. Furnivall, p. 40.

63. 9. Fitzherbert shows how a township that is worth twenty marks a-year may be made worth £20, and the ground-work of his plan is to enclose the land. "By enclosing," he says, "a farmer shall save meat, drink, and wages of a shepherd; the wages of the swineherd, the which may fortune to be as chargeable as his whole rent; and also his corn shall be better saved from eating or destroying by cattle."

63. 12. Harman, 1567 (E. E. Text Soc., ed. Furnivall, p. 82), speaks of "lewtering lusks and lazy *lorrels*," and in Pierce Plowman's Crede we find in line 750, "lordes sones lowly to þo *losells* aloute," and in l. 755, "and leueþ swiche *lorels* for her lowe wordes."—See Note in Prompt. Parv. *s.v.* Lorel. Levins (Manip. Vocab. 1570) translates *lorel* by *nebulo*, *scurra*.

Courts for presenting nuisances are generally the greatest nuisances themselves. Under the semblance of justice, they often retard its execution. The members, or jury who compose them, do not want the power, but they want the independence to act right.—M.

63. 14. "In Bridewell a number be stript," etc. Although all the editions I have been able to examine read "lesse worthie than *theefe* to be whipt," I suspect the correct reading to be "lesse worthie than *theese* to be whipt." The mistake might easily occur through the similarity of the old *s* and *f*. The meaning, as the lines read at present, is not very clear, but if we adopt the suggested reading, the sense becomes at once apparent:—"In Bridewell many are stripped for flogging who do not deserve it so much as these."

63. 16. "Take them"=arrest them.

63. 18. "Mo," lit.=more; but also used in the sense of *others*. "This use of *mo* is not common, but there are a few examples of it. Thus in Specimens of English, ed. Morris and Skeat, we have at p. 47, l. 51,

> "Y sike for vnsete
> Ant mourne ase men doþ *mo*,"

i.e. 'I sigh for unrest, and mourn as *other* men do.' And on the next page (48, l. 22) we have

> 'Mody meneþ so doþ *mo*,
> Ichot ycham on of þo,'

i.e. 'The moody moan as *others* do; I wot I am one of them.' Somewhat similar is the expression *oþer mo*, where we should now say *others as well*, Piers Plowman, C. Text, Passus v. 10."—Rev. W. Skeat, in note to l. 1039 of Chaucer, Clerke's Tale, Clarendon Press Series. *Mo* is also used in the same sense in 67, 11, p. 154.

"Verlets," originally a servant to a knight, below page or squire, though often used in French Romance as equivalent to a squire. "Pages, *varlets*, ou damoiseaux: noms quelquefois communs aux *ecuyers*."—Cotgrave. Ducange (Gloss. M. et I. Lat.) has: "*Valeti valecti* appellati vulgo magnatum filii, qui necdum militare cingulum consecuti erant: vassallorum filii *vassaleti* dicti." Levins (Manip. Vocab.) says: "Varlett, *verna*." See Wedgwood, Dict. Eng. Etymology, *s.v.* Valet.

63. 19. "Ruleth the roste;" to *rule* the *roast* is to preside at the board, to assign what share one pleases to the guests; hence it came to mean to domineer, in which sense it is commonly used in our old authors. See Nares, s.v.

64. 1. With this description of an envious neighbour compare Langland's picture of *Invidia* (Envy) in Piers Plowman, B. Text, E. E. Text Soc., ed. Skeat, Passus v. l. 76.

64. 3. "His hatred procureth," etc., his hatred takes pains to bring bad to worse, his friendship is like that of Judas who, etc., *i.e.* is selfish.

64. 9. "His lips out of frame," *i.e.* are out of order, are not kept in order. Cf. the expression "loose in the haft."

64. 12. "Spials;" so Spenser, Faery Queene, i. 4:

> "And privie *spials* plast in all his way."

Levins (Manip. Vocab.) has "Spyall, *arbiter*."

64. 17. "Would'st thou not be glad to have the niggardly rascally *sheepbiter* come by some notable shame."—Shakspere, Twelfth Night, Act ii. sc. 5.

"Who is in this closet? let me see (*breaks it open*). Oh, *sheep-biter*, are you here?"—Shadwell, Bury Fair, 1689.

64. 18. "Coxcombe:" see Cotgrave, s.v. *Effeminé*, *Enfourner*, *Fol*, *Lambui*.

64. 20. Davus is the common name in Terence for the cunning, plotting servant.

64. 21. Thersites, the ugliest and most scurrilous of the Greeks before Troy. He spared in his revilings neither prince nor chief, but directed his abuse especially against Achilles and Ulysses. The name is often used to denote a calumniator. Cf.

"When rank Thersites opes his mastiff jaws,
We shall hear music, wit, and oracle."
Shakspere, Troilus and Cressida, Act i. sc. 3.

64. 22. "Shall swell like a tode." Cf. 65, 6.

64*. "To hold a candle to the devil is to assist in a bad cause or an evil matter."—Ray. Hazlitt (English Proverbs, p. 407) gives "'Tis good sometimes to hold a candle to the devil." Thus we find an anonymous correspondent writing to John Paston: "for howr Lords love, goo tharow with Wyll Weseter, and also plese Chrewys as ye thynke in yow hert best for to do; for it is a comon proverbe, 'A man must sumtyme *set a candel befor the Devyle*;' and therfor thow it be not alder most mede and profytabyl, yet of ij harmys the leste is to be take."—Paston Letters, ed. Gairdner, ii. 73.

64*. 7. At Canterbury is a representation of Master Shorne holding up his hand in a threatening attitude at the Devil, who is in a boot.

64*. 8. "False birds can fetch the wind;" an expression taken from hawking. To *fetch the wind*, to *take the wind* (Bacon), and to *have the wind* are various forms of the same expression, the meaning of which is to gain or take an advantage. We still use the expression "to get to windward of another," meaning to get the better or advantage of him. Mavor reads, "false *words* can fetch the wind," *i.e.* slander will spread as though borne on the wind. I do not, however, know on what authority he has adopted this reading, as the text of 1577 gives "birds."

65. The following poem on Evil Tongues is from a MS. of the 15th century, edited for the Percy Soc. by the late Mr. T. Wright, 1847: "A man that con his tong stere,
He ther not rek wer that he go."

"Ittes knowyn in every schyre,
Wekyd tongges have no pere;
I wold thei wer brent in the fer,
That warke men soo mykyll wo.

Ittes knowyn in every lond,
Wekyd tongges don gret wrong,
Thei make me to lyyn long,
And also in myche car.

Ȝyf a man go in clothes gay,
Or elles in gud aray,
Wekyd tongges yet wyl say,
Wer cam the by therto?

Ȝyf a man go in cloys ill,
And have not the world at wyl,
Wekyd tongges thei wyll hym spyll,
And seyd he ys a stake, lat hym goo.

Now us to amend God yeve us grace,
Of repentens and of gud grace,
That we mut se hys glorius face.
Amen, Amen, for charyte."

65. 1. There is a smoothness in the versification of this sonnet, and a succession of imagery, though drawn from common sources, which we do not often find in Tusser. He has made a good use of the figure *erotesis*.—M. Compare Milton, Lycidas, 45:

"As killing as the canker to the rose,
Or *taint-worm* to the weanling herds that graze."

66. 1. Janus, an old Italian deity, the god of the sun and the year, to whom the month of January was dedicated.

66. 5. Ver=Spring, Æstas=Summer, Hyems=Winter.

66. 7. "Delaide;" so in Spenser, Faery Queene, ix. 30. "But to *delay* the heat," and in Prothalamium 3:

"Zephyrus did softly play
A gentle spirit, that lightly did *delay*
Hot Titan's beames."

66. 9. Alluding to the thirteen revolutions of the moon in the year.

67. It appears from the Books of the Stationers' Company, on the authority of Warton (Hist. of Eng. Poetry, vol. iii. p. 428) that a licence was granted to T. Hackett, in the year 1562, to print "A Dialogue of Wyvynge and Thryvynge of Tusshers with ij lessons for olde and yonge."

67. 2. "Bolted out," a term taken from the language and usage of millers, who use the word "to bolt" of the separation of the bran from the flour. Cf. Chaucer, Nonnes Prior's Tale, 415:

"But yit I can not *bult it to the bren*."

And Spenser, Faery Queene, iv. 24:

"He now had *boulted* all the floure."

"Time and nature will *bolt out* the truth of things."—D'Estrange. "To *boulte out* the truth in reasoning, *limare veritatem in disceptatione*."—Baret's Alvearie. A "Bolting Cloth" is the name in Lincolnshire for a cloth used for sifting meal in mills. See Peacock's Glossary, *s.v.* There was a term "boultings" or "boltings," used of private arguings of cases in some of the Inns of Court. "Boulter, a sifter."—Coles' Dict. 1676.

67. 3. "Could the way to thriue." *Could* is here used in its old sense of *knew*, or *understood*. A.S. *cunnan*, to know; *ic can*, I know; *ic cuðe*, I knew.

"To stay himselfe in some good plot," etc.; compare 10. 8.

67. 5. "Of this and that;" cf. 62. 10.

67. 6. "The blacke oxe neare trod on thy fut:" a proverbial expression, meaning, you have experienced misfortune close at home.

In Peacock's Glossary of Manley, etc. (E. D. Soc. 1877), we have: "The *Black Bull's* trodden on him;" that is, he is in a very bad temper. And the following passage from Bernard's Terence is quoted: "Prosperitie hangs on his sleeue; the *black oxe* cannot tread on his foot."

"Venus waxeth old; and then she was a pretie wench, when Juno was a young wife; now crowes foote is on her eye, and the *black oxe* hath trod on her foot."—Lyly's Sapho and Phao, 1584, ed. 1858, i. 199.

Mr. George Vere Irving (Notes and Queries, 3rd Ser. xii. 488) remarks that this expression is at this day frequently used in Scotland in reference to a person who has experienced misfortune. See Hazlitt's Eng. Proverbs, p. 359.

67. 8. "It is too much we dailie heare," etc. This proverbial expression occurs in the *Townley Mysteries*, p. 86, as—

"A man may not wive,
And also thrive,
And all in one year."

67. 11. "As *mo* have bin;" compare note on 63. 18.

67. 18. "The good wiues husband weares no breech." So in a song in the MS. of the 15th cent. quoted above, the heading of which is

"*Nova, Nova*, sawe yow ever such,
The moste mayster of the hows weryth no brych."

The burden of the song being

"Lest the most mayster wer no brych."

67. 20. The same reply is attributed to Thales. See his life in Diogenes Laertius, Bk. i. 26.

67. 22. "Yyng men, I red that ye be war,
That ye cum not in the snar;
For he is browt in meche car,
That have a shrow onto his wyfe.

In a panter I am caute,
My fot his pennyd, I may not owt;
In sorow and car he his put,
That have, etc.

With a qwene yif that thou run,
Anon it is told into the town;
Sorow he hath both up and down,
That have, etc.

Song in MS. of 15th century quoted above.

"Feareth me," that is, it frightens me, I fear, as in "me liketh" = it pleases me, I like.

67. 23. "As good a shrew is as a sheepe," etc. This proverb appears in *Epistolæ Hoelianæ*, ed. 1754, p. 177, in a letter dated 5th February, 1625-6, as "It is better to marry a shrew than a sheep." In Taylor's Pastorall, 1624, we have "A shrew is better than a sheep."

68. William, the first Lord Paget, and the patron of Tusser, married Anne, daughter of Mr. Prestin, of the County of Lancaster; and to her it is most probable the Book of Huswifery was dedicated, and not to Margaret, the daughter of Sir H. Newton, and lady of Thomas, Lord Paget.

68. 8. "By their fruits ye shall know them, do men gather grapes of thorns or figs of thistles?"

69. 1. The rime in the last two lines is most remarkable; apparently *thriue* is pronounced *threw*, as Mr. Ellis contends.

69. 6. From the last two lines of this stanza it would appear that Tusser was a widower at the time when he wrote this Address to the Reader, or at least when he first wrote on the subject of Huswifery.

72. "A description of Huswife," etc. This antithetical description seems to have been introduced, in order that it might correspond with the description of Husbandry, chapter 8, p. 16.—M.

73. 1. According to Fitzherbert, the farmers' wives must have been patterns of diligence and industry, and a variety of duties devolved upon them which have since ceased to be required, or have fallen with more propriety upon the other sex. They had to measure out the quantity of corn to be ground, and see that it was sent to the miller. The poultry, swine, and cows were under their charge; and they superintended the brewing and baking. The garden was peculiarly the care of the farmer's wife. She had to depend upon it for various herbs which are no longer in use, but which could not be dispensed with when spices were rare and costly. Besides pot-herbs, strewing-herbs were required for the chambers, and herbs possessing medical virtues. The list of fruits at this date was confined to a few of indigenous growth, which were but little improved by skill and management. Tusser directs his housewife to transplant into her garden wild strawberries from the woods. All the writers on rural economy during this period recommend the farmer's wife carefully to attend to her crop of flax and hemp. When, however, Fitzherbert asserts that it is a wife's duty "to winnow all manner of corn, to make malt, to wash, and to make hay, shear corn, and, in time of need, help her husband to fill the muck-wain or dung-cart, drive the plough, to load hay, corn, and such other, to go to market and sell butter or pigs, fowls or corn," it is to be presumed that he had in his view the smallest class of yeomen, who had no hired servants.

73. 5. "Reason their cace," that is, gossip and argue over their circumstances.

73. 8. "Home is home, be it never so ill." Ballad licensed in 1569-70. Clarke (Paræm. 1639, p. 101) has with us, "home is home, be it never so homely." On the other hand, Heywood, in his Epigrams, 1562, says:

"Home is homely, yea, and to homely sometyme,
Where wives' footestooles to their husbandes' heads clime."

73. 13. "Familie"=household. Compare chap. 9, st. 12.

74. 5. "Maides, three a clock," etc. Compare Romeo and Juliet, Act iv. sc. 4, 3—

"The second cock hath crow'd,
The curfew bell hath rung, 'tis three o'clock."

"Lay your bucks," *i.e.* get ready the washing tubs. Compare: "Throw foul linen upon him as if it were going to *bucking*."—Shakspere, Merry Wives of Wind., Act iii. sc. 3. Buck-basket, the basket in which linen is carried to the wash. "Bouck-fatt, a washing tub."—Upton Inventories, p. 28. Cf. "And for I can so wele wasche and so wele *bowke*, Godde has made me his chaumberere."—The Pilgrimage of the Life of the Manhode, f. 21*b*., MS. in Libr. of St. John's Coll. Camb. "'I *bucke* lynen clothes to scoure of their fylthe and make them whyte, *Je bue*. Bucke these shyrtes, for they be to foule to be wasshed by hande, *buez ces chemises, car elles sont trop sallies de les lauer a sauon*.'—Palsgrave. 'Buée, lie wherwith clothes are scowred; also a *buck* of clothes; *Buer*, to wash a *buck*, to scowre with lie; *Buandiere* f., a laundresse, or buck-washer.'—Cotgrave. To *buck* is to cleanse clothes by steeping them in lye: see *Buck* in Webster, Nares, Wedgwood, etc."—Rev. W. W. Skeat, note to P. Plowman, B. Text, xiv. 19.

76. 1. The hours of meals varied at different dates. In the Myrour of Our Lady, ed. Blunt, p. 15, we read: "At houre of tyerse [9 A.M.] labourers desyre to haue theyr dyner."

In Chambers's Book of Days, i. 96, we read that Gervase Markham, in 1653, makes the ploughman have three meals, viz. breakfast at 6 A.M., dinner at half-past 3 P.M., and supper at 6 P.M. See also note to 85. 1.

77. 8. In the Library of Caius Coll. Camb. is a volume of Tracts, No. 286, one of which, published in 1555, An Account of the Cruelties of the King of Spain, has as its motto: "Beware of Had I wiste." This is also the title of a poem in the Paradyce of Daynty Deuyses, 1578. It is quoted by Sir Simon D'Ewes (Diary, etc., ii. 366):

"Telle neuere the more thoug thou myche heere,
And euere be waare of *had-y-wist.*"
Babees Book, ed. Furnivall, p. 264, l. 72.

77. 20. See note on ch. 10. 46.

78. 4. "Beware that ye geue no persone palled drynke, for feere
Hit mygtt brynge many a man in disese durynge many a yere."
—John Russell's Boke of Norture, in Babees Book, p. 13.

"Sowre ale, and dead ale, and ale the whiche doth stande a tylte is good for no man."—Andrew Boorde, Regimen of Health.

"Of ale and beer, as well as of wine, we find various kinds mentioned. There were single beer, or small ale, which could do little more than quench thirst,—and double beer, which was recommended as containing a double quantity of malt and hops,—and double-double beer, which was twice as strong as that,—and dagger-ale, which, as the name implies, was reckoned particularly sharp and dangerous,—and bracket, a kind of ale which we are unable distinctly to describe. But the favourite drink, as well as the chief article of vulgar debauch, was a kind of ale commonly called huffcap, but which was also termed 'mad dog,' 'angel's food,' 'dragon's milk,' and other such ridiculous names, by the frequenters of ale-houses: 'and never,' says Harrison, 'did Romulus and Remus suck their she-wolf with such eager and sharp devotion as these men hale at huffcap, till they be as red as cocks, and little wiser than their combs.' The higher classes, who were able to afford such a luxury, brewed a generous liquor for their own consumption, which they did not bring to the table till it was two years old. This was called March ale, from the month in which it was brewed. But the servants had to content themselves with a more simple beverage that was seldom more than a month old. A cup of choice ale was often as richly compounded with dainties as the finest wines. Sometimes it was warmed, and qualified with sugar and spices; sometimes with a toast; often with a roasted crab or apple, making the beverage still known under the name of Lambs'-wool; while to stir the whole composition with a sprig of rosemary, was supposed to give it an additional flavour. The drinks made from fruit were chiefly cider, perry, and mum. Those that had formerly been made from honey seem to have fallen into disuse in consequence of the general taste for stronger potations; metheglin being now chiefly confined to the Welsh. A simple liquor, however, was still used in Essex, called by Harrison, somewhat contemptuously, 'a swish-swash,' made of water with a little honey and spice, but 'as differing,' he says, 'from true metheglin as chalk doth from cheese.' He informs us, moreover, that already the tapsters of England had learned to adulterate their ale and beer with pernicious compounds."—Pict. Hist. of England, ii. 883.

"In the parish of Hawsted, Suffolk, the allowance of food to the labourer in harvest was, two herrings per day, milk from the manor dairy to make cheese, and a loaf of bread, of which fifteen were made from a bushel of wheat. Messes of potage made their frequent appearance at the rustic board."—Knight, Pict. Hist. of England, i. 839.

79. Harrison gives an account (pp. 153–4) of the following kinds of bread made in England: 1. Mainchet, "commonlie called white bread, in Latine *Primarius panis.*" 2. Cheat "or wheaton bread, so named bicause the colour therof resembleth the graie [or yellowish] wheat [being cleane and well dressed,] and out of this is the coursest of the bran (vsuallie called gurgeons or pollard) taken. The raueled is a kind of cheat bread also, but it reteineth more of the grosse, and lesse of the pure substance of the wheat." 3. Brown bread, of which there were two kinds, viz. (*a*) of whole meal unsifted, (*b*) pollard bread, with a little rye meal, and called Miscelin or Meslin. "In champeigne countries much rie and barleie bread is eaten, but especiallie where wheat is scant and geson."

81. 2. "Baies." Halliwell prints this word as *baics* in his Dictionary, defining it as "chidings, reproofs," and giving as his authority Hunter's Additions to Boucher.

81. 3. "Droie." See Note in Prompt. Parv., s.v. *Dryvylle* and *Deye.* Probably a corruption of *droile;* a scullion, kitchen-boy, or servant of all-work.—M. Droie also occurs in Stubbes' Anatomie of Abuses, 1583.

84. 2. "In some places it [the malt] is dried at leisure with wood alone, or strawe alone, in other with wood and strawe togither; but of all, the strawe dried is the most excellent. For the wood dried malt when it is brued, beside that the drinke is higher of colour, it dooth hurt and annoie the head of him that is not vsed thereto, bicause of the smoake. Such also as vse both indifferentlie, doo barke, cleaue and drie their wood in an ouen, therebv to remooue all moisture that shuld procure the fume, and this malt is in the second place, and with the same likewise, that which is made with dried firze, broome, etc.; whereas, if they also be occupied greene, they are in maner so preiudiciall to the corne, as is the moist wood."—Harrison, Description of England, ed. F. J. Furnivall, Part I. p. 157.

84. 6. See Note on ch. 19. 39.

85. 1. "The husbandmen dine at high noone as they call it, and sup at seuen or eight."—Harrison, Part I. p. 166.

85. 5. Though all the standard editions read "chaps walking," may it not be a misprint for "chaps wagging," that is, mouths craving?—M.

85. 16. "Enough is a plentie." Cf. "Mesure is medcyne þouȝ þow moche ȝerne."—Piers Plowman, Passus i. 35. "But mesure is a meri mene, þouȝ men moche ȝerne."—Richard the Redeles, E.E. Text Soc., ed. Skeat, ii. 139. "Measure is treasure."—Dyce's Skelton, ii. 238, 241. "Enough is as good as a feast."—Gascoigne's Posies, 1575.

86. 3. "Chippings." The "Chippings of Trencher-brede" in Lord Percy's household were used "for the fedynge of my lords houndis."—Percy Household Book, p. 353. "Other ij pages . . . them oweth to *chippe* bredde, but too nye the crumme."—Household Ordin. pp. 71–2. In the *Regimen Sanitatis Salerni*, ed. 1634, p. 71, we are warned against eating crusts, because "they ingender a dust cholor, or melancholly humours, by reason that they bee burned and dry."

86. 10. "Call quarterly seruants to court and to leete," that is, call to account.

88. 7. "Lurching," cf. footnote to 23. 3, p. 61.

89. 2. "Bandog," cf. note on ch. 10. 19.

89. 12. "Guise."

> "For he was laid in white Sheep's wool
> New pulled from tanned Fells;
> And o'er his Head hang'd Spiders webs
> As if they had been Bells.
> Is this the *Country Guise*, thought he?
> Then here I will not stay."
> Ballad, K. Alfred and the Shepherd.
>
> "'Tis thy *Country Guise*, I see,
> To be thus bluntish still."—Ibid.

"The Norman *guise* was to walke and jet up and downe the streets." —Lambert's Peramb. of Kent, 1826, p. 320.

90. 2. The Skreene was a wooden settee or settle, with a high back sufficient to screen the sitters from the outward air, and was in the time of our ancestors an invariable article of furniture near all kitchen fires, and is still seen in the kitchens of many of our old farm-houses in Cheshire. The meaning of the two lines:

> "If ploughman get hatchet or whip to the skreene,
> maides loseth their cock if no water be seene,"

is, "if the ploughman can get his whip, ploughstaff, hatchet, or anything he wants in the field to the fireside (*screen* being here equivalent to *fireside*) before the maid has got her kettle on, then she loses her Shrove-tide cock, which belongs wholly to the men."

"Plough Monday." "The Monday next after Twelfth-day, when our Northern plow-men beg plow-money to drink; and in some places if the plowman (after that day's work) come with his whip to the kitchin hatch, and cry 'cock in pot' before the maid says 'cock on the dung-hill,' he gains a cock on Shrove-Tuesday."—Coles' Dict. 1708. "Among the rural customs connected with the anniversary of Christmas were those of Plough-Monday, which fell on the first Monday after Twelfth-day. This was the holiday of the ploughmen, who used to go about from house to house begging for plough-money to drink. In the northern counties, where this practice was called the fool-plough (a corruption perhaps of *yule*-plough), a number of sword-dancers dragged about a plough, while one of the party, called the Bessey, was dressed for the occasion like an old woman; and another, who was the fool of the pageant, was almost covered with skins, and wore the tail of some animal dangling down his back. While the rest danced, one of these odd personages went among the spectators, rattling a box, and collecting small donations; and it is said that whosoever refused to pay had the plough dragged to his door and the soil of his threshold ploughed up."—Pict. Hist. of England, ii. 894.

90. 3. "Shroftide." The Hen is hung at a Fellow's back who has also some Horse Bells about him, the rest of the Fellows are blinded, and have Boughs in their Hands, with which they chase this Fellow and his Hen about some large Court or small Enclosure. The Fellow with his Hen and Bells shifting as well as he can, they follow the sound, and sometimes hit him and his Hen, other times, if he can get behind one of them, they thresh one another well favour'dly; but the Jest is, the Maids are to blind the Fellows, which they do with their Aprons, and the cunning Baggages will endear their Sweet Hearts with a peeping hole, while the others look out as sharp to hinder it. After this the Hen is boil'd with Bacon, and store of Pancakes and Fritters are made. She that is noted for lying a Bed long or any other Miscarriage, hath the first Pancake presented to her, which most commonly falls to the Dog's share at last, for no one will own it their due.—T.R.

"Let glad Shrove Tuesday bring the pancake thin
Or fritters rich with apples stored within."

Oxford Sausage.

90. 5. "Wake Day." The Wake-day is the day on which the Parish Church was dedicated, called So, because the Night before it, they were used to watch till Morning in the Church and feasted all the next day. Waking in the Church was left off because of some abuses, and we see here it was converted to wakeing at the Oven.—T.R. "Similar to the church-ales, though of a still more ancient origin, were the Wakes. It had been the custom, on the dedication of a church, or the birth-day of a saint, for the people to assemble on the night previous, to hold a religious vigil in the open air; and, as they remained all night occupied in devotional exercises, this practice was called a wake. Such a method of spending the night, however, soon gave place to very different employments; and feasting, riot, and licentiousness became the prevailing characteristics of these vigils. These concourses, also, from every neighbouring town and parish, naturally suggested the expediency of improving such opportunities for the purposes of traffic; and hence the wakes gradually became fairs, which in some places they still continue to be."—Pict. Hist. of England, ii. 897.

"Flawnes;" a kind of pancake was also so called. Nettleham feast at Easter is called the *Flown*, possibly from *flauns* having been formerly eaten at that period of the year: but see Babees

Book, p. 173, where Flawnes are stated to be "*Cheesecakes* made of ground cheese beaten up with eggs and sugar, coloured with saffron, and baked in 'cofyns' or crusts."

"Bread an chese, butere and milk,
Pastees and *flaunes*."—Havelok, ed. Skeat, 644.

For flaunes.

"Take new chese and grynde hit fayre,
In morter with egges, without dysware;
Put powder þerto of sugur, I say,
Coloure hit with safrone ful wele þou may;
Put hit in cofyns þat ben fayre,
And bake hit forthe, I þe pray."
Liber Cure Cocorum, ed. Morris, p. 39.

90. 6. A goose used formerly to be given at harvest-home, to those who had not overturned a load of corn in carrying during harvest.—M.

90. 7. "Fyrmente is made of whete and mylke, in the whiche, yf flesshe be soden, to eate it is not co*m*mendable, for it is harde of dygestyon; but whan it is dygested it doth nowrysshe, and it doth strength a man."—Andrew Boorde's Dyetary, E.E. Text Soc. ed. F. J. Furnivall, p. 263. The following recipe for making Furmenty is from the Liber Cure Cocorum, ed. Morris, p. 7:

Furmente.

Take wete, and pyke[1] hit fayre (and clene)
And do hit in a morter shene;
Bray hit a lytelle, with water hit spryng[2]
Tyl hit hulle, with-oute lesyng.
þen wyndo[3] hit wele, nede þou mot;
Wasshe hit fayre, put hit in pot;
Boyle hit tylle hit brest, þen
Let hit doun, as I þe kenne.
Take now mylke, and play hit up
To hit be thykkerede to sup.
Lye hit up with yolkes of eyren,[4]
And kepe hit wele, lest hit berne.[5]
Coloure hit with safron and salt hit wele,
And servys hit forthe, Syr, at þe mele;
With sugur candy þou may hit dowce,
If hit be served in grete lordys howce.
Take black sugur for mener menne;
Be ware þerwith, for hit wylle brenne.[5]

The following recipes for the manufacture of Furmenty are given in Pegge's Forme of Cury, pp. 91 and 121: 1. For to make Fur-

[1] pick. [2] sprinkle. [3] winnow. [4] eggs. [5] burn.

menty, "Nym[1] clene wete, and bray it in a morter wel that the holys[2] gon al of and seyt[3] yt til it breste and nym yt up, and lat it kele[4] and nym fayre fresch broth and swete mylk of Almandys or swete mylk of kyne and temper yt al, and nym the yolkys of eyryn,[5] boyl it a lityl and set yt adoun and messe yt forthe wyth fast venyson and fresch moton." 2. For to make Formenty on a Fischeday, "Tak the mylk of the Hasel Notis, boyl the wete wyth the aftermelk til it be dryyd, and tak and colour yt wyth Saffroun, and the ferst mylk cast therto and boyle wel and serve yt forth." In Mr. Peacock's Glossary of Manley, etc., we have: "Frumerty, a preparation of creed-wheat[6] with milk, currants, raisins and spices in it."

91. 1. To make Aqua Composita, chap. 223: "Take of Sage, Hysope, Rosemarie, Mynt, Spike or Lauender leaues, Marioram, Bay leaues, of each like much, of all foure good handfulles to one galon of liquour. Take also of Cloues, Mace, Nutmegs, Ginger, Cinnamon, Pepper, Graines, of each a quarter of an ounce, Liquorice and Annise, of each halfe a pound: beat the spices grosse,[7] and first wash the herbes, then breake them gently betweene your hands. Scrape off the barke from the Liquorice, and cut it into thin slices, and punne[8] the Annise grosse, then put altogether into a gallon or more of good Ale or Wine, and let them steepe all night close couered in some vessell of earth or wood, and the next morning after distill them with a Limbecke or Serpentine. But see that your fire be temperate, and that the head of your Limbecke be kept colde continually with fresh water, and that the bottom of your Limbecke bee fast luted with Rye dough, that so Ayre issue out. The best Ale to make Aqua Composita of is to be made of Wheate malte, and the next of cleane Barley malte; and the best Wine for that purpose is Sacke."—Cogan's Haven of Health, ed. 1612, pp. 222–3.

92. 4. A *Cockney*, the derivation of which word has been much disputed, appears to me clearly to come from the verb to *cocker*, to *cock*, by contraction, as in this passage. A *cockney*, therefore, is one who has been brought up effeminately, and spoilt by indulgence, whether a native of the city or of the country.—M.

"The original meaning of *cockney* is a child too tenderly or delicately nurtured, one kept in the house and not hardened by out-of-doors life; hence applied to citizens, as opposed to the hardier inhabitants of the country, and in modern times confined to the inhabitants of London. The Promptorium Parvulorum, and the authorities cited in Mr. Way's note, give '*Coknay*, carifotus, delicius, mammotrophus'; 'To bring up like a *cocknaye*, mignoter.' 'Delicias facere, to play the *cockney*.' Cf. 'Puer in deliciis matris nutri-

[1] take. [2] hulls. [3] seethe. [4] cool. [5] eggs.
[6] wheat simmered until tender. [7] not fine, coarse. [8] beat, pound.

tus, Anglice, a *cokenay*.'—Halliwell. '*Cockney*, niais, mignot.'—Sherwood. The Fr. *coqueliner*, to dandle, cocker, fedle, pamper, make a wanton of a child, leads us in the right direction."—Wedgwood, Etymol. Dict. "A *cockney*, a childe tenderly brought up; a dearling. *Cockering*, mollis illa educatio quam indulgentiam vocamus."—Baret's Alvearie, 1580.

94. In chapter 62 of the First Part of this work, p. 139, we had a comparison between good and bad husbandry, and we are here presented with a contrast between good and bad huswifery.

94. 2. Compare Taming of the Shrew, Act iv. sc. 3, 57:

"With scarfs and fans and double change of *bravery*."

94. 8. "Good huswiferie *canteth*." The ed. of 1573 reads "*franteth*," the meaning of which is "to be careful, economical."

95. 1. For boys the practice of music would be degrading, except as a profession; and even for girls, however fashionable it may be, it is generally worse than useless, as it occupies that time which ought to be devoted to much more important purposes.—M.

95. 2. "Least homelie breaker," etc., that is, lest an inexperienced teacher ruin the mind of the pupil, as an unpractised horse-breaker will spoil a promising colt.

95. 3. "Well a fine," a phrase meaning to a good purpose, a good result.

95. 5. "Cocking Mams," that is, over-indulgent mothers. "A father to much *cockering*, Pater nimis indulgens."—Baret's Alvearie, 1580. See Note to 92. 4.

"Shifting Dads," that is, fathers who are constantly shifting their children from one school to another.

97. 1. "Assone as a passenger comes to an Inne the Host or Hostesse visit him; and if he will eate with the Host or at a common table with others, his meale will cost him sixe pence, or in some places but foure pence (yet this course is lesse honourable and not used by gentlemen); but if he will eate in his chamber he commands what meate he will, according to his appetite, and as much as he thinkes fit for him and his company."—Fynes Moryson's Itinerary, 1617, Part III. p. 151.

97. 3. "To purchase linne." To purchase Lynn, by petty savings, seems to have been a proverbial mode of expression, used in ridicule of stinginess.

97. 5. "You are on the high way to Needham."—Ray.

98. 1. The braggadocios and coxcombs of the day would use their daggers to carve with, which were perfectly harmless for any other purpose. Forks were yet strangers to an English dinner-table. Knives were first *made* in England, according to Anderson, in 1563. A meat-knife of Queen Elizabeth's, mentioned in Nichols's "Progresses," had "a handle of white bone and a conceyte in it." In the same work we read of "a dozen of horn spoons in a bunch," as the instruments "meetest to eat furmenty porage with all;" also of "a folding spoon of gold," and "a pair of small snuffers, silver-gilt."—Pictorial History of England, ii. 856.

98. 4. "Go toie with his nodie." The edition of 1573 reads "go toy with his noddy, with ape in the street," and more recent editions read "go toy with his noddy-like ape in the street." This reading has been adopted by Dr. Mavor. Peacock's Gloss. gives "Noddipol a sillie person. 'Whorson *nodipol* that I am!'—Bernard's Terence, 43. 'A verye *nodypoll* nydyote myght be ashamed to say it.'—The Workes of Sir Thomas More, 1557, p. 209."

99. 3. "Fisging." The Rev. W. Skeat, in his note to Piers Plowman, C. Text, Passus x. l. 153, "And what frek of þys folde *fiskeþ* þus a-boute," remarks: "*Fisketh*, wanders, roams. As this word is scarce, I give all the instances of it that I can find. In Sir Gawayne and the Grene Knight, ed. Morris, l. 1704, there is a description of a foxhunt, where the fox and the hounds are thus mentioned:—

'& he *fyskez* hem by-fore · þay founden hym sone'—

i.e. and he (the fox) runs on before them (the hounds); but they soon found him. 'Fyscare abowte ydylly; Discursor, discursatrix, vagulus vel vagator, vagatrix.'—Prompt. Parv. p. 162. 'Fiskin abowte yn ydilnesse; Vago, giro, girovago.'—Ibid.

'Such serviture also deserveth a check,
That runneth out *fisking*, with meat in his beck [*mouth*].'—
Tusser, Five Hundred Points, etc., ed. Mavor, p. 286.

'Then had every flock his shepherd, or else shepherds; now they do not only run *fisking about* from place to place, . . but covetously join living to living.'—Whitgift's Works, i. 528. 'I *fyske*, ie fretille. I praye you se howe she *fysketh* about.'—Palsgrave. '*Trotière*, a raumpe, fisgig, *fisking* huswife, raunging damsell.'—Cotgrave.

'Then in cave, then in a field of corn,
Creeps to and fro, and *fisketh* in and out.'
Dubartas (in Nares).

'His roving eyes rolde to and fro,
He *fiskyng* fine, did mincyng go.'
Kendalls's Flower of Epigrammes, 1577 (Nares).

'Tom Tankard's cow . . . .
Flinging about his halfe aker, *fisking* with her tail.'
Gammer Gurton's Needle, i. 2.

'*Fieska*, to *fisk* the tail about; to *fisk* up and down.'—Swedish Dictionary, by J. Serenius. '*Fjeska*, v.n. to fidge, to fidget, to *fisk*.'—Swed. Dict. (Tauchnitz)."

100. 3. In the Rolls of Parliament, at the opening of the Parliament of 2 Rich. II. in the year 1378, we find—"Qui sont appellez *Bacbyters* sont auxi come chiens qi mangeont les chars crues," etc. In the Ancren Riwle (Camden Soc. ed. Morton), p. 86, are described two kinds of *backbiters*, who are defined generally as "Bacbitares, þe biteð oðre men bihinden"; the two kinds are 1. those who openly speak evil of others, and 2. those who under the cloak of friendship slander others. The latter is stated to be far the worse. In an Old Eng. Miscellany (E. E. Text Soc. ed. Morris), p. 187, we are told that "Alle *bacbytares* heo wendeþ to helle."—Rev. W. W. Skeat, note to P. Plowman, B. v. 89.

"The friend doth hate." The edition of 1585 reads, evidently by a misprint, *fiends*.

102. 1. "Roinish," lit. scurvy, hence coarse, rough. "*Rongneux*, scabbie, mangie, scurvie."—Cotgrave. It occurs twice in the "Romaunt of the Rose," ll. 988 and 6190. In the form *rinish*, signifying "wild, jolly, unruly, rude," it is found among the Yorkshire words in Thoresby's Letter to Ray, reprinted by the Eng. Dial. Soc. "Rennish," in the sense of "furious, passionate," which is in Ray's collection of North-country words, is, perhaps, another form of the word.

105. 16. "Still presently," *i.e.* always as close at hand.

106. 15. "In vsing there his will," that is, in doing so he acted of his own free will.

106. 16. "Scene"=appeared, showed himself.

107. 1. "Do show" (to who thou wouldst to know). The meaning is perfectly clear, but the manner in which it is expressed is very curious. We may paraphrase it thus: "doth show to him whom thou wishest to teach."

107. 4. Compare Psalm ciii. 15, 6.

108. 1. "Let gift no glorie looke," that is, in giving alms look for (expect) no praise or earthly reward for so doing.

108. 2. "Provoke"=urge.

111. In the edition of 1577 the arrangement of this chapter is somewhat different. The Latin verses are first printed by themselves, and headed "Sancti Barnardi dicta," and after comes the English version, with the following title: "Eight of Saint Barnardes verses, translated out of Latin | into english by this Aucthor for one kind | of note to serue both ditties." The translation in the "Paradise of Dainty Devices," mentioned by Mason, is by Barnaby Rich, under the signature of "My Luck is Loss." The following is the first verse, transcribed for comparison with Tusser's version:

"Why doth each state apply itself to worldly praise?
And undertake such toil, to heap up honour's gain,
Whose seat, though seeming sure, on fickle fortune stays,
Whose gifts are never prov'd perpetual to remain?
But even as earthen pots, with every fillip fails:
So fortune's favour flits, and fame with honour quails."

111. 5. "Carle." M. Licinius Crassus, surnamed Dives, or the Rich, one of the first Roman Triumvirate, and celebrated for his avarice and love of the table.

111. 6. "O thou fit bait for wormes!" In the Treatise of Vincentio Saviolo, printed in 1595 with the title "Vincentio Saviolo his

Practise. In two Bookes. The first intreating of the use of the Rapier and Dagger. The second of Honor and Honorable Quarrels," the printer's device has the motto: "O wormes meate: O froath: O vanitie: why art thou so insolent." Compare "As you Like it," Act iii. sc. 2, 59, "Most shallow man! thou worm's meat!"

112. 1. "For fortunes looke." In editions of 1573 and 1585 the reading is "For fortune, look." It is evident that these verses were written at the time when our author first retired from court, and that they were appended to this work long after. They allude to recent events, to "fatal chance," and to other circumstances, which would have been obliterated from the mind after the lapse of so many years.—M. See Tusser's Autobiography, ch. 113, stanza 14, p. 208.

112. 4. "Too daintie fed;" that is, to one who has been accustomed to luxury, and high living.

112. 5. "If court with cart, etc." If one, who has been a courtier, must put up with the life of the country.

113. 5. "What toesed eares." *Toese*, or *touze*, to worry (as a dog does a bear), properly used of the dressing of wool, and thence metaphorically, as in Spenser, Faerie Queene, xi. 33,

"And as a beare, whom angry curres have *touz'd*:"

to the dog who pulls the fell off the bear's back. Cf. the old name for a dog, *Towzer*. Coles renders *tose* or *toze* by "*carpo, vellico*." Baret, Alvearie, 1580, gives, "to Tosse wooll, *carpere lanam*." Compare chap. 99. 4, p. 189, "so *tossed* with comorants," which is spelt *toesed* in the ed. of 1577, and *teazed* in those of 1580 and 1585.

"What robes." The livery or *vestis liberata*, often called robe, allowed annually by the college.—Warton, Hist. of Eng. Poetry.

Penny-ale is common, thin ale. It is spoken of in Piers Plowman, ed. Skeat, Passus xv. l. 310, as a most meagre drink, only fitted for strict-living friars. It was sold at *a penny a gallon*, while the best ale was *four pence*.

"Peny ale and podyng ale she poured togideres
For labourers and for lowe folke, þat lay by hym-selue."
Piers Plowman, B. Text, Passus v. 220.

113. 6. "Sundrie men had plagards then." See remarks in Biographical Sketch.

"The better brest," etc. On these words Hawkins, in his Hist. of Music, ed. 1853, ii. 537, remarks: "In singing, the sound is originally produced by the action of the lungs, which are so essential an organ in this respect, that to have a *good breast* was formerly a common periphrasis to denote a *good singer*." Cf. Shakspere, Twelfth Night, Act ii. sc. 3, "By my troth, the fool hath an excellent breast." Halliwell quotes:

"I syng not musycall
For my *brest* is decayd."—Armonye of Byrdes, p. 5.

Ascham, in his Toxophilus, says, when speaking of the expediency of educating youths in singing: "Trulye two degrees of men, which have the highest offices under the king in all this realme, shall greatly lacke the vse of singinge, preachers and lawyers, because they shall not, without this, be able to rule theyr *brestes* for euerye purpose."—Lond. 1571, fo. 86; and in Strype's Life of Arch. Parker it is stated that "In the Statutes of Stoke College, Suffolk, founded by Parker, is a provision in these words: 'of which said queristers, after their *breasts* are changed, will the most apt of wit and capacity be holpen with exhibitions of forty shillings.'"

113. 8. Nicholas Udall was the author of our oldest known comedy "Roister Doister." He was born 1505, and was Master first at Eton and afterwards at Westminster, at both of which places he became notorious for the severity of his punishments. He wrote several dramas, now lost, one of which, "Ezekias," was acted before Queen Elizabeth at Cambridge, and, in all probability, "Roister Doister" was intended to be performed by his pupils.

113. 11. As to Tusser's pedigree see letter from the Windsor Herald, in the Biographical Sketch.

113. 12. "Tiburne play." Tyburn appears from authentic records to have been used as a place of execution in the time of Edward III. and probably before. See also stanza 35 post. There was another place of execution, in the parish of St. Thomas-a-Waterings, in Southwark, called for distinction Tyburn *of Kent*. See Pegge's Kenticisms, ed. Skeat, Proverb 11, and Dr. Johnson's Poem of London, l. 238, and the note on it in Hales's Longer Eng. Poems, 1872, p. 313.

113. 16. "A towne of *price*." A common expression in old English, meaning of high estimation, noble. See Halliwell, s.v.

113. 18. "Norfolk wiles," etc. The East Anglians were noted for their litigious propensities. Fuller, in his Worthies, says, "Whereas *pedibus ambulando* is accounted but a vexatious suit in other counties, here (where men are said to study law as following the plough-tail) some would persuade us that they will enter an action for their neighbour's horse but looking over their hedge." An Act was passed in 1455 (33 Henry VI. cap. 7) to check the litigiousness of the district: "Whereas, of time not long past, within the city of Norwich, and the counties of Norfolk and Suffolk, there were no more but 6 or 8 attornies at the most that resorted to the King's Courts, in which time great tranquillity reigned in the said city and counties, and little trouble or vexation was made by untrue and foreign suits. And now so it is, that in the said city and counties, there be fourscore attornies or more, the more part of them having no other thing to live upon but only his gain by the practice of attorneyship, and also the more part of them not being of sufficient knowledge to be an attorney, which come to every fair, market, and other places, where is any assembly of people, exhorting, procuring, moving and inciting the people to attempt untrue foreign suits for small trespasses, little offences and small sums of debt, whose actions be triable and determinable in Court Barons; whereby proceed many suits, more of evil will and malice than of the truth of the thing, to the manifold vexation and no little damage of the inhabitants of the said city and counties, and also to the perpetual destruction of all the Courts Baron in the said counties, unless convenient remedy be provided in this behalf; the foresaid Lord the King considering the premises, by the advice, assent and authority aforesaid, hath ordained and established, that at all times from henceforth there shall be but six common attornies in the said County of Norfolk, and six common attornies in the said County of Suffolk, and two common attornies in the said City of Norwich, to be attornies in the Courts of Record; and that all the said fourteen attornies shall be elected and admitted by the two Chief Justices of our Lord the King for the time being, of the most sufficient and best instructed, by their discretions." East Anglians were frequently called "Barrators," that is, incitors to lawsuits (O.Fr. *bareter*, to deceive, cheat).

113. 21. "Diram sell." West Dereham Abbey, near Downham, Norfolk, founded by Hubert Walter, Archbishop of Canterbury, for Præmonstratensian canons.

113. 27. Faiersted, a parish about four miles from Witham, and near our author's birthplace.

113. 31. The plague, to which Tusser evidently alludes, according to Maitland, raged in London in 1574 and 1575. It must have been subsequent to 1573, as the edition of that date does not contain this or the following stanza.

113. 32. This and the preceding stanzas were first introduced in the edition of 1580.

113. 33. Cf. "The rank is but the guinea stamp,
A man's a man for a' that."—Burns.

113. 35. "Cocking Dads." Cf. ch. 95, stanza 5, p. 186.

113. 36. "Of hir or him." See note on ch. 62, stanza 6.

113. 37. "L'homme propose, Dieu dispose."

113. 31. "Or for to iet," etc. "The Normane guise was, to walke and *jet* up and downe the streetes, with great traines of idle serving men following them."—Lambarde's Peramb. of Kent, Reprint of 1826, p. 320. "*Jetting* along with a giant-like gate."—Tom Tel-Troth's Message, New Shak. Soc. ed. Furnivall, p. 125. "Rogue, why winkest thou? Jenny, why *jettest* thou?"—R. Holme, Names of Slates, Bk. iii. ch. v. p. 265. "*Item*, That no scholler be out of his college in the night season, or goe a *Jetting*, and walke the streetes in the night season, unlesse he goe with the Proctors, uppon the payne appointed in the ould Statutes of the University, which is not meate. And they declare that it is the auncient custome, that the Proctors shall not goe a *Jetting*, without the licence of the Vice Chancellor, unlesse it be in Time of some suddayne danger or occasion."—Cole's MSS. vol. 42, in the British Museum.

ADDITIONAL NOTES.

Those signed J. B. *are by* MR. J. BRITTEN, F.L.S.

---

21. 14. Cotgrave, *s.v. Laisser* and *Houseau*, has an exactly parallel expression: "*Il a laissé ses houseaux*, he hath tipped up the heeles, or is ready to doe it; he hath got him to his last bed; he is even as good as gone; he is no better then a dead man." The Catholicon Anglicum also gives "Top ouer tayle, *precipitanter*: to cast tope ouer tayle, *precipitari*."

34. 21. Turner (Names of Herbes) says the currant tree is called "in some places of England a *Rasin* tree."—J.B.

37. 1. See also Swainson's Weather Folklore, pp. 40-42.—J.B.

39. 5. "Beets," although joined here with "bleets," no doubt refers to the common beetroot, *Beta vulgaris*, Linn. Gerard had the "White or Yellow Beete" in his garden.—J.B.

39. 16. This is no doubt *Helminthia echioides*, Linn., of which Parkinson (*Paradisus*) gives a good description and figure under this name, and says, "The leaves are onely used . . . for an herbe for the pot among others." Lyte's reference is to some other plant which has "a purple flower."—J.B.

39. 20. The first portion of the note on p. 266 refers to a Cryptogam called Liverwort, having nothing to do with the plant meant by Tusser.—J.B.

39. 22. It is still much grown in some districts, as in Lincolnshire (where it is called "Marquerry"), being boiled and eaten as spinach.—J.B.

39. 24. The plant referred to in the quotation from the Prompt. Parv. is not that meant by Tusser.—J.B.

39. 30. Lupton (Book of Notable Things, v. 89) speaks of "Primroses, which some take to be Daisies."—J.B.

39. 40. The wild tansey is not Tusser's plant.—J.B.

40. 17. "Sea holie." *Eryngium maritimum*, Linn. "The leaves are good to be eaten in sallads."—Langham's Garden of Health. "The young and tender shoots are eaten of divers either raw or pickled."—Parkinson, *Theatrum Botanicum*, 1640, p. 988.—J.B.

43. 4. "There are many sorts of Colombines, as well differing in forme as colour of the flowers, and of them both single and double carefully noursed up in our gardens, for the delight both of their forme and colours."—Parkinson, *Paradisus*, 1629, p. 271.—J.B.

51. 32. Compare the expression in the Paston Letters, i. 390, "Writan in my slepyng tyme at after none, on Wytsonday."

56. 44. "For Mihelmas spring," that is, "for fear of injuring the young plants, etc., at Michaelmas."

57. 3. There is no doubt Mr. Skeat is right; compare "Centory must be gotten betweene our Lady dayes."—Langham's Garden of Health. The date is not uncommon in Herbals.—J.B.

GLOSSARY.

Those words which occur only in the edition of 1557 *are marked with an asterisk.*

The references are to the Chapters and Stanzas; thus, 36/23 *means page* 36, *stanza* 23. *The usual abbreviations are used.*

Ad, 36/23, *v. imp.* add.

Addle, 51/6, *v.* increase in bulk.—T.R. Icel. *odlask* = to gain, earn. "Adylle, *adipisci, acquirere.*"—Cath. Anglicum.

Adue, 3/8, *int.* adieu, farewell.

Aduise, 10/41, *s.* care, notice. "Take aduise of thy rent" = make preparations for paying your rent, by laying by for that purpose.

Afoord, 99/4, *v.* afford.

After claps, 49/*d*, *s. pl.* disagreeable consequences.

> Whane thy frende ys thy foo,
> He wolle tell alle and more too;
> Beware of after clappes!
>
> MS. Lansd. 762, f. 100.

After crop, 18/20, *v.* extract a second crop from the land.

Aile, 35/31, *v.* affects, is the matter with. A.S. *eglan.*

Aker, 10/14, *s.* acre.

Alexanders, 40/1, *s. pl.* the horse parsley. "*Alexandre*, the hearb great parsley, Alexanders or Alisaunders."—Cotgrave. See Lyte's Dodoens, p. 609.

All in all, 4/2, the principal point.

Alley, 15/35, *s.* paths, walk.

Allow, 33/30; Alow, 15/32, *v. pr. t.* recommend, approve of. O. Fr. *alouer*, from Lat. *laudare.*

Aloft, 33/56, *adv.* up.

Alowe, 114/2, *adv.* low down, deep; cf. 113/23. Cf. "Why somme be *alowe* and somme alofte."—P. Plowman, B. Text, xii. 222.

Ambling, 95/2, *adj.* trotting, cantering.

Amends, *110/58, *s.* reparation, amendment.

Amisse, 89/13, *adv.* amiss, wrong.

Amitie, 9/18, *s.* friendship.

Andrew, 48/19, St. Andrew's Day, 30th November.

Among, 1/5, *adv.* at times; 27/4, euer among = constantly, always.

Anker, 13/5, *s.* anchor.

Annis, 45/1, *s.* anise. Lat. *anisum.*

Anoieng, 48/11, *v.* injuring, damaging. O. Fr. *anoier*, from Lat. *nocere.*

Anue, 10/37, *adv.* anew, again.

Aperne, 17/4, *s.* an apron. Fr. *naperon*, a large cloth, from Lat. *nappa.* O. Fr. *appronaire* = a woman's apron; *appronier* = a blacksmith's apron. "Barmeclothe or naprun."—Prompt. Parv.

Aqua composita, 91/1, see note.

Araid, 48/22, *pp.* kept in order, regulated. O. Fr. *arraier.* A.S. *geræдan* = to get ready.

Arbor, 35/45, *s.* an arbour. O. Fr. *herbier.*

Armer, 2/4, *s.* help, assistance.

Arse, 51/4, *s.* buttocks, hind part. A.S. *ears, ærs.*

As, 57/47, which.

Assai, 1/4, *s.* trial. O. Fr. *assai.*

Asunder, 17/11, *v.* break asunder or in pieces.

Atchine, 69/1, *v.* finish, complete. O. Fr. *achiever.*

Athit, 16/6, *adj.* (?), "ill-breeders."—Mavor. Ill-conditioned.—Wright's Prov. Dict.

A too, 17/9, *adv.* in two, asunder.

Attainted, 75/8, *pp.* tainted; the expression "touched" is also in use. O. Fr. *attaint*, from Lat. *attingere.*

Attonemēt, 106/11, *s.* atonement.

Auke, 62/13, *adj.* unlucky (*lit.* backward, inverted, confused). "Awke or wronge, *sinister.*" — Prompt. Parv.

Aumbrie, 75/2, *s.* cupboard, pantry. See Prompt. Parv. s.v. *Awmebry.* L. Lat. *almonarium.* See also Wedgwood, s.v. *Ambry.*

Auailes, p. 2, *v. pr. t.* is useful or profitable.

Auens, 39/1, *s.* herb bennet—*geum urbanum.* Welsh *afans.* The roots gathered in the spring and put into ale give it a pleasant flavour.

Auise Avouse, 55/4, "is French jargon for *assure* yourself, *take care.*"—Mavor.

Auouch, 10/12, *v.* own, acknowledge. "I'll avouch it to his head."—Shak. Mids. Night's Dream, i. 1.

Awe, 56/2, *s.* August.

Ayer, 16/20, *s.* air.

B.

Baggage, 21/21, *s.* foul stuff, perhaps from Fr. *bagasse.*

Baggedglie tit 16/6, worthless beasts, baggagely.

Baies, 81/2, *s. pl.* chidings, reproof. Halliwell has this word, misspelt *baies*, as from Hunter's additions to Boucher.

Bailie, 10/18, *s.* bailiff, steward. Lat. *bajulus.* Fr. *bailli.*

Baiting, 85/2, feeding, eating.

Balke, *s.* "What is in some places called a mier bank, being narrow slips of land between ground and ground."—T.R. A.S. *balc.* Welsh *valc*, a strip of land. "A *balke* or banke of earth ranged or standing up betweene two furrowes."—Baret's Alvearie. Halliwell, s.v. Balk, refers to this passage and explains Balke as a piece of timber.

Ball, 95/2, *s.* a common name for a horse. In the Prompt. it is applied to a sheep, and in the Privy Purse expenses of Henry VIII. p. 43, to a dog.

Band, 56/17, *s.* bands or ropes of straw.

Bandes, 9/24, *s.* bonds, engagements.

Bandog, 10/19, *s.* a dog always tied up on account of his fierceness; according to Bewick a species of mastiff crossed with a bull-dog. Dutch *band-hond.*

Bane, 81/6, *s.* poison.

Bane, 46/23, *s.* ruin. A.S. *bana.* O. Icel. *bani.*

Banish, 9/29, *v.* free, clear.

Banket, 28/3, *v. pr. t.* feast, banquet.

Barberies, 34/3, *s.* barberry; *berberis vulgaris*, Linn.

Barberlie, 51/4, *adv.* like a barber.

Bare, 74/6, *adj.* uncouer your bare = strip the clothes off and whip you.

Barelie, 56/23, *s.* barley.

Bargaine, 16/3, *s.* contract, agreement.

Barth, 33/26, *s.* shelter. "Barth, ground floor, floor."—Spurrell's Welsh Dict. "A warm place or pasture for calves or lambs.—Ray. "A place near the farm-house well-sheltered."—T.R.

Bartilmewtide, 57/47, St. Bartholomew's Day, 24th August.

Bassel, 42/1, Bazell, 50/34, *s.* basil, much used in cookery, especially in France. *Ocymum basilicum.*—Gerard's Herball. So called probably from its being used in some royal (βασιλικον) medicine or bath.

Baulme, 42/2, *s.* balsam, contracted from Lat. *balsamum.*

Bauen, 57/33, *s.* light loose faggots. O. Fr. *baffe*=a faggot. "Baven, the smaller trees whose sole use is for the fire."—Skinner.

Bayted, 64*/7, *pp.* baited.

Beare off, 17/2, *v.* ward off, keep off.

Beare out, 16/10, *v.* keep off, protect from.

Beares, 20/1, *v. pr. t.* provides, furnishes.

*Bease, 57, *s. pl.* beasts, cows.

Beastlie, 20/2, *adj.* stupid, careless.

Beath, 23/9, *v.* to place before the fire, to straighten by heating.

Beck, 46/28, *s.* beak.

*Beclip, 30, *v.* anticipate, surprise.

Bedstraw, 19/40, *s.* clean straw.

Beene, 51/22, *s.* property, wealth. Fr. *bien.*

Beere, 96/84, *s.* bier.

Beetle, 22/1, *s.* a wooden club or mallet, its head hooped with iron, and studded all over with nails, used for splitting wood.

Beggerie, 10/40, *s.* beggary, poverty.

Begilde, 57/27, Beguilde, 10/56, *pp.* cheated, disappointed.

Begon, 99/5, *pp.* begun.

Behoouing, 2/5, *adj.* belonging, proper to.

Bellifull, 46/27, *s.* sufficiency, satisfaction.

Bent, 112/3, *pp.* inclined, disposed.

Beshreawd, 102/7, *pp.* ruined, cursed. Connected with the *shrew* mouse, to which deadly qualities were at one time attributed.

Bestad, 113/23, *pp.* circumstanced, situated.

Bestowe, 16/34, *v. imp.* place, arrange.

Betanie, 45/3, *s.* the plant Betony, *Betonica officinalis*, Linn.

Betwix, 74/2, *adv.* between. A.S. *betwix*.

Bewraies, 108/4, *v. pr. t.* betrays.

Bex, 37/12, *s. pl.* beaks. Fr. *bec*, pl. *becs*.

Biefe, 21/11, *s.* beef.

Big, 33/36, *s.* teat, pap. A.S. *bige*, a bosom.—Bailey's Dict. 1735. It also occurs in Gifford's Dialogue on Witches, 1603.

Bil, 17/8; Bill, 33/22, *s.* billhook.

Bilde, 95/6, *v.* build.

Billet, 53/12, *s.* chopped-up wood.

Bin, 107/1, *pp.* been.

Blabs, 100/3, *s. pl.* chatterboxes, talkative persons. "*Cacqueteur, babillard, baquenaudier, bavard.* A *blab*, a long tongue: one that telleth whatsoever he heareth."—Nomenclator, 1585.

Blade, 19/14, *s.* blades of grass.

Blaze, 108/4, *v.* spread abroad the report of, *blaze* abroad. Cf. Spenser, F. Q., I. xi. 7. A.S. *blæsan*, to blow.

Blenge, 100/3, *v.* blenge, mix.

Blessed thistle, 44/1, *s.* so called from its supposed power of counteracting the effects of poison; *Carduus benedictus*.

Blew, 43/3, *adj.* blue.

Blindfild, 90/3, *adj.* blindfold.

Blisse, 2/3, *v.* bless, praise.

Block in the fier, 10/57, a block of wood in the fire.

Blocks, 17/11, *s. pl.* blocks of wood, trunks and stumps of trees.

Bloodwort, 39/4, *s.* bloody-veined dock, *Rumex sanguineus*.

Blouse, 16/37, *s.* red-faced wife or girl. "A girl or wench whose face looks red by running abroad in the wind and weather is called a *blouz*, and said to have a *blouzing* colour."—Kennett, MS. Lansd. 1033. See also Thoresby's Letter to Ray, E.D. Soc. B. 17.

Blowne, 2/10, *pp.* reported.

Bobbed, 113/5, *pp.* pouting.

Boddle, 51/11, *s.* "a weed like the Mayweed, but bears a large yellow flower."—T.R. From Dutch *buidel*, a purse, because it bears *gools* or *goldins*, gold coins, Dutch *gulden*, a punning allusion to its yellow flowers.

Boies, 57/34, *s. pl.* boys.

Bold, 2/9, *v. pt. t.* embolden, encourage.

Bold, 63/22, *adj.* proud.

Boll, 83/2, *s.* washing-bowl, tub.

Bolted, 67/2, *pp.* sifted, examined. Bolted-bread = a loaf of sifted wheat meal mixed with rye. See *Bolt* and *Bolting-cloth* in Peacock's Gloss. of Manley and Corringham.

Boollesse, 34/4, *s.* bullace, small tartish plums, black or yellow. Called in Cambridgeshire "Cricksies." "I believe the word to be Celtic: Irish *bulos*, a prune, Breton *polos*, a bullace, Gaelic *bulaistear*, a bullace, a sloe."—Note by Rev. W. W. Skeat. "A bullace, frute, *pruneolum*."—Manip. Vocab.

Boone, 62/17, *s.* request, prayer.

Boord, 23/12, *s.* boards, planks.

Boorde, 88/1, *s.* the table, meals.

Bootie, 48/14, *s.* booty, prey.

Borough, 33/7, *s.* burrows, warren. A.S. *beorg*, *beorh*.

Botch, 74/5, *v. imp.* patch.

Botles, 43/3, *s.* chrysanthemum. "Boyul or bothule, herbe or Cowslope, *Vactinia*."—Prompt. Parv.

Bots, 45/22, *s. pl.* a disease (worms) troublesome to horses. Gaelic *botus*, a bott; *boiteag*, a maggot.

Bottle, 21/15, *s.* the leathern bottle.

Bowd, 19/39, *s.* weevil, *Curculio granarius*; bowd-eaten = eaten by weevils. "Bowde, malte worme." "Malte bowde or wevyl."—Prompt. Parv.

Bowe, 17/13, *s.* bow.

Bows, 36/12, *s. pl.* boughs, sticks. A.S. *bog*, *boh*.

Brag, 19/14, *s.* boast, sham, pretence; 94/16, value, estimation.

Braggeth, 62/1, *v. pr. t.* boasts, brags. Welsh *bragiaw*. Fr. *braguer*.

Brake, 15/33, *s.* underwood, ferns, etc. Brakes, "Their light firing in Norfolk, that is wherewith they bake and brew."—T.R.

Brall, 77/11, *v.* quarrelling, scolding.
Bralling, 101/4, *adj.* brawling, quarrelsome.
Brank, 19/20, *s.* Buck-wheat. *Polygonum fagopyrum.* "*Brance*, bearded red wheat."—Cotgrave. "*Brance*" occurs in Pliny's Hist. Nat. xviii. c. 7.
Brats, 81/6, *s. pl.* children.
Brauling, 48/15, *s.* quarrels, contention.
Braue, 94/2, *adj.* fine, grand.
Brauerie, 9/12, *s.* show, boast.
Brawne, 31/2, *s.* brawn, originally the flesh of the wild boar, but used for flesh generally. O. Fr. *braon*, *braion.*
Brawneth, 16/22, *v. pr. t.* fatteneth.
Breaching, 2/11, *s.* breaking, breach.
Breadcorne, 19/20, *s.* "leguminous crops."—Wright's Dict.
Breaker, 95/2, *s.* horse-breaker.
Breaketh his credit, 10/37, fails to do what he has promised.
Breakhedge, 15/36, *s.* trespassers and others who break down fences, or make gaps in hedges.
Breathely, 33/38, *adj.* worthless. See Halliwell, s.v. Bretheling.
Brecke, 16/16, *s.* breach, gap. A.S. *brecan*, to break.
Breede, 10/31, *v.* cause, generate.
Breeders, 12/2, *s. pl.* good time for breeding.
Breeding, 2/10, *s.* origin, source.
Breers, 113/2, *s. pl.* briars, thorns, hence troubles and difficulties.
Bremble, 36/23, *s.* bramble, briar.
Brest, 11/7, *v.* nurse.
Brest, 113/6, *s.* voice. See note.
Breth, 107/4, *s.* breath.
Bribing, 10/27, *v.* thieving, stealing. "I *bribe*, I pull, I pyll."—Palsgrave. See Mr. Skeat's note to P. Plowman, xxiii. 262.
Brineth, 75/8, *v. pr. t.* cure with brine or salt.
Brooketh, 94/10, *v. pr. t.* endures, allows.
Brothell, 10/20, *v.* riotous, dissipated. See Halliwell, s.v. Brethel.
Brows, 33/11, feed on, nibble. O. Fr. *brouster* from *broust*, a sprout. "Yode forth abroade unto the greenewood to *browze* or play."—Spenser, Shep. Cal. May. "*Browse*, or meat for beastes in snowtyme. *Vesca.*"—Huloet.
Brue, 15/33, *v.* brew. A.S. *briwan.*
Brush, 17/14, *s.* underwood, brushwood.
Brushed cote, 49/*b*, a beating; cf. "a dusted jacket."
Buck, 50/13, *s.* buckwheat. Dutch *boekweit.*
Buckle, 96/84, *v. imp.* prepare, get ready; cf. *buckle to.*
Bucks, 74/5, *s. pl.* a quantity of linen washed at once, a tub-full of linen ready for washing. *Bouckfatt*, a washing-tub (Unton Inventories, p. 28). Lay your bucks = get your linen ready for washing.
Buglas, 39/5, *s.* bugloss, *Lycopsis arvensis*, Linn.
Buie, 3/8, *v.*; Buieng, 56/4, buy.
Bulchin, 33/36, *s.* a bull-calf.
Bullimong, 19/30, *s.* a mixture of oats, peas and vetches, or buckwheat. Possibly a corruption of Lat. *pulmentum.*
Burch, 92/4, *s.* the rod, birch.
Burrage, 39/7, *s.* borage. *Borago officinalis.* The flowers were supposed to be cordial and excitative of courage, especially if infused in wine; whence the derivation Celtic *borr*, pride, *borrach*, a haughty man.
Burs, 63/16, *s. pl.* the burdock. "*Bourre*, the downe or hairie coat, wherewith divers herbs, fruites, and flowers are covered."—Cotgrave.
Bushets, 37/19, *s. pl.* small shoots from bushes.
Busht, 42/1, *adj.* thick, spreading.
Buttrice, 17/4, *s.* a farrier's tool used in shoeing horses to pare the hoofs.
Buttrie, 89/5, *s.* pantry, cupboard.
Buzard, 46/28, *s.* buzzard.
By and bie, 57/15, *adv.* presently.

C.

Cabben, 16/23, *s.* house, sty.
Cace, 67/26, *s.* case, point.
Cadow, 46/28, *s.* jackdaw. "*Cadesse*, Daw, Jackdaw." — Cotgrave. "Cad-dow, a Jackdaw or Chough, Norfolk."—Bailey's Dict. See note in Prompt. Parv., s.v. Cadaw.
Calling, 9/1, *s.* station in life.
Camamel, 42/3, *s.* Camomile. Lat. *chamæmelum.* Greek χαμαιμηλον, earth-apple, from the smell of its flowers.

Campe, 22/24, *v.* to play football. A.S. *camp*=a contest. See Ray's Glossary, E. D. Soc. p. xvi.

Campers, 22/24, *s. pl.* football players. See note.

Campions, 43/5, *s.* Red Lychnis or Campion, *Lychnis diurna.*

Candlemas, page 77, footnote 5, *s.* 2nd February, so called from the great number of lights used on that day, being the feast of the Purification of the Virgin Mary.

Canteth, 94/8, *v. pr. t.* ? scanteth, *i.e.* is economical. The edition of 1573 reads *franteth*, which is a Somerset word meaning *to be careful.* Canteth, according to Halliwell, means "divides," *i.e.* does not use up everything at once, but only what is wanted for the time.

Canuas, 57/54, *s.* canvas.

Capitaine cheefe, 10/19, head or chief captain.

Capon, 31/3, *s.* a castrated cock.

Careles, 35/4, *adj.* unwilling, not anxious.

Carkas, 26/4, *s.* corpse, body. Fr. *carcasse.*

Carke, 113/15, *v.* to be anxious. "I carke, I care, I take thought, *je chagrine.*" — Palsgrave. "Waile we the wight whose absence is our *carke.*"—Spenser, Shep. Cal. November.

*Carnels, 101, *s. pl.* seeds of the haw, briar, etc. Cf. ch. 18. st. 48 and 36. 12.

Carrege, 56/21, *s.* carrying home.

Carren, 18/36, *s.* carrion, carcasses, M.E. *caroigne.* Fr. *charogne*, from It. *carogna*, Lat. *caronem.*

Carrenly, 19/36, *adj.* rotting, putrifying.

Cart gap, 56/13, *s.* the openings for carts to pass from one field to another.

Cartwrite, 58/5, *s.* cartwright.

Cast, 10/41, *v.* to count up, reckon.

Cast, 20/3, *v. pr. t.* to clean the threshed corn by casting it from one side of the barn to the other, that the light grains and dust may fall out. For this purpose is used a *skuttle*, q.v.

Cast, 33/52, *v. imp.* give over, throw up.

Casting, 65/8, *adj.* that throw up the earth as they burrow through it.

Cater, 10/16, *s.* caterer, provider. "*Cater* a steward, a manciple, a prouider of Cates."—Baret's Alvearie. "Cates, dainty provisions."—Bailey's Eng. Dict. 1737.

Cawme, 56/15, *adj.* calm, settled.

Challenge, 72/1, *v.* claim. O. Fr. *chalenger.*

Champion (title), *s.* plain open country. Fr. *champagne*, from Lat. *campania*, from *campus* = a field. "Worstershire, Bedfordshire, and many other well-mixt soiles, where the Champaigne and couert are of equall largeness."—G. Markham, Husbandman's Recreations, c. i.

Champions, 16/2, *s. pl.* inhabitants of counties where lands are open and unenclosed.

Chancing, 9/30, *v.* happening, falling out.

Chapman, 19/27, *s.* bargainer, dealer. A.S. *ceapman.*

Charge, 84/2, *s.* trouble, expense. Compare All's Well that Ends Well, ii. 3, 121: "She had her breeding at my father's charge."

Charged, 10/8, *pp.* burdened, busy, anxious.

Charges, 23/6, *s. pl.* works, troubles.

Charuiel, 45/4, *s.* the plant Chervil. *Chærophyllum temulentum*, Linn. Whence A.S. *cærfille*, Fr. *cerfeuil.*

Chaunting, 16/31, *v.* crying, yelling.

Cheanie, 2/6, Jeanie, Jennie.

Cheere, 22/28, *v.* enjoy oneself.

Cheere, 57/26, *s.* enjoyment, merriment.

Chees, 48/20, *s.* cheese. Lat. *caseus*; whence O.H. Ger. *chasi*, A.S. *cêse.*

Chein, 17/10, *s.* chain.

Cherie, 33/58, *s.* cherry. Lat. *cerasus*; whence A.S. *cirse*, Fr. *cerise.*

Chikins, 38/33, *s. pl.* chickens, young fowls.

Chinke, 46/27, *s.* money. A word formed from the sound of coin *jingling* together.

Chip, 57/32, *s.* wood-choppings.

Chippings, 86/3, *s. pl.* fragments of bread. "*Chapplis*, bread-chippings."—Cotgrave.

Choised, 57/34, *pp.* selected, chosen. Fr. *choix*, choice.

Chopping, 57/40, *s.* exchange, barter. "Choppe and chaunge, *mercor.*"—Huloet. A.S. *ceapan.*

Churle, 10/50, *s.* an ill-bred, disagreeable person. A.S. *ceorl*, a freeman of the lowest rank.

Cinqfile, 45/5, *s.* cinquefoil. *Potentilla*, Linn.

Clap, 10/22, *s.* blow, stroke; "at a clap" = at once.

Clapper, 36/25, *s.* a rabbit burrow or warren. "Cony hole or *clapar*." —Palsgrave. "A *clapper* for conies, *i.e.* a heap of stones, earth, with boughes or such like wherinto they may retire themselves."—Minsheu. Fr. *clapier*. L. Lat. *clapa*.

Clarie, 39/9, *s.* meadow sage. *Salvia pratensis*.

Clauestock, 17/20, *s.* a chopper for splitting wood.

Cleerely, 16/25, *adj.* clear.

Clicket, 77/9, *v.* chatter. "If I disturb you with my *clicketten*, tell me so, David, and I won't."—C. Dickens in David Copperfield. "A tatling huswife, whose *clicket* is ever wagging."—Cotgrave.

Clim, 56/23, *s.* ? Clement.

Clime, 57/30, *v.* climb. A.S. *climban*.

Clod, 113/37, *s.* earth, hence = landed property.

Clog, 89/1, *s.* charge, duty.

Closet, 14/3, *s.* retirement, seclusion.

Closeth, 62/5, *v. pr. t.* incloses, fences in.

Closier, page 2, *s.* enclosures. Fr. *closure*.

Clot, 33/24, *s.* clods. A.S. *clûd*. "Clodde or clotte lande, *occo*."—Huloet.

*Cloughted, 89, *pp.* See Clouted.

Clout, 67/16, *s.* piece of cloth. A.S. *clût*, a little cloth. Mid. Eng. *clout*, *clutian*, *clutien*, to patch.

Clouts, Cloutes, 17/10, *s.* an instrument similar to the *plowstaff*, shod with iron and used for breaking large clods, etc.

Clouted, 17/6, *pp.* "having the Axletree armed with Iron plates."—T.R. O. Fr. *clouet*, dimin. of *clou*, a nail, from Lat. *clavus*. See Nares, s.v. Clout.

Coast, 63/7, *s.* country, district. O. Fr. *coste*, from Lat. *costa*, a rib, side.

Coast man, 36/22, *s.* masters of coasting vessels.

Cobble, 74/5, *v. imp.* patch, mend.

Cock, 53/4, *v. imp.* put into cocks, or small stacks.

Cocking, 95/5, *adj.* over-indulgent.

Cockle, 46/13, *s.* the weed corn-rose, *Agrostemma githago*, Linn. Cockle or Cokyl is used by Wycliffe and other old writers in the sense of a weed generally.

Cockneies, 92/4, *s. pl.* spoilt or effeminate boys. See note, and Halliwell, s.v. Cockney.

Cocks, 57/16, *s. pl.* small conical heaps of hay or corn.

Codware, 19/26, *s.* all plants that bear pods (or cods); peas, beans, etc. "Pescodde, *escosse de poix*."—Palsgrave. A.S. *codd*. Welsh, *cod*, *cwd*, a small bag.

Coeme, Coome, 17/7, *s.* a measure of half a quartern. A.S. *cumb*.—Somner. "There is no such word in A.S. as *cumb*; it is one invented by Somner, so that the (so-called) A.S. *cumb* is really derived from Eng. *coomb*."—Note by Rev. W. W. Skeat.

Cofer up, 10/61, *v.* to hoard up, lock up.

Cofers, 16/4, *s. pl.* money-boxes.

Cog, 63/14, *v.* cheat, defraud. "Cog a dye, to load a die."—Cotgrave. "A cogger, *un pipeur*. To cogge, *piper*."—The French Schoolemaster, 1636.

Coile, 4/1, *s.* bustle, hard work; cf. Fr. *cuellie*, a mob, tumult.

Cold, 91/2, *adj.* cooling.

Cole, 57/31, *s.* turf, peat.

Colewort, 39/10, *s.* or collet, cabbage. *Brassica oleracea*, Linn.

Collembines, 43/4, *s. pl.* columbine. Lat. *columbina*, adj. from *columba*, a pigeon, from the resemblance of its nectaries to the heads of pigeons in a ring round a dish, a favourite device of ancient artists.—Dr. R. A. Prior.

Comfort, 19/19, *s.* strength, fertility.

Commodities, 37/17, *s. pl.* advantages.

Compact, 111/1, *pp.* composed. Lat. *compactus*, from *compango*. "Love is a spirit all *compact* of fire."—Venus and Adonis, 149.

Compas, 47/3, *s.* manure, compost. O. Fr. *compost*, from Lat. *compositum*.

Compassing, 56/1, *s.* manuring.

*Compast, 11, *pp.* manured.

*Compound, 11, *v. imp.* agree, arrange.

Confer, page 2, *v.* compare. Lat. *conferre.*

Confound, 67/27, *v.* destroy, spoil.

Conie, 15/20, *s.* a term of endearment.

Conies, 63/10, *s. pl.* rabbits. Welsh *cwning.* Irish *coinni.* Lat. *cuniculus,* cognate with Lat. *cuneus* (what cleaves, a wedge), and comes from the Sanskrit root *khan* = to dig.—Palmer.

Conserue, 91/3, *s.* preserve.

Constancie, 9/23, *s.* consistency, firmness.

Conster, 113/34, *v.* understand.

Conteemne, 106/7, *v. pr. t.* despise. Lat. *contemnere.*

Continue, 19/35, *v.* to breed from, to keep up stock from.

Contrarie, 67/25, *v. imp.* oppose, contradict.

Cooples, 10/6, *s.* couples, husband and wife.

Coosen, 63/14, *v.* cheat, swindle. Shakespere's *cozen.*

Copie, 47/8, *s.* coppice.

Coresie, 19/24, *s.* annoyance, trouble.

Cornet plums, 34/7, *s.* cornel plums, cornel cherries.

Corneth, 75/8, *v. pr. t.* preserve and season, cure.

Corps, 53/1, *s.* body.

Cost, 32/5, *s.* coast, country. See Coast.

Costmarie, 42/4, *s.* costmary, called also ale-cost, *Balsamita vulgaris.*

Cote, 58/11, *v.* cogitate, reflect.

Coted, 2/8, *v. pt. t.* took note of, wrote down. "Howe scripture shulde be *coted* (quoted)."—Skelton, Colin Clout, l. 758.

Count, 10/21, *v.* reckon, "be to counte" = be of account, be worth.

Counterfait, 94/29, *adj.* counterfeit, sham, false.

Coursest, 55/4, *adj.* coarsest.

Court, 86/10, *s.* account, examination.

Cousleps, 42/5, *s. pl.* cowslips.

Couert, 63/5, *s.* covert, underwood.

Couertlie, 9/5, *adv.* closely.

Cowlaske, page 4, *s.* diarrhœa in cattle. See Fletcher's Differences, 1623, p. 33. Laske, *v.* = to re*lax*, slacken. See Glossary to "William of Palerne," E. E. Text Soc. edit. Skeat.

Coxcombe, 64/18; Coxcome, 10/48, *s.* The cap of the licensed fool had often on the top a cock's head and comb and some of the feathers. Therefore he "strives for a coxcome" = he will only succeed in proving his own folly.

Crabs, 15/17, *s. pl.* crab apples.

Cracketh, 10/37, *v. pr. t.* half breaks, injures.

Cradle, 17/14, *s.* "A three-forked instrument of wood, on which the corn is caught as it falls from the sithe."—T.R.

Crake, 18/21, *v.* brag, boast. Dutch *kraaken.*

Crakers, 51/4, *s. pl.* boasters.

Cram, 113/15, *v.* feed up, satisfy.

Creake, 47/2, "to cry creak" = "to be afraid," "to desist from any object, to repent."—Halliwell.

Credit crackt, 4/1, credit or trust broken.

Creekes, 49/4, *s. pl.* corners, seek creekes = hide herself.

Creekes, 38/26, *s. pl.* servants.

Creepinglie, 9/32, *adv.* stealthily, by degrees.

Cresies, 40/5, *s.* cress. Fr. *cresson.* M. Lat. *crissonum* from Lat. *crescere,* to grow, "a celeritate crescendi."

Crome, 17/19, *s.* "Like a dung-rake with a very long handle."—T.R.

Crone, 56/46, *v. imp.* pick out the crones, *i.e.* the old ewes. The meaning is, weed out your flocks.

Crones, 12/4, *s. pl.* "Ewes, whose teeth are so worn down that they can no longer keep their sheep-walk."—T.R.

Crooked, 57/46, *adj.* deformed.

Croppers, 18/19, *s.* the best or most productive crops.

Croppers, 19/20, *s. pl.* persons who extract crop after crop from the land.

Crosse, 46/9, *s.* a cross-piece.

Crosse, 9/29, *v.* happen, result unfavourably.

Crosses, 9/29, *s.* troubles, misfortunes.

Crosserowe, page 3, *s.* called also Christcrossrow; the alphabet. "A is the name of the first letter in the *Crosrowe.*"—Baret's Alvearie.

Crotch, 51/10, *s.* "a curved weeding tool."—T.R.

Crotches, 60/11, *s. pl.* crutches. A.S. *cryce.* L. Lat. *croccia, crucca.* H. Ger. *krücke.*

Crotchis, 57/51, *s. pl.* crooks, hooks. O. Fr. *croche.*

Crowchmas, 50/36, *s.* St. Helen's Day,

3rd May, being the feast of the Invention of the Holy Cross.
Crowe, 46/9, *s.* crowbar.
Cubboord, 89/5, *s.* cupboard.
Culters, 17/10, *s. pl.* coulters.
Cumbersome, 10/13, *adj.* troublesome, vexatious, oppressive.
Cummin, 45/6, *s.* cumin, a plant resembling fennel, cultivated for its seeds, which have a bitterish warm taste, and are used like those of anise and carraway. Arabic *kammûn.* Hebrew *kammôn.*
Cunnie, 36/25, *s.* rabbit.
Currant, 10/44, *adj.* current coin, good coin.
Currey, 61*/2, *v.* gain by flattery. On the origin of this phrase see "Leaves from a Word-Hunter's Note Book," by Rev. A. S. Palmer, p. 63.
Custome, 77/1, *s.* custom, habit; of custome = as a matter of course.
Curtesie, 9/8, *s.* courtesy, respect.

D.

*Dabblith, 27, *v. pr. t.* make wet and dirty.
Dads, 95/5, *s. pl.* fathers.
Daffadondillies, 43/7, *s. pl.* daffodils. *Narcissus pseudonarcissus*, Linn.
Daieth, 62/8, *v. pr. t.* names some future day for payment, *i.e.* buys on credit.

> "The moste part of my debtters have honestly payed,
> And they that were not redy I have gently *dayed.*"
> Wager's Cruell Debter, 1566.

*Dainty, 94, *adj.* difficult, lit. choice, excellent.
Dallops, 54/5, *s. pl.* "A patch or bit of ground lying here and there among the corn."—T.R. 57/17, "Tufts of corn such as are commonly seen where dung-heaps have stood too long, or in shady places."—T.R.
Damsens, 34/8, *s. pl.* damsons, contracted from *damascene* = the *Damascus* plum.
Dank, 22/11, *adj.* damp, wet.
Dare, 2/7, *v.* pain, grieve. A.S. *daru*, hurt.
Darnell, 65/1, *s.* darnel, the plant *Lolium perenne.* "Darnell or Iuraye in Englishe also called Raye."—Dodoens, Newe Herball, 1578.
Darth, 63/24, *s.* dearth, dearness of food, etc.
*Daunger, 90/8, risk.
Daw, 99/2, *s.* simpleton, sluggard.
Day, 57/8, *s.* day-work, time-work.
Dead, 78/4, *adj.* flat (beer). Cf. "Pallyd, as drynke, *emortuus.*" — Prompt. Parv.
Deaw, 56/48, *s.* dew, damp.
Deckt, 106/2, *pp.* adorned, beautified.
Defende, 86/7, *v.* avoid, prevent.
Deintily, 19/37, *adv.* dearly.
Delaide, 66/7, *pp.* tempered, moderated.
Delue, 21/19, *v. imp.* dig. A.S. *delf*, *delfan* = to dig, from Goth. *dailjan* = to deal, divide. Cf. Ger. *thal*, Eng. *dale.*
Deluing, 36/17, *pr. p.* burrowing.
Depart, 10/56, *v. imp.* give away, part with.
Descant, 68/5, *v.* comment. O. Fr. *deschanter*, from L. Lat. *discantare.*
Despaire, 57/10; Dispaire, 63/9, *s.* injury, damage.
Despight, 106/12, *s.* despite.
Det, 113/38, *s.* debt.
Detanie, 45/8, *s.* Dittany or Pepperwurt, apparently a corruption of Lat. *dictamnus*, of which Dodoens says:—"It is fondly and unlearnedly called in English Dittany. It were better in following the Douchemen to call it Pepperwurt."—Book v. c. 66. Welsh *Ddittain.*
Dew-retting, 16/25, *s.* steeping flax by leaving it out all night on the grass. See Water-retting.
Diall, 68/7, *s.* sundial.
Dible, 46/24, *s.* a planting or setting stick, a dimin. of *dib* = *dip* and allied to *tip* = a sharp point. "*Debbyll*, or settyng stycke."—Huloet.
Dicing, 10/40, *s.* gambling.
Didall, 17/19, *s.* "A triangular spade, as sharp as a knife, excellent to bank ditches, where the earth is light and pestered with a sedgy weed."—T.R.
Dide, 113/11, *v. pt. t.* died.
Digest, 11/4, *v.* quiet, sooth.
Dight, 23/19, *pp.* prepared, treated. A.S. *dihtan.*
Dike, 3/7, *s.* ditch, dike, fence. A.S. *dic.*
Dill, 44/3, *s.* dill. A.S. *dil. Antheum graveolens.*

Dippings, 86/3, *s. pl.* dripping, grease, etc., collected by the cook.
Discharge, 53/3, *v.* relieve you of the trouble.
Discurtesy, 9/19, *s.* incivility, rudeness.
Dispaire, 57/53, *v.* injure, depreciate.
Dissurie, 113/26, *s.* the strangury.
Distaffe, 67/15, *s.* distaff.
Docking the dell, 10/40, dissipation. See Grose's Dict. s.v. *Dock.*
Docks, 17/11, *s. pl.* weeds.
*Dockes, 27, *s. pl.* ?
Dole, 33/16, *s.* share.
Doles, 48/6, *s. pl.* boundary marks, either a post or a mound of earth; also, a balk or slip of unploughed ground.
Dolt, 33/37, *s.* stupid, fool.
Don, 106/21, *pp.* done.
Doo of, 33/39, *v. imp.* get rid of.
Doong, 19/29, *s.* dung, manure.
Doong Crone, 17/7, *s.* a crook or staff with hooked end for drawing dung.
Doonged, 53/21, *pp.* dunged, manured.
Doted, 2/8, *v. pt. t.* became foolish, was silly. Fr. *dotter*, *radoter*, to dote, rave.—Cotgrave. Cf. Piers Plowman, "Thou *doted* daffe."
Doughtful, 114/3, *adj.* doubtful.
Douse, 10/7, *s.* strumpet, prostitute; the same word as *Doxy*. Halliwell, s.v. Douce, quotes this passage, and renders *douse* by "a pat in the face," but s.v. Dowse he gives the correct meaning.
Dout, 87/7, *s.* danger, risk, difficulty.
Doues, 56/24, *s. pl.* doves, pigeons.
Dowebake, 79/2, *s.* dough, underbaked bread.
Drab, 77/5, *s.* sloven, loose woman.
Dragons, 45/7, *s.* the herb Serpentine, Serpentarie, or Dragonwort.
Dredge, 16/13, *s.* a mixture of oats and barley. "Dragge, menglyd corne (drage or mestlyon), *mixtio*."—Prompt. Parv. See Notes.
Drest, 49/8, *pp.* treated.
Dreue, 35/42, Driue, 33/42, *v.* follow you up, press you.
Dreuils, 113/12, Driuell, 79/1, *s.* wasters, spendthrifts.
Drift, 10/13, *s.* end, aim, design, 113/39, course, such drift to make = to drift along in such a manner.
Drines, 53/20, *s.* dryness.
Drinke corn, 18/24, *s.* barley.
Driping, 35/14, *v.* dripping on, keeping wet.
Driue, 16/20, *v.* drive out of their hives for the purpose of taking the honey.
Droie, 81/3, *s.* a drudge, servant. See note in Prompt. Parv. s.v. *Deye.*
Drousie, 89/4, *adj.* the drowsy, the sleepy.
Drout, 14/3, *s.* drought, dry weather.
Drowseth, 62/13, *v. pr. t.* droops, gives way.
Drudge, 7/1, *s.* slave, mean servant.
Duck, 55/6, *s.* docks, dockweed.
Dun, 82/2, *pp.* finished, done for.
Dy, 35/24, *s.* a die, as close as a dy = as close as possible.

E.

Earthes, 35/50, *s. pl.* a ploughing. A.S. *earian*. Lat. *arare*, to plough. In the Catholicon Anglicum we find "A dayserth or daysardawe, *juger*, *jugerum*." See also Ray and Halliwell, s.v. *Arders.*
Easeth, 94/9, *v. pr. t.* indulges, pleases.
Eaw, 67/24, *s.* ewe.
Eb, 14/5, *s.* ebb. A.S. *ebba.*
Ech, 57/23, *adj.* each.
Edder, 33/13, *s.* "Such fence wood as is commonly put upon the top of Fences and binds or interweaves each other."—T.R.
Edish, 18/4, *s.* stubble after the corn is cut. Roughings. · *Edisc* is an old Saxon word signifying sometimes *roughings*, *aftermathes.* See Glossaries, B 15, B 16, E. D. Soc.
Edmond, St., 20/12, St. Edmund's Day, 20th November.
Eie, 57/9, *s.* eye, attention.
Eiebright, 44/5, *s.* common eyebright, *Euphrasia officinalis*, formerly much used as a remedy for diseases of the eye.
Eies, 113/4, *s. pl.* eyes.
Eke, 66/6, *adv.* also, too, A.S. *eac*, *ec.*
Elfe, 113/14, *s.* creature; 86/11, a servant.
Elues, 22/3, *s. pl.* young cattle.
Embraid, 112/7, *v. imp.* upbraid, abuse.
Embrings, 12/6, *s. pl.* the Ember-days, being the Wednesday, Friday, and Saturday after the first Sunday in Lent, the feast of Whitsuntide, the 14th September, and the 13th December.

Endiue, 91/2, *s.* endive.
Enuite, 16/32, *v.* invite, call.
Er, 56/21, *adv.* ere, before. Er an = ere than = before that.
Erecting, 1/1, *pr. p.* sustaining, strengthening.
Erie, 57/11; Ery, 18/17, *adj.* every.
Estate, 10/3, *s.* condition, position.
Etch, 36/3, *s.* stubble, edish, q.v.
Exceptions, 19/25, *s. pl.* differences, distinctions.
Exeltred, 17/6, *adj.* furnished with an axle-tree.
Expulsed, 1/4, *v. pt. t.* expelled, drove away.
Extolst, 111/6, *v. pr. t.* praise, extol.
Ey, 99/2, *s.* attention, forgetting his eye = neglecting his duty by staring or gaping about. See Eie.

F.

Fall, 35/32, *v. pr. t.* are born.
Falleth, 20/1, *v. pr. t.* falls off, loses flesh.
Falt, 35/43, *s.* fault.
Fansies, 2/13, *s.* fancies, whims.
Fare, 2/5, *s.* treatment.
Fare, 33/33, *v.* farrow, litter.
Fare, 10/32, *v.* prosper, fare. A.S. *faran.*
Farnesse, 14/4, *s.* distance, length.
Fasting daie, 10/51, *s.* a day on which it was forbidden to eat food of any description.'
Fat, 18/34, *adj.* fattened beasts.
Fat, 57/54, *s.* vat, vessel.
Fats up, 15/28, *v. pr. t.* fattens up.
Fautie, 99/2, *adj.* faulty.
Fauoreth, 52/24, *v. pr. t.* help, improve.
Fay, 77/4, *s.* faith, word. O. Fr. *fei.*
Feaw, 56/48, *adj.* few, a few.
Feawe, 50/1, *adj.* little time, while. A.S. *feawe*, few.
Fees, 33/12, *s. pl.* pay, reward.
Feft, 113/33, *pp.* enfeoffed, endowed.
Fellowes, 57/9, *s. pl.* companions, mates. O. Icel. *félagi*, a companion.
Fellowlie, 10/55, *adj.* friendly, neighbourly. Cf.

> "Mine eyes . . .
> Fall *fellowly* drops."
> Tempest, Act v. sc. i. 64.

See also Abbot's Shaksperean Grammar, § 447.
Fence, 63/2, *s.* defence, protection.
Fenell, 39/13, *s.* fennel. *Fœniculum vulgare.*
Fennie, 35/44, *adj.* mouldy, vinewed. "*Moisi*; mouldy, hoary, vinowed." —Cotgrave.
Ferme, 10/13, *s.* farm.
Fermer, 19/18, *s.* farmer.
Fetches, 64/2, *s. pl.* tricks, stratagems. Harrison, Descript. of Eng., has: "it be a vertue to deal without anie suspicious *fetches*," p. 115, ed. 1587.
Fetherfew, 43/9, *s.* feverfew. So named from its supposed febrifugal qualities. A.S. *feferfuge.*
Fetters, 17/21, *s. pl.* chains for the feet.
Fewell, 50/30, *s.* fuel. O.Fr. *fouaille*, from L. Lat. *focale*, from Lat. *focus*, a hearth.
Fide, 21/21, *pp.* purified, cleansed.
Fie, 20/21, *v.* cleanse. Icel. *fægja.* Cf. Ger. *fegen.*
Fieing, 53/18, *v.* cleaning out.
Feying, "Cleaning a Ditch or Pond, so as the water may come clear."—T.R. See *Fie.*
Fiemble, 55/8, *adj.* a corruption of *female*, the female hemp.
*Fierbote, 65, *s.* the right to take wood for burning. See Peacock's Gloss. of Manley and Corringham, E.D.S.
Filbeards, 34/9, *s. pl.* filberts. Various derivations have been given for this word: one, the most probable, from *full* and *beard*, referring to the long *beard* or husk with which it is provided: cf. Ger. *bart-nusz* = *bearded nut.*
Filbellie, 10/40, *s.* extravagance in food.
Filchers, 10/54, *s. pl.* pilferers. Scot. pilk = to pick. "She has pilkit his pouch."—Jamieson.
Filcheth, 63/13, *v. pr. t.* steals, pilfers.
*Fildes, 38, *s. pl.* fields.
Fisgig, 77/8, *s.* a worthless fellow: a light-heeled wench.—Craven. "A fisgig, or fisking housewife, *trotière.*" —Howell, 1660. Still in use in Lincolnshire.
Fishdaie, 10/51, *s.* a day in which fish is allowed to be eaten, but no flesh.
Fitchis, 53/11, *s. pl.* tares, vetches.
Fitly, 92/3, *adj.* suitable, fit.
Flacks, 50/16, *s.* flax. A.S. *fleax.* O. H. Ger. *flahs.*
Flaies, 18/3 *s. pl.* flails.
Flap, 85/7, *s.* a stroke with the flail.

Flawnes, 90/5, *s. pl.* "A custard, generally made in raised paste. Fr. *flan*, a custard or egg-pie." "A *flawne* or custard."—Baret's Alvearie, 1580.

Fleering, 64/17, *v. pr. p.* laughing, grinning. "To *fleer* and scorn at our solemnity."—Shakspere, Rom. and Jul. i. 5. "I *fleere*, I make an yvell countenaunce with the mouthe by vncoveryng of the tethe."—Palsgrave.

Fleming, 37/22, Flemming, 18/37, *s.* Dutchmen, Dutch coasting traders.

Flixe, 18/41, *s.* a flux.

Floted, 49/1, *v. pt. t.* skimmed off the cream. "Flet, as mylke or other lyke, *despumatus*."—Prompt. Parv. "*Escrémé*, fleeted as milk."—Cotgrave.

*Flotte, 72/*e*, *pp.* skimmed.

Flower, 52/14, *s.* ? floor.

Flower armor, 43/10, *s.* The "floure gentill or purple velvet floure."—Lyte's Dodoens, p. 168. Fr. *Floramor*, in Cotgrave *la noble fleur*, from its resemblance to the plumes worn by people of rank. *Amaranthus tricolor*.

Flower gentle, 43/12, *s.* a species of Amaranth. *Amaranthus spinosa*.

Flower de luce, 43/11, *s.* Iris, or flower-de-luce. Fr. *fleur-de-lis*. A plant of the genus *Iris*, in particular *Iris pseudacorus*, the yellow Iris or water flag.

Foison, 35/4; Foyzon, 113/37, *s.* plenty. "Foyzon is winter food."—T. R. Fr. *foison*, from Lat. *fusionem*, from *fundere*. Cotgrave gives "*Foison*: f. store, plentie, abundance, great fullnesse, enough." The word still exists in the Scotch *foison* or *fusion*, and the adj. *fusionless* or *fissenless*. Forby explains it as "Succulency, natural nutritive moisture," as *e.g.* "there is no *foison* in this hay."

Foistines, 57/5; Foistnes, 21/5; Foystines, 20/5, *s.* mustiness, mould. O. Fr. *fust*, a cask, *fusté*, tasting or smelling of the cask, musty.

Foisty, 19/39, *adj.* musty.

Fondlie, 10/26; Fondly, 67/9, *adv.* foolishly. *Fon* = to play the fool. Jamieson, Scott. Dict.

For, 9/9, *prep.* in spite of, regardless of.

For, 9/18. Here and in numerous instances in Tusser *for* means "for fear of," "to prevent."

Forbearer, 13/3, *s.* one who refuses.

Forborne, 13/2, *pp.* withheld, refused.

*Forehorse, 94, *s.* one who is always in advance with his work, never behindhand; the opposite to a procrastinator.

Forke, 22/9, *s.* pitchfork, hayfork.

*Fornight, 51, *s.* a fortnight.

Forrough, 16/15, *s.* furrow. A.S. *furh*.

Foyson, 10/6, *s.* plenty. See Foison.

Fough, 102/5, *interject.* faugh! phew! an exclamation.

Fraid, 2/8, *v. pt. t.* frightened, made afraid.

Fraie, 53/22, *s.* quarrel, fray.

Fraight, 113/24, *s.* freight, cargo.

Frailnesse, 10/62, *s.* frailty, uncertainty.

Frame, 57/1, *v.* make.

Framed, 2/15, *pp.* arranged, composed.

Fransie, 88/4, *s.* madness.

Fraud, 62/15, *v.* obtain by fraud.

Fraught, 64/5, *pp.* laden, freighted.

Fray, 77/4, *s.* disturbance, trouble.

Freat, 23/2, *v. imp.* be vexed.

Freat, 51/11, *v.* damage, decay, eat away.

> "As doth an hidden moth
> The inner garment *fret*."
> Spenser Faery Queene, ii. 34.

See Wedgwood's Dict. s.v. Fret.

Freeseth, 35/1, *v. pr. t.* freezes. A.S. *freosan*. O. Icel. *friosa*. Dan. *fryse*.

Frier, 86/14, *s.* friar.

Fritters, 90/3 *s. pl.* small pancakes with apples in them. "Frytoure, *lagana* (a pancake)."—Prompt. Parv. "A fritter or pancake; a kind of bread for children, as *fritters* and wafers."—Baret's Alvearie, 1580.

Froth, 35/3, *adj.* tender, perhaps originally = pulpy.

Frower, 17/8, *s.* a frow, an iron instrument for rending or splitting laths. Also called *Frommard*.

Fumetorie, 44/7; Fumentorie, 91/3, *s.* Fumitory. *Fumaria officinalis*, so called from its rank disagreeable smell: formerly used as an antiscorbutic: it is called *erthesmok* [earthsmoke] in MS. Sloane 5, f. 5.

Furmentie pot, 90/7, *s.* hulled wheat boiled in milk, and seasoned with cinnamon, sugar, etc. See note.

G.

Gadding, 10/51, *v.* going about gossipping.

Gaffe, 22/18, *v.* man, gaffer. "Formerly a common mode of address, equivalent to *friend, neighbour.*"—Halliwell.

Gage, 94/13, *s.* pawn, sweepeth to gage = hurries to pledge or place in pawn.

*Gage, 53, *v.* assert, maintain.

Galling, 57/31, *v.* causing sore or bare places.

Gallond, 19/42, *s.* gallon.

Gap, 113/20, *s.* an opening, cause.

Gaping, 57/45, *pr. p.* being greedy, grasping.

Garlike, 21/12, *s.* garlic.

Garmander, 42/8, *s.* germander. Fr. *gamandrée*, from Lat. *chamædrys.*

Garsong, 33/41, *s.* boy, lad. Fr. *garçon.*

Gasing, 99/1, *pr. p.* gazing, staring.

Gate, 64/17, *s.* walk, gait.

Gayler, 86/11, *s.* guardian, housekeeper.

Geanie, 2/6, *adj.* profitable, useful. A.S. *gægn*, fit, suitable. Robert de Brunne in his History of England, 3376, has, "a *geiner* way" = a more direct advantageous way. Scot. *gane*, fit, useful. Lanc. *gainest* way = the shortest cut.

Geld, 15/17, *v.* castrate, spay.

*Gentiles, 17, *s. pl.* gentle-folk.

Gentilie, 9/14, *adv.* kindly, with proper respect.

Gentils, 49/*c*, *s. pl.* gentles, maggots.

Gentlenes, 102/7, *s.* gentlemanly manners.

Gently, 102/7, *adv.* as gentlemen, in a gentlemanly manner.

Gentrie, 113/33, *s.* true nobility.

Gesse, 113/1, *v. imp.* guess, believe.

Gest, 4/2, *s.* a guest. A.S. *gest.*

Get, 9/5, *v.* earn.

Gettings, 9/5, *s.* earnings.

Giddie braine, 10/23, *adj.* giddy, unsteady.

Giles, 113/18, *s. pl.* traps, deceits.

Gillet, 50/30, *s.* lad. Gael. *gille, giolla*, a lad. Halliwell gives "an instrument for thatching" as the meaning in this passage, but why, I do not know.

Gillian spendal, 23/18, wasteful, careless housekeeper.

Giloflowers, 15/42, *s. pl.* carnations, pinks. Fr. *giroflée*, from Lat. *caryophyllus*, a clove, from the clove-like smell of the flowers.—Wedgwood.

Gin, 10/19, *s.* trap.

Ginnes, 106/22, *s. pl.* means, contrivances.

Ginnie, 90/5, Jenny.

Ginny, 33/38, *s.* a name for a filly. Mavor reads Jilly.

Gise, 97/4, *s.* fashion, way.

Gloues, 57/9, *s. pl.* gloves.

God night, 18/49. A phrase equivalent to "it is all over," "it is too late.

Goef, 55/4, *s.* the stack or rick.

Goeler, 46/4, *adj.* "The Goeler is the yellower, which are the best setts, old roots (of hops) being red."—T.R. A.S. *geolewe.*

Gofe, 56/20, *s.* rick, stack. In Addit. MS. 1295, a Lat. Eng. Vocab. written in Norfolk in the 15th century, occur "*Gelimo*, to golue, *Ingelimum*, golfe." Palsgrave gives "a *goulfe* of corne."

Gofe ladder, 17/1, *s.* a ladder for hay ricks.

Gole, 114/3, *s.* goal, prize.

Goom, 33/59, *s.* gum.

Goordes, 41/5, *s. pl.* gourds. Lat. *cucurbita.*

Gossep, 94/7, *s.* gossips, companions.

Got, 113/16, *pp.* caught.

Gotten, 10/4, *pp.* earned, acquired.

Gould, 3/3, *s.* gold, money.

Goue, 57/10, *pp.* laid up in the barn in the straw. Another form of *Goaf.* "*Goulfe* of corne, so moche as may lye betwene two postes."—Palsgrave. Dan. *gulve* = to lay corn sheaves on the floor, from Dan. *gulv*, a floor.

Gouing, 57/23, *v.* laying up in the barn in the straw. See Goue.

Graffing, 46/10, *s.* grafting. O. Fr. *grafe*, from Lat. *graphium*, a pencil, from the resemblance of the graft to a pointed pencil.

Grassebeefe, 12/4, *s.* beef of an ox fattened upon grass.

Grate, 10/29, *s.* prison (grating).

Greaseth, 68/2, *v. pr. t.* bribes, enriches.

Great, 57/8, by great = task or piece-work, in contradistinction to *day*-work.

Greedie gainfull, 2/13, *adj.* greedy for gain.
Greefe, 89/8, *s.* trouble, worry.
Gregorie, 46/2. St. Gregory's Day, 12th March.
Grinstone, 17/8, *s.* grindstone.
Gromel, 45/9, *s.* the plant Gromwell. *Lithospermum arvense*, Linn.
Grosest, 19/18, *adj.* heaviest, thickest, Fr. *gros.*
Grosse, 18/18, *adj.* coarse.
Grossum caput, 95/1, a blockhead, stupid.
Grotes, 33/46, *s. pl.* money (groats). L. Ger. *grot* = a large piece (of money), so called because before this coin was issued by Edward III., the English had no larger silver coin than the penny.
Gruch, 57/19; Grutch, 86/2, *v.* grudge. O. Fr. *grouchier*, to grumble.
Grutching, 10/8, *s.* grumbling.
Guise, 89/12, *Guyse, 5, *s.* habit, custom.
Gunstone, 10/19, *s.* a ball of stone, used in heavy artillery before the introduction of iron shot.—Nares' Gloss.
Gutted, 46/4, *pp.* taken off from the old roots.
*Gutting, 27, *v.* cutting up, making ruts in.

H.

Haberden, 23/12, *s.* "that kind of cod which is usually salted."—Nares. ? Aberdeen haddocks.
Hacking, 53/15, *v.* hewing down, cutting of trees.
Had I wist, 77/8, lit. "had I known:" foole had I wist = foolish and useless regrets.
*Haft, 60, *v. imp.* "Act like a miser, be a niggard. The sentence then reads 'Be not niggardly towards God of the goods He sends you.' *Haft*, to grasp (an extension of the verb *to have*), and hence to save, be a niggard, is preserved in *hafter*, a miser, saver; which see in my Notes to P. Plowman, l. 197, p. 117. See nine examples of this word in Skelton, ed. Dyce, ii. 108." —Note by Rev. W. W. Skeat. The word, however, seems to bear even a stronger meaning, for Cooper, in his "Thesaurus," 1584, has "*Cauilla*, a mocke, a scoffe, an haftyng question, a cauill." The words "haft not to godward" thus may mean "do not grumble at, find fault with, or question the justice of what God sends you."
Haie, 63/24, *s.* hay. A.S. *haga.*
Haier, 57/51, *s.* cloth made of goats' hair.
Haile, 15/34, *adj.* sound, strong. A.S. *hǽl.*
Hailoft, 89/6, *s.* hay-lofts.
Haithorne, 34/28, *s.* hawthorn. A.S. *hagaþorn* from *haga* = hedge, haw. Ger. *hagedorn.*
Hallomas, 23/1, *s.* the Feast of All Saints. Hallowmas, *i.e.* All Saints' Day, Nov. 1, was, in Tusser's time, ten days nearer the winter solstice than now.
Hallontide, 21/1. All Saints' Day, 1st November.
Handsome, 48/18, *adj.* useful, ready, *handy.* A.S. *hand*, *hond*, the hand. Prompt. Parv. gives "handsum, *manualis.*"
Handsomly, 21/24, *adv.* neatly, trimly.
Hardhead, 71/4, *adj.* hardy, brave.
Hardlie, 10/50, *adv.* with difficulty.
Harlots, 74/4, *s. pl.* tramps, vagrants, or disreputable characters of either sex. "An harlott, *balator*, *rusticus.*"—Cathol. Anglicum.
Harmes, 16/15, *s.* in harm's way, in danger.
Harolds Booke, 113/11. *s. pl.* the Books of the College of Heralds.
Hart, 19/13, *s.* strength, fertility.
Harted, 48/17, *pp.* provided with a good heart, or, as we should now say, a good bottom; strengthened.
*Harthe, 65, *s.* hearth.
Hartilie, 10/55, *adj.* hearty.
Hartstong, 45/10, *s.* the Heartstongue, *Ceterach officinarum*, so called from the shape of the frond.
Hastings, 18/32, *s. pl.* an early variety of peas, "soone ripe, soone rotten." —D. Rogers' Naaman.
Hauke, 56/44, *s.* hawking, falconry.
Haunt, 67/14, *v.* follow, pursue, be accustomed. O. Fr. *hanter*, to pursue.
Haunting, 16/31, *adj.* frequenting, in the habit of coming.
Hauocke, 77/3, *s.* havoc, waste.
Hawe, 36/13, *s* the berries of the hawthorn, hips.
Hawme, 55/14, *s.* haulm, straw.

"Haulm, straw left in an esh or gratten; stubble, thatch. Sax. hælme, *culmus*, *calamus*. Icel. halmur, *palea*."—Bish. Kennett's MS. Ray gives "haulm or helm, stubble gathered after the corn is inned."

Hazard, 23/11, *s.* danger.

Heale, 19/37, *v.* to recover, be cured.

Healthsom, 11/S, *adj.* healthy, invigorating.

*Heare, 41, *s.* hair.

Hearesaie, 2/10, *s.* hearsay, report.

Hearie, 49/7, *adj.* hairy, full of hairs. A.S. *hær*. O. Icel. *här*, hair.

Heate, 76/2, *pp.* heated, hot.

Heawers, 47/8, *s. pl.* woodcutters. A.S. *heawan*, to cut.

Hed, 89/9, *s.* head, mind.

Hedlonds, 52/17, *s. pl.* headlands.

Hew, 112/1, *s.* colour, "changed hew" = have changed, become unfavourable.

Hew prowler, 35/25. "Hugh Prowler is our Author's name for a night-walker."—T.R.

Hid, 2/11, *s.* care, heed. A.S. *hédan*.

Hier, 23/9, *s.* business, duty.

Hight, 113/3, *v. pt. t.* was called, named. O. Eng. *higt*, *higte*. A.S. *hâtte* from *hatan*, to call, name.

Hilback, 10/40, *s.* cover back, *i.e.* clothes, extravagance in dress. Kennett, MS. Lansdowne 1033.—Halliwell A.S. *hilan*, *helan*, to cover.

Hindring, 88/3, *v.* injuring, damaging.

Hir, 35/51, *poss. pr.* their. A.S. *heor*.

Hobbard de Hoy, 60/3, *s.* a lad approaching manhood. "Hober-de-hoy, half a man and half a boy."—Ray's Gloss.

Hogscote, 17/21, *s.* a pen or sty for hogs.

Holds, 33/40, *v. pr. t.* equals, gains equal.

Holiokes, 43/15, *s. pl.* hollyhocks. A.S. *holihoc*.

Homelie, 1/2, *adj.* plain, homely, unpretending.

Hone, 46/9, *s.* "a common rubber or whetstone."—T.R.

Honie, 106/4, *adj.* sweet.

Horehound, 45/11, *s.* horehound. A.S. *hara-hune*, or possibly a corruption of Lat. *urinaria*, the plant being considered a sovereign remedy in cases of strangury and dysuria.

Horselock, 17/21, *s.* shackles for horses' feet.

Horseteeme, 17/10, *s.* team of horses.

Hostis, 10/8, *s. pl.* entertainers.

Householdry, 9/11, *s.* furniture and articles for domestic use.

Houell, 52/8, *s.* barn, outhouse.

Houen, 49/4, *pp.* swelled. A.S. *hebban*, *hefan* (pp. *hofen*), to heave, raise. O. H. Ger. *hevan*.

Hower, 107/4, *s.* hour.

Howse, 57/31, *v. imp.* house.

Hoy, 57/13, *v. imp.* drag, frighten, drive away by crying, "hoy, hoy!"

Hull, 36/23, *s.* holly.

Huluer, 48/10, *s.* holly. O. Icel. *hulfr*.

Hurtilberies, 34/13, *s. pl.* the hurtleberry or whortleberry, bilberry.

Hutch, 10/47, *s.* money chest or box. A.S. *hwæcca* = chest, an unauthorised (? invented) form, due to Somner. O. Fr. *houche*.

I.

*Iayle, 88, *s.* a gaol, prison.

Ictus sapit, 2/8. Lat. Prov. See Notes.

Indian eie, 43/16, *s.* the Pink, so called from the eye-shaped marking of the corolla.

Inholder, 97/1, *s.* innkeeper.

Inned, 23/19, *pp.* saved, housed.

Intreating, 88/5, *s.* treatment.

Invest, 11/8, *v.* surround.

Ise, 111/2, *s.* ice.

Isop, 42/9, *s.* hyssop. A name assigned in the Authorised Version of the Bible to the caper.

Ist, 5/3, is it.

Iuie, 50/6, *Iuye, 42, *s.* ivy. A.S. *ifig*.

J.

Jack, 17/20, *s.* a horse or wooden frame upon which wood is sawn.

Jack, 85/10, *s.* a drinking vessel containing half a pint according to Grose, and quarter of a pint according to Pegge, and Peacock's Gloss. of Manley and Corringham.

Jade, 17/3, *s.* an ill-tempered horse.

Janting, 87/3, *v.* driving. Cotgrave gives another form of the word in English. "*Iancer vn cheual.* To stirre a horse in the stable till hee sweat withall; or (as our) to iaunt; an old word." "Jaunt" is found in Romeo and Juliet, ii. 5, 26,

"What a *jaunt* have I had!" and in line 53 of the same scene:

"To catch my death with *jaunting* up and down."

Cf. also Richard II. v. 5, 94.

Jarring, 88/3, *s.* quarrelling, scolding.

Jerke, 64*/9, *s.* stroke, blow. See *Yerke.*

Jet, 113/38, *v.* strut about, walk proudly. Fr. *jetter.*

"Along the streetes as he doth *jetting* passe,
His outside showes him for an inward asse."

Rowland's Knave of Hearts, 1613.

Jettie, 68/1, *v.* walk or strut about.

Jobbing, 37/12, *v.* pecking. "As an ass with a galled back was feeding in a meadow, a raven pitched upon him, and their sate *jobbing* of the sore."—L'Estrange's Esop.

John Baptist, 12/4. The feast of St. John the Baptist, 24th June.

Jornie, 57/38, *v. pr. t.* go on a journey, start.

Just, 57/10, *adv.* neatly, trimly.

K.

Karle hempe, 15/24, *s.* the male hemp. See Glossary of Manley and Corringham (E. D. Soc. No. VI.), by E. Peacock.

Keies, 89/3, *s. pl.* keys, locks.

Kell, 57/51, *s.* hop-kiln.

Kerue, 113/32, *v.* (carve), set out, arrange.

Kest, 11/3, *v. imp.* cast, turn.

Kiffe, 10/30, *s.* kith, kindred, relations.

Kinde, 46/20, *s.* nature, natural way. A.S. *cynd.*

Kirnels, 36/13, *s. pl* pips, seeds. A.S. *cyrnel.*

Knacker, 58/5, *s.* a cart, collar and harness maker, chiefly employed by farmers.

Knackes, 86/7, *s. pl.* knickknacks, trifles.

Knap, 85/11, *v. imp.* rap, knock.

Knauerie, 9/13, *s.* roguery, craft, deceit.

Knede, 74/5, *v. imp.* knead. A.S. *cnedan.* O. H. Ger. *chnetan.*

Kniueles, 98/1, *adj.* having no knives. "When knives were not laid for the guests, as at the present period, they would use their daggers to carve with, which were harmless as to any other purpose."—Mavor.

Knot, 22/22, *s.* flower-beds laid out in fanciful shapes. See Bacon's Essay Of Gardens, ed. W. A. Wright, p. 189: "As for the making of *knots*, or figures, with divers coloured earths, that they may lie under the windowes of the house, on that side, which the garden stands, they be but toyes." Compare also Love's Labour's Lost, i. 1, 249: "Thy curious-*knotted* garden;" and Milton's Paradise Lost, iv. 242:

"Flowers worthy of Paradise, which not nice art
In beds and curious *knots*, but nature boon
Pour'd forth profuse."

And Shakspere, Richard II. iii. 4, 46.

Knotted, 42/13, *adj.* jointed. "The *knotted* rush-ringes, and gilte Rosemaree." — Spenser, Shep. Cal. November.

L.

Lackey, 87/3, *s.* servant, messenger.

Lag, 20/15, *v. pr. t.* pilfer, steal.

Lagged, 36/25, *pp.* caught.

Laggoose, 85/4, *s.* laggard, lazy.

Laie, 4/1, 9/32, *v.* plan, intend, purpose.

Laie, 35/46, Lay, 35/48, *s.* untilled land, grass land, lea.

Laier, 63/4, *s.* soil, ground.

Laier, 20/27, *s.* beds, litter.

Lammas, 50/36, *s.* Lammas Day, the 1st August. A.S. *hlâfmaesse.* O. Eng. *loafmas*, the bread-feast or feast of first fruits.

Lamming, 35/21, *s.* lambing.

Lams, 51/1, *s.* lambs

Langdebiefe, 39/16, *s.* Wild bugloss. See Mr. Britten's note, p. 266.

Larkes foot, 43/18, *s.* Larkspur, or Larksclaw. *Delphinium*, Linn.

Lash, 63/20, *s.* dirt, mud; leaue in the lash = leave in the lurch, or, perhaps, in the snare, trap. See next word.

Lash, 10/15, *s.* the leash in which an animal is caught or held, hence "to run in the lash" = to fall into the snare.

Lasheth, 23/18, *v. pr. t.* lavisheth, wastes.

Lashinglie, 9/6, *adv.* lavishly, freely.

Lash out, 9/6, *v.* lavish, spend.

Laster, 85/10, *s.* is no laster = will not or does not last, *i.e.* is soon broken.

Launders, 83/2, *s. pl.* washers, laundresses.

Lauender cotten, 42/12, *s.* the Garden cypres, *Chamæcyparissus.*—Lyte's Dodoens, ed. 1578, p. 29.

Lauender spike, 42/11, *s.* spike lavender, *Lavandula spica*, from M. Lat. *lavendula*, from *lavare* = to wash, as being the plant used to scent newly-washed linen, whence the expression of "laid up in lavender." The essential oil distilled from this plant, which is nearly allied to the common Lavender, is called in French Essence d'Aspic, and in English Oil of Spike. It is used in porcelain painting and in veterinary medicine. See Pharmacographia, p. 430.

Lawe, 56/2, *s.* rule, for a lawe = as a rule.

Laxe, 19/41, *s.* looseness, diarrhœa. See Cowlaske.

Lay, 10/60, *v. pr. t.* plan, try.

Lay land, 33/49, *s.* untilled lands. "Lay lande, *terre nouvellement labourée.*"—Palsgrave.

Lead, 56/14, *s.* a cauldron, copper, or kettle. Gaelic *luchd* = a pot, kettle. "That stemede as a forneys of a *leede.*"—Chaucer, Prologue to C. T. l. 202. "Make þe broys in þe *led.*"—Havelok, ed. Skeat, 924.

Lease, 33/49, *s.* a pasture. "A lease is a name used in some countries for a small piece of ground of two or three acres."—T. R. O.E. *leswen*, to pasture, from A.S. *lǽsu*, a pasture, *lǽswian*, to pasture.

Leaueled, 46/7, *pp.* levelled, measured.

Leauens, 89/10, *s. pl.* the barm and meal laid together for fermentation: *to lay the leavens or leavance* = to put them together for that purpose. See Halliwell, s.v. Leavance.

Leese, 56/47, *v. imp.* lose, miss.

Leete, 86/10, *s.* a manor court.

Lemmans, 40/2*a*, *s. pl.* lemons. Arabic *laimûn*.

Lent stuffe, 56/36, *s.* provisions for Lent.

Lesse, 2/8, *s.* lease, term. Fr. *lais*, *laissement*, the lease or instrument by which a holding of any kind is let (*laissé*) to a tenant.

Let, 57/50, *s.* hindrance, obstacle.

Letted, 23/2, *pp.* hindered, delayed.

Lettis, 39/18, *s.* lettuce. Lat. *lactuca*, from Greek γαλα, gen. γάλακτος, milk, and ἔχω, to contain, through *lattouce*, an older form (still retained in Scotland).

> "Letuce of lac derivyed is perchaunce;
> Ffor mylk it hath or yeveth abundaunce."
> Palladius on Husbondrie, E. E. Text Soc. ed. Lodge, 51/216.

Leuer, 50/9, *adv.* sooner, rather. A.S. *leófer*.

Lick, 23/6, *v.* lick themselves.

Licoras, 45/13, *s.* liquoras.

Licour, 22/23, *s.* water, drink.

Lide, 113/3, *v. pt. t.* lay, was situate.

Lie in the dust, 10/32, cease, be done away with.

Lieng alonge, 19/25, lying at a distance.

Linage, 113/3, *s.* lineage, family.

Lightly, 46/20, *adv.* easily.

Likest, 35/34, *adj.* most likely, promising.

Lillium cum-vallium, 43/20, *s.* Lily of the valley, or Lily-convally. Lat. *Lilium convallium*, a name taken from Canticles ii. 1, "I am the lily of the valleys."

Line, 17/5, *s.* rope (?).

Ling, 57/36, *s.* a fish (*Lota molva*) resembling a cod, but longer and more slender. When salted, it is extensively used for food in Scotland and Ireland. Fr. *lingue*, O. Dutch, *linghe*.

Linne, 97/3, *s.* the town of Lynn. "To purchase Lynn" seems to have been a proverbial mode of expression used in ridicule of stinginess.—Mavor.

Linnen, 94/13, *s.* linen.

Litherly, 85/8, *adj.* lazy, idle.

Lively spide, 3/2, quickly seen.

Liuerwort, 39/20, *s.* so called from the *liver* shape of the thallus. Lyte (Dodoens, ed. 1587, p. 411) tells us it is "a sovereign medicine against the heate and inflammation of the liver."

Loiterers, 2/6, *s. pl.* hangers on, dependents.

*Lone, 10, *s.* a loan, grant from God.

Longing, 16/10, *s.* desire, what it requires.

Longwort, 39/19, *s.* lungwort, *Pulmonaria maculosa*.

Looke, 5/1, 10/4, *v.* look for, seek, expect.

Loose, 57/22, *v. pr. t.* lose, waste.

Lop, 33/13, *s.* the faggot wood of a tree.

Lordlie, 112/3, *adv.* to live in a lordly or grand style.

Losels, 63/12, *s. pl.* worthless, abandoned fellows. Prompt. Parv. has "Lorel or losel, or ludene, *lurco.*"

Louage, 45/12, *s.* Lovage. *Ligusticum Scoticum*, Linn.

Lowe, 23/24, *adj.* not advanced, if Spring is taken to mean the *season*; or, not grown up, if Spring is the *young grass.*

Lowe, 63/11, *adv.* low, feeding so lowe =to allow the flocks to eat the pasture too low or short.

Lower, 20/17, *v.* scowl, look discontented.

Lubberlie, 9/16, *adj.* lazy, idle. "Thither this lusking *lubber* softly creeped." *Tom Tel Troth's Message*, New Shak. Soc. ed. F. J. Furnivall, p. 128. "*Baligaut, m.* an vnweldie *lubber*, great lobcocke, huge luske, mishapen lowt, ill-fauoured flabergullion."—Cotgrave.

Lubbers, 57/22, *s. pl.* louts, awkward fellows. Welsh *llob* = a heavy lump, *llabi* = a looby. Gaelic *leobhair* = a lubber.—Wedgwood.

Lug, 87/4, *v.* drag, draw.

Lurched, 23/3, *pp.* robbed of their food, being left in the *lurch.*

Lurching, 88/7, *s.* greediness. L. Lat. *lurcare*, to swallow food greedily. "To *lurch*, devour, or eate greadily, *ingurgito.*"—Baret's Alvearie. Cf. Bacon's Essays, xlv.

Lurke, 86/1, *v.* idle, loiter about.

Lurketh, 62/9, *v. pr. t.* lounge, dawdle about. The same as Lusk. Harman, p. 82, speaks of "lewtering luskes and lazy lorrels."

Lust, 15/10, *s.* desire.

Lustie, 60/5, *adj.* strong, lusty.

M.

Mads, 50/4, *s. pl.* maggots, worms. Another form of *moth.*

Magget the py, 49/9, the magpie. See note.

Maides, 90/3, *s. pl.* maidens, girls.

Maierom, 42/13, *s.* marjoram, from Lat. *majorana*, with the change of *n* to *m*, as in "Holm, Lime," etc.

Maine, 19/17, *adj.* = *meint*, i.e. *mixed* wheat. See *Mung* or *muncorn* in Halliwell.

Mainecombe, 17/3, *s.* a comb for horses' manes.

Maine sea, 14/4, the ocean, the high sea. Cf. the expression "the Spanish main."

Male, 102/4, *s.* mail-bag, portmanteau, or sack.

Mallow, 33/6, *s.* the field mallow.

Mams, 95/5, *s. pl.* mothers, mammas.

Manerly, 85/11, *adj.* polite, decent.

Mar, 95/2, *v.* spoil, ruin.

*Marefoles, 53, *s. pl.* fillies.

Marke, 17/17, *s.* marking tool.

Marres, 20/14, *v. pr. t.* spoils, interrupts.

Marrow, 57/40, *s.* a mate, companion. "Marwe, or felawe yn trauayle or mate, *socius, compar, sodalis.*" —Prompt. Parv. See Towneley Mysteries, p. 110, and quotations in Craven Glossary and Jamieson.

Marsh men, 17/19, *s. pl.* farmers in the fen and marshy country.

Martilmas, 12/3. The feast of St. Martin, 11th November. See Notes.

Mast, 63/5, *s.* the fruit of the oak and beech and other forest trees. A.S. *mæst.* Ger. *mast*, from Gothic *matan*, to nourish.

Mastlin, 63/23, *s.* mixed corn. See Mestlin.

Mates, 113/30, *s. pl.* companions.

Mawdlin, 49/c, *s.* Magdalene.

Mawdelin, 42/14, *s.* Maudlin. *Balsamita fœminea.*—Gerard's Herball.

Meade, 63/3, *s.* meadow. A.S. *mǽd*, *meadu*, genitive, *meadewes.*

Meake, 17/14, *s.* "a hook at the end of a handle five foot long."—T.R. "A *meag* or *meak*, a pease-hook." —Ray. Also in Coles' Dict. 1676.

Meane, 113/25, *s.* means, help.

Meanie, 2/6, *adj.* many.

Measling, 16/23, becoming measly. "*Masyl* or *mazil*, sekenesse."—Prompt. Parv.

Measure, 68/9, *v.* be moderate, be within measure.

Meated, 17/12, *pp.* fed.

Meateth, 62/7, *v. pr. t.* feeds, supports.

Medcin, 33/19, *s.* medicine.

Meedeful, 87/7, *adj.* thankful.

Meedes, 106/4, *s. pl.* meadows. See Meade.

Mendbreech, 89/6, *s.* one who sits up late at night to mend his clothes.

Mercurie, 39/22, *s.* Mercury, or Good King Henry, is largely grown by cottagers in Lincolnshire. This plant, the *Chenopodium bonus henricus* of botanists, bears tender young leaves resembling spinach, which, when cooked, are but little inferior in flavour to the finest asparagus. It is a robust-growing perennial, and, when once planted in deep, rich soil, requires no further cultural attention than a dressing of well-decomposed manure during the winter.

Mestlen, 37/21, *s.* a mixture of wheat and rye. "Mastilþone, *bigermen, mixtilio.*"—Cath. Ang. "*Framois*, meslin of oats and barlie mixed." "*Meteil*, messling or misslin, wheat and rie mingled."—Cotgrave.

Mew, 36/26, *s.* a cage for moulting.

Michel, 33/22, Mihel, 57/25, Mihell, 12/4, *s.* Michaelmas. The feast of St. Michael and All Angels, 29th September.

Michers, 10/15, *s. pl.* lurking thieves, skulkers. "Mecher, a lytell thefe, *larronceau.*"—Palsgrave. Now common as a term for a truant. Cf. Shak. 1 Henry IV. ii. 4: "Shall the blessed sun of heaven prove a *micher* and eat blackberries."

Mickle, 68/1, *adj.* great, much.

Mier, 107/4, *s.* mire, filth. A.S. *myre.*

*Mier, 38, Mierie, 113/27, *adj.* filthy, muddy.

Mihelmas, 57/44, Michaelmas.

*Millons, 72/*c*, *s. pl.* melons. See Musk Million.

Mind, 68/5, *v.* notice, comment on.

Mind, 63/1, *v. pr. t.* intend, have in mind, wish.

Minion, 66/4, *adj.* pleasant, agreeable, favourite. Fr. *mignon.* L. Lat. *mignonetus, gratissimus, minna*, love.

Minnekin, 10/20, *adj.* little, perhaps with the idea of the modern contracted form "minx."

Miring, 23/3, *v.* being stuck in bogs.

Mis, 16/8, *v.* want, be without.

Mischiefe, 23/4, *v.* hurt, injure.

Mischieued, 10/36, *adj.* unfortunate, ruined.

Misdeeme, 30/3, *v.* misjudge. A.S. *deman*, to judge.

Mislike, 23/16, *v.* displease, not suit.

Mistle, 33/12, *s.* mistletoe. A.S. *mistel.* O.H. Ger. *mistil.*

Mitch, 17/17, *adj.* large.

Mite, 63/20, *s.* the smallest piece. A.S. *mite.*

Mo, 33/57, *adj.* more, others. A.S. *má.*

Moether, 17/13, Mother, 16/14, *s.* a girl. A woman and her mawther = a woman and her daughter. "Moder, servaunte or wench."—Prompt. Parv.

Mogwort, 45/15, *s.* mugwort, *Artemisia vulgaris*, Linn.

Moile, 4/1, *v.* to work hard, drudge. Lat. *moliri*, to struggle. "In the earth we *moile* with hunger, care and paine."—Mirror for Magist. ed. 1610.

Molding, 55/4, *v.* becoming musty, or mouldy.

Mome, 62/3, *s.* blockhead, fool. "A gull, a ninny, a *mome.*"—Florio, p. 81. "A youth will play the wanton, and an olde man proove a *mome.*"—Drayton, Skeltoniad.

Mone, 67/1, *s.* complaint, lamentation.

Moooeth, 94/7, *v. pr. t.* moves or exerts herself, plans.

Mother, 16/14, *s.* a girl. See Moether.

Moulspare, 17/18, *s.* mole spear.

Mow, 17/19, *s.* stack of hay or corn. A.S. *muwa.* L. Lat. *mugium.*

Mowles, 36/17, *s. pl.* moles.

Mowse, 38/3, *v. pr. t.* mouth, bite.

Mowth, 57/25, *v.* eat.

Muck, 51/13, *s.* manure.

Mulley, 57/46, a common name for a cow in Suffolk.

Mungrels, 46/3, *s. pl.* cur dogs, mongrels. A.S. *mengan*, to mix, hence an animal of a mixed breed, a hybrid.

Musk Million, 40/8, *s.* the musk melon. "Pickled cowcombers I have bought a pecke for threepence, and *musk mellions*, there hath beene cast five or sixe loads of them in one day to their hogs."—Taylor's Works, 1630. See Lyte's Dodoens, p. 590.

Myslen, 16/11, *s.* mixed corn. Mestlyone or monge corne or dragge.—Prompt. Parv. See Dredge and Mestlen.

N.

Nads, 17/9, *s.* an adze.

Naile, 17/8, *s.* nails.

Nall, 17/4, *s.* an awl.

Naughtie, 53/20, *adj.* useless, unfit.
Naughtly, 10/4, *adv.* by unfair or improper means.
Nauewes, 41/6, *s. pl.* wild navew. *Brassica napus*, L. Fr. *naveau*, from *napellus*, dimin. of *napus* = the rape.
*Nawlt, 32, ? *nawt*, nothing.
Neat, 50/28, *s.* cattle. A.S. *neât*, horned cattle.
Neatherd, 63/2, *s.* herdsman, the man who attends to the cattle.
Needams shore, 97/5. "A punning proverb recorded in Ray; and signifying that waste and extravagance bring a man to want or need."—Mavor.
Needfullie, 9/15, *adv.* necessarily.
Ne forte, 23/10, Latin, lest by chance.
Nep, 39/24, *s.* cat mint, a contraction from the Lat. *nepeta*.
Nest, 11/6, *v.* nestle, settle.
*Nestling, 41, *v.* harbouring, supporting.
Nettie, 68/1, *adj.* natty, neat. O. Fr. *net*, from Lat. *nitidus*.
Nice, 102/1, *adj.* careful, particular.
Nick, 98/4, *v.* cut, notch.
Nie, 16/4, *adj.* near, convenient.
Nips, 113/5, *s. pl.* pinches.
Niggerly, 27/4, *adj.* niggardly, miserly. Icel. *hnöggr*, sparing, miserly. Cf. Ger. *knicker*, a niggard.
Nittes, 21/23, *s. pl.* the eggs of a louse or other insects. A.S. *hnitu*.
Noble, 16/16, *s.* noble, a gold coin of the value of 6*s.* 8*d.*
Noddies, 18/20, Nodie, 98/4, *s. pl.* simpletons, fools.

"Ere you come hither, proove I was somebody,
The king delighted in me, now I am a *noddy*."
Damon and Pythias, i. 174.

Noe, 7/4, *s.* Noah.
Noiance, 16/8, *s.* injury, trouble.
Noie, 52/15, *v. pr. t.* are injurious, noxious.
Noieth, 57/13, *v. pr. t.* suffer harm or injury.
Noisome, 10/8, *adj.* injurious, damaging.
Norfolk wiles, 113/18, "Essex miles, Suffolk stiles, Norfolk wiles, many men beguiles."—Old East Anglian saw. See note.
Nowles, 36/17, *s. pl.* the hillocks, little mounds. A.S. cnoll, *cacumen*. "Nolle, *idem quod* nodul."—Prompt. Parv.
Noy, 53/15, *v.* hurt, are injurious. See Noie.
Noyer, 13/2, *s.* one that hurts or injures.
Nurteth, 20/28, *v. pr. t.* poke or push with the horns. ? connected with Fr. *nuire*, Lat. *nocere*. Halliwell quotes from Gawayne *nirt* = a cut, hurt.
Nurture, 10/57, *s.* training.

O.

Of, 106/12, *prep.* through, in consequence of.
Of, 106/2, *prep.* out of, from.
Of, 19/22, *prep.* after.
Of, 64*/4, *prep.* with, by means of.
Ofcorne, 86/5, *s.* offal or waste corn.
Office, 99/2, *s.* duty. Lat. *officium*.
Oke, 19/31, *s.* oaks. A.S. *Æc*.
Ope gap, 16/36, hedge or fence breakers.
Open, 16/38, *v.* bark, open his mouth.
Opprest, 19/29, *pp.* troubled, laden.
Opte, 113/22, *v. pt. t.* opened.
*Or and, 18, before. Cf. Er an.
Orach or Arach, 39/26, *s.* Orach. *Atriplex sativa alba. Atriplex sativa purpurea.*—Gerard's Herball, ed. 1633.
Orderlie, 9/8, *adv.* in due order.
Orengis, 40/4*a*, *s. pl.* oranges. Arabic, *nârandj*. L. Lat. *arantia*, from its first title, *pomum aurantium*, golden apple.
Otemell, 46/26, *s.* oatmeal. A.S. *âta*, oat, and *mæl*, meal.
Otes, 46/13, *s. pl.* oats.
Othing, 94/6, one thing.
Out, 16/17, *adj.* outdoor, open air.
Ouercome, 53/4, *v.* manage, keep up with.
Ouerly, 23/21, *adv.* all over.
Over reaching, 2/11, cheating, deceiving.
Ouerthwart, 46/9, *prep.* across. A.S. *oferþweorh*. O. Eng. *outhwar*, *thweorh*. O. Norse, *thwert*.
Ox bowes, 17/10, *s. pl.* the bow of wood which goes round the neck of an ox.
Oxboy, 63/15, *s.* the boy who attends to the cattle.
Oxteeme, 17/10, *s.* team of oxen.
Oxyokes, 17/10, *s. pl.* yokes for oxen.

P.

Pad, 17/21, *s.* padlock.
Paggles, 43/25, *s. pl.* cowslip, primrose,

paigles. In Suffolk the *Cuckoo flower*. See note.

Paier, 17/13, *s.* pair, couple.

Paine, 3/1, *s.* pains, trouble.

Painfull, 77/15, *adj.* painstaking, careful.

Painfull, 2/13, *adj.* full of trouble, requiring care.

Painted, 5/3, *pp.* adorned; the *sermo ornatus* of Cicero.

Paltrie, 57/30, *adj.* poor, worthless.

Panel, 17/5, *s.* a pannier. A *pannel* and *ped* have this difference: the one is much shorter than the other, and raised before and behind, and serves for smaller burdens; the other is longer and made for Burdens of Corn. These are fastened with a leathern Girt called a Wantye.—T.R.

Parasites, 10/27, *s. pl.* flatterers, hangers on.

Pare, 2/7, *v.* injure, damage, impair.

Pared, 46/4, *pp.* cleaned and cleared of all superfluous roots.

Partition, page 2, *s.* division.

Pas, 48/6, *v. pr. t.* care. "As for these silken-coated staves, I *pass* not."—Shakspere, 2 Henry VI. iv. 2.

Pask, 46/2, *s.* Easter. Lat. *Pascha*.

Passeth, 102/3, *v. pr. t.* think, reflect. See Pas.

Pasties, 90/7, *s. pl.* pies.

Patch, 51/32, *s.* originally a fool, jester, here = the farm labourer. Ital. *pazzo*, which Florio ("New Worlde of Wordes") defines as "foolish, fond, mad, rash, doting, rauing or simple. Also a foole, a gull, an idiot, a mad man, a naturall." By some, however, it is derived from the *patched* or motley coat of the jester.

Patches, 53/2, *s. pl.* places where the shearer has cut the skin of the sheep, wounds.

Pates, 63/9, *s. pl.* persons.

Pauncies, 43/24, *s.* pansies, heartsease. "There's *pansies*, that's for thoughts." — Shakspere, Hamlet, iv. 5.

Pay, 77/11, *v.* pay home = give a strong, sharp blow.

Peake, 67/27, *v.* to look thin or sickly, "Dwindle, *peak* and pine."—Shakspere, Macbeth, i. 3.

Pearch, 87/5, *v.* perch, roost.

Peasebolt, 18/38, *s.* "pease in the Hawm or Straw."—T.R.

Peaseetch, 19/5, *s.* the aftermath of a crop of peas. See Etch.

Peasefed, 18/27, *adj.* fed on peas.

Peason, 53/9, *s. pl.* pease.

> "Prick *peason* and beanes, if thy garden be dry,
> At change of the moone, and in beautiful skye."
>
> Almanack, 1615.

Peccantem, 35/28. See note.

Peck, 17/12, *s.* a peck measure.

Ped, 17/5, *s.* a pannier, a large capacious basket, in which fowls, eggs, fish, etc., are hawked about the country. Peder, a small farmer (Lincoln), "Pedde, idem quod panere, *calathus*."—Prompt. Parv. "Pedder, *revolus*, *negociator*."—Cathol. Anglic. See also Halliwell, sub. voc.

Peeces, 2/7, *s.* pieces, in parts.

Peele, 75/6, *v.* strip. "*Peler*. To bauld, or pull the haire off; also to pill, pare, barke, unrinde, unskin."—Cotgrave.

Peeler, 35/51, *s.* an impoverisher.

Peeling, 33/51, *s.* impoverishing.

Pelfe, 55/1, *s.* apparatus, implements.

Peneriall, 39/29, *s.* penny-royal. *Mentha pulegium*, from Lat. *puleium regium*, through Dutch *poley*, in the old Herbals called *puliol royal*; its Latin name being derived from its supposed efficacy in destroying *fleas* (*pulices*). See Pliny (b. xx. cap. 54).

Penie, 2/13, *s.* penny, money.

Penurie, 9/6, *s.* destitution, want.

Perareplums, 34/18, *s. pl.* some variety of plum either lost or unknown (if not a misprint).

Perceley, 39/28, *s.* parsley. A.S. *petersilige*. Lat. *petroselinum*.

Percer, 17/6, *s.* a piercer, gimlet.

Perie, 18/48, *s.* perry.

Perle, 96/28, *s.* pearl, jewel, ornament.

Perseneps, 41/8, *s. pl.* parsnips. Spelt in the old herbals *Pasnep* and *Pastnip*, from Lat. *pastinaca*.

Pester, 48/14, *v.* overcrowd with stock, abbreviated from O.Fr. *empestrer* = to entangle the feet or legs, to embarrass, from Fr. *pasturon*, L.Lat. *pastorium*, a fetter by which horses are prevented from wandering in the pastures.

Pestring, 53/11, *v.* being in the way or troublesome. "*Empestrer*, to pester, intricate, intangle, trouble, incomber."—Cotgrave.
Petigree, 113/11, *s.* pedigree, genealogy.
Pewter, 85/11, *s.* pewter vessels.
Philip and Jacob, 51/1. The feast of Saints Philip and James, 1st May.
Phraies, 113/8, *s.* phrase, language.
Pickle, 56/17, *s.* condition, state.
Piddling, 56/48, *v.* "going about pretending to work but doing little or nothing, as after illness a man is said to go *piddling* about, though as yet unable to do much."—Halliwell.
Pie, 53/3, *s.* magpie.
Piggen, 16/14, *s.* pigeons.
Pike, 17/15, *s.* a pitching fork with two or three prongs for cocking corn not put into sheaves.
Pilch, 15/39, *v. pr. t.* pilfer. See also Filchers.
Pilcrowe, page 2, *s.* the mark ¶. "Pylcrafte in a booke, *asteriskus.*" —Prompt. Parv.
Pilferie, 9/4, *s.* theft, fraud. O. Fr. *pelfrer*, to plunder.
Pinched, 10/30, *pp.* in straitened circumstances, in need or want.
Pinching, 9/6, *adj.* extreme, pressing.
Pinching, 97/3, *s.* economy.
Pinwood, 17/20, *s.* pegwood, *i.e.* wood that does not split, for making wooden pins or pegs of.
Pionées, 45/16, *s. pl.* The peony. *Pæonia corallina.* The seeds of this plant were used as a spice, and also as a medicine. See note in Liber Albus, p. 351.
Pismier, 110, *s.* ant.
Pitch and pay, 113/24, pay ready money.
Placing, 56/32, *v.* arranging, stacking.
Plagards, 113/6, *s. pl.* commissions, instruments.
Planked, 17/2, *pp.* boarded.
Plantine, 44/10, *s.* Plantain. The Water-plantain was formerly regarded as a specific against hydrophobia: from *planta*, sole of the foot, from the shape of the leaf.
Plash, 36/15, *v. imp.* to lower and narrow a broad-spread hedge by partially cutting off the branches and entwining them with those left behind. "*Plesser*, to plash, fould, to bow, or plait young branches one within another; also to thicken a hedge, or cover a walke, by plashing."—Cotgrave. In 36/15 it means to *pleach* down a hedge over the burrow, so as to protect it.
Pleasure, 7/6, *v.* to please.
Plight, 16/34, *s.* condition.
Plot, 9/7, *s.* piece of ground, farm.
Plot, 12/1, *s.* plan, rule.
Plough Monday, 90/2. The Monday next after Twelfth Day. See note.
Ploughstaff, 17/11, *s.* an instrument like a paddle for cleaning a plough, or clearing it of weeds, stalks, etc.
Plowmeat, 47/12, *s.* food made of corn.
Plowwrite, 58/5, *s.* plough wright.
Plump, 19/41, *v. imp.* throw in.
Pod, 17/6, *s.* "a box or old leather bottle nailed to the side of the cart to hold necessary implements, or perhaps grease."—Mavor. Cf. Ped.
Poke, 16/3, *s.* a bag, sack, "buy a pig in a poke" = to buy without seeing what one is buying.
Poling, 35/45, *s.* supporting with poles.
Pollard, 19/16, *s.* a mixture of bran and meal.
Pollenger, 35/13, *s.* pollard trees, brushwood.
Pompions, 41/7, *s. pl.* pumpkins. Fr. *pompon.*
Poppie, 45/17, *s.* poppy. A.S. *papig.*
Poret, 39/31, *s.* a scallion; a leek or small onion. O. Fr. *porette.* Lat. *porrum*; called *Porrectes* in the Forme of Cury, p. 41.
Porkling, 19/34, *s.* young swine. Cf. *Bulchin*, q.v.
Posie, 97/1, *s.* a poetical inscription. Udal writes it *poisee.* "There was a superscription or *poisee* written on the toppe of the crosse."—St. Luke, c. 23.
Pot, 15/43, *s.* the pot for cooking purposes.
Pottage, 76/2, *s.* pottage, soup. Fr. *potage.*
Pottle, 21/12, *s.* a pottle, a measure of two quarts.
Pouch, 62/16, *s.* pocket, purse. A.S. *pocca.*
Poucheth, 35/46, *v. pr. t.* pockets.
Pound, 113/21, *v.* fight, beat.
*Powlinges, 66, *s. pl.* the branches or shoots of pollard trees. Still called *Pollengers.*

Practise, 73/13, *s.* practice, experience.
Practisie, 19/5, *s.* conduct, practices.
Praies, 113/18, *s.* praise.
Prating, 64/27, *s.* talking, chattering.
Pray, 113/25, *s.* prey, booty, plunder.
Preferment, 10/57, *s.* advancement, assistance.
Prentise, 92/4, *v.* apprenticeship, business.
Prentiships, 60, *s. pl.* periods of seven years, that being the duration of an apprenticeship, or 'prenticeship.
Prest, 56/43, *adj.* ready.
Prest, 63/7, *adj.* neat, tidy. Tusser Redivivus says, "An old word for Neat or Tight; I suppose comes from women being *strait-laced.*" Ital. *presto.* O. Fr. *prest,* Fr. *prêt.*
Prest, 49/8, *pp.* pressed. Fr. *presser.*
Pretie, 86/7, *adj.* pretty, dainty. A.S. *prætig.*
Preuenting, 10/62, *pr. p.* anticipating. Lat. *prevenire,* to go before.
Price, 113/16, *s.* renown, high estimation. Lat. *pretium.*
Pricketh, 77/22, *v. pr. t.* makes proud or puffs up.
Pricking, 67/16, *v.* embroidering, doing fancy work.
Pride, 19/12, *s.* excessive richness. "The ground having his *pride* abated in the first crop."—G. Markham.
Prie, 35/15, *s.* privet.
Prim, 15/42, *s.* another name for the "privet;" called also "primwort."
Prime, 14/3, *s.* the time of the new moon, as change is the time of the full moon.
Prime grass, 35/18, *s.* earliest grass. See footnote.
Priuie, 10/12, *adj.* aware, acquainted.
Priuie, 15/42, *s.* privet. *Ligustrum vulgare.*
Procureth, 64/3, *v. pr. t.* contrives, brings about.
Promooters, 64/11, *s. pl.* informers.
Prooue, 46/1, *v. imp.* try, have some experience of.
*Prouision, 4, foresight. Lat. *providere.*
*Pullein, 37, Pullen, 87/5, *s. pl.* poultry, fowls. "Pullayne, poullane, *poullaille.*" — Palsgrave. See also Pulter.
Pullet, 63/16, *s.* chicken.
Pulter, 21/9, *s.* fowl keeper or breeder. "*Poullailler, m.* a poulter or keeper of pullaine."—Cotgrave.
Pultrie, 21/9, *s.* poultry.
Purkey Wheat, 19/17, maize.
Purloiners, 10/54, *s. pl.* thieves, pilferers. Spelt "*pro*loiners" in edit. of 1577.
Purse penniles, 10/28, *adj.* a purse without a penny, empty pursed.
Purslane, 40/10, *s.* water purslane. *Portulaca domestica.* — Gerard's Herball, ed. 1633. From *porcellus,* a little pig; the plant being a favourite food of swine.
Put to, 10/30, *v.* place.
Puttocks, 38/33, *s. pl.* kites, hawks. "Puttok, bryd, *milvus.*"—Prompt. Parv. In 99/3 the meaning is, voracious fellows.

Q.

Quaile, 15/34, *v.* fail.
Quaile, 91/6, *s.* be shaken.
Quamier, 33/56, *s.* quagmire, bog. O. Eng. quavemire.
Queenes gilleflowers, 43/27, *s.* the Dame's Violet, also called Rogue's or Winter gilliflower. *Hesperis matronalis,* L.
Queere, 113/6, *s.* choir. "Queere, *chorus.*"—Cath. Anglicum.
Quickset, 18/33, *s.* quickset hedge.
Quick setted, 35/45, *pp.* enclosed with a quickset hedge.
Quieter, 63/22, *adv.* more easily, quietly.
Quight, 114/2, *adv.* completely, entirely.
Quite, 15/7, *v. pr. t.* requite, repay.

R.

Rabetstock, 17/20, *s.* a rabbet-plane, a joiner's tool for cutting rabbets.
Rable, 22/17, *s.* crowd, number.
Rage, 113/35, *adj.* wild, dissipated.
Raise, 9/16, *v.* stir up.
Rampions, 40/12, *s.* rampion, *rapuntium.*—Gerard's Herball.
Ranke, 53/17, *adj.* strong, rank.
Ranker, 10/6, *s.* ill-feeling, quarrelling.
Raskabilia, 10/54, *s.* packs of rascals. Cf. Mid. Eng. *rascaille.* "Rascalye, or symple puple, *plebs.*"—Prompt. Parv.
Ratling, 19/34, *s.* the rattle.
Rawing, 16/25, *s.* the aftermath of a Meadow Water.—T.R. "Raweyne,

hey, *fenum serotinum*."—Prompt. Parv. See also Rowen.

Reame, 3/3, *s.* kingdom, country. O. Fr. *realme*, *reaume*.

Reasnable, 10/14, *adj.* fair, equitable, reasonable.

Reastie, 20/2, *adj.* rusty, rancid. "Reest as flesche, *rancidus*."—Prompt. Parv. "I *reast*, I waxe ill of taste, as bacon."—Palsgrave. See Wedgwood, s.v. Reasty.

Recken, 10/43, *v.* to compute, count.

Redele, page 3, *s.* riddle. "Rydel or probleme, *enigma*."—Prompt. Parv. A.S. *rǽdelse*.

Reeded, 51/5, *pp.* thatched with reeds.

Reeding, 2/10, *s.* reading, study. A.S. *rǽdan*.

Reeke, 10/24, *v.* smoke. A.S. *rêcan*.

Refraine, 48/1, *v.* stop, prevent.

Rehersed, 45/1, *pp.* mentioned, named. Fr. *reherser*, properly to go over again like a harrow (Fr. *herce*) over a ploughed field.

Reisons, 34/21, *s. pl.* currants. "Raysouns of Corante."—Pegge's Forme of Cury, ed. 1780, p. 16.

Relent, 23/11, *v.* become soft.

Rendrit, 24, *v.*=render it, *i.e.* return, requite it.

Rent, 55/7, *pp.* torn, plucked.

Rept, 18/43, *pp.* reaped, gained.

Resdue, 48/19, *s.* residue, remainder. Fr. *résidu*. Lat. *residuum*.

Respe, 15/27, Respies, 44/12, *s.* Raspberries.

Respit, 70/4, *s.* rest, respite.

Restfull, 106/2, *adj.* full of rest, resting.

Retcheles, 10/23, *adj.* reckless, careless. A.S. *recceleas*.

Revengement, 9/18, *s.* revenge.

Rew, 45/18, *s.* rue.

Rife, 98/1, *adj.* abundant, common.

Rifle, 17/14, *s.* "a rifle or rufle is no more than a bent stick standing on the butt of a sithe-handle."—T.R. Now called a *bale*.

Rigging, 16/37, *pr. p.* making free with, knocking about.

Rigs, 15/37, *v. pr. t.* make free with.

Ringle, 33/54, *v. imp.* ring, put rings through the snouts.

Ringling, 16/32, *v.* ringing of swine to prevent their tearing up the ground.

Riping, 37/7, ripening.

Rikes, 53/10, *s. pl.* ricks. A.S. *hreac*, a heap.

Rise, 40/5*a*, *s.* rice.

Rishes, 75/6, *s. pl.* rushes. A.S. *risce*. Lat. *ruscum*.

Riuet, 19/16, *s.* bearded wheat. "Dog-wheat, a bearded species, called in Mark-lane, *rivets*."—Forby.

Rode, 57/36, *s.* harbour.

Roinish, 102/1, *adj.* mean, rough, coarse. Fr. *rogneux*. "The roynish clown."—Shakspere, As You Like It, ii. 2.

Roister like, 98/3, blustering. "They ruffle and *roist* it out." Harrison's Eng. ed. F. J. Furnivall, New Shakspere Soc. Pt. 1, p. 77. "This is the very *royster* that gagg'd and bound me, Sir."—The Reformation, 1673.

Rokat, 40/13, *s.* garden rocket. Fr. *roquette*. *Eruca sativa*.—Gerard's Herball, ed. 1633.

Roong, 15/29, *pp.* have rings put through their noses to prevent them from tearing up the ground.

Roperipe, 92/3, *s.* one old enough to be flogged. "Deserving of hanging."—Howell, 1660.

Roste, 63/19, *s.* rule the roste=domineer, have the sway. According to Richardson equivalent to "*rule the roost*," an expression of which every farm yard would supply an explanation.

Rottenly, 18/11, *adj.* rich, crumbly.

Roule, 17/8, *s.* a rule, measure.

Roules, 10/54, *v.* roll in, bring in.

Rowe, 36/12, *s.* row, a rowe=in a row.

Rowen, 57/25, aftermath of mown meadows. "*Rowen* is a field kept up till after Michaelmas, that the corn left on the ground may sprout into green."—Bailey's Dict. See Rawing above, and Rawings in Ray's Gloss.

Rowleth, 46/15, *v. pr. t.* roll. O. Fr. *roler*, Ger. *rollen*, from Lat. *rotulare*.

Rubstone, 17/14, *s.* a sandstone for a scythe. "The rub or buckle stone which husbandmen doo occupie in the whetting of their sithes."—Harrison, Description of England, Pt. 2, p. 64.

Rudenes, 2/9, *s.* want of refinement, plainness, homeliness.

Ruffen, 98/3, *s.* ruffian, scoundrel.

Runciuall peas, 41/9, *s. pl.* marrow-fat

peas. Supposed to be derived from Span. *Roncesvalles*, a town at the foot of the Pyrenees, where gigantic bones of old heroes were pretended to be shown; hence the name was applied to anything of a size larger than usual.

Runnagate, 77/17, runaway. "White-livered *runagate*." — Shakspere, Richard III. iv. 4.

Runt-wood, page 78, foot-note 3, *s.* stumps of underwood. "Neither young poles nor old *runts* are suitable for building."—Holland.

Rydgis, 16/9, *s. pl.* ridges.

S.

Sad, 17/12, *adj.* disappointed, vexed.

Saddle, 35/37, *s.* the saddle, riding. We still say "a saddle horse," "a cart horse," meaning a horse for riding or carting.

Saile, 113/23, *s.* sail, beare low saile = to live humbly or economically. "Than bear so *low a sail*, to strike to thee."—Shakspere, 3 Hen. VI. v. 1. Cf. also 3 Henry VI. iii. 3.

Sallets, 40/1, *s. pl.* salads.

Sallow, 22/26, *s.* a species of willow. A.S. *salig.*

Salue, 4/2, *s.* ointment, salve.

Sampire, 40/6, *s.* samphire. *Crithmum marinum.*—Gerard's Herball, 1633.

"Half way down,
Hangs one that gathers *samphire*, dreadful trade."

Shakspere, Lear, iv. 6.

Saver, 10/10, *s.* scent, inkling.

Sauer, 77/3, *s.* a person to look after and see that things are not wasted.

Sauerie, 39/35, *s.* savoury. Fr. *savorée.* Lat. *satureja.*

Sauerlie, 9/3, *adj.* frugal, gained by saving.

Sauin, 45/22, *s.* savin. *Juniperus sabina*, Linn.

Sawsie, 113/35, *adj.* saucy, impudent.

Saxefrage, 44/13, *s.* saxifrage. Lat. *saxifraga*, from *saxum*, a rock, and *frango*, to break, being supposed to disintegrate the rocks, in the crevices of which it grows, and thence to dissolve stone in the bladder. Called in Scotland *Thirlstane*, which has the same meaning.

Scaberd, 102/2, *s.* scabbard.

Scamble, 51/7, *v.* scramble for.

Scant, 56/52, *adj.* scarce, wanting.

Scant, 113/24, *adv.* scarcely. So in Bacon's "Table of Coulers," I. "The Epicure that will *scant* indure the Stoic to be in sight of him." Cf. also Romeo and Juliet, i. 2.

Scanted, ii. 14, *adj.* limited, stinted, grudged. Cf. also note to 51/15.

Scape, 97/1, *v.* escape, get off.

Scare, 56/13, *v. imp.* drive away.

Scotch, 33/17, *v. pr. t.* cut, hew.

Scoutwatch, 10/19, *s.* watch, guard.

Scowles, 10/23, *v. pr. t.* scowls, frowns, is ill-tempered.

Scrall, 49*c*, *v. pr. t.* crawl. "To scrall, stir, *motito*."—Coles' Lat. Dict. "And the river shall *scral* with frogs."—Wiclif, Exodus viii. 3.

Scrauling, 49/9, *pr. p.* crawling.

Scruplenes, page 4, *s.* scruples, scrupulousness. Lat. *scrupulus*, a little stone such as may get into a traveller's shoe and distress him; hence, a source of doubt or distress.

Sea holie, 40/17, *s.* sea-hulfer, sea-holm; a plant of the genus *Eryngium* (*E. maritimum*). A.S. *hulfer*, holly.

Sealed, 17/18, *adj.* certified, stamped.

Seame, 21/2, *s.* a quarter of corn. A.S. *seam.*

Secresie, 9/20, *s.* secrets, private concerns.

Sedge collars, 17/12, *s. pl.* collars made of sedge or reeds.

Seede, 51/12, *v.* obtain seed from.

Seede cake, 90/7, "a festival so called at the end of wheat-sowing in Essex and Suffolk, when the village is to be treated with seed cakes, pasties, etc."—Warton.

Seeith, 19/41, *v. imp.* boil.

Seeke, 10/24, *v.* seek, "their dinners to seeke" = their dinners have to be sought, *i.e.* are lacking.

Seelie, 48/21, *adj.* silly, simple. A.S. *sælig.* O.L. Ger. *salig.*

Seene, 95/1, *adj.* practised, experienced.

"Its a schoolmaster
Well *seen* in music."

Shakspere, Taming of Shrew, i. 2.

Seene, 106/16, *v. pt. t.* appeared. Lat. *visus est.*

Seeth, 78/5, *v. imp.* boil.

Seeue, 17/3, *s.* sieve, sifter.

Seggons, 85/6, *s. pl.* poor labourers. "*Seg-head*, a blockhead."—Craven

Glossary. Cf. *Segger*, Chester Plays, ii. 51.

Sell, 113/21, *s.* cell, abbey.

Semsters, 86/7, *s. pl.* needlewomen, seamstresses. A.S. *seamestre.*

Seruice-trees, 34/24, *s. pl.* more correctly spelt *Servise-tree*, from Lat. *cervisia*, its fruit having from ancient times been used for making a fermented liquor, a kind of beer.

Seruiture, 99/1, *s.* servant, attendant.

Set, 36/25, *v. imp.* plant round, set.

Set, 35/45, *s.* the young shoots.

Setteth, 10/60, *v. pr. t.* risks. "Setteth his soule upon sixe or on seauen" = "risks his soul on the cast of a die."

Seuer, 15/40, *v. imp.* separate, sort.

Seuerall, title, *adj.* inclosed land, divided into fields by fences. L. Lat. *separalis.*

Sewe, 15/17, *v. imp.* drain. Cf. sewer. Welsh, *sych*, dry. Cf. Lat. *siccus.* See Pegge's Kenticisms.

Shackles, 17/21, *s. pl.* shackles. A.S. *scacul.* Dutch, *schakel*, a link of a chain.

Shack time, 16/30, *s.* the time during which the shaken-out grain remains on the ground after harvest. "*Shack*, Norfolk, a general common for hogs, from the end of harvest till seed time. To go at *shack*, to go at large." — Coles' Dict. 1676. Brockett's Glossary gives: "*Shack*, *shak*, to shed, or shake, as corn in harvest. Then *shack-fork*, a shake-fork." "*Shacking-time*, the season when malt is ripe."—Kersey's Eng. Dict. 1715. Wedgwood (Eng. Etym.) says: "Shack is the shaken grain remaining on the ground when the gleaning is over, the fallen mast (Forby). Hence to *shack*, to turn pigs or poultry into the stubble field to feed on the scattered grain. *Shack*, liberty of winter pasturage, when the cattle are allowed to rove over the tillage land." Forby gives "*Shack*, sb. the acorns or mast under the trees." Compare the provincial "Shucks," the pods or shells from which peas have been *shaken*, or, as it is frequently called, "*shook.*"

Share, 52/1, *v.* shear.

Shares, 17/10, *s.* plough shares.

Sharing, 17/16, *adj.* shearing.

Shaue, 17/6, *s.* spokeshave.

Sheawd, 102/7, *pp.* shown, displayed.

Shed, 57/7, *v.* lose the grains of corn.

Sheepebiter, 64/17, *s.* a thief, lit. a wolf, a cant phrase. See Halliwell, s.v.

Shent, 57/45, *pp.* ruined, disgraced. A.S. *scendan.*

Shere, 3/7, *s.* shire, county. A.S. *scire.*

Shift, 9/39, *v.* manage, fare.

Shift, 104/1, *s.* excuse, makeshift.

Shifting, 95/5, *adj.* changing, often removing.

Shifting, 10/27, 10/33, *v.* trickery, cheating, acting shiftingly.

Shiftingly, 9/26, *adv.* by tricks or mean shifts.

Shock, 56/20, *s.* a certain number of bundles or sheaves of corn (in some parts twelve). "A *shocke* of wheate, *meta tritici.*"—Withal's Dict. 1608.

Shock, 57/10, *v. imp.* collect into *shocks* or heaps of twelve sheaves.

Shod, 17/6, *pp.* tired.

Sholue, 17/1, *s.* shovel.

Shoo, 102/2, *s. pl.* shoes. A.S. *sceo*, a shoe, pl. *sceon.*

Shot, 113/40, *s.* expense, reckoning.

Showreth out, 14/3, *v. pr. t.* is showery, rainy weather.

Shreaw, 16/17, *s.* thief, rascal, 67/24, *s.* shrew, scold. See Shrew.

Shred pies, 31/3, *s. pl.* mince pies, the meat being cut up into *shreds.* A.S. *screádan*, small pieces. "No matter for plomb-porridge or *shrid pies.*" —Sheppard's Epigrams, 1651.

Shrew, 64*/6, *s.* scold. "Shrewe, *pravus.* Schrewyd, *pravatus*, *depravatus.*"—Prompt. Parv.

Shroftide, 90/3, *s.* Shrove Tuesday, the day before the first day of Lent.

Shrouing, 90/3, *s.* to be merry, probably derived from the sports and merriment of Shrovetide. See Halliwell, s.v. Shrove.

Shut, *v.* 51/5, shoot, throw; 37/13, shoot out, spring up.

Sieth, 35/25, *s.* scythe. A.S. *siðe.*

Siethes, 39/39, *s. pl.* chives, spelt in Hollyband's Dict. 1593, *sieves*, from Fr. *cive*, *Allium fissile*, L.

Sirops, 91/3, *s. pl.* sirups.

Siszers, 17/4, *s.* scissors.

Sithe, 17/14, *s.* scythe.

Skare, 2/7, *v.* frighten. Icel. *skirra*= to drive away.
Skared, 69/4, *pp.* frightened, cheated of.
Skavel, 17/19, *s.* a kind of spade, having its sides slightly turned up, used in draining, and cleaning narrow ditches. Compare *scuffle*, a garden hoe, and *shovel.*
Skep, 17/3, *s.* a basket made of rushes or straw.
Skill, 113/38, *s.* plan, design.
Skillesse, 112/4, *adj.* simple, homely.
Skirrets, 40/19, *s. pl.* the water-parsnip. *Sium latifolium*, contracted from *skirwort*, its older name, a corruption of *sugar-wort.* Ger. *zuckerwurzel.*
Skreene, 90/2, *s.* fire-screen. See note.
Skreine, 17/16, *s.* sieve, screen. O. Fr. *escrein.*
Skuppat, 17/19, *s.* a spade used in draining and making narrow ditches. Belgian *schup*, a spade.
Skuttle, 17/16, *s.* a screen for cleaning corn, *i.e.* a large broad and shallow shovel for casting threshed corn from one side of the barn to the other that light grains and dust may fall short.
Slab, 15/35, *s.* the outside cut of sawn timber.
Slabbered, 48/20, *pp.* dirtied, beslobbered. L. Ger. and Dut. *slabbern.*
Slained, 106/15, *pp.* slain, murdered, but perhaps we should read *stained.*
Slake, 1/4, *v.* to slacken.
Slapsauce, 98/2, *s.* "a parasite."—Minsheu. "A lickedish, a lickerish fellow, a *slapsawce.*" — Nomenclator, 1585.
*Slapt, 72*e*, *pp.*
Slea, 107/3, *v.* slay, kill. A.S. *slean.*
Sled, 17/11, *s.* sledge, truck. Ger. and Dutch *slede.* Icel. *sledi.* A.S. *slidan*, to slide.
Slept, 90/1, *pp.* slipt, forgotten, omitted.
Slise, 35/20, *v. imp.* slice, cut.
Sliuers, 23/1, *s. pl.* pieces of split wood, chips. A.S. *slifan.*
Slugging, 75/1, *s.* lying late in bed.
Sluts, 75/5, *s. pl.* slovens, slatterns. Ger. *schlutte.* Dutch *slet.*
Smack, 57/24, *s.* a pleasant repast.
Smalach, 45/20, *s.* celery, or water parsley. The *small ache* or parsley as compared with the *hipposelinum* or great parsley.
Small nuts, 34/22, Smal nuts, 33/57, *s.* hazel nuts.
Snagdragons, 43/30, *s. pl.* snapdragons, so called from its corolla resembling the *snap* or snout. Dut. *sneb* of some animal. Called by Lyte "Calf's snowte."
Snorting, 9/16, *adj.* snoring, sleepy. A.S. *snora*, a snoring.
Snudgeth, 62/2, *v. pr. t.* is economical or saving, or, works quietly or snugly. In Lanc. *snidge.* A.S. *snid.* Danish *snedig*, cunning. "Thus your husbandrye, methincke, is much more like the life of a covetous *snudge*, that ofte very evill proves, then the labour of a goode husbande, that knoweth well what he doth."—Ascham, Toxophilus, p.6.
Sockle, 35/30, *v. imp.* suckle, provide with milk.
Sod, 22/27, *pp.* boiled.
Soketh, 19/2, *v. pr. t.* wets, soaks.
Soles, 17/21, *s. pl.* a collar of wood, put round the neck of cattle to confine them to the post.
Sollen, 89/13, *adj.* sullen, sulky.
Soller, 57/5, *s.* garret, loft, or upper room. "*Solarium*, an upper room, chamber, or garret which in some parts of England is still called a *sollar.*"—Kennett, Gloss. p. 134.
Sooth, 10/61, *v.* to flatter.
Sops in wine, 43/31, *s.* a kind of pink resembling a carnation; the clove pink. "The rose and speckled flowre cald sops-in-wine." — The Affectionate Shepheard, 1594.
Sorell, 39/36, *s.* sorrell. Fr. *surelle*, a dimin. from L. Ger. *suur*=sour, from the acidity of the leaves. *Rumex acetosa*, L.
Sost, 48/20, *pp.* dirty, foul. "Of any one that mixes several slops, or makes any place wet or dirty, we say in Kent, he makes a *soss.*"—Kennett MS.
Souse, 12/5, *s.* pigs' feet and ears pickled.
Soutage, 57/51, *s.* bagging for hops, or coarse cloth. See More's MS. Additions to Ray's North Country Gloss.
Southly, 16/20, *adv.* facing the south.
Sowce, 19/37, *v. imp.* steep in brine, pickle.
Sower, 35/51, *adj.* sour.
Spare, 112/3, *v.* economize, be sparing.

Spareth, 10/35, *v. pr. t.* are economical, save.
Spars, 33/16, *s. pl.* rafters.
Speedfull, 52/13, *adj.* useful, profitable.
Speeding, 2/10, *s.* progress, success.
Speered, 84/5, *pp.* sprouted, a term in malting. "I *spyer* as corne dothe whan it begynneth to waxe rype, *je espie.*"—Palsgrave.
Spent, 15/41, *pp.* used, consumed.
Sperage, 40/18, *s.* asparagus. Lemery in his Treatise on Foods, 1704, gives as the etymology: *ab aspergendo*, sprinkling, because 'tis convenient to water them!
Spials, 64/12, *s. pl.* spies. Fr. *épier.* O. Fr. *espier*, whence our *espy*, *spy*. Low Lat. *espia*.
Spide, 2/9, *v. pr. t.* beheld, saw.
Spight, 57/13, *s.* as a spite or grief to.
Spight, 97/6, *v.* spite, be unpropitious.
Spil, 102/6, *v. pr. t.* spoil, ruin.
Spilled, 50/6, Spilt, 56/54, *pp.* ruined, spoilt. A.S. *spillan*.
Spring, 48/11, *s.* young buds of felled underwood.
Spurlings, 12/5, *s. pl.* smelts. "Spurlin, a smelt, Fr. *esperlan.*"—Skinner. Sparling, smelts of the Thames.—Brockett's N. C. Glossary. "First a sprat, then a small sparling, then a sparling."—R. Holme, p. 325.
Squatteth, 16/38, *v. pr. t.* sit or crouch down. Welsh *yswatian*, to squat, lie flat.
Squier, 10/57, *s.* squire, gentleman.
Stadled, 48/8, *pp.* "to stadle a Wood is to leave at certain distances a sufficient number of young trees to replenish it."—T.R.
Staddles, 47/9, Stadles, 48/9, *s. pl.* young growing trees left after cutting underwood.
Staid, 2/8, *v. pt. t.* kept, detained.
Staie, 10/7, *s.* means of support.
Staie, 19/40, *v.* prevent, stop.
Staied, 60/9, *adj.* steady, staid.
Stalfed, 21/11, *adj.* stall-fattened.
Stamp, 18/48, *v. imp.* bruise, pound.
Stands thee upon, 10/39, are suitable, proper for. To *stand* a person *on* is *to be incumbent* upon him, *it is his duty.*—Wilbraham, Gloss. of Cheshire Words, 1818.
Star of Bethlehem, 43/34, *s.* Star of Bethlehem. *Ornithogalum umbellatum*, a bulbous plant having a white star-like flower, like pictures of the stars that indicated Our Lord's birth.
Star of Jerusalem, 43/35, *s.* perhaps sunflower or turn-sole. Ital. *girasole*, familiarized into *Jerusalem*.
Stay, 113/31, *s.* rest, quiet.
Steade, 63/3, *s.* in steade = to advantage.
*Stede, 19, *v.* suffice, profit.
Steelie, 19/12, *adj.* hard, firm.
Steepe, 46/6, *adj.* a steepe = steeply.
Steeres, 36/8, *s. pl.* oxen in their third year. A.S. *steor*.
Sterue, 103/4, *v.* starve, perish. A.S. *steorfan*.
*Steruelings, 50, *s. pl.* half-starved animals.
Stick, 16/34, *v. imp.* to stick boards = to arrange them neatly one upon another with sticks between.—T.R.
Still, 33/53, *v. imp.* quiet, stop from growing.
Still, 44/1, *v.* distill.
Still, 50/33, *s.* a still. Lat. *stilla*, a drop.
Stinted, 95/4, *pp.* appointed, settled.
Stirre, 77/6, *v.* move quickly, bestir herself.
Stitchwort, 45/23, *s.* stitchwort, chickweed, *Stellaria media*, Linn.
Stocke gilleflowers, 43/36, *s.* now shortened to stock, from stock, the trunk or woody stem of a tree or shrub, added to *gilliflower* to distinguish it from plants of the pink tribe, called, from their scent, *Clove-gilleflowers*.
Stocks, 22/13, *s. pl.* young trees.
Stoutnesse, 9/9, *s.* force.
Stouer, 20/16, *s.* winter food for cattle, fodder from thrashed corn, whether straw, chaff, or colder (broken ears of corn), from the Old French *estavoir*, *estovoir*, *estouvier*, A.N. *estovers*, or *estouvoir*, which denotes, according to Roquefort (Glossaire de la langue Romane), 'provision de tout ce qui est nécessaire.'
Strangenes, 3/1, *s.* strangeness.
Strawforke, 17/1, *s.* a pitchfork.
Strawisp, 19/38, *s.* wisps of straw.
Streight waies, 113/8, *adv.* at once.
Strike, 16/9, *v. pr. t.* striking is the last ploughing before the seed is committed to the earth.—M.
Strike, 17/1, *s.* a bushel measure. "Robert Webb of Shottre oweth me iiij*s.* iiij*d.* lent hym in money

for making ix *strycke* and a half of malt."—Will of John Cocks of Stratford-on-Avon, dated May 27th, 1600.

Stripe, 57/5, *s.* "beating upon a Hurdle or some other rough thing."—T.R.

Stroieng, 48/17, *s.* destruction, injury. O. Fr. *(de)struire.* Lat. *struere.*

Stroken, 35/31, *pp.* stroked, kindly treated.

Strowing, 42/1, *adj.* for strewing.

Stroyal, 10/23, *s.* waste all, wasteful.

Stub, 35/9, *s.* stump, buie at the stub = buy on the ground. A.S. *stybb*, allied to Lat. *stipes.*

Stub, 33/47, *v. imp.* grub up.

"And badd hym take a mattock anon,
And *stubbe* the olde rote away,
That had stonde there many a day."

MS. Cantab. Ff. ii. 38, f. 129.

Stud, 33/16, *s.* the uprights in a lath and plaster wall. "In manie places there are not above foure, six, or nine inches between *stud* and *stud.*"—Harrison, Pt. 1, p. 233.

Stur, 62/6, *v.* move about, exert.

Sturs, 63/16, *s. pl.* disturbances, commotions.

Substanciallie, 9/23, *adv.* in reality, truly.

Subtiltie, 9/17, *s.* cunning, artfulness, deceit.

Sucker, 23/4, *s.* assistance, help, succour.

Suckerie, 91/2, Suckery, 39/38, *s.* succory, the wild endive, chicory. Fr. *chicorée*, often replaced by fraudulent dealers with dandelion roots, *Cichorium Intybus*, L.

Sudgerne, 10/8, *v.* settle down. Fr. *sojourner.* Cf. Barbour's Bruce, E. E. Text Soc. ed. Skeat, 6/26, 16/47, and 20/356.

Suer, 84/3, *adj.* sure, careful. O. Fr. *seur, segur.* Lat. *securus.*

Suerty, 9/24, *s.* being security or surety.

Suite, 18/49, *s.* description, kind.

Suretie, 10/28, *s.* security, bail.

Swage, 113/26, *v.* assuage.

Swatches, 57/18, *s. pl.* rows or ranks of barley, etc.

Swathes, 55/2, *s. pl.* the line of grass or corn cut and thrown together by the scythe in mowing. Cotgrave gives: "*Gerber des javelles* to bind corne of *swath* into sheaues, to sheaue vp corne." "*Fœni striga.* Monceaux de foin par ordre. The *swathe* or strake of grasse, as it lyeth mowne downe with the sithe." —Nomenclator.

Sweate, 56/20, *s.* a sweating, *i.e.* feel the effects of the heat.

Sweete Johns, 43/33, *s.* a species of *Dianthus* or pink, called also *Sweet John's-wort.*

Swerue, 96/42, *s.* fail, depart.

Swill, 78/5, *s.* hog's-wash.

Swim, 10/59, *v.* to abound, to overflow.

Swinge, 52/16, *v. imp.* cut down with the long swinging scythe used for that purpose.

T.

Tack, 12/3, Tacke, 76/3, *s.* substance. A tough piece of meat is said to have plenty of *tack* in it.

Taile, 77/8, *s.* back.

Taint wormes, 65/3, *s. pl.* "A small red spider called *taint* is by the country people accounted a deadly poison to cows and horses."—Sir T. Browne.

Tale, 83/4, *s.* tally, reckoning.

Talent, 59/9, *s.* the gifts and powers entrusted by God. Of course the reference is to the Parable.

Tallie, 78/2, *s.* score, bill, charge.

Tallwood, 53/12, *s.* wood cut for billets. "Tall woode, pacte wodde to make byllettes of, *taillee.*"—Palsgrave.

Tampring, 17/16, *v.* tempering, mixing, thus the Bible speaks of "*untempered* mortar."

Tane, 66/1, *pp.* taken.

Tanzie, 39/40, *s.* tansy, *Tanacetum vulgare*, Linn.

Tapple up taile, 21/14. See notes, pp. 253 and 317.

Tarie, 16/11, *v.* delay, keep back.

Tarragon, 40/21, *s.* tarragon. *Tragum vulgare.*—Gerard's Herball. Used for perfuming vinegar in France. O. Fr. *targon.*

Tarrie, 85/1, *v.* wait for, await.

Tawnie, 43/3, *adj.* yellowish.

Ted, 54/1, *v.* to spread abroad new-cut grass. "I teede hay, I tourne it afore it is made in cockes, *je fene.*" —Palsgrave.

Tedder, 10/9, *s.* tether, "live within one's tether" = "within the limits of one's income."

Teddered, 16/33, *pp.* tethered, tied up.

Teemes, 58/6, *s. pl.* teams.

Tell, 50/30, *v. imp.* count.

Temmes lofe, 16/11, *s.* "that made of a mixture of wheat and rye out of which the coarser bran is taken." —T.R. "*Miche*, a fine manchet; the country people of France call so also a loafe of boulted bread or *tems* bread."—Cotgrave.

Temper, 91/2, *s.* condition.

Tend, 10/39, *v. imp.* attend.

Tendance, 56/53, *s.* attention, care.

Tendeth, 62/3, *v. pr. t.* attends to, looks after.

Tere, 19/30, *s.* tares.

Thacke, 53/12, *s.* thatch, roof covering. "Erige, holme or *thacke*."—Huloet, 1552. "Thakke, *tegmen, tectura*." —Vocab. MS.

Thacker, 36/24, *s.* thatcher. "A proud *thacker* of Theeva would laugh them to scorn." — Pilkington's Works, 381.

Thee, 10/8, *v.* thrive, prosper. "A very late example of this word; at this time it was nearly obsolete. A.S. *théon*, to thrive, flourish.

> "God that sittis in trinite,
> Gyffe thaym grace wel to *the*
> That lystyns me a whyle."

MS. Cantab., Ff. v. 48, f. 47.

Theeuerie, 86/12, *s.* dishonesty.

Thencrease, 21/2, for the encrease = the increase, gain.

Thend, 19/40, for "the end."

Thetch, 57/32, *s.* thatch.

Thicker, 74/2, *adv.* more frequently.

Thies, 49/*c*, *s. pl.* thighs, limbs. A.S. *theoh*. Icel. *thio*.

Thiller, 17/4, the shaft-horse, also the last horse in a team. A.S. *thil*, a pole or shaft. "Thylle horse, *veredus*."—Prompt. Parv.

Thoes, 19/40, *pr.* those.

Thon, 110, the one.

Thorow, 15/15, *v.* pass through.

Thother, 110, the other.

Thresh, 90/3, *v. imp.* whip, thrash.

Thresher, 86/13, *s.* a duster of furniture.

Thrift, page 3, *s.* fortune, success, prosperity. Icel. *thrif*.

Thriftie, 59/1, *adj.* thrifty, economical.

Thrift's ladder, 57/30, *s.* the ladder or road to fortune.

Thry-fallowing, 56/1, *s.* "the third fallow; perhaps also cross-fallowing."—Mavor. "The third plowing of a summer fallow."—T.R.

Thwack, 18/3, *v. imp.* thump, beat together.

Tiburne stretch, 113/35, an execution. See note.

Tide, 63/2, *pp.* tied, fastened.

Tidie, 57/22, *adj.* "An old word signifying neat, proper, or in season, from the word Tide."—T.R.

Tieth, 56/19, *s.* tithe.

Tilman, 16/4, *s.* farm labourers, ploughmen, etc.

Tilth, 4/2, *s.* tillage, cultivation. A.S. *tilð*, from *tilian*, to till.

Tilth, 47/2, the ground tilled.

Tilture, 38/21, *s.* tillage, cultivation.

Time, 39/41, *s.* thyme. Greek θυμος, from θυω, fumigate, and identical with Lat. *fumus*, from its being used in sacrifices.

Timelie, 55/9, *adv.* in time.

Timely, 16/19, *adv.* early, soon.

Tine, 50/18, *s.* wild vetch or tare, a plant that *tines* or encloses and imprisons other plants. *Vicia hirsuta*.

Tith, 56/12, *s.* tithe.

Tithers, 10/52, *s. pl.* payers of tithes.

Tithing, 10/52, *s.* paying tithes or dues.

Tits, 15/6, *s. pl.* horses. The phrase "a nice *tit*" is still in use.

Titters, 50/18, *s. pl.* a noxious weed amongst corn.

Tittle tattle, 22/3, chattering, gossipping.

To, 18/6, *prep.* for, as.

Tode, with an R, 62/17, *s.* See note.

Toesed, 113/5, *pp.* pulled, pinched. Cf. "to *tease*, or card wool." A.S. *tæsan*, to pull, pluck.

Toieng, 61/1, *pr. p.* playing, amusing ourselves.

Toies, 57/34, *s. pl.* amusements, occupations.

Toile, 2/11, *s.* labour, work.

Tolleth, 55/12, *v. pr. t.* takes toll.

Ton, ... tother, 55/8, the one . . . the other.

Tone, 10/10, the one.

Tooteth, 94/2, *v. pr. t.* looks or strives anxiously. "*Tooting* and prying." —Taylor's Workes, 1630, i. 119.

Toppingly, 49/1, *adj.* ?

Tost, 2/11, *v. pt. t.* agitated, harassed. Cf. *tease*.

Touch, 57/43, *s.* faith, honour, to keep touch, to keep faith, perform a promise. The phrase occurs in the

Ballad of "George Barnwell," line 42.

Traie, 17/16, *s.* a mason's hod.

Traine, 32/2, *s.* draw. Fr. *trainer*, from L. Lat. *trahinare*, from Lat. *trahere*.

Transpose, 59/10, *v.* arrange, dispose of.

Trauell, page 2, *s.* labour, work. Fr. *travail*.

Trauerse, 59/2, *v.* start upon, proceed upon.

Treachery, 9/27, *s.* breach of faith, perfidy.

Treene, 85/10, *adj.* wooden.

Treu, 112/2, *adj.* true.

Trick, 15/35, *adj.* neat, clean, tidy.

Tricketh, 94/5, *v. pr. t.* dresses up, furnishes.

Trickly, 73/3, *adj.* neat, tidy.

Trim, 23/9, *v.* repair.

Trim, 3/2, *adv.* quickly, at once, easily. A.S. *trum*.

Trimlie, 57/34, *adv.* neatly, cleanly.

Trinkets, 17/5, *s. pl.* porringers (Halliwell), Ray gives: counterfeits and trinkets, *s. pl.* porringers and saucers. Cheshire. See note in Prompt. Parv.

Triue, 59/2, *v. pr. t.* (for contrive), attempt, try.

Troffe, 17/9, *s.* a trough.

Trope, 28/2, *s.* a phrase. From Greek τροπὸς, a turning, lit., the use of a word or expression in a different sense from that which properly belongs to it.

Troth, 1/1, *s.* truth. See an article on the derivation of this word in "Leaves from a Word Hunter's Note Book," by Rev. A. S. Palmer, 1876, p. 73.

Trowleth, 59/6, *v. pr. t.* helps on, moves towards. Welsh *troliaw*, to *troll* or trundle.

Trudge, 73/20, *v.* go, be spent.

Trudgeth, 10/21, *v. pr. t.* labours, journey's far.

Trull, 36/4, *s.* girl, lass.

Trustilie, 9/22. *adv.* confidingly.

Tullie, 111/5, Cicero.

Tumb, 106/15, *s.* the tomb, grave.

Tumbrel, 16/7, *s.* a tumbril, a dung-cart.

Turfe, 52/12, *s.* turf, peat. "Turfe of flagge, swarde of the erthe, *cespes*." — Prompt. Parv. "A Turfe, *cespes*."—Cathol. Angl.

Turnebroch, 80/2, *s.* Before the introduction of *jacks*, spits were turned either by dogs trained for the purpose, or by lads kept in the family, or hired, as occasion arose, to turn the spit, or *broach*. These boys were the *Turn-broaches*. See Halliwell.

Turn up, 46/18, *v.* deck, ornament.

Twelftide, 90/2, *s.* Twelfth Day, *i.e.* January 6th, twelve days after Christmas. "At the city of New Sarum is a very great faire for cloath at *Twelftyde* called Twelfe Market." — Aubrey's Wilts. MS. Roy. Soc. p. 333.

Twifallow, 50/23, *v. imp.* till twice, plough twice. See Trifallow.

Twiggers, 35/28, *s. pl.* first-class breeders. See Halliwell, s.v.

Twigging, 35/28, *s.* fast breeding.

Twinlings, 35/28, *s. pl.* twins (according to Dr. Mavor, but see note).

Twinning, 35/28, *s.* bearing twins.

Twise, 59/11, *adv.* twice.

Twitcher, 17/17, *s.* instruments used for clinching the *hog-rings*.—Mavor.

Twitchis, 53/2, *s. pl.* wounds, cuts.

U.

Undeskanted, 10/39, *pp.* untalked of.

Undoeth, 10/46, *v.* ruins, destroys.

Unfainedlie, 9/38, *adv.* unfeignedly, in truth.

Vnlustie, 19/24, *adj.* poor.

Unmeete, 57/5, *adj.* unfit. A.S. *unmæte*.

Vnsauerie, 9/15, *adj.* wasteful, ruinous.

Vnshaken, 16/34, *adj.* perfect, in good order, free from *shakes*.

Vnspilt, 16/8, *pp.* not wasted.

Vntackle, 23/6, *v.* unyoke.

Vntangled, 57/50, *pp.* freed from the hop vines.

Vnthrift, 6/3, *s.* a prodigal, spendthrift.

Unthriftely, 9/30*, *adv.* wastefully.

Usher, 10/17, *s.* doorkeeper. O. Fr. *ussier*, *huissier*, from *uis*, *huis*, a door.

V.

Vaine, 18/8, *s.* liking, fancy.

Vainfull, 2/13, *adj.* vain, fickle.

Valerian, 45/24, *s.* Valerian. *Valeriana officinalis*, Linn.

Vance, 113/7, *v.* advance.

Vantage, 3/7, *s.* advantage, profit.
Vegetiue, 55/7, *adj.* belonging to the plant.
Vent, 19/27, *s.* sale, disposal. Fr. *vente*, from Lat. *vendere, venditum*, to sell. "There is no *vent* for any commoditie except wool."—Sir W. Temple.
Venter, 83/4, *v.* venture, risk.
Ventrest, 19/35, *v. pr. t.* risk, venture.
Vergis, 19/42, *s.* verjuice, the juice of crab-apples, or other unripe fruit." Fr. *verjus*, from *vert*, green and *jus*, juice.
Verie, 92/4, *adj.* true, real.
Verlets, 63/18, *s. pl.* rascals, scoundrels. O. Fr. *varlet, vaslet*, now *valet.*
Vermin, 33/7, *v.* to destroy the vermin.
Vew, 113/24, *s.* view, sight.
Vewe, 75/7, *v.* view, examine.
Vice, 64/19, *s.* buffoon. The fool or punchinello of old shows. "Light and lascivious poems, uttered by these buffoons or *vices* in plays."—Puttenham, ii. 9, p. 69.
Villeny, 9/21, *s.* unfair or mean treatment.
Vitleth, 97/1, *v. pr. t.* eats, dines.
Vittels, 57/39, *s. pl.* provisions, food.
Voyd, 64*/4, *v.* avoid.

W.

Wadling, 35/45, *s.* wattling, wattled fence. "Wattles are wood slit." —T.R.
Wadmus (? Wadmul), page 37, note 1, a very thick, coarse kind of woollen cloth, made originally of Iceland wool. Icel. *vadmâl.* Halliwell, s.v. *Wadmal.*
Wag, 87/3, *s.* messenger.
Waid, 113/40, *pp.* considered, reflected on.
Waieth, 99/5, Waith, 101/5, *v. pr. t.* considers, reflects.
Waight, 56/24, *v. pr. t.* watch, wait about.
Waighls, 10/42, *s.* weights, measures.
Waight, 99/1, *v.* attend or wait at table.
Waine, 48/22, *v. imp.* fetch, bring, lit. to convey in a *wain* or wagon.
Waine, 16/7, *s.* waggon. A.S. *wæn, wägen.*
Wake day, 90/5, *s.* a village festival, kept originally on the day of the dedication of the parish church. See note.
Walke, 48/17, *s.* pasturing.
Wallow, 102/2, *v. pr. t.* make dirty, cover.
Wand, 33/45, *v. imp.* inclose with poles.
Wanteth, 94/8, *v. pr. t.* is in want.
Wantey, 17/5, *s.* a rope or leathern girdle, by which burdens are tied to the back of a horse; *wamb-tie*, a belly-band.
Wanton, 90/5, *s.* merry girl. O.E. *wantowen*, from *wan-*, prefix signifying lack or *want*, and *togen*, pp. of *teon*, to educate.
Wardens, 34/26, *s. pl.* a large baking pear. "I would have him roasted like a *warden*."—Beau. and Flet.
Warely, 114/2, *adv.* carefully, warily.
Wares, 22/19, *s. pl.* productions.
Warily, 10/34, *adv.* discreetly, cautiously. A.S. *wær.*
Warrener, 33/7, *s.* the keeper of a warren.
Wart, 113/5, *v. pr. t.* wert, wast.
Waster, 79/1, *s.* wasteful.
Water furrow, 19/7, *v. imp.* draw furrows across the ridges in the lowest part of the ground to act as drains or water-courses. "A watir furre, *elix*."—Cathol. Anglicum.
Water-retting, 16/25, *s.* retting is the process of steeping flax in water to separate the fibres. "Rettyn tymber, hempe or other like, *rigo, infundo.*" —Prompt. Parv.
Wayest, 10/4, *v.* considerest.
Weather, 57/5, *v. imp.* dry in the open air.
Weene, 67/12, *v. pr. t.* think. A.S. *wenan.*
Webster, 15/17, *s.* a weaver. A.S. *webbestre*, a female weaver.
*Wedehoke, 79, *s.* a weeding tool.
Weeles, 36/31, *s. pl.* snares or traps for fish made of osiers or twigs. "A *weele*, a wicker net, wherewith fishes being once entred, there is no way for them to get out; a bow net."—Nomenclator.

> "There plenty is of roches, bleakes, or eeles,
> Which fishermen catche in their nets and weeles."
>
> Newe Metamorphosis, 1600.

Wefte, 84/1, *s.* a loss.
Well a fine, 113/9, to a good end or purpose.
Welthines, 10/36, *s.* plenty, wealth.
Wenches, 57/34, *s. pl.* girls.

Wennel, 20/28, *s.* a calf just *weaned.* "A lambe, or a kidde, or a *weanell* wast."—Spenser, Shep. Cal. September.

Wether, 90/7, *s.* weather.

Wheat plums, 34/27, *s. pl.* a large fleshy plum, sometimes called the bastard Orleans plum.

Wheele ladder, 17/6, *s.* "probably a frame on the side of a cart to support hay or corn when the load is to be increased."—Mavor.

Whelpe, 95/2, *s.* child.

Whereas, 21/25, *adv.* wherever.

Whight, 15/12, *adj.* white.

Whinnes, 53/12, *s. pl.* whin. furze.

Whipstock, 21/14, *s.* the handle of a whip.

> "Bought you a whistle, and a *whip-stalk* too,
> To be revenged on their villainies."
> Span. Tragedy, iii. 180.

Whist, 64*/10, *v.* be silent, be hushed. "Keepe the *whisht*, and thou shalt heare it the sooner."—Terence in Eng. 1641.

Whit, 2/4, *s.* a point, no whit, not in the slightest degree. A.S. *wiht*, a creature, thing. Gothic *waiht.*

Whitch, 35/6, which sort.

Whit leather, 17/4, *s.* leather dressed with alum, salt, etc., remarkable for its pliability and toughness. "I think I'm as hard as a nut, and as tough as *whit-leather.*"—Howitt.

Whitemeat, Whitmeat, 47/20, *s.* eggs, milk, butter, cheese, etc.

Wicket, 77/9, *s.* mouth.

Wight, 3/6, *s.* person, man. A.S. *wiht.* Gothic *waiht.*

Wild otes fantasie, 9/30*, the fancies or excesses of youth. Cf. "sowing his wild oats."

Wiles, 113/18, *s. pl.* tricks, deceits.

Wilfull, 35/4, *adj.* ready, hasty.

Wimble, 17/6, *s.* auger. "An auger or *wimble*, wherwith holes are bored, *terebra* and *terebrum.*" — Baret's Alucarie, 1580. *Gimlet* is the dimin. from *wimble.*

Wine, 51/21, *v. imp.* win, make to please.

Wit, 16/3, *s.* sense, good judgment. A.S. *witt.*

Wither, 57/20, *v.* dry.

Wonne, 75/3, *pp.* managed, made up.

Wood, 13/5, *adj.* mad. A.S. *wod.*

Woodrofe, 44/17, *s.* sweet woodruff, *Asperula odorata.* A.S. *wudurðfe.*

Woodsere, 51/6, *s.* the month or season for cutting wood; but see next word. "If wood be cut after the sunne decline from us till he come to the equinoctial (which time they call *woodsere*), it will never grow againe"—Heydon, Def. of Astrology, 1603.

Woodsere, 53/15, *s.* "By woodsere is meant decayed or hollow Pollards." —T.R.; but in his note to this passage he says, "Woodsere is the season of felling wood."—T.R.

Woorser, 10/32, Worser, 63/15, *adv.* worse, a double comparative. A.S. *wyrsa.*

Woorth, 112/7, *s.* in worth = for what I am worth, *i.e.* as I can, what I can get.

Wot, 94/4. *v. pr. t.* ye know not what, an indefinite expression.

Wote, 10/21, *v. pr. t.* know. A.S. *witan*; *pt. t. Ic wat,* I know.

Wounder, 2/2, *s.* wounder, slayer. A.S. *wundian*, to wound.

Wrall, 101/4, *v. pr. t.* quarrel.

Wraught, 113/35, *pp.* supplied, furnished.

Wrauling, 92/1, *s.* quarrelling.

Wrecke, 114/2, *v.* wreak, vent. A.S. *wrecan.*

Wrest, 11/1, *v.* turn, force away.

Wrest, 10/61, *v.* steal away, plunder.

Wresting, 89/13, *s.* struggling for, fighting for.

Wright, 68/1, *v.* write.

Wringer, 2/13, *s.* extortioner.

Write, 86/10, *v. imp.* mark, write the name on.

Wud, 33/16, *s.* wood. A.S. *wudu.*

Wull, 35/21, *s.* wool. A.S. *wull.* Gothic *wulla.*

Y.

Yarn, 21/13, *v. pr. t.* earn. A.S. *gearnian.*

Yeane, 33/21, *v.* bring forth young. A.S. *eanian.*

Yeerlie, 63/21, *adv.* ? = yarely, readily. A.S. *gearu.* O.L. Ger. *garu.*

Yerke, 64*/9, *v.* kick, wince. "They flirt, they *yerk*, they backward fling."—Drayton. "*Tire*, a kick, yark, jerk, jert."—Cotgrave.

Also from Benediction Books ...

Wandering Between Two Worlds: Essays on Faith and Art
Anita Mathias
Benediction Books, 2007
152 pages
ISBN: 0955373700

Available from www.amazon.com, www.amazon.co.uk
www.wanderingbetweentwoworlds.com

In these wide-ranging lyrical essays, Anita Mathias writes, in lush, lovely prose, of her naughty Catholic childhood in Jamshedpur, India; her large, eccentric family in Mangalore, a sea-coast town converted by the Portuguese in the sixteenth century; her rebellion and atheism as a teenager in her Himalayan boarding school, run by German missionary nuns, St. Mary's Convent, Nainital; and her abrupt religious conversion after which she entered Mother Teresa's convent in Calcutta as a novice. Later rich, elegant essays explore the dualities of her life as a writer, mother, and Christian in the United States--Domesticity and Art, Writing and Prayer, and the experience of being "an alien and stranger" as an immigrant in America, sensing the need for roots.

About the Author

Anita Mathias was born in India, has a B.A. and M.A. in English from Somerville College, Oxford University and an M.A. in Creative Writing from the Ohio State University. Her essays have been published in The Washington Post, The London Magazine, The Virginia Quarterly Review, Commonweal, Notre Dame Magazine, America, The Christian Century, Religion Online, The Southwest Review, Contemporary Literary Criticism, New Letters, The Journal, and two of HarperSanFrancisco's The Best Spiritual Writing anthologies. Her non-fiction has won fellowships from The National Endowment for the Arts; The Minnesota State Arts Board; The Jerome Foundation, The Vermont Studio Center; The Virginia Centre for the Creative Arts, and the First Prize for the Best General Interest Article from the Catholic Press Association of the United States and Canada. Anita has taught Creative Writing at the College of William and Mary, and now lives and writes in Oxford, England.

"Yesterday's Treasures for Today's Readers"

Titles by Benediction Classics available from Amazon.co.uk

Religio Medici, Hydriotaphia, Letter to a Friend, Thomas Browne

Pseudodoxia Epidemica: Or, Enquiries into Commonly Presumed Truths, Thomas Browne

Urne Buriall and The Garden of Cyrus, Thomas Browne

The Maid's Tragedy, Beaumont and Fletcher

The Custom of the Country, Beaumont and Fletcher

Philaster Or Love Lies a Bleeding, Beaumont and Fletcher

A Treatise of Fishing with an Angle, Dame Juliana Berners.

Pamphilia to Amphilanthus, Lady Mary Wroth

The Compleat Angler, Izaak Walton

The Magnetic Lady, Ben Jonson

Every Man Out of His Humour, Ben Jonson

The Masque of Blacknesse. The Masque of Beauty,. Ben Jonson

The Life of St. Thomas More, William Roper

Pendennis, William Makepeace Thackeray

Salmacis and Hermaphroditus attributed to Francis Beaumont

Friar Bacon and Friar Bungay Robert Greene

Holy Wisdom, Augustine Baker

The Jew of Malta and the Massacre at Paris, Christopher Marlowe

Tamburlaine the Great, Parts 1 & 2 AND Massacre at Paris, Christopher Marlowe

All Ovids Elegies, Lucans First Booke, Dido Queene of Carthage, Hero and Leander, Christopher Marlowe

The Titan, Theodore Dreiser

Scapegoats of the Empire: The true story of the Bushveldt Carbineers, George Witton

All Hallows' Eve, Charles Williams

The Place of The Lion, Charles Williams

The Greater Trumps, Charles Williams

My Apprenticeship: Volumes I and II, Beatrice Webb

Last and First Men / Star Maker, Olaf Stapledon

Last and First Men, Olaf Stapledon

Darkness and the Light, Olaf Stapledon

The Worst Journey in the World, Apsley Cherry-Garrard

The Schoole of Abuse, Containing a Pleasaunt Invective Against Poets, Pipers, Plaiers, Iesters and Such Like Catepillers of the Commonwelth, Stephen Gosson

Russia in the Shadows, H. G. Wells

Wild Swans at Coole, W. B. Yeats

A hundreth good pointes of husbandrie, Thomas Tusser

The Collected Works of Nathanael West: "The Day of the Locust", "The Dream Life of Balso Snell", "Miss Lonelyhearts", "A Cool Million", Nathanael West

Miss Lonelyhearts & The Day of the Locust, Nathaniel West

The Worst Journey in the World, Apsley Cherry-Garrard

Scott's Last Expedition, V1, R. F. Scott

The Dream of Gerontius, John Henry Newman

The Brother of Daphne, Dornford Yates

The Downfall of Robert Earl of Huntington, Anthony Munday

Clayhanger, Arnold Bennett

The Regent, A Five Towns Story Of Adventure In London , Arnold Bennett

The Card, A Story Of Adventure In The Five Towns , Arnold Bennett

South: The Story of Shackleton's Last Expedition 1914-1917, Sir Ernest Shackketon

Greene's Groatsworth of Wit: Bought With a Million of Repentance, Robert Greene

Beau Sabreur, Percival Christopher Wren

The Hekatompathia, or Passionate Centurie of Love, Thomas Watson

The Art of Rhetoric, Thomas Wilson

Stepping Heavenward, Elizabeth Prentiss

Barker's Delight, or The Art of Angling, Thomas Barker

The Napoleon of Notting Hill, G.K. Chesterton

The Douay-Rheims Bible (The Challoner Revision)

Endimion - The Man in the Moone, John Lyly

Gallathea and Midas, John Lyly,

Mother Bombie, John Lyly

Manners, Custom and Dress During the Middle Ages and During the Renaissance Period, Paul Lacroix

Obedience of a Christian Man, William Tyndale

St. Patrick for Ireland, James Shirley

The Wrongs of Woman; Or Maria/Memoirs of the Author of a Vindication of the Rights of Woman, Mary Wollstonecraft and William Godwin

De Adhaerendo Deo. Of Cleaving to God, Albertus Magnus

Obedience of a Christian Man, William Tyndale

A Trick to Catch the Old One, Thomas Middleton

The Phoenix, Thomas Middleton

A Yorkshire Tragedy, Thomas Middleton (attrib.)

The Princely Pleasures at Kenelworth Castle, George Gascoigne

The Fair Maid of the West. Part I and Part II. Thomas Heywood

Proserpina, Volume I and Volume II. Studies of Wayside Flowers, John Ruskin

Our Fathers Have Told Us. Part I. The Bible of Amiens. John Ruskin

The Poetry of Architecture: Or the Architecture of the Nations of Europe Considered in Its Association with Natural Scenery and National Character, John Ruskin

The Endeavour Journal of Sir Joseph Banks. Sir Joseph Banks

Christ Legends: And Other Stories, Selma Lagerlof; (trans. Velma Swanston Howard)

Chamber Music, James Joyce

Blurt, Master Constable, Thomas Middleton, Thomas Dekker

Since Yesterday, Frederick Lewis Allen

The Scholemaster: Or, Plaine and Perfite Way of Teachyng Children the Latin Tong , Roger Ascham

The Wonderful Year, 1603, Thomas Dekker

Waverley, Sir Walter Scott

Guy Mannering, Sir Walter Scott

Old Mortality, Sir Walter Scott

The Knight of Malta, John Fletcher

The Double Marriage, John Fletcher and Philip Massinger

Space Prison, Tom Godwin

The Home of the Blizzard Being the Story of the Australasian Antarctic Expedition, 1911-1914, Douglas Mawson

Wild-goose Chase , John Fletcher

If You Know Not Me, You Know Nobody. Part I and Part II, Thomas Heywood

The Ragged Trousered Philanthropists, Robert Tressell

The Island of Sheep, John Buchan

Eyes of the Woods, Joseph Altsheler

The Club of Queer Trades, G. K. Chesterton

The Financier, Theodore Dreiser

Something of Myself, Rudyard Kipling

Law of Freedom in a Platform, or True Magistracy Restored, Gerrard Winstanley

Damon and Pithias, Richard Edwards

Dido Queen of Carthage: And, The Massacre at Paris, Christopher Marlowe

Cocoa and Chocolate: Their History from Plantation to Consumer, Arthur Knapp

Lady of Pleasure, James Shirley

The South Pole: An account of the Norwegian Antarctic expedition in the "Fram," 1910-12. Volume 1 and Volume 2, Roald Amundsen

A Yorkshire Tragedy, Thomas Middleton (attrib.)

The Tragedy of Soliman and Perseda, Thomas Kyd

The Rape of Lucrece. Thomas Heywood

Myths and Legends of Ancient Greece and Rome, E. M. Berens

In the Forbidden Land, Henry Savage Arnold Landor

Across Unknown South America, by Arnold Henry Savage Landor

Illustrated History of Furniture: From the Earliest to the Present Time, Frederick Litchfield

A Narrative of Some of the Lord's Dealings with George Müller Written by Himself (Parts I-IV, 1805-1856), George Müller

The Towneley Cycle Of The Mystery Plays (Or The Wakefield Cycle): Thirty-Two Pageants, Anonymous

The Insatiate Countesse, John Marston.

Spontaneous Activity in Education, Maria Montessori.

On the Art of Writing, Sir Arthur Quiller-Couch

The Well of the Saints, J. M. Synge

Bacon's Advancement Of Learning And The New Atlantis, Francis Bacon.

Catholic Tales And Christian Songs, Dorothy Sayers.

Two Little Savages: Being the Adventures of Two Boys who Lived as Indians and What they Learned, Ernest Thompson Seton

The Sadness of Christ, Thomas More

The Family of Love, Thomas Middleton

The Passing of the Aborigines: A Lifetime Spent Among the Natives of Australia, Daisy Bates

The Children, Edith Wharton

A Record of European Armour and Arms through Seven Centuries., Francis Laking

The Book of the Farm: - Detailing The Labours Of The Farmer, Steward, Plowman, Hedger, Cattle-Man, Shepherd, Field-Worker, and Dairymaid. (Volume I). by Henry Stephens

The Book of the Farm: - Detailing The Labours Of The Farmer, Steward, Plowman, Hedger, Cattle-Man, Shepherd, Field-Worker, and Dairymaid. (Volume II). by Henry Stephens

The Book of the Farm: - Detailing The Labours Of The Farmer, Steward, Plowman, Hedger, Cattle-Man, Shepherd, Field-Worker, and Dairymaid. (Volume III). by Henry Stephens

The Naturalist On The River Amazons, by Henry Walter Bates

and many others…

Tell us what you would love to see in print again, at affordable prices!
Email: **benedictionbooks@btinternet.com**

www.ingramcontent.com/pod-product-compliance
Lightning Source LLC
LaVergne TN
LVHW102005210926
848483LV00009B/45
9781849020893